The Rings of Allah

by

Lee Boyland

authorHOUSE

1663 LIBERTY DRIVE, SUITE 200
BLOOMINGTON, INDIANA 47403
(800) 839-8640
www.authorhouse.com

© 2004 Lee Boyland
All Rights Reserved.

No part of this book may be reproduced, stored in a retrieval system, or transmitted by any means without the written permission of the author.

First published by AuthorHouse 09/02/04

ISBN: 1-4184-2727-6 (sc)
ISBN: 1-4184-2728-4 (dj)

Library of Congress Control Number: 2004105029

Printed in the United States of America
Bloomington, Indiana

This book is printed on acid-free paper.

Acknowledgements

My wife and editor, Vista, without whose support, dedicated editing, and character development this book would not have been published.

Patti Barbã for review and input on the medical instruments used in a diagnostic center. Also thanks to my friends who have read earlier drafts and offered encouragement, with special thanks to Dr. Arlie Cole, Larry Runyon, and Jack Wiles.

Last, but not least, thanks to Greg Jones, Dale Preston and the rest of the AuthorHouse team who helped a novice author though the maze of publication and promotions.

Foreword

This novel is not about understanding Islam or the Middle East. It is a fictional story about nuclear weapons, al-Qaeda terrorists, and what they could do with them. However, to understand al-Qaeda, one must have a cursory understanding of Islam and associated history.

The plot of *The Rings of Allah* is interwoven with historical events and persons. Brief summaries of these events are included in order to tell a story spanning 64 years. The last half of the introduction deals with Islam, and contains a sketch of its history. A chapter is devoted to the Soviet-Afghanistan war, because it was the birthplace of today's Islamic terrorists and al-Qaeda.

Scenes containing explanations of basic nuclear physics and descriptions of processes used to enrich uranium are included for readers who like technical detail. Reading over these passages will not degrade the story. Detailed information pertaining to uranium and uranium enrichment is provided in Appendix A.

America's use of two types of atomic bombs – to bring an end to World War II – continues to be a touchy subject. Consequently, one of America's greatest technological achievements, the Manhattan Project, has been relegated to a dusty shelf in the basement of our nation's history. The prolog includes a brief description of the Manhattan Project's history and scope, and references to the Project occur throughout the book.

Readers of *The Rings of Allah* will have gained a better understanding of certain terms currently found in news articles: such as *centrifugal separation of uranium, enriched uranium, and highly enriched uranium (HEU)*. A new term is introduced that has yet to make its appearance in the mainstream press – *gun-type atomic bombs*. Hopefully, readers will also acquire a better understanding of the mindset of Islamic terrorists and the meanings of frequently used Arabic words. The author wishes to clarify in advance that the text may contain variations in the spellings of Arabic words and names. This phenomenon exists because spellings differ depending upon the resource materials used for research. A list of the main fictional characters is included at the end of the book.

The Rings of Allah is a fictional account of Islamic terrorists using old Soviet atomic test devices to attack America. Such an event is not as far fetched as it might appear. After the Soviet Union collapsed one live atomic bomb was found in its underground test tunnel at the Semipalatinsk test range; where it had been abandoned before it could be tested. This incident has been documented, and rumors exist of two more that are still there.

Could a real attack employing nuclear devices actually occur in America? You bet it can. As the reader will see, it is not difficult to build a gun-type atomic device, if one has enough highly enriched uranium. Is HEU available? The following amounts of HEU were reportedly recovered by the U.S. and Russia in 2003: Yugoslavia - 100 pounds; Romania - 30 pounds; and Bulgaria - 37 pounds. More than enough HEU to make one gun-type atomic bomb.

The concept of the Soviet Little Boy uranium bomb team is the fictional product of the author's imagination, as are all subsequent non-historical events contained in this novel. *The Rings of Allah* is not intended to be a prophetic work; however one can surely imagine "what if" the movie *Tora, Tora, Tora* – depicting Pearl Harbor's surprise attack – had been published as a novel in the spring of 1941

While the *Rings of Allah's* plots are fictional, the threat it foretells is real. The story told in *The Rings of Allah* could really happen. The plot is entirely feasible and the technology has existed since 1945.

I love the greatness of America – our way of life and the diversity of our ethnic backgrounds. The potential for our collective progeny to lose their rightful heritage and become enslaved by an archaic, fanatical, Islamic government is unthinkable. This novel is my "wake up call" to all who love liberty, democracy, and freedom of Church and State. In short – America – our way of life is in peril. There are people in our midst whose sole purpose is to destroy all freedoms that Americans hold dear. We as a people must support and encourage our government to take every possible action to protect our way of life, educate the public to the threat, protect the public through greater vigilance, and use all possible means nationally and internationally to encourage peace loving Muslims to eliminate those murderous radicals who corrupt their religion and would rule the world.

God bless America.

Lee Boyland
Melbourne, Florida

"They will target the joints of your economy until you stop your injustice and aggression."
— Usama bin Laden

Prologue

The Manhattan Project

The history of nuclear fission and the atomic bomb began in the fall of 1938 with the splitting of the first uranium atom at the Kaiser Wilhelm Institute in Berlin, Germany. Soon scientists around the world were adding their discoveries to the rapidly growing body of information. Nuclear fission dangled the promise of a new energy source greater than any known to date. To some countries such as Germany – then Nazi Germany ruled by Adolph Hitler – it held the promise of becoming a mighty weapon.

Word of the potential danger of an "Atomic Bomb" arrived in America with scientists fleeing Hitler's "New Order." Among them were three refugee Hungarian scientists: Leo Szilart, Eugene Wigner, and Edward Teller, who were able to convince Albert Einstein of the danger of a Hitler Atomic Bomb. Albert Einstein with the help of Szilart, Wigner, Teller, and Alexander Scahs wrote his famous "dangers of uranium fission letter" to President Roosevelt. Sachs, who was also a friend and economic advisor to President Roosevelt, delivered the letter into the president's hand on October 11, 1939.

Immediately recognizing that a Hitler Atomic Bomb would lead to world conquest, President Roosevelt wasted no time in ordering the establishment of a government committee to fund American universities engaged in uranium research. The task was given to the Office of Scientific Research and Development (OSRD), which formed an Atomic Committee, code name S-1. Twelve months later $300,000 had been disbursed to sixteen research groups. The thrust of all of the research was to find a means to separate sufficient quantities of fissionable materials suitable to build an atomic bomb.

By 1942, five different technologies had been identified as practical methods to produce fissionable material. Two of the methods involved the theoretical use of nuclear reactors to convert uranium-238 into plutonium-239. However, no such reactor existed. The other three – gaseous diffusion, centrifugal diffusion, and electromagnetic isotope separation (EMIS) – were experimental separation technologies for the extraction of the uranium-235 isotope from uranium metal that contained 0.7 % uranium-235. None of these technologies offered assurance that they could be turned into production facilities for the large quantities of fissionable isotopes required to manufacture nuclear weapons.

By May, 1942 the S-1 Committee, unable to choose a technology or technologies, because all were equally risky, made a courageous and bold decision to prepare a report recommending that all five technologies should be put into production at the same time. The recommendation was sent to Army Chief of Staff, General George C. Marshall; Secretary of War, Henry L. Stimson; and Vice President Henry A. Wallace. All three men approved the report and forwarded it to the president, who quickly returned it with "O.K., FDR" written in one corner.

Thus began the greatest scientific, engineering, and

manufacturing effort in the history of mankind.

OSRD Director, Dr. Vannevar Bush, recommended that the project be transferred to the U.S. Army Corps of Engineers (COE), for transition from research and development (R&D) to full-scale production. President Roosevelt concurred, and the project was transferred to the Army COE in June 1942. The COE formed a new special district to manage the secret project, named the "Manhattan District," under the direction of Colonel James C. Marshall. Control of the research groups remained with OSRD. Colonel Marshall had mistakenly assumed that the scientific and engineering work necessary to start construction of production facilities was completed. He quickly determined that was not the case – nothing was ready for production. Colonel Marshall, a highly qualified engineer, was reluctant to commit to starting construction on facilities before the technology was proven – sound engineering practice in normal times. But this was not a simple engineering project and these were not normal times. It quickly became apparent to the president's advisors that a strong, qualified, decisive leader was needed to spearhead this enormous war effort.

Secretary of War Stimson selected a candidate, U.S. Army Colonel Leslie Groves, who was approved by the president. Graduated fourth in his 1918 class at West Point, Colonel Groves was currently Deputy Chief of Army Construction, responsible for controlling construction work amounting to $600 million per month. Colonel Groves was also the liaison officer for the COE Manhattan District, and as such had provided advice to Colonel Marshal in the areas of procurement, plant location and selection of contractors. When on September 17, 1942 Colonel Groves was informed by his boss, Major General Brehon Somervell, that he had been appointed Chief of a new program, "The Manhattan Project," America's atomic bomb project came into being. Colonel Marshall remained head of the COE Manhattan District, which ultimately became part of The Manhattan Project.

On September 23, 1942 newly promoted Brigadier General Leslie Groves officially took charge of the Manhattan Project. Under Groves' leadership, the Manhattan Project had total responsibility for all science, engineering, processes and construction of production facilities required to deliver the atomic bomb – its mission was to build "THE BOMB," and win the war.

During the next two years, land was acquired and three new cities built to provide housing for the personnel needed to build and operate the massive facilities required for production of atomic bombs. Vast facilities were created including: Oak Ridge, Tennessee, encompassing fifty-four thousand acres, for uranium separation; Los Alamos, New Mexico, located in a high valley called a "mesa" surrounded by mountains, for a bomb design laboratory; and Hanford, Washington, six hundred square miles, for plutonium production.

General Groves built production facilities for technologies that had yet to be developed (using components not yet invented); marshaled the resources of major universities; obtained the assistance and support of America's greatest corporations (many of which placed the future of their companies at risk for the project); and gathered the greatest group of scientists, engineers and inventors ever assembled.

American leadership, ingenuity and determination prevailed. Technical problems were solved – many at the last minute. THE BOMB project finally came together in early 1945, when sufficient uranium-235 and plutonium-239 was produced at Oak Ridge to construct three atomic bombs at the Los Alamos laboratory.

General Groves leadership, tenacity and management ability provided America with the means to end World War II. Control of THE BOMB allowed America to lead the world into the nuclear age under democracy rather than tyranny.

The Manhattan Project advanced science; accelerated development of new technologies and manufacturing processes; created new materials, products and industries; established the nuclear power industry; and propelled America into the role of world leader – the first superpower.

The history of The Manhattan Project[*] should be a part of every school's required curriculum; for it is truly an inspiration and a testament to America's greatness.

---

[*] *The Manhattan Project: the Untold Story Of The Making Of The Atomic Bomb*, Stephane Groueff, Bantam Books, Inc., 1967

Introduction

The year was 1945. The Unites States had won the war with Japan by dropping two entirely different types of atomic bombs on Hiroshima and Nagasaki. The American war machine, the greatest in the history of mankind, was being disassembled. While the new U.S. President, Harry S. Truman, and the nation dreamed of peace, Joseph Stalin dreamed of empire. America was the world's first true superpower, and Stalin could not allow this to last – he too must have *THE BOMB*.

In 1943 Joseph Stalin initiated the Soviet atomic bomb development program. After Germany's and Japan's surrender, Stalin directed resources into the Soviet's version of the Manhattan Project, with orders for scientists and engineers to develop a Soviet atomic bomb. Stalin had two major advantages: first he knew that both atomic bomb designs would work – Hiroshima and Nagasaki had establish that; and second, his intelligence agencies had provided him access to the American atomic bomb designs. The Soviet Union detonated its first atomic bomb, an exact copy of America's plutonium bomb, the "Fat Man," at the Semipalatinsk Test Range, Kazakhstan in August 1949.

America's Fat Man was not the first atomic bomb dropped. "Little Boy," a uranium atomic bomb, was dropped on Hiroshima, Japan, August 6, 1945 – followed by the Fat Man dropped on Nagasaki three days later. The Little Boy was a simple, inefficient uranium atomic bomb that had limited military use; but its simplistic design and portability make it an ideal weapon for rogue nations, Islamic fundamentalists, and terrorists. Did the Soviets also attempt to duplicate the Little Boy? The plot of this novel is based upon a fictionalized account of such an effort and subsequent events caused by it.

Islamic fundamentalism has replaced communism as the free world's chief antagonist. Failure by leaders of both communist and capitalist governments to recognize the enormous threat posed by virulent Islamic fanatics has upset the balance of power and created a major threat to the civilized world.

Looking back at the cold war, one can see a form of stability in leaders, who had no desire to die for a cause. All had assets and populations that would be forfeited as a result of nuclear war. For this basic reason, the seemingly insane strategy of Mutually Assured Destruction (MAD) proved – for half a century – to be a sound deterrent to nuclear war.

Much has been written and many commentators have espoused their interpretation of Islam (which means submission). Yet the true nature of Islamic belief continues to be generally confusing to most westerners.

The Islamic faith, now the second largest religion in the world in terms of numbers of believers (over one billion), was founded by the Prophet Muhammad. Muhammad ibnu Abdillah was born in Mecca in the year 569 or 570 CE. A member of the Quraish tribe, Muhammad earned his living as a trader, and was known by his people as "*al-Amin,*" the trustworthy one.

At the age of 40, Muhammad claimed that while he sought seclusion to meditate in a cave located approximately three miles north of Mecca, the angel Gabriel came to him, with the first of many revelations. In the twenty-three years that followed, Muhammed continued to receive revelations that compelled him to recite (orally to an audience) the message of Islam: first to his immediate family, including his beloved first wife, Khadija; and eventually to deliver *Allah's* (in Arabic Allah means "the God") message to all of mankind.

Muhammad is said to have received the first eighty-six revelations in Mecca. In 622 the *hijra*, from Mecca to Medina (about 280 miles north-east of Mecca) occurred. The word *hijra* does not mean "flight" or "migration," but rather the more general meaning of "breaking of old ties." Muhammad received the remaining twenty-eight revelations in Medina. Muhammad could neither read nor write, but his followers wrote down their memory of his oral messages on any available materials (later referred to as fragments): pieces of paper, stones, palm leaves, bits of leather, and even on their own bodies.

Some twenty years after Muhammad's death, the third Caliph (successor to Muhammad), Uthman, collected the fragments; then summoned the men with memories of Muhammad's recitations and had them compiled into a text – which became know as "The Quran." After the text was compiled, Uthman ordered all of the fragments burned. The Quran contains one hundred-fourteen chapters called "Surahs" of various lengths. Collectively, the Surahs, which are not in chronological order, are comparable in length to the Christian New Testament. Muslims believe that the Quran contains the exact words of Allah as revealed to the Prophet.

Mohammed believed that Islam was for all mankind. There was no place in Islam for idolaters – they would have to convert to Islam or perish. Therefore it followed that others must be made to listen to Islam's teaching by force. A charter drawn up by Mohammed after he had moved to Medina shows that the brotherhood of Islam came before all other commitments and family ties. A believing father may have to slay an unbelieving son. Islam was a brotherhood that bound all Muslims together for all purposes, with Allah and his Prophet the final judge in all disputes.

The Prophet Muhammad died in 632 CE without naming a successor. His loyal companion and father-in-law, Abu Bakr (632-634) was elected by the tribal counsel to be the Prophet's successor: with the title of *khalifat rasul-Allah,* which means deputy or successor of the Messenger of Allah (*i.e.* Caliph). The Caliph assumed Muhammad's authority as teacher and head of the community – the temporal and spiritual leader. Bakr was followed by Umar (634-644), whose daughter was married to Muhammad; Uthman (644-656), who had married Muhammad's daughter Ruqayya; and then by Muhammad's cousin and son-in-law, Ali (656-661), who had married Muhammad's daughter Fatima.

Caliphs were elected by tribal leaders. The first four were either related to the Prophet Muhammad by blood or marriage. Ali was followed by Mu'awiya (660-680), who was the first non-related Caliph, and founder of the Umayyad Caliphs. Mu'awiya aligned himself by marriage with the most powerful tribe in Syria. He secured his Caliphate by using the powerful Syrian army, which he realized was the glue holding the Arab empire together. By securing a pledge from the army to support his son, Yazid, as the next Caliph, Mu'awiya effectively bypassed election and established hereditary succession.

Opposition flared to Yazid I's (680-683) inherited succession. The Shias, who believed that Caliphs must be descendants of Muhammad, invited the Prophet's grandson (Ali's and Fatima's son), Husain, to come from Mecca to Kufa to claim the Caliphate. En route to Kufa, Husain's party was attacked by an Umayyad force (sent to intercept him) at Kerbala. There on the banks of the Euphrates River, Husain and most of his family and followers were slaughtered in the battle on October 20, 680.

With the assassination of Husain came Islam's first schism. The Islamic faith split into two major sects: the majority sect was Sunni, and the minority sect was Shi'ite or Shia. Each sect recognized a different legitimate successor to the Prophet Muhammad. Sunnis believed that the Caliph should be elected; while the Shi'ites believed that the successor must be related to the Prophet by blood or by marriage. Shi'ites observe the anniversary of Husain's death, the day of 'Ashura – the tenth day of Muharram – as a day of public mourning. Additional interpretations within each major sect have resulted in many sub-sects. The Arab Islamic Empire peaked in the thirteenth century, and then fragmented. The office of the Caliph was placed in abeyance by the last Caliphate congress held in Cairo, Egypt in 1926.

In 1979 the United States had its first major encounter with the radical Muslim world. In February of that year, U.S. President, Jimmy Carter subjected America to international embarrassment and opened the door to the fury of radical Islam. Ayatollah Khomeini, Iran's exiled Islamic leader, was returning home from France amidst negative public opinion and demonstrations against the country's leadership. Carter encouraged the Iranian military to remain in its barracks when the Ayatollah arrived – an incident, which led to uncontrolled, massive demonstrations supporting Khomeini and sparked the Iranian revolution. Iranian students, inflamed by Khomeini's return, seized the American Embassy on November 4, 1979, and took approximately ninety people hostage inside the embassy. Fifty-two of the hostages remained in brutal captivity until the crisis came to an end with the inauguration of President Reagan on January 20, 1981.

In the 1980s during Mikhail Gorbachev's perestroika, the last official Muslim suppression occurred. Official Soviet policy considered Islamic traditions and beliefs to be the enemy of modernization, and a focal point for anti-Russian movements in Central Asia.

America and Great Britain, concerned with winning the Cold War, intervened in the Soviet-Afghan war in the 1980s. By supporting the Afghan Mujahedeen (holy warriors), they hoped that Islamic unrest would spread throughout Soviet Central Asia. No thought was given to the long-term consequences – which unfortunately have proven the old saying, *"The Devil you know is better than the Devil you don't,"* to be correct.

Radical Islamic fundamentalists have no plans to reform corrupt and unjust governments; no plans to provide jobs, education, training, or medical care; and no plans for democratic participation in government. Rather they seek to recreate the *khalifat* (Caliphate or Muslim Empire). They seek to impose *sharia* (Islamic law) on their people, not to create a free society, but rather to control their subjects. Extremists reject science and most of what history has taught us. They wish to revert to a society based upon life in the seventh century. Afghanistan ruled by the Taliban was a (so called) "model for the fundamentalist ideal Islamic State," which included: repression of women; a sadistic penal code; total control of the population; and a restrictive dress code.

Islam under fundamentalist rule has been stripped of its true values. Muhammad's teachings of searching for self improvement and spiritual growth have been replaced with a system so petty that it defines piety: for women, as wearing a burka that covers her ankles; and for men, the length of their beard.

Radical fundamentalists have hijacked Islam and are racing down the path toward worldwide destruction of Islam's true values. Short of war, only Islam itself can defeat radical Islamic fundamentalists. Unfortunately,

Islam has chosen to act in the style of the United Nations: explaining, justifying, rationalizing, and apologizing for a dictator's or radical's inhumane actions. By failing to actively denounce and confront Islamic radicals, because they are Muslims, greater Islam is allowing its radicals to drag their religion and their people into an abyss. The MAD (Mutually Assured Destruction) strategy that deterred nuclear war for half a century has no meaning to Islamic radicals: who, with nothing to loose, are willing to die and let anyone who opposes them – and some who support them – die for their cause.

Two radical Sunni-Islamic sects have exerted great influence on Central Asia's radical Islamic fundamentalists' movement – Deobandism and Wahhabism. The traditions of both sects adhere to the belief that seizure of power is the only way to impose *sharia* and change social behavior. Once power is forcibly seized, an Islamic state will naturally follow.

Deobandism is a Sunni-Islamic sect that was founded in British controlled India in the nineteenth century. Deobandism teachers spread their radical teachings to Afghanistan and Pakistan. Deobandi madrassahs (schools) established in Pakistan, trained the founders of the Taliban; and are also credited with reintroducing the militant version of jihad in the latter half of the twentieth century.

Wahhabism followed Saudi Arabian militants to Afghanistan. Wahhabism, a distortion of Islam, known as "Islamism," is a sect that considers itself to be the purest form of Islam. Intolerant of other forms of Islam and unwilling to accommodate other religions, Islamism teaches a narrow view of the world. Wahhabists fiercely oppose anything viewed as *bida*, an Arabic word, usually muttered as a curse against any change or modernization that deviates from the fundamental teachings of the Quran. The Wahhabism sect is named for Muhammad bin-Abd al-Wahhab, an 18th-century tribal leader, whose descendants are known as Wahhabists. An alliance between the Wahhabi religious movement and the House of Saud founded the kingdom of Saudi Arabia in 1932. Members of the Wahhab family continue to hold prominent positions in Saudi Arabia to this day.

Saudis themselves do not use the term Wahhabi, preferring to refer to themselves as *Unitarians* – believers in one indivisible deity. Saudi's religious establishment, the *Ulema,* imposes strict segregation of the sexes, an absolute prohibition of the sale and consumption of alcohol, a ban on women driving, and many other social restrictions. Rules are enforced by the religious police, the *Mutawa*, who patrol streets and shopping centers looking for anyone breaking the rules. Telephones, radio broadcasts, and public education for women are condemned as innovations of the Devil. There are no movie theaters in Saudi Arabia, because they promote unhealthy mingling of the sexes. Wahhabists believe their faith should be spread at all cost. No ground should be given to conquered people. All should convert or perish. According to Defense Minister Prince Sultan, ". . . Saudi Arabia, as the birthplace of Islam, will not allow [Christian] churches to be built on its land. . . . Islam is the only accepted religion in Saudi Arabia, home to the faith's holiest shrines in Mecca and Medina."[*]

The end of the Soviet-Afghan war was closely followed in 1991 by the collapse of the Soviet Union, which granted the five Central Asian republics independence: Kazakhstan, Kyrgyzstan, Tajikistan, Turkmenistan, and Uzbekistan. Sealed behind the iron curtain, Central Asians knew little about the outside world. Their ideology dated back to the 1920s. Into this vacuum rushed mullahs teaching Deobandism and Wahhabism, and creating the political turmoil that exists in Central Asia today.

Before citizens of the free world can make rational decisions regarding how to deal with Islam and radical Islamism, they must understand the ideologies and needs of Islam and the Central Asian people. Their lands are tribal: where loyalties belong to the kinsmen, tribal brothers and religion – not the current nation's flag.

Attempts to deal with Muslims in Central Asia by using western philosophy and ideology are a classic mistake. Central Asians have not acquired western values, and therefore have neither understanding nor ability to respond to western offers. Understanding the culture of Middle and Central Asia and Islam is vital to avoiding a worldwide religious war.

Can the rest of the world peacefully co-exist with Islam? That will be determined by future events. Statements made by Khalid Khawaji,[**] a self-proclaimed companion of Usama bin Laden in the early days of Afghan resistance may provide some insight:

". . . We in the Umma, the Muslim world, believe – not unjustifiably if one studies history – that American and

---

[*] *Orlando Sentinel*, March 11, 2003.

[**] Quoted from a *Special to the Los Angeles Times*, (reprinted in *Florida Today*, March 9, 2003), Khalid Khawaji, a former senior intelligence officer for Pakistan's Inter-Service Intelligence (ISI) from 1985 to 1987, described the Islamic view of church and state.

British rulers, with their laser-guided bombs of mass terror, want to subjugate others who do not wish to be ruled. . . .You believe in the separation of church and state. We believe Allah's words as revealed in the Quran are sufficient to govern our life – the church is the state, if you will. . . ."

Part I

DISCOVERY

Saravo, Russia, Winter 1990

The old man stood staring out the window, looking down at the desolate town with its snow covered streets. It was cold, well below zero, and a strong wind was blowing from the north. Turning from the window he returned to his lumpy bedside chair where he took the hand of Anya, his ailing wife. How, he wondered, after 48 years had they come to this?

The small, fifth floor apartment was frigid; the heat was neither dependable nor adequate. Food was scarce and they were only able to have two meager meals a day. His pension was insufficient to sustain a comfortable life, and he had not received his stipend for over three months. Tomorrow he would have to stand in line most of the day in the bitter cold to obtain a share of what food might be available. Maybe tomorrow there would be fresh tea for the kettle he had just put on to boil.

With his mind numbed by the cold, and consumed with bitter memories he stared once again out the frosty window. "Nothing to see," he muttered, no sun, just snow and an occasional patch of snow clouds against a gray sky. Like other frigid mornings in frozen secret places, doing secret work – *still secret* even now after Perestroika. Haunting secrets from atomic weapons Design Bureau-11. So much disclosed. So much still hidden – abandoned successes and failures. Experiments and tests at the Semipalatinsk Test Range in Kazakhstan, the first Soviet nuclear weapons test site, left frozen in time. Caves, tunnels, bunkers, test sites, a lifetime devoted to now unwanted things.

Startled from his reverie by the whistle of the teakettle, the old man grasped his wife's work worn hand and shook her awake. "Tea, my dear, that's what we need. Warm us. Yes, warm us," he said as he rose to make tea. *More water than tea these days*, he thought. The absence of rubles to purchase necessities meant that tealeaves were used more than once. Not so, when his work had top priority, and food and vodka were plentiful.

Anya coughed. *Vodka*, he thought, *a bit in her tea would be good. Our one cheap luxury*, he smiled as he topped off both cups and tucked the bottle under his arm.

"Drink Anya, take this warm cup in your hands and warm yourself my love," he muttered as he pressed the steaming cup into her gnarled hands and helped raise them to her feverish lips.

Satisfied that she was drinking, he sank again into his bedside chair with the Vodka bottle open on the table beside him. Looking up, his gaze fell again on the window and then wandered round the shabby room. Photos of his youth hung crooked on the faded walls. Memories framed in pealing paint and water stained wallpaper.

So much promise we had then, such bright futures, full of party loyalty and pride of country. Going to make a difference for Mother Russia. Teach the Capitalists that the Communists were their equals, their betters. Russia must have "THE BOMB." Change the entire fabric of civilization doing secret work . . . his waking thoughts turned into dreams as he slipped into vodka-induced slumber. Back to the glory days of his youth when he was a young engineer working in Arzamas-16, the home of the Soviet atomic bomb, and often at the Semipalatinsk Test Range in Kazakhstan.

Ivan Zeldovich completed his bachelor's degree in mechanical engineering and received an advanced degree in physics in 1939 from the Kharkov Physicotechnical Institute. There he had assisted V. A. Maslov and Vladimir Shpinel, research fellows, who filed a patent application in October 1940: "On the Use of Uranium as an Explosive and as a Poisonous Substance." The invention proposed: to separate a number of sub critical parts of uranium-235 in a bomb with neutron-proof partitions made of explosives; and to destroy these partitions by an explosion. While this invention had little to do with a genuine atomic bomb, it did provide a career path for Ivan into the Soviet atomic bomb project.

In the early 1940s, Joseph Stalin, General Secretary of the Communist Party, had begun receiving intelligence reports indicating that nuclear research to develop an "Atomic Bomb" was under way in Germany, America and Britain. Russian Professors Ioffe, Kapitsa, Khlopin, and Vernadsky successfully convinced Stalin that a Soviet atomic bomb could be developed relatively quickly. Stalin then took the first steps toward obtaining THE BOMB and initiating what was to become the Cold War. In the spring of 1942 Stalin ordered formation of a top-secret atomic weapons development program and a small nuclear research project. Igor Kurchatov, a young and relatively unknown, but promising research physicist was appointed as project leader along with Yakov Zeldovich as number two scientist.

Ivan Zeldovich's work on uranium at the Kharkov Physicotechnical Institute, though not earth shaking in importance, did draw attention, because uranium was the key to producing THE BOMB. As a bright young research fellow possessing a near photographic memory, Ivan was selected – drafted might be a better word – by Yakov Zeldovich, a distant cousin, to become a member of Igor Kurchatov's newly formed atomic weapons program. In 1943 Kurchatov became director of Laboratory No. 2, which was located on the outskirts of Moscow. Later names for Laboratory No. 2 included, LIPAN, and the Kurchatov Institute of Atomic Energy to honor its first director. In Ivan's present-day Russia the Institute was simply called the Russian Research Center.

3

As progress on developing THE BOMB accelerated, Ivan Zeldovich was drawn deeper into the ultra secret world of atomic bomb research. When a new bomb design group, Design Bureau-11, was formed, Ivan was transferred to the Bureau that was being assembled in Saravo: a sleepy town located 400 km east of Moscow at the confluence of the Satis and Sarovka Rivers. In 1946 Saravo was renamed Arzamas-16, and became the Soviet's first ultra secret atomic weapons city – a city that existed on no Soviet map. Sometimes referred to as "Los Arzamas" (a play-on-words reference to the American nuclear weapons lab at Los Alamos), Arzamas-16 became the first of 10 ultra secret cities in the Soviet Union – none of which appeared on any Soviet maps. It was in this climate of secrecy that Ivan met and married his wife, Anya, the daughter of a Russian scientist.

In keeping with Stalin's directive to match or outdo America in all things, work at Arzamas-16 was patterned after Soviet intelligence reports on America's two atomic bomb designs – "Little Boy," a pure uranium bomb, dropped on Hiroshima, August 6, 1945; and "Fat Man," a plutonium bomb, dropped on Nagasaki three days later. Ivan, with his extensive experience in uranium research was assigned to the Arazamas-16 team with orders to duplicate America's Little Boy uranium bomb.

As work advanced on developing both bombs, Soviet intelligence eventually gleaned sufficient data to enable the plutonium bomb team to successfully duplicate and detonate a Fat Man type bomb. Further pursuit of developing a uranium bomb was summarily abandoned, the bomb team purged, and the lower ranking personnel reassigned to work in obscurity: either as junior scientists, engineers, simple lab assistants, or even as common laborers in bomb production plants.

At first Ivan whispered bitter complaints to Anya about being removed from the day-to-day excitement associated with being a member of one of the competing atomic bomb development teams. "I miss my old friends," he would tell his wife when remembering shared camaraderie with his colleagues. None-the-less, over time he and Anya simply learned to be grateful to be alive. Especially when they watched a fellow scientist and his family vanish in one of Stalin's purges.

In recent years Ivan's bitterness had been replaced with an obsession for the power of nuclear fission and his early experiences with uranium. Memories of his research played and replayed in his thoughts and dreams; and were as fresh in his mind today as they were the day he was forced to retire from Design Bureau-11. With no one, not even Anya, to share his deepest secrets, Ivan silently reveled in the thought that he was one of a select few who possessed knowledge of the wonders of atomic fission and atomic bombs.

Dark dreary days like this one fueled his memories. He dreamed of the past and of the key to both bomb designs – the radioactive element uranium: an element with the chemical symbol U that spontaneously decays into another element by the emission of alpha particles. The uranium atom can also spontaneously split into two new atoms: a process called fission, in which a naturally occurring neutron is captured by its nucleus.

Natural uranium is found in many types of ores and is extracted and concentrated by conventional mining processes. Uranium metal is obtained from ores. Once known by the code word "tuballoy," Uranium is composed of three isotopes of uranium: 99.295% uranium-238, 0.7% uranium-235, and 0.005% uranium-234. Uranium metal looks similar to stainless steel when first processed. Upon exposure to air at room temperature, uranium metal first oxidizes to a golden color; then continues to oxidize until its color is blue-black or black. Exposure to the dust from the oxide coating, which is toxic when inhaled or ingested, causes heavy metal poisoning. At elevated temperatures uranium becomes pyrophoric (burns like a magnesium flare when raised to high temperatures).

The Little Boy type bomb required almost pure uranium-235 – code named "oralloy." Uranium-235 is obtained by chemically and physically separating the small amount (0.7 %) of the lighter uranium-235 isotopes from the naturally occurring uranium metal. Uranium-235 (obtained from the separation process) is divided into two general classes: 3.5% – 5% uranium-235 (suitable for use in a nuclear reactor), referred to as "enriched uranium," or EU; and 80% or greater uranium-235 (suitable for use in a fission atomic bomb), referred to as "highly enriched uranium," or HEU.

The other American bomb, the Fat Man, required a specific isotope of plutonium (chemical symbol Pu), plutonium-239. Unlike uranium, which occurs naturally in earth's minerals, plutonium is a man-made radioactive element, produced from unranium-238 in a nuclear reactor: where the uranium-238 captures a neutron and becomes uranium-239; which decays by beta emission to neptunium-239; which decays by beta emission to plutonium-239.

Separation of uranium isotopes in large quantities to make an atomic bomb was a technically complicated process that required enormous capital resources. Through American and British secrets obtained by Stalin's efficient intelligence network, Soviet researchers were able to reduce the time and cost required for their atomic research. Secret documents ferreted by Soviet spies provided evidence that America had developed designs for four methods of uranium separation: gaseous diffusion, centrifugal separation, thermal diffusion, and electromagnetic isotope separation (EMIS or calutron). Two of these processes, gaseous diffusion and calutrons were initially constructed at Oak Ridge, Tennessee.

The large amount of uranium-238 hexafluoride residue from the American uranium separation processes was referred to as "depletealloy." While depletealloy was unsuited for use in atomic bomb design, it eventually found a future use as "Depleted Uranium Kinetic Energy Penetrators" used in American anti-tank and anti-armor ammunition in the 1991 Gulf War and later battles.

The reason America never seriously considered centrifuge technology was initial impression and expediency. As soon as General Leslie Groves was officially appointed Director of the Manhattan Project on September 23,1942, he toured across America to size up the various groups working on uranium separation technologies. General Groves was a man of action, who always got the job done on time. It was natural that he would gravitate to other men of action, and judge the value of competing technologies by the drive and leadership ability of team leaders. General Groves looked for teams that had an individual or leader, who was the "spark plug" – the "can do" individual, who believed in and championed the technology. Centrifuge technology was being developed at Westinghouse Research Laboratory in Pittsburgh and the University of Virginia. Grove's assessment was that both groups were working at a relaxed academic pace, and did not grasp the urgency of the project. There was no spark plug in the centrifuge team. Centrifuge technology was dropped a short time later (additional information about the Manhattan Project's technology used to separate unanium-235 is provided in Appendix A.).

Soviet scientists initially chose the centrifugal uranium separation method. They considered the gaseous diffusion method to be more complicated and expensive. Another reason for the choice may have been that Yuli Khariton, a leading Soviet nuclear weapons scientist, recognized as the father of the Soviet Union's atomic bomb, had proposed separating isotopes of uranium in a centrifuge, and had provided a quantitative basis for the process. Much speculation occurred when it was learned that the American's had chosen gaseous diffusion as their primary process.

Centrifuge separation technology required that the gasified uranium hexafluoride be placed into a centrifuge: a spinning tube that revolved at high speed around its center axis. Spinning action of the tube caused the heaver uranium-238 molecule to move outward and concentrate along the outer wall of the spinning tube. The lighter uranium-234 and uranium-235 molecules were concentrated in the center of the tube, where they could be removed and fed into the next centrifuge tube. Like gaseous diffusion, one centrifuge fed another, which fed another. The entire process was known as a "cascade." Thousands of sequential centrifuges are required to obtain enough HEU for an atomic bomb. While gaseous diffusion technology required a massive facility, Soviet scientists thought that multiple centrifuges could be operated in a smaller facility, and still produce sufficient quantities of HEU required to build an atomic bomb.

Soviet scientists estimated that the centrifuge process would also require less power, approximately 1/10 of that required for the gaseous diffusion process; however, centrifugal separation turned out to be far more difficult than anticipated. Ultimately the Soviets put the project on hold and, like the Americans, began construction on a massive gaseous diffusion facility at Verkh-Neyvinsk: which became Sverdlovsk-44, another ultra secret Russian city, located 50 kilometers from Yekaterinburg in the Ural Mountains.

The Soviets did not completely abandon pursuit of the centrifuge process. In 1945 they captured, Dr. Gernt Zippe, the Austrian scientist, sometimes referred to as the "father of the centrifuge," and forced him to work on the Soviet's atomic bomb in Moscow. In order to obtain Dr. Zippe's full cooperation, the Soviets agreed that if Dr. Zippe successfully constructed a uranium centrifuge separation facility he would be released. Dr Zippe capitulated and designed and supervised the construction and operation of what was later considered by some to be the greatest centrifuge technology the world had ever known.

In 1952 the Soviets released Dr. Zippe and allowed his return to West Germany, where he shared his centrifuge technology with the West German Government. Eventually the CIA took Dr. Zippe to America were he was debriefed by the Atomic Energy Commission and military scientists. Employed at the University of Virginia for a period of time, he eventually returned to West Germany and worked for the German company Degussa.

Ivan, who had long been interested in Dr. Zippe's work, had read with interest a 1990 news item reporting that Karl Heinz Schaab, one of Zippe's students and himself a former Degussa employee, had been convicted by a German court in 1990 of selling uranium enrichment centrifuge technology to Iraq. A crime that earned him a minor sentence of time served – some 15 months in prison. *So,* Ivan had thought after reflecting on the story, *atomic secrets are worth something after all, but at what a risk! In Russia, in my time, a man like Schaab would simply have disappeared.*

Thoughts of purges and persons who had disappeared always brought frightening memories to Ivan's mind of Lavrenti Beria, head of the

Soviet's atomic bomb project. Lavrenti Pavlovich Beria began his political career during the Russian Revolution. He later became director of the secret police in Georgia. In 1938 Stalin appointed him to be first Commissar for Foreign Relations, and head of the Commissariat for Internal Affairs (NKVD) – the predecessor of the Committee for State Security (KGB).

Through an intelligence memorandum received from Beria in the spring of 1942, Joseph Stalin learned of America's atomic bomb development program, and became interested in Soviet Russia having THE BOMB. On February 11, 1943, Stalin authorized the State Defense Committee to establish a scientific and technical research program on the use of atomic energy. Lavrenti Beria was appointed to head the entire project called, the "First Main Directorate" (later the Soviet Ministry of Medium Machine Building), with Yuli Kurchatov remaining as scientific director and Yakov Zeldovich the number two scientist. Beria brought to his new position all the ruthlessness he had displayed as head of the NKVD and KGB. Up to the time of his arrest and subsequent execution in 1953 for a failed attempt to succeed Stalin, following Stalin's death, Beria remained one of the most feared men in the Soviet Union – second only to Joseph Stalin.

Obsessed with security, Soviet intelligence dictated that secrecy was best obtained by compartmentalizing information. Rightly so, considering how easily Soviet intelligence penetrated the American defense industry and laboratories. Only top Soviet administrators and scientists knew the scope of the entire atomic bomb project. The written history of the Soviet atomic bomb project only recorded successes. Failures were simply deleted from the records, along with senior project scientists and administrators. Unlike American and British scientists, a few of whom thought they had the right to share top secret information with another country, Soviet scientists understood security – and the penalties for breaking security rules.

Ivan, like most surviving bomb scientists, still feared Soviet intelligence and respected security. Even now thoughts of Beria and his tactics made Ivan uneasy. Rumor had it that in 1949, Lavrenti Beria, while deciding how prizes for Russia's first successful atomic bomb detonation were to be awarded, used the punishment plan for unsuccessful projects to determine those scientists who would receive awards. Scientists, who would have been shot for failure, received the title of "Hero of Socialist Labor" for success. Scientists, who would have been given maximum prison terms for failure, were awarded the "Order of Lenin," and so forth down the line.

Pressure to achieve results was intense. Ivan's uranium team worked many long hours exhausting themselves in their efforts to be the first to produce a workable bomb design. Like the Americans, Soviet scientists were exploring new technologies fraught with technical challenges and safety hazards. Environmental concerns had not yet been conceived. In many cases radioactive materials were haphazardly disposed of. Ivan often worried about the health of the men who had worked in the uranium separation facilities and at the test sites. Back then, time was of the essence, and precautions for exposure minimized. Safety became secondary to technical progress.

Soviet scientists knew that plutonium was the preferred "fissile" material – a term applied to the fissionable isotopes suitable for creating an atomic explosion – for an atomic bomb. Their main priority was developing a plutonium bomb. The uranium bomb was their backup. However, converting uranium into plutonium had not yet been accomplished in the Soviet Union. Stalin needed a functioning atomic bomb to be equal to the Americans – the type did not matter.

Facing the same technical problems encountered by the Americans in their gaseous diffusion plant (perhaps learning from the American's problems and solutions), Beria ordered the construction of a Soviet version of the American calutron facility at Sverdlovsk-44. The Soviet facility incorporated the American's alpha and beta calutron technology; and was expected to quickly produce enough HEU to construct and detonate one bomb.

The precise degree of purity of uranium-235 required to sustain the supercritical chain reaction needed for a nuclear detonation was unknown. In 1939 Soviet scientists Yuli Khariton and Yakov Zeldovich had presented a paper that formulated the conditions for a nuclear explosion, and estimated its destructive force at the Leningrad Physicotechnical Institute. In 1941, on the basis of still approximate values for the nuclear constants, Khariton, Zeldovich, and Isaak Gurevich, determined the critical mass of uranium-235. However the value was not exact.

In the late spring of 1945 the Americans had enough uranium-235 for one bomb. They determined that the Little Boy design was so simple they did not have to test a prototype device before dropping it on Hiroshima. This decision in no way meant that they underestimated the required purity or the amount of required uranium-235 fissile material.

Soviet scientists knew the design principal used in the Little Boy. G. N. Flerov and K. A. Petrzhak had discovered the spontaneous fission of uranium, and Flerov had made calculations regarding the functioning of a gun-type bomb.

An atomic bomb or atomic device requires a rapidly increasing chain reaction called a "supercritical reaction." While a nuclear reactor requires a self-sustaining reaction called a "critical reaction." A critical reaction is a self-sustaining nuclear chain reaction. When one atom splits and releases a neutron, causing another atom to split and release a neutron, causing another atom to split and release a neutron – a self-sustaining critical reaction has occurred. A nuclear reactor is said to have "gone critical" when a self-sustaining chain reaction has been achieved. A "sub critical reaction" is one in which the chain reactions die out. In other words, the chain reaction is not maintained.

A "prompt critical reaction" is an increasing chain reaction in which one fission produces more than one fission in a controlled manner. In a nuclear reactor, control rods that absorb neutrons regulate the prompt critical fission reaction. A prompt critical reaction occurs when a nuclear reactor increases its power level. Once the new power level is achieved, control rods are adjusted to bring the reaction back to critical. Without control rods, the fission reaction increases (runs away) until the uranium core of the reactor melts and deforms: leaving highly radioactive molten metal slag. If the reactor's containment vessel ruptures, fission products can be released. Such a runaway is popularly referred to as "The China Syndrome": a name coined from the title of a movie depicting a fictional account of runaway reactor. An event that later became a reality when Russia's Chernobyl nuclear reactor went into an uncontrolled prompt critical reaction and melted, rupturing, the containment vessel. Nuclear reactors use enriched uranium (EU), which cannot sustain the supercritical fission reaction required to produce an atomic explosion. Nuclear reactors cannot blow up and make an atomic explosion, because they do not contain HEU (fissile material).

A uranium-235 supercritical chain reaction requires HEU. One fission produces, for example, three fissions that produce three more for a total of nine – nine produces twenty-seven, twenty-seven produces eighty-one, *etc.* These chain reactions result in a nuclear detonation. The yield of the detonation will depend on the length of time the fissile material remains in a supercritical mass configuration. The length of time that the mass remains supercritical is measured in nanoseconds. One nanosecond is one billionth of a second, or 1×10^{-9} second. A typical implosion device will complete its supercritical chain reaction in thirty nanoseconds.

When the uranium-235 atom splits, it creates two new atoms that are called "fission products" – examples are *tellurium, iodine, xenon,* and *cesium.* Most fission products are unstable isotopes that are radioactive and decay to form new atoms by releasing one of the following: a positive charged alpha particle; a negatively charged beta ray; a neutron; or gamma radiation.

A supercritical mass has to be assembled very quickly, just how quickly was the Soviet's problem. Ivan's bomb team knew that the supercritical mass concept was valid – Hiroshima had established that. Spontaneous fission is continuously occurring in highly enriched uranium (HEU). Therefore the components making up the supercritical mass of HEU must remain separated by some distance in order to prevent starting a chain reaction. How to assemble the sub critical components into a supercritical mass was the problem. How many sub critical components should be used – two, three? The more sub critical components used the more complicated the assembly mechanism. The shape of the subcomponents dictated the assembly method – or visa versa.

Ivan's team was in the process of evaluating various designs for sub critical components, when they received the order to prepare a critical mass uranium experiment. A sphere is the best shape or geometry for a critical or supercritical mass. Enough HEU had been produced to make a test device, and Beria wanted to satisfy Stalin's desire to become a nuclear super power. Ivan's team had succeeded in developing an HEU component design, and had quickly chosen a method of assembly, but the team lacked confidence in the design. Data had to be obtained pertaining to assembly of sub critical mass components into a supercritical mass.

The team decided to conduct a test to determine parameters for assembly of sub critical components. The test, conducted with maximum instrumentation, used a critical mass geometry that would not produce a nuclear yield. But the test was expected to provide necessary data to proceed with the design. The critical mass design was a small sphere of HEU that did not have enough HEU to form a supercritical mass. The test sphere consisted of two halves – two hemispheres that were propelled together at a known velocity to form the sphere and create a critical mass. Each hemisphere was mounted on a small sled. The sleds were mounted facing each other on opposite ends on a track; and were driven into each other at a known velocity by means of compressed air.

Ivan Zeldovich had been on the test team in 1947 for the first critical mass test that resulted in incomplete assembly of the sphere. The two hemispheres, fabricated from HEU, had not completely combined as expected. Analysis of test data showed that as the two sub critical components approached each other a chain reaction began, releasing enough heat to melt the components before they touched – leaving a hot, radioactive slag on the ground. The team had set up the test device in a narrow canyon on the Semipalatinsk test range. The canyon's walls could be collapsed, burying the radioactive slag. *Many undocumented things were buried on the test range – this was just one of them,* Ivan thought.

Anya coughed, breaking his reverie. Turning toward her, he again saw her pale face and wondered how much longer she could survive these harsh conditions. After covering her with a blanket he went to the kitchen to reheat the teakettle. Another cup of tea would be good for her.

Sitting down near her in the apartment's shabby living room, his mind returned to his previous musings. A second test in 1948, also conducted under extreme secrecy in another test range canyon, achieved complete assembly of the critical mass. The senior scientists on his team were delighted that now they had sufficient data to proceed with a uranium atomic bomb design. They had determined that the enriched uranium used in the tests had to be increased to at least 90% uranium-235. They used the American assembly method, but the configuration of the sub critical components needed improvement. America's Little Boy had not achieved the predicted yield; because a supercritical mass had pre-detonated before the components had completely come together.

The proper specification for highly enriched uranium had finally been determined. Sufficient quantities of HEU were now available; because Soviet scientist had boosted their calutron's output to HEU, by using the enriched uranium output from the centrifuge and gaseous diffusion facilities as feedstocks. Ivan's team made several new improved designs and selected the most promising five for testing. Components were ordered for each of the five designs. Component assembly techniques were tested, using deplete alloy components. The new supercritical mass designs allowed the uranium-235 components to completely combine. An external neutron source had also been designed that would increase the yield by increasing the number of initial fissions. Each initial fission created an increasing chain reaction referred to as "generations."

The initial fission or fissions are the first generation. The resulting fissions are the second generation. It follows that the more fissions in the first generation the greater the yield. One initial fission would produce 3 that would produce 9, then 27, then 81. The series continues until the bomb explodes. If a million initial fissions occurred in the first generation, the progression would be 1,000,000, 3,000,000, and 9,000,000. The more effective the neutron source the larger the number of fissions in the first generation.

Ivan rose to the sound of the kettle and poured more tea and vodka. Seeing Anya once again settled with her cup in hand, he fell asleep in his chair.

The following day on the way to the food line Ivan met his old friend and fellow engineer, Georgi Akademii. Ever mindful of security neither man referenced the past during their weekly public meetings in the long line. It wasn't until much later in the day that the two old comrades felt comfortable, quietly talking of secret things in the privacy of one or the other's apartment. Settled now at Georgi's table with bags of that day's purchased food in front of them, they began what had become routine over the years – drinking and sharing fresh news, rumors and repeating over and over memories of their experiences and adventures.

Georgi, who had been a member of the plutonium bomb team and was present for the successful detonation of his team's bomb, "First Lightning," was obsessed with the history of Soviet nuclear testing. As often as not, he started every visit with Ivan bemoaning the fact that nothing was being done to test new bombs. "You know that nothing has been done since the last Soviet underground nuclear weapons test in 1989," Georgi always said.

Ivan nodding in agreement, sipped his vodka and sat back to listen to the history once again, as though he never tired of hearing it.

"Yes, but we really put one over on the Americans in 1963 when we agreed to sign the limited test ban treaty. The treaty banned atmospheric testing before the Americans could start their second major test program in the Pacific. Our test data really gave us an advantage over them in electromagnetic pulse (EMP) technology," Ivan commented.

"I guess that made up for the Cuban missile fiasco," Georgi bragged.

"That's right. We completed 60 atmospheric tests in 1962. Our first shot was over 60 megatons (MT). As I remember, the Americans were not ready to test their high yield designs. They were planning a second Pacific test series for the late 1960s, but Comrade Chairman Khrushchev outsmarted them by agreeing to the Limited Test Ban Treaty in July of 1963. The Americans did test 36 warheads in the low kiloton to low megaton range in their OPERATION DOMINIC test series conducted in the Pacific. Their last test, STARFISH PRIME, was a 1.5 MT high altitude atmospheric detonation near Johnson Island that created an EMP wave causing a power loss on the island of Oahu, Hawaii 800 miles away."

"Did you know," Georgi asked, "that we were developing a 100 MT bomb? It was named 'Tsar Bomba' and weighed 27 tons."

The Soviet's nuclear weapons program, like the American's, had been interrupted with a series of voluntary moratoriums: November 1958 to August 1961; December 1962 to March 1964; August 1985 to October 1987; and November 1989 to October 1990. President Gorbachev, seeking to reach accommodations with the U.S., was about to order a fifth moratorium in anticipation of the Comprehensive Test Ban Treaty.

"I tell you Ivan, we can not just stop testing. We have too much at stake in the nuclear weapons program for it to be reduced; but funding is being drastically cut and personnel are being retired, reassigned or just let go. That means a lot more fellows like us will be out of work and standing in line for food, waiting for meager scraps like these on the table," Georgi ranted while gesturing with a flourish at the few bags on the table.

For awhile the two friends sat silently looking at each other, until Georgi suddenly sat forward in his chair with some news of what might be happening to some of the cut personnel. "I have heard that all may not be bad for those fellows. Rumor has it that some of our top nuclear scientists have been offered high paying positions in Iran, Iraqi and Libya," Georgi said. "Imagine Ivan, giving our secrets to some foreign government. What would Beria have done to them in the old days?"

Then Georgi mentioned hearing from a mysterious man, identifying himself as KGB, who had been contacting personnel from the old Design Bureau-11. "When he first approached me, I thought he might be looking for traitors who were leaving to work for foreign governments. But no, strangely enough, the man inquired only about the location of weapon components and fissile material that may have been abandoned, misplaced or forgotten. He showed no interest in engineers and scientists. Instead he said that anyone helping to find what he called 'orphans' would be well rewarded with rubles and commodities not available to the masses. What do you suppose they are really looking for? " he asked Ivan as he poured them another drink. "We were too busy trying to design a working bomb to be worried about left-over materials and where they were put."

Again the old friends simply sat and looked at one another. Both dismayed by the idea someone would actually be interested in remnants of a time so long ago. Then prompted anew by thoughts of long ago events Georgi and Ivan began talking about their personal experiences with disposal of certain wastes and leftover components from development projects.

Accountability was not a high priority in the Soviet Union of the late 1940s. When a test or project was completed it was time to move on – salvage only what might be needed for the next task. "We could always go back and retrieve anything of value when it was needed. Could we not?" Georgi asked. "That is if any of us ever took the time to think about the equipment and where it had been left."

"Yes," Ivan agreed, "some of the time we were not even sure if it was safe to go back where something had been left to retrieve it. I remember how hard we tried to teach the technicians at the test site about basic worker safety?"

"Yes, we did, and do you remember what a miserable time I had when I was assigned to teach them basic nuclear physics?" asked Georgi.

"You made it so simple. I never could understand why it was so difficult for them to grasp the basic concepts."

By now the old friends were well into their cups and had begun their usual rambling – each about their own favorite subject. "Yes, you taught them the basics," Ivan said, knowing full well Georgi was about to repeat a lecture almost verbatim to one he had given so many years ago at the test site. Ivan poured another drink and again settled back to listen.

"Yes, I started with the atom, which is made up of three major components: a proton that has a positive electrical charge; a neutron that has no electrical charge; and an electron that has a negative electrical charge. I then told them that the proton and neutron are in the center of the atom called the nucleus, and that the electron orbits around the nucleus. Our solar system was my model. The nucleus would be the sun and the electron the earth. After that I covered the definition of an element – a substance, which consists wholly of atoms having the same number of protons in the nucleus. The atom of the simplest element, hydrogen, I explained, is also the lightest element. Its atom is comprised of one proton and one orbiting electron. Continuing on, I spoke of the next lightest element, helium, which has two protons and two neutrons in its nucleus with two orbiting electrons. . . ."

Ivan's mind had drifted off. He suddenly became aware that Georgi was reaching the end of his lecture. Talk then shifted to the test range, the excitement, and their adventures in the early days of the nuclear weapons program. Now looking back, they realized that whatever hardships they had endured went unrecognized at the time. Most remarkable, they remembered how little physical security had been there, considering the secrecy of the projects. The test range had not been fenced in and the guards were lax in their duties, except when senior officers were present.

All during Georgi's lecture Ivan had felt something tugging at the corner of his mind. The feeling started with the reference to the KGB man. At first his breath had caught in his throat as it often did when, unbidden, the specter of Beria would come to mind. Choking back memories, he had quickly erased Beria's image, until now when once again the KGB man and his quest for "orphans" came to mind. The secrecy surrounding the way his team had been disbanded always made Ivan wary of questions relating to his work with the team. Over his spectacles, Ivan watched Georgi rambling on about some test or other and wondered, *what do you know about my team's test devices or equipment? "Orphans," if you like, that might have been left from my project. I know far more about yours. I think you talk too much my friend. Over the years I have told you little to nothing. I have spoken of other work I did at Arzamas-16, but never the bomb team. Yes, we were told to say nothing. My very life depended upon it. But what were you told? Let us see just how much you do remember about the circumstances surrounding the disbanding of my team.*

"Georgi, do you remember the summer of 1949?" Ivan asked.

"Yes, we were franticly trying to get First Lighting ready for its test. We worked day and night until the test. I witnessed the test, you know. I will never forget the brilliant light. It was terrifying and fascinating. I do not think any of us knew what to expect. We thought we did. Nothing could have prepared us for the actual event. When it happened it was overpowering. I was both scared and exhilarated. I first told myself, 'We did it,' and then I shuddered and wondered, 'What have we done?' Does this seem strange to you?"

"No. I saw the second test in 1951 and had much the same emotions. What did you do after the first test?"

"Well, there was a lot of Vodka," Georgi snorted and laughed, then continued, "Parties everywhere. Then I was sent back to Arzamas-16 with the rest of our team. We were very busy, and you know that Yuli Khariton and Yakov Zeldovich received the Hero of Socialist Labor medal, the only Jews in Soviet history to receive the highest Soviet civilian honor?"

"Yes, all of you must have been very proud of your accomplishments."

"Yes, I was, and I still am. I have always been hesitant to ask you about your situation, but now I guess it is O.K. to do so after all of these years."

"I am not sure what you mean, Georgi," Ivan said hoping his friend was referring to the disbanding of Ivan's team, and trying to draw Georgi out about what he knew. *After my team's failure to achieve the first atomic bomb detonation, we all simply disappeared. Then slowly over the next year some of us gradually reentered the atomic weapons project.* In all the years since, Georgi and Ivan had never discussed that awful time: awful and shameful for Ivan for he felt like such a failure. *This is the first time the subject has come up. I am very curious to know what Georgi was told.*

Georgi poured them another drink, looked rather embarrassed and shifted somewhat nervously in his chair as he spoke, "Well, when we returned to Arzamas-16 the whole team was taken to a conference room: where Comrade Lavrenti Beria first congratulated us for our achievement; then ordered us to forget everything pertaining to your team − never mention its name or any of the team members. I was very happy to see you later that year, but of course I could not say so. Over the years I have read much about the work our team did on First Lighting, but never saw any reference to what your team was doing. All I know is that the team simply disappeared and apparently no record of its existence was ever documented."

"Yes, well I was not considered to be responsible and was allowed to continue with the program, but I never was going to be given great responsibilities again. I was very bitter at first, but then Anya and I learned to be grateful just to be alive"

So, it is as I thought. You know nothing my friend. Nothing more than that there was a team and you were told to forget that. This is good. Better still is the idea that I might know something about "orphans." I must give this some serious thought, Ivan decided. Suddenly anxious to change the subject, he turned the conversation to the present and how bad things were. All kinds of rumors were circulating. Many were about Afghanistan losses, others about the Soviet government loosing control of its republics. Satisfied that he had put thoughts of the past out of Georgi's mind, Ivan gathered up his food bags, said goodbye, and somewhat unsteady from the vodka, slowly returned to his apartment.

The weather became worse the next day, and the apartment grew even colder. More snow fell. Anya remained in bed to keep warm. Ivan resumed his practice of staring out of the window, but today there was a definite purpose behind his thoughts. *If what Georgi said is true, and there was value in old components from the 1940s, I might remember something that could help Anya and me out of our present state of misery. What,* he wondered, *happened to the components for the five atomic devices we never tested?*

Components for the five new atomic devices began to arrive at Semipalatinsk in the spring of 1949. Ivan had helped store them in a remote underground bunker complex. Extreme secrecy surrounded the arrival of the components. Testing was scheduled to begin in September. The uranium enrichment process had been improved. Enough high quality HEU fissile material was available to fabricate the five atomic test devices, with calculated yields ranging from 20 kilotons (KT) to 30 KT each. One kiloton is the equivalent of one thousand tons of trinitro-toluene (TNT) explosive. Each of the five devices would test a different supercritical component shape called "geometry." The team had used the American method of assembling the sub critical components into a supercritical mass. Extensive testing using components fabricated from uranium-238 had been conducted with a cannon and experimental sabot ammunition. Yields were estimated; and the tests would provide data to evaluate the effectiveness of the polonium-beryllium neutron source.

The chief scientist was a nervous man, who would become almost paralyzed with fear at the thought of failure. This fear was the basis for his decision to have five test devices ready prior to testing. One of the five had to work. Beria would conceal failure of unsuccessful tests; as long as there was another device to test that could work. Ivan had no way of knowing that the chief scientist had serious reservations about one of the device's geometry; nor that he had decided that the questionable device would not be tested if one of the other four achieved a high yield.

Rumor had it that the other Soviet team, Georgi's team, working on the plutonium bomb design, was about to catch up. Obtaining sufficient quantities of plutonium-239 was the critical path to success; and that required a nuclear reactor capable of converting uranium-238 into plutonium-239. At 6 P.M. Moscow time on December 25, 1946 at the Kurchatov Institute, the first Soviet nuclear reactor went critical; and the first self-sustaining nuclear chain reaction in the Soviet Union was achieved. The Kurchatov reactor, originally operated at a power level of 10 watts, was a graphite-moderated reactor based on the American Hanford 305 reactor design. Eventually Kurchatov had upgraded its power level to 24 kilowatts. In 1948 Soviet prisoners constructed a larger graphite moderated plutonium production reactor in another secret city, Chelyabinsk-40 – later know as Chelyabinsk 65. The Chelyabinsk reactor produced 100 grams per day and provided the plutonium-239 fissile material for the early Soviet atomic bombs. Four additional reactors were added to the Mayak production facility. By spring 1949 there was sufficient plutonium-239 fissile material to construct an implosion bomb.

At 7 A.M. on August 29, 1949, the Soviet Union tested its first atomic bomb at the Semipalatinsk test site using plutonium-239 as the fissile material. Plutonium-239 is a superior fissile material, requiring only about one third the amount of HEU needed for a uranium bomb. The devise, designated First Lighting, was mounted on a tower with a yield of 22 KT. Many years later American and Soviet scientists learned that First Lightning, which the Americans had named "Joe" for Joe Stalin, was an exact copy of the American Fat Man. Joe later became known as "Joe-1." When the second Soviet device was detonated September 24, 1951, with a yield of 38 KT, the Americans named it "Joe-2."

Failure was not a good thing in the Soviet Union, especially when Lavrenti Beria was in charge. Thus, all record of the Little Boy type uranium bomb team was deleted from the formal record. First Lighting became the first successful nuclear detonation conducted by the USSR. The Plutonium team became the core of the Soviet nuclear weapons program. The Soviets eventually produced 1,000 metric tons of highly enriched uranium, and continued to use HEU in future soviet implosion nuclear weapons. Immediately following the successful First Lightning test, Ivan's team was disbanded. Key scientists disappeared and lower ranking personnel like Ivan were reassigned. Ivan escaped the purge and was able to remain employed with minor responsibilities until he retired in 1985.

Noises from the kitchen brought Ivan back to the present. His wife was preparing their meager dinner. Joining her at the table, they discussed their situation and future. Ivan mentioned Georgi's tale of the man who was offering to pay a reward for certain abandoned items. Anya asked if he knew where such items could be found. *As recently as a year ago I would have severely chastised her for such a question,* he thought, but now he held his tongue. Maybe tomorrow his pension would be paid.

Five days later, after hours spent remembering the last days before his team was disbanded, he again met Georgi Akademii on the way to the food line. This time Ivan was armed with the sure knowledge that he had a very valuable secret. He thought he knew what had been done with the components of his team's five devices. With his food purchases made and anxious to return to Anya, who was suffering terribly from the cold, Ivan found the courage to speak openly to Georgi of the orphan hunter as they walked home through the frozen streets.

"Georgi," he said, "I have thought of your friend the orphan hunter, and cannot think now of any waste materials that might be considered valuable. But I would like to know how to contact this fellow to learn more of what they are looking for." In response Georgi said that he had written down a Moscow number one could call and leave a message. He would give Ivan the number, which was written on a piece of paper in his wallet, when they could get out of the cold inside the foyer of Ivan's apartment building. Now, with the prized telephone number clutched safely in his gloved hand, Ivan watched as Georgi walked away in the blowing snow. *He knows nothing about my team's devices,* Ivan thought trying to reassure himself that his secret was safe. *No one must benefit from this memory, but my Anya and me.*

That night after another bland supper, Ivan lay huddled with Anya in their bed in the small, drafty bedroom and wondered, What happened to the components for the five test devices in the years since 1949? Had anyone found and removed them from storage in the remote underground bunker at the Semipalatinsk Test Site? Could they still be there? If so, what condition are they in? His last thoughts before sleep were stories of the warmth of Cuba. Wouldn't it be wonderful to live there?

The next morning he was haunted by thoughts of the five devices. How could he go about finding out if they were still there? *Only one way, I must go there and see. But how?* he thought, *I have no funds, or a travel permit required for such a trip.* He spent the day, and the next several days contemplating this issue. Could the components have been forgotten? It was possible. Georgi confirmed what I was told. All records pertaining to my team were destroyed, and the key personnel purged. Yes, it was possible. The components could still be there – forgotten with no remaining record.

For several more days he pondered the possibilities. If the components were still there, could he find the underground bunker entrance after all of these years? What would the components be worth? How much should he ask for them? Millions of rubles, he still could not think in these terms. *If I do get millions of rubles, where would we go?* The questions kept coming. Anya noticed his change in attitude and inquired as to the cause.

"Ivan, you are troubled, what is the matter?" Anya asked.

How much should he tell her? Secrecy was a must. Others might remember the storage bunker. What would be the penalty if he was caught? "Nothing important dear, I am concerned about Georgi and his family."

Finally he decided. He would call the phone number for the orphan hunter and feel him out. Later that day while Anya slept, Ivan called the Moscow number; and left a brief message that he may know about an abandoned item, and that he would call again the next day after 2 pm.

Afghanistan-Soviet War

It began on April 27, 1978, with a bloody pro-Soviet leftists' military coup, the "Great Saur Revolution," which established a Communist government, the "Democratic Republic of Afghanistan." Headed by President Nur M. Taraki, the new Afghanistan government quickly established a military and economic treaty with the Soviet Union. Sweeping changes followed. The most unsettling to fanatical Islamic leaders were those changes that concerned land distribution, and emancipation of women. Both of which threatened to undermine tribal culture, and to destroy ancient Afghanistan social structure.

Unpopular from the start, the Communist led government was immediately challenged by armed Islamic resistance fighters. Bloody purges swept the officer ranks of the Army. The city of Herat rose in open revolt in March 1979. Forces loyal to the new Communist government advanced and occupied the city. While the Communist led Afghan Air Force bombed the city, the Afghan Army's 17th Division's infantrymen mutinied, and most joined the rebellion. Over 5,000 people died in the fighting, including some 100 Soviet citizens.

By the end of 1979, the size of the Afghan Army had been reduced from about 90,000 to about 40,000. Soldiers, units and entire brigades deserted to the Islamic resistance. Half of the officer corps was purged, executed or deserted. The Prime Minister, Hafizullah Amin, seized power and executed President Taraki in September 1979. President Amin faired no better than his predecessor. The Soviet Politburo watched in dismay as its new Communist state disintegrated.

Insurrection was not tolerated in the Soviet Union. Soviet military might had subdued the Ukraine, East Germany, Hungary, and Czechoslovakia. Afghanistan would be no exception. The Soviet General Staff was directed to start intervention planning.

In an effort to catch western governments off guard, the Soviets launched their 1979 Afghanistan invasion; with a massive military airlift into the capital, Kabul, on Christmas Eve. Soviet advisers conducted acts of sabotage by blocking arms rooms and disabling equipment. Soviet airborne and *Spetsnaz*, Soviet Special Forces, seized key airfields, government and communications sites in Kabul. Also seized was the *Salang Tunnel,* the highest tunnel in the world at 3,363 meters (11,034 ft.). Salang provides the only practical passage through the *Hindu Kush Mountains* on the road between the city of Mazar-e-Sharif, near the Soviet border and Kabul. Soviet ground invasion forces crossing into Afghanistan met little resistance and occupied the main cities. President Amin was killed and replaced with Babrak Karmal, a pro-Soviet faction leader. A new Afghan puppet government, People's Democratic Party of Afghanistan (PDPA) was installed.

The Soviets modeled their Afghanistan invasion after their take-over of Czechoslovakia. For several months the take-over proceeded on schedule. Most military experts assumed that Islamic Afghani rebels would be subdued; however, some skeptics recalled that the British had not faired well in their Afghanistan war. Rebellious Afghani forces continued to grow under the subversive leadership of fanatical Islamic leaders.

Soon things began to go horribly wrong. Instead of the resistance ending, it had only begun. Two months after the invasion, on the night of February 23, 1980, the population of Kabul, almost in its entirety, climbed on their rooftops and chanted with one voice, *"Allah Akbar,"* God is Great: An act of defiance that was repeated throughout the countryside. The Afghan warrior society sent thousands of Islamic fanatics against the Soviet invader. The ten-year Afghanistan/Soviet War had begun.

During the next nine years, Soviet troops fanned out over Afghanistan: fighting the *Mujahedeen,* Islamic holy warriors, in a costly, protracted guerrilla war. A war that continued throughout the reign of four Soviet General Secretaries – Brezhnev, Chernenko, Andropov and Gorbachev. A conflict that would not officially end until May 15, 1989, with the departure of the last Soviet soldier.

Resistance to the PDPA and Soviet domination of Afghanistan became a holy war or *jihad* – Islam against Communism – Islamic values against the infidel's. Afghan Mujahedeen, jihad holy warriors were fierce, brave fighters, but were too few in numbers to defeat the Soviet army. A call for help echoed throughout the Islamic world.

Neighboring Pakistan with its predominantly Muslim population was one of the first to heed the call. Having declared itself an Islamic Republic and promulgated its first constitution, Pakistan had established a parliamentary form of government in 1956. Two years later General Ayub Khan became the first of a succession of military rulers, and rewrote Pakistan's constitution to allow himself wide-ranging executive powers. Over the next ten years warring factions along the India and Pakistan border battled over control of East Pakistan. In 1966 the General signed the *Tashkent Cease-fire Declaration* with India's Prime Minister. Bitterness over the agreement, which Pakistanis considered a submission to India, brought about General Ayub Khan's abdication of power to General Yahya Khan in 1969. Pakistan's foreign minister, Zulfikar Ali Bhutto, resigned and formed the Pakistan People's Party (the PPP).

General parliamentary elections in March 1970 brought about a political impasse between East Pakistan, supporters of the majority Awami League, and West Pakistan, which had voted for Bhutto's PPP. With India's help, East Pakistan separated from Pakistan and formed Bangladesh in 1971. Four days later, General Yahya Khan was deposed. Bhutto took over West Pakistan's government until his own arrest in 1977 by General Zia-ul-Haq.

During General Zia's term, Pakistan was placed under martial law and profited from the Soviet's Afghanistan invasion. Quick to realize the possibility of turning Pakistan into the leader of the Muslim world, Zia used Pakistan's Inter-Services Intelligence agency, the ISI, to foster plans for Islamic opposition to communism in Central Asia.

Eager to establish a strategic buffer state against their Cold War nemesis, the Soviet Union, the United States donated military equipment and aid to Pakistan. Through Pakistan's secret service, the U.S. began channeling money to a newly emerging group of hard-core Islamic fanatics, the "Taliban." American aid, while strengthening Pakistan's economy and the growth of the private sector, did little to establish democratic or economic reforms. When Zia died in a suspicious plane crash in 1988, Zulfikar Ali Bhutto's daughter, Benazir Bhutto, succeeded him as Prime Minister. Accused of corruption and dismissed in 1990, Benazir was replaced by Nawaz Sharif. He too was dismissed in 1993. In

1996 Benazir returned, only to be deposed again the following year on the same charges. Sharif was then reinstated.

The northern border between Pakistan and Afghanistan proved to be a vital lifeline for Afghani rebels, and ultimately a hot bed for the fermentation of fanaticism and terrorism. In the ten-year period following the beginning of the Soviet/Afghanistan war, numerous training camps sprang up along the border near the Pakistani town of Peshawar. Islamic recruits from Muslim countries and around the world met each other in these camps; where they exchanged views, and learned about each other's Islamic movements. In addition to training fighters, these camps became defacto universities for Islamic radicalism.

In the mid 1980s, America's CIA director, William Cassey, working with Zia and Pakistan's ISI to combat the spread of communism, committed CIA support to the ISI's long-standing initiative to recruit radical Muslims from around the world; and to bring them to Pakistan to fight with the Afghan Mujahedeen. Cassey also obtained funding and approval to provide the Mujahedeen with American-made shoulder launched Stinger anti-aircraft missiles – effective against Soviet helicopters and planes – and U.S. advisers to train the guerrillas.

Blinded by the need to win the Cold War against the Soviets, America failed to recognize the threat created by funding the Mujahedeen. Thousands of radical fighters brought together for training were also exposed to a form of Islamic fundamentalism unknown in most of the Muslim world. America had unwittingly given these volunteer radicals an opportunity to create their own agenda, and ultimately to turn against their sponsors. The Cold War had given way to what analysts were quick to name the "New Great Game": a game in which Russia, China and the United States were fighting for influence over the people of Central Asia. Shortsighted help for the militants had planted the seeds for an even more ominous game – the world wide Islamic terrorist movement.

In addition to providing weapons and advisers to the Afghan Mujahedeen, the CIA, through MI6 (Britain's equivalent to the CIA), conceived of a plan to attack supply bases in the Soviet Republics of Tajikistan and Uzbekistan. Command of the attacks, the first of which occurred in March 1987, was assigned to Mujahedeen leader, Gulbuddin Hikmetyar, a favorite of Pakistan's ISI. Afghan Mujahedeen soldiers crossed the Amu Darya River, entered Tajikistan and attacked villages with rockets.

Between 1982 and 1992, some 35,000 Muslim radicals from 43 Islamic countries in the Middle East, North and East Africa, Central Asia and the Far East passed their baptism under fire fighting for the Afghan

Mujahedeen. Pakistan established and funded hundreds of fundamental Islamic schools, known as *madrassahs*, along the Afghan border: where many thousands of foreign Muslim radicals came to study; and to fall under the influenced of Islam's most fanatical sub-sects – Deobandism and Wahhabism. Wahhabism is an ideology so puritanical in its dogma, that it effectively replaced communism as the root of anti-Western ideology. Madrassahs continue to operate in the 21st century, and tens of thousands of their graduates continue to wreak havoc throughout the world.

Resistance to the Soviet's 1978 take-over of Afghanistan required more than just fighters. Funding to support the rebellion had to be obtained. Saudi Arabia, among other Islamic nations met the challenge. However, Saudi Arabia was on the verge of experiencing its own Islamic rebellion. On November 20, 1979, 500 radicals seized the Grand Mosque in Mecca and killed thousands of pilgrims. As titular protector of Islamic pilgrims and worshipers, the royal family was being severely ridiculed by Central Asian governments, and more significantly, the *Ulema*, the body of scholars who dictate Islamic theology. Saudi forces captured and beheaded sixty-three of the rebels responsible for the killings. If Saudi leaders wished to sustain their legitimacy as guardians of Islam's holy places, Mecca and Medina, a greater show of force was required. In addition Islamists, devout in their puritanical adherence to Wahhabism, began openly criticizing the royal family, and its Saudi advisors, for publicly succumbing to the self-indulgent temptations of western life – liquor, fast cars, and women.

Something had to be done to save face for the house of Saud, a traditional adherent to the Wahhabism form of Islam. Support for the Afghan uprising against communism proved to be the perfect conduit for Saudi Arabia to rid itself of the radicals; to coalesce with other Islamic nations; and more importantly, to appear to be sincere in their adherence to the Wahhabism faith.

Prince Turki bin-Faisal, the head of the Saudi Intelligence Service, the *Istakhbara*, was under pressure from Pakistan's ISI to provide a royal prince to lead the Saudi contingent in support of the Islamic revolution. Such a move would have shown the Islamic world the royal family's commitment to the jihad: a commitment, which by the end of 1979 had only been demonstrated through funding; and by providing a token number of Bedouin tribesmen, students, and taxi drivers to fight in the rebellion. The Saudis had shown some support by sending Abdul Rasul Sayyaf, an Afghan Islamic scholar, to Peshawar to promote Wahhabism; but, no members of the royal family were to be found roughing it, living in the harsh conditions of the training camps. Fighting in the Afghan mountains and being martyred for Allah held no appeal for the royals.

The Saudis solved their 1979 controversy with the Ulema by allowing Wahhabism clerics more control over the social, economic, and educational development of Saudi Arabia's kingdom; and by funding the export of Wahhabism to Pakistan and throughout the Muslim world. The Saudi government funded billions of dollars to finance fundamentalist religious madrassahs in Pakistan and to build Wahhabist-oriented mosques from the Balkans to Indonesia. Sixty percent of the mosques built in America were Wahhabi-funded. Emerging from these schools and mosques are millions of militant Muslims filled with a vitriolic dogma, and spouting vicious anti-American anti-Semitic teachings.

A river of charitable money flowed from wealthy Saudis to *al-Qaeda, Hamas, the Palestinian Authority* and other radial groups throughout the Muslim world. For years the Saudi government turned a blind eye to the problem. In an agreement cut with the House of Saud, the wealthy were expected to donate to "charities," which would directly fund the extremists. The *quid pro quo* was a promise from the fanatics not to direct terrorist's wrath against the House of Saud and other interest in Saudi Arabia.

One notably prominent Saudi, who openly funded the Afghan rebels, was Mohammed bin Laden, a Yemen born billionaire. Mohammed bin Laden built a business empire based in Saudi Arabia by obtaining contracts to renovate and expand the Holy Mosques of Mecca and Medina. Mohammed bin Laden, a close friend of King Faisal, had twenty wives and fifty-four children. Each wife had a separate house. Mohammed bin Laden's fourth wife, a Syrian, had one child, Usama bin Laden. Usama, which means "lion like" in Arabic, had little contact with his siblings. Like many Arab children of his class, young Usama spent most of his early life isolated in a world filled with tutors and servants. His Syrian mother was a sophisticated and well-traveled woman who refused to wear a burka and favored *Chanel* suits.

Mohammed bin Laden, who reportedly died in 1968, left 13-year-old Usama $80 million dollars. In his early years, Usama behaved like many western young men – seeking fun, drinking heavily, and nightclubbing in Beirut. Party animal or not, Usama inherited his father's skill for making money and used his inheritance to amass a great fortune of his own.

Usama bin Laden graduated from King Abdul-Aziz University, in Jidda, with a degree in civil engineering. He then started work on a master's degree in business administration; but eventually switched to Islamic studies where he apparently fell under the influence of one of Islam's most puritanical dogmas – Wahhabism. Like a born-again

Christian, Usama embraced Wahhabism with a passion: a religion which punishes those who enjoy any music other than the drum, and can put a man to death for drinking or sexual misconduct. With his long flowing beard and standing an imposing 6 feet 5 inches tall, Usama towered above his contemporaries, who remember him as a quiet and pious individual, but hardly one destined for greatness.

At the University, Usama met Abdullah Azam, a Jordanian Palestinian, who later ran the offices of the World Muslim League, and the Muslim Brotherhood in Peshawar, in northern Pakistan. As a center for Arab-Afghans, Peshawar's population grew to include: Philippine, Moros; Uzbeks from Soviet Central Asia; Arabs from Algeria, Egypt, Saudi Arabia and Kuwait; and Uighurs from Xinjiang, China. All were there to fight with the Mujahedeen.

In 1979 Usama answered the Afghan rebels call to arms, and traveled to Peshawar to help in the fight against the Russian "infidels." Usama Bin Laden, although not a royal, was close enough to the royals and certainly wealthy enough to lead the Saudi contingent. Prince Turki bin-Faisal, the head of the Saudi Intelligence Service, under pressure from Pakistan's ISI to provide a royal prince to lead the Saudi contingent, had found his man. Usama bin Laden, a natural leader and brilliant organizer, was on a religious mission – and Afghanistan became his obsession. Usama became friends with Saudi's Prince Turki bin-Faisal and Pakistan's General Hameed Gul, head of the ISI.

Former CIA station chief in Pakistan, Milt Bearden, has been reported to have said that Arab sympathizers like bin Laden, " . . . were bringing in up to $25 million dollars a month . . . to underwrite the war . . . an extra $200 to $300 hundred million dollars a year." Separating fact from the frequent fiction of Arab rhetoric is difficult. Despite the stories highlighting his Afghanistan exploits, bringing in money was apparently the limit to bin Laden's combat experience. Reports imply that he spent most of the war fundraising in Peshawar. Even though a heroic mythology developed around him, it has been reported that Usama only fought in one important battle.

Recognizing that the Afghan Mujahedeen lacked infrastructure and manpower, Usama bin Laden set about solving both problems. Working with his college friend, Abdullah Azzam, a gifted storyteller and leader of the Palestinian Muslim Brotherhood, who had formed Maktab al-Khidmatlil-mujahedeen al-Arab (commonly known as the Afghan bureau, the Office of Services, or al-Kifah, or MAK), to recruit freedom fighters. MAK advertised throughout the Arab world for young Muslims to come and fight in Afghanistan, and set up branch recruiting offices all over the world – including in the U.S. and Europe.

Azzam, through his al-Kifah network, established major centers in Atlanta, Boston, Brooklyn, Chicago, New Jersey, Pittsburgh, and Tucson with subsidiary centers in thirty more American Cities. Al-Kifah published a full color Arabic language magazine, *Al-Jihad*, which featured gory battle stories featuring young mujahedeen *shahids* (martyrs) and attacks against Americans, Christians and Jews for their crimes against Islam. *Al-Jihad* had a reported circulation of 50,000 with half in America.

Bin Laden, the Saudi financier and MAK's single largest financial backer provided travel funds for new recruits and set up facilities to train them. Experts on guerilla warfare, sabotage, and covert operations were obtained to augment training.

Bringing his business and some of his engineers, workmen and equipment with him, bin Laden moved to Peshawar in 1982: where he helped build roads and depots for the Mujahedeen. In 1986, he helped build the *Khost* tunnel complex deep under the mountains close to the Pakistan border: A project funded by the CIA to provide a major arms storage depot, training facility and medical center for the Mujahedeen. Bin Laden set up his first training camp for Arab Afghans in Khost. The Arab Afghans were beginning to accept this lanky, wealthy and charismatic Saudi as their leader. Perhaps it was there too that bin Laden, who grew up in a culture that fostered the belief that the very existence of the West was an affront to Islam, first saw his destiny as being the uniting force behind all Muslim lands to re-establish the original *Caliphate* of a millennium ago.

In the late 1980s bin Laden split with MAK co-founder Azzam; and in 1988, joined Mohammed Atef (al-Qaeda's future military commander) to form *al-Qaeda* (the base) to continue the work of the jihad. While Azzam continued to focus on support for Muslims in Afghanistan, bin Laden turned his attention to carrying the holy war to other countries. In late 1989 Abdullah Azzam died in a car bomb explosion, which was generally blamed on a rival Afghani faction. Several rumors circulating at the time tied bin Laden to the assassination.

During this period, bin Laden furthered the growth of al-Qaeda by traveling throughout the Islamic world, funding other fundamentalist groups, and establishing contacts with other extremists, who were founding and leading other terrorists groups. He also established contacts with various intelligence organizations, including the Soviet KGB.

On September 28, 2001, BBC's Richard Engel interviewed *Gamaa Islamiya* (Islamic Group) leader, Ibrahim, a student at Egypt's University of Assiout, the heart of the Islamic activism in Egypt. In the interview, which was conducted in Cairo, Ibrahim, a recent graduate of one of Bin

Laden's guerrilla training camps, recounts how he met Usama bin Laden while on a pilgrimage to Saudi Arabia. He remembered bin Laden as a devoted young man who loved his religion. Although bin Laden was prosperous, he dressed humbly and kept the company of people with no money. When Ibrahim was ready to leave Saudi Arabia, bin Laden gave him a bag stuffed with Egyptian currency: money to be used to set up a military camp in the hills near Assiout as a step towards converting Egypt to an Islamic government.

By early 1989 it was clear that the Soviets were going to withdraw from Afghanistan. Soon after that withdrawal, fighting erupted among Mujahedeen factions. Disillusioned with inter-tribal bickering for supremacy, bin Laden returned to Saudi Arabia in 1990. With Afghanistan behind him Usama turned to his new obsession, al-Qaeda, which by then he considered his life's work. In Usama's mind America was the prime enemy of his vision of Islam. Destruction of the U.S. through al-Qaeda became his ultimate goal. He dreamed of an all Islamic world ruled by pure Unitarian governments. A man of action, Usama began translating his dreams into action. Experience had taught him that Muslims did not like to criticize Muslims in front of the west; and that liberals in the west could produce a rationalization to excuse any behavior. Keenly aware that stable governments, be they Islamists or Capitalists, would go to any extreme to maintain the *status quo*, Usama pushed the Saudis government to its limit. By stirring up fanatical adherents to his vitriolic Islamic views; and by criticizing the Saudi royal family for their failure to adhere to the puritanical ways of Wahhabism, Usama gave Saudi leaders no choice but to take some action against him.

Opposing fanatics requires strong leadership that is willing to do whatever it takes. Unfortunately this sort of leadership only occurs after the fanatics have caused tremendous devastation and turmoil. When confronted by bin Laden's extremism and his open criticism of the royal family, Saudi Arabia took the "out of sight out of mind" line of least resistance – and did nothing more than simply expel him. While all Muslims are not fanatics, failing to publicly condemn the actions of Islamic fanatics like Usama bin Laden is tantamount to an endorsement. Undeterred by his banishment, Usama, who was always a cunning long-range planner, had also established a presence in Africa's Sudan; where he freely set about exporting his terrorists throughout the world.

Peshawar, Pakistan 1988

One of the oldest historic cities in Pakistan, Peshawar is located near the Afghan border and the Khyber Pass. So old that its origins are lost in antiquity, Peshawar has had almost as many names as it has had rulers. Founded over 2,000 years ago by the Kushan Kings of Gandhara, a region of ancient India and now in northwestern Pakistan, Peshawar was first known as "Lotus Land." Other names included the "City of Flowers," and the "City of Grain." At one time a revered center of the Buddhist civilization, the city became an important place of pilgrimage.

In the sixteenth century the Mogul emperor Babar built a fort in the city, which was then named "Begam." Under the Moguls, Begam became "The Place at the Frontier," and was given its current name, "Peshawar," by the Babar's son Akbar. For many centuries traveling Afghan merchants led their camels there every autumn to deal in dried fruits, wool, woolen products, rugs, carpets, sheepskin coats, lambskin caps and cloaks.

Over the years the city became home to many universities, making it not only a center of commerce, but also a center of learning. With its history as a gathering place for learning and trade, it follows that Peshawar and its outskirts would become a gathering place for Islamic fundamentalist – some of whom were bent on revolution. In 1979, when the Afghanistan war began, Peshawar became an Islamic "Woodstock" – a gathering place where Moslem youth from around world came to express their unbridled hatred against the established order.

* * * *

Colonel Kamal Hussain of Pakistan's ISI was waiting at the table in the small coffee house on the western side of Peshawar for Mohammed al-Mihdar. At 48, Colonel Hussain was a trim man of medium build with a neatly groomed mustache and hair. Today he was wearing a light brown suit – he rarely wore a uniform. Sipping his coffee, Hussain was pleased with the nest egg he was accumulating. *War with the Soviets will not last much longer. I must take maximum advantage of the remaining time to earn as many commissions as possible from various antagonists,* he thought.

Pakistan's support last year of Mujahedeen leader Gulbiddin's foolish attacks on villages in Soviet Tajikistan and Uzbekistan had, in the Colonel's opinion, been a waste of time. But they had provided him the opportunity to establish a secret and beneficial relationship with certain KGB border guards. Smuggling had always been a way of life in the region, and war between Afghanistan and the USSR provided greater

29

opportunities to gain wealth. He had made several good KGB contacts, the best being Lieutenant Colonel Alexei Valek.

While still commanding a border guard's unit in Uzbekistan, Valek had earned substantial commissions from opium smugglers, and additional fees from the sale of Soviet arms to Colonel Hussain for the Mujahedeen. Alexei Valek had been transferred back to Moscow where he had been promoted to Colonel. There he had become a junior member of a practical, one might say self serving, group of senior KGB officers: men who saw the end of the Soviet empire coming and planned to be prepared when it arrived. Hussain saw in Valek a way to further increase his growing wealth. Through Valek, Hussain could act as intermediary to parties, who wished to acquire Soviet items of value.

Mohammed al-Mihdar approached the table. He was of medium height and thin, with a light complexion for a Saudi, and had a carefully trimmed beard. Hussain estimated him to be 29 years old. Mohammed was wearing clothes of good quality that blended well with the local dress. His appearance had changed little since their last meeting over a year ago.

"Allah be praised," Mohammed said in a hushed voice, "It is good to see you my friend."

"Praise be to Allah, it is good to see you Mohammed. Everything goes well with your war against the infidel Soviets?"

"Yes Kamal, we are winning and expect to drive the infidel dogs from our land by next year. Usama, Allah bless him, is concerned about rivalry among the Mujahedeen leaders, who are already quarreling over how to govern Afghanistan after the victory. He is forming a new organization to be known as "al-Qaeda" that will defeat the real Satan, the United States. Our al-Qaeda brothers will spread the true faith around the world; and establish camps that will train thousands of fighters from all lands. Fighters who will first join our brothers throughout Afghanistan, then return to their homelands carrying the message of jihad with them."

"That will require enormous funds Mohammed. Are such funds available?"

"Yes, Allah be praised, our Saudi brothers will provide Usama with funds to carry out his holy mission."

"How can I be of service Mohammed?"

"Praise be to Allah, thank you for asking. We are still receiving excellent infidel weapons from the Great Satan; however, this will not last once the Soviet dogs have been pushed from our land. Usama has already directed that Russian and American weapons be hidden for future use. We understand that you have contacts with persons in the Soviet Union, who can provide weapons, materials and technical information pertaining to nuclear, biological and chemical weapons. We are seeking such information and items, especially nuclear weapons."

"Yes Mohammed, I may know of one or two such individuals; however, they will require a substantial commission for assisting. The items themselves will be expensive."

"Allah be praised, funds are no problem, and you must also receive a commission for your services."

"If you insist, thank you Mohammed. I will arrange for you to meet a KGB officer, Colonel Alexei Valek, who may have knowledge of such items. The meeting will have to be in another country."

"*Allah Akbar*, thank you for your assistance. I await your instructions for a time and place for such a meeting with this Valek."

Mohammed al-Mihdar, born in Riyadh in 1959, was the fifth, and favorite son of a wealthy Saudi businessman and close associate to the Crown Prince. Mohammed was raised in a privileged environment. During his teens, Mohammed had accompanied his father on many business trips to Arab and western lands. He obtained his undergraduate degree at King Abdul-Aziz University, in Jidda. While at King Abdul-Aziz University he fell under the influence of an Imam and became a fanatical member of the Wahhabist sect of Islam. In fact, he followed much the same path as that trod earlier by Usama bin Laden. Later, one of Mohammed's distant relatives, Khalid al-Mihdar would participate in the attack of September 11, 2001.

In pursuit of his graduate degree, Mohammed moved to America where he attended Harvard and received his Master's Degree in International Economics. After Harvard, he studied engineering and physics at MIT and obtained a doctorate degree in physics. Highly intelligent, Mohammed was a quiet, soft-spoken man with piercing dark eyes and a light complexion: allowing him to pass as westerner when clean-shaven and dressed in western clothes.

Zawar Kili Training Camp Eastern Afghanistan 1988

Usama bin Laden, Mohammed Atef – al-Qaeda's military chief – Mohammed al-Mihdar, and Ayman al-Zawahri were discussing plans for the destruction of the Great Satan, America. Ayman al-Zawahri, an Egyptian and bin Laden's doctor and spiritual adviser, was considered by many to be the brains behind al-Qaeda and the mastermind of many of its most infamous operations: including attacks on two US embassies in Africa in 1998; and the September 11, 2001 attacks against New York and Washington.

"Allah be praised, for we are being shown the path to achieve our goal," bin Laden said. "It is Allah's will that we bring the message of the Prophet Mohammad to the unbelievers in the Great Satan. To do so we must first destroy the infidel's government. With Allah's guidance, let us find the method to do so."

"Thanks be to Allah for this opportunity," interjected al-Zawahri, "for we are truly blessed to be given the means to accomplish his mission. The Great Satan is strong. We must not engage him in open battle. Instead, we must destroy what he holds most precious – *his money and his economy.*"

"Allah be praised, I agree, we could not win a direct military battle. But we can attack America's military personnel and equipment, such as housing or ships, with a small cell of our fighters," commented Mohammed Atef.

"Allah bless you, what are your thoughts on this matter," bin Laden asked Mohammed al-Mihdar the newest member of his inner circle of trusted advisors.

Mohammed al-Mihdar, a Saudi with his master's degree in International Economics, had discussed these issues with al-Zawahri. Both had agreed that causing damage to the American economy could be accomplished, but would require detailed coordination and a long-term plan. A series of actions would be required over several years, each having more impact than the previous one. Americans, they concluded, apparently did not brood over things. Instead they shrugged off setbacks and continued on – an ability, which is both a blessing and a curse. Being able to move on after adversity, allowed America's economy to ride over obstacles without a major long-term effect. On the other hand, it could allow al-Qaeda to execute a number of operations before the seriousness of the attacks would be recognized. Much credit for this major chink in American armor had to be given to the press, who constantly blamed the president, if he was a Republican, or the government for the world's problems. It seemed to Mohammed that Allah was guiding the American's press corps to help establish the true faith in that godless land. *Well, control by the press would have to go once America converted to Islam,* Mohammed thought.

"May Allah bless you Usama," al-Mihdar said. "I have given much thought to this question. The American economy appears stronger than it is. In fact, they are loosing their industrial base at a rapid rate, and will continue to do so as China's grows. Theirs' is a most wasteful economy, which spends billions of dollars a year on gambling. They have lost the notion of spirituality and only live in sin. They have let their agricultural out-put fall off, and it will continue to decline. The lazy dogs prefer to purchase food, rather than expend the effort to grow it. Most of the fabulous American economy is a myth, consisting of providing services, not producing goods. Their economy is based on financial speculation. They seek jobs that can be performed in plush offices. While they proclaim to be a Christian nation, their real God is the dollar. To severely cripple and eventually destroy the Great Satan, we must undermine and destroy their economy."

"By the grace of Allah let us make it so," commented al-Zawahri. "To do so we must establish cells of our brothers throughout the Great Satan's land. All brothers must become law-abiding members of the community and not attract attention. First, we should find and train brothers, who can successfully operate businesses that will provide funding and the basis for future operations. As our plans develop we can guide our enterprises to provide specific resources when required. Slowly we will build a network of cells that have many purposes – purposes that only we shall know."

"Allah be praised for you insight. It shall be done," bin Laden said.

Bin Laden switched the topic to more immediate matters. Turning to Mohammed Atef he asked, "What is the status of the fighting and our weapons stockpile?"

"The Soviet dogs have lost their will to fight. The Great Satan's Stinger missiles have worked well against the Soviet helicopters. Without the helicopters the cowardly dogs no longer want to follow us into the mountains where their armor is useless. We are stockpiling weapons, Stingers, small arms, mortars, artillery ammunition, RPGs, and SA-7s in the caves. We will continue to obtain and hide American weapons of all types as long as they are available. I estimate that the Soviet dogs will be completely gone within a year."

"We are thankful to Allah," commented al-Zawahri. "The dogs may be more than gone, the Soviet Union is in danger of breaking up. It is time for us to start planning how best to take advantage of such a break up. The Soviet economy is in shambles. People are hungry and no work can be found. We should be able to take advantage of this decline and purchase many of the things we will need. It may be possible to obtain chemical or biological agents, or even a nuclear weapon. If such opportunities appear, we must be prepared to act upon them quickly. We will need trained technicians to handle them, and safe and secret storage sites. Once we obtain such weapons, we can formulate plans for their use."

"Allah be praised for you wisdom. We shall make plans as you suggest. Are there any other issues to be discussed?" asked Usama.

"There are two," Mohammed al-Mihdar said. "First, I had a meeting with Colonel Kamal Hussain of the ISI. He is making arrangements for me to meet with a renegade KGB Colonel, who may be able to supply us with materials to construct or obtain actual chemical, biological or even nuclear weapons. According to Kamal, some senior KGB, military and civilians are beginning to realize that the Soviet Union is coming apart. They may be eager to sell items that we require. I will know more after I meet with the KGB Colonel."

"Allah bless you, Mohammed," commented bin Laden.

"As Allah wills. Second, here in camp we have a student trainee from America, who is very bright and a dedicated follower of the Prophet. He has a degree in business administration from Harvard, and has almost completed a doctorate degree in nuclear physics from the California Institute of Technology in America. When he returns he should complete his studies in one of their semesters. His family is Egyptian, but he is an American citizen by birth. His father and mother were killed in an automobile accident three years ago, and he has a small inheritance that he is using to attend the university. He should be encouraged to gain knowledge of nuclear weapons. After graduation he should obtain employment where he can gain such knowledge. Then he can assist us in the use of such a weapon – should we be able to obtain one."

"Thanks be to Allah. This is a technology that you understand, Mohammed, so you shall be responsible for preparing for such an opportunity. You may proceed with your protégé as you have suggested. Funds will be made available to ensure his success. He is not to be told of the nature of our plans until it is necessary. With Allah's guidance, you will succeed. What is the name of this future brother?" asked Usama.

"His name is Ralph Eid," replied Mohammed.

Ralph Eid was born in New York in 1961. After graduating from New York University, he was accepted at Harvard where he obtained a Masters in Business Administration. His father and mother had immigrated to the America in the 1950s and started a successful rug emporium in the upper east side of New York City. Ralph was a late baby, born when his mother was in her mid forties. His older sister had returned to Egypt before Ralph was born, and he hardly knew her. His parents had become naturalized United States citizens after he was born.

Ralph was raised in a Muslim environment and spoke fluent Arabic and Farsi. A tall, well built, handsome young man, with light skin for an Egyptian, Ralph had black curly hair and dark laughing eyes. His cheerful personality and winning smile could, according to his elementary school teachers, charm the most miserable curmudgeon. In truth he lived a somewhat charmed life as a child. His parents adored him, and he was devoted to his mother, who teased him by calling him "My Darling Omar": because one of his father's rug clients had compared his handsome features to Omar Shariff, the movie star.

Fate dealt Ralph a bitter hand though, when both parents were tragically killed in a 1985 automobile accident on the Long Island Expressway. The intoxicated driver of the other vehicle, the 18-year-old son of a powerful politician, escaped serious punishment by only receiving a sentence of one hundred days community service. The event left Ralph bitterly angry, which brought him to the attention of an al-Qaeda recruiter at his mosque. Driven by that anger, Ralph embraced radical Islam. With no family left in New York, Ralph had moved to Oakland, California to work on his Ph.D. in nuclear physics, and to pursue his deep seated desire to avenge his parent's death by striking at the American establishment.

Gamaa Islamiya Safe House, Cairo, Egypt Spring 1989

Mohammed al-Mihdar sat in the walled in garden sipping tea. Colonel Alexei Valek was due to arrive within the hour. Mohammed disliked dealing with arrogant Russians almost as much as dealing with Americans. Both were infidels, but Allah forgive him, it was necessary. Kamal had told him the Russian was a greedy pig, but resourceful and produced results. Valek was part of that secret network of Soviet KGB, military officers, and bureaucrats, which had adopted the name "The Group." Preparing for the end of the Soviet Union, they were grabbing what booty they could while there was still time. It was late morning and Mohammed enjoyed the peace of the garden. His bodyguard gave him the signal that his guest had arrived.

A tall well built man with closely cropped blond hair and piercing blue eyes entered the garden. He was wearing a poorly fitted dark suit, typical of Russian clothes. Mohammed estimated his height to be 180 cm and his weight to be 91 kg.

"Mr. al-Mihdar, I am Colonel Alexei Valek, we have a mutual friend. Could you please name him and his agency?"

"May Allah be with you Colonel Valek. Our mutual ISI friend, Colonel Kamal Hussain said you were a cautious man, and that is prudent. Come, sit and please call me Mohammed. Will you join me in some tea? . . . Has Kamal's tile floor been repaired yet?"

"Yes, tea, thank you. I am Alexei. Kamal sends his regards and requests that I provide any assistance you require. Unfortunately Kamal has not been able to obtain a Spanish tile in the proper color."

"Yes, I knew he was having trouble with the green color, but I thought it was Italian tile."

"You are correct, it was an Italian tile, but the color was blue."

Alexei thought Mohammed was young, perhaps 30 or 35 – it was hard to tell with some Arabs – and wondered, *Does he and this al-Qaeda bunch have any concept of what they were getting into?* "I understand you are seeking chemical, biological and even nuclear weapons. Do you have qualified technicians who understand the dangers in handling and storing such things? Handling biological agents requires sealed rooms with special filters and decontamination equipment – chemical agents require much the same. Leakage can occur during transportation and storage. Nuclear . . . well, that is an entirely different set of problems – radiation shielding and the possibility of interaction between warheads causing a chain reaction. In addition to qualified technicians, proper instruments to make measurements are required. Such things are very expensive."

Just as condescending and arrogant as I assumed he would be, Mohammed thought. "Yes, we do understand the problems you mention. We will be seeking instructors to train our fighters in these things. We plan to recruit students from technical universities, who will be able to properly handle the items we seek. Storage facilities are being prepared in several places. Funding is not a problem."

He may not be as naïve as I first thought. "I am very pleased to learn that you have considered these things. We have had inquires from other groups that have no concept of the technical difficulties and do not wish to be told of them. You must understand that we cannot be linked to the sale of such things. Security and secrecy are most important to both of us."

The Russian pig makes a good point. "Usama bin Laden, our leader, limits knowledge of the overall plan to a very few trusted lieutenants. Each group will only know the details of its assignment. Al-Qaeda will take years to train fighters and to send them to their destinations. We plan to establish cells in many countries, including America. I believe you call this system compartmentalization. As to funding, Usama has been responsible for the majority of the Mujahedeen funding. This funding will be available to al-Qaeda. I tell you these things, because you must be made to understand that al-Qaeda is several years away from directly engaging in activities. Al-Qaeda, which means "The Base" in our language, will be exactly that, a base for operations in many places. Our fighters will spread out over the globe. Some will take up residence and become members of the local communities. We may not call upon them for years. Usama thinks in terms of years."

Cautious not to disclose too much information to the Russian, Mohammed deliberately neglected telling Alexei the true meaning of al-Qaeda, which initially referred to a "computer database" Usama bin Laden had established. Al-Qaeda, "The Base," originally was a computer database that contained the names and contact information for many of the mujaheddin fighters.

Alexei, who sat sipping his tea and fervently wishing that some good Vodka was available, attempted to show no emotion to Mohammed's revelations. *This Arab may be a serious player. Although I have never met Usama bin Laden, I have received reports that he is a major force in the Mujahedeen, a very competent organizer, and the conduit of Saudi funding. I wonder if I can get him to shed some more light on his relationship with al-Qaeda and his relationship with bin Laden.* Having decided it was time to fish for more details Alexei asked, "Mohammed, can you tell me a little about yourself."

"Allah be praised, I have had the good fortune to attend the American university, Massachusetts Institute of Technology, and to obtain a doctorate's degree in Physics and a master's in International Economics from Harvard."

"I am not surprised, you appear to be *very well educated*. Your long-range plans make sense. Placing hidden fighters in other countries – we call them "sleepers"– is a sound strategy."

Mohammed thought that he had told the Russian infidel just enough, maybe even too much. It had been decided that the Russians must be told enough to gain their respect.

Alexei decided to take Mohammed and the al-Qaeda organization seriously. He would make a full report to his leader, Lieutenant General Valrie Yatchenko, upon his return to Moscow. "I am aware of what you are seeking and will advise you when we have located items of interest. Some of the items, shall we refer to them as *antikvaryat*, 'antiques,' may cost many millions of dollars. We will prefer payment in U.S. dollars."

"Allah be praised, we will be most interested in any antiques that you may find. From now on we shall refer to you as the antique broker; and I shall be the antique collector, Ahmed al-Hijazi. What shall we call you?"

"This is a good system. I will be "Sergey," and the business *Volga Antiques*."

"The price is not a problem. When do you think some of these antiques may be available?"

"That is hard to say. As you may know, the Soviet Union is starting to unravel. There is still strict control of most of the laboratories and storage depots. If our projections are correct, things will start to change in the next two years. We will contact you when we have an item of interest."

"Allah be with you," Mohammed said, and waved his hand toward the exit to indicate that the meeting was over.

With farewell amenities complete Alexei departed the house, and as was his practice scanned the traffic for a tail out the rear window of the taxi. There was none. Returning to the Soviet Embassy, Alexei spent the remainder of the day performing the "cover" duties specified in his travel orders. Lt. General Valrie Yatchenko was able to use normal KGB duties and assignments to allow members of The Group to move about without causing suspicions. Each member would receive a percentage of fees earned: the residual would be placed into an operating fund. If the Soviet Union did crumble, The Group could move to another location and continue operations or retire.

The Chinese are correct. Crisis does also mean opportunity, Alexei thought as he got out of the car near the embassy building.

Moscow, Spring 1989

Alexei Valek entered Lt. General Valrie Yatchenko's office at precisely 9 A.M. General Yatchenko was a thin fit man of 59 years with closely cropped gray hair, and a couple of centimeters taller than Valek. Number three officer of the KGB, Valrie Yatchenko, unlike his superiors, did not believe communism and the present way of life would survive Mikhail Gorbachev's pandering to the west. "When the ship is sinking, the first to the life boats have the best chance to survive," was one of the General's favorite sayings. General Yatchenko was the founder and leader of The Group.

"Good morning Alexei Valek, you seemed to have survived your trip to Egypt."

"Good morning General, yes, my trip went well. You have read my report regarding my assignment."

"Yes, excellent report, it covered everything. Tell me about the Arab." The Group's activities were not reported in writing. The general would prepare an encrypted summary of Alexei's verbal report.

"Mohammed al-Mihdar is an educated man, Ph.D. in physics from MIT and a Masters in International Economics from Harvard. He represented himself as one of Usama bin Laden's inner circle. Our reports are correct, bin Laden has formed an organization to be know as *al-Qaeda*, which means "The Base" in Arabic. Bin Laden expects the Mujahedeen to splinter into factions as our troops pull out – just as we have predicted. At bin Laden's orders, al-Qaeda has already begun to store weapons for later use. Al-Qaeda, through bin Laden, will continue to receive Saudi funding and will set up training camps for radical Islamic fighters from many countries. Bin Laden plans to set up sleeper cells in various countries and is in no hurry to use them. I got the impression that he has a long-term plan and the resources and patience to implement it. These trained fighters will export Wahhabism to other countries. I have not met bin Laden; but from all reports, he and his group of fanatics are totally dedicated to creating an

Islamic empire based upon Wahhabist beliefs – which is a scary prospect for all of us.

"Al-Mihdar said they have funds available to purchase equipment and expressed interest in chemical, biological and nuclear ordnance. Kamal has told me that this is true. I mentioned the dangers associated with these items and al-Mihdar provided reasonable answers. My major concern is the items being traced back to us. If bin Laden or al-Qaeda uses a Soviet weapon of mass destruction it will be traced back to us, and we will have no place to hide. We must consider the risk, versus the rewards – which will be the greatest. I made no commitment to al-Mihdar. In the future, we will refer to his want list as 'antiques.' He will be the antique collector, and I will be the antique broker. I told him we would contact him when we found antiques of interest, but not to expect any activity for at least a year."

The General considered this while Alexei poured two glasses of vodka. After a toast to The Group, the General said, "Alexei, you have done well. You are correct, we must be very careful in dealing with a terrorist organization like al-Qaeda. It is better to deal with a state such as Iran, Iraq or Syria. Let them pass the weapons through to the terrorists groups they sponsor. On the other hand, bin Laden has direct access to Saudi funding. We may want to make an exception. Did al-Mihdar request technical assistance?

"No, I do not think Russian advisors would be welcome in Afghanistan."

"True, but we could provide Cubans or East Germans. Let us suggest this to Kamal, who can pass the suggestion on as his idea to bin Laden or al-Mihdar."

"Very good idea General, that should get us some eyes and ears in this al-Qaeda bunch."

"I like your term 'antiques.' You will be our point of contact with al-Qaeda. I have already started the process of identifying lost or misplaced components. We are referring to them as 'Orphans,' that may be available. I have agents questioning scientists and engineers about abandoned material and equipment. My agent covering Saravo has instructions to identify personnel who may be approachable. I will instruct him to make preliminary contacts."

Berkley, California, Spring 1989

The newly graduated Ralph Eid, Ph.D. was quite pleased with his progress. He expected to be offered a position at the Laurence Livermore National Laboratory, Livermore, California: One of the Department of Energy's two main nuclear weapons development laboratories, which were operated for the Department of Energy by his new alma mater, the University of California. Whether he would be able to gain access to nuclear weapons information was unknown. The lab was also engaged in extensive research in the management and disposal of radioactive waste or "rad waste." He had received a phone call from Mohammed al-Mihdar congratulating him for earning his doctorate's degree. Mohammed had told him that all of his brothers were proud of his accomplishments and would follow his progress with interest. Mohammed was especially pleased when told about the pending job at Livermore Labs and requested confirmation when it happened.

Two weeks later the offer arrived from Livermore Labs. Dr. Ralph J. Eid was offered the position of Research Scientist Grade 200, assigned to the low level radioactive waste project. A security clearance was required and necessary forms were included with the letter. The forms were to be returned to the security office as soon as possible. Ralph sent a telegram, announcing his new job, to Uncle Saleh – who was in fact Mohammed al-Mihdar – in Riyadh, Saudi Arabia.

The next day Eid received a telephone call from Mohammed, who was extremely pleased about the position at Livermore Labs. Mohammed instructed Eid to purchase a house in the area that would provide a secure meeting place. Funds were being deposited in his bank account to cover the house purchase and other items. Coded progress reports were to be mailed to Ralph's Uncle Saleh in Riyadh.

Ralph decided to complete the security forms, drive to the Livermore Labs to deliver them, and then do some house hunting. Three days later, on a clear Monday morning he left his apartment in Oakland and drove through the mountains on Interstate 580 toward Livermore. Livermore Labs, a large sprawling complex, was on the south side of I-580. After stopping at the gate, providing identification and showing a copy of his offer letter, Ralph was directed to the security office. There a security officer reviewed the forms and told him he would probably be granted an interim secret clearance in the next few weeks. A final clearance would be issued within a few months. Next Ralph reported to human resources, where he completed the usual employment forms. One of the secretaries told him about a new housing development that was closing out on Highland Road. Furnished models were for sale.

After leaving the labs Ralph turned north from I-580 onto Tassajara Road, and then right onto Highland. Three miles further into the foothills, he found Rancho Nuevo and turned into the entrance, where he located the model homes. Rancho Nuevo was built into the side of the mountain. Each street was terraced, so that the houses appeared to be stair-stepped up the side of the hill. The last model home, named according to the sign the

"Sorrento," was at the end of the street with no house above it. A salesman greeted him when he entered the model and showed him the house: which consisted of three bedrooms, a large family room, kitchen, dining room and living room, and on the back a patio that overlooked the valley. An adobe block wall enclosed the lot. While the salesman prattled on about real estate values, schools and other trivia, Ralph considered his priorities. No one could look down onto the house. The rear faced a valley: making it all but impossible to use a laser to monitor conversations held inside the back rooms. The wall provided privacy. Yes, this would do nicely. The fact that it was completely furnished was a bonus.

Ralph sat down to discuss purchase with the salesman. The price had just been reduced to $350,000. Ralph said he would take it, if the price included all closing costs. He would pay $250,000 in cash and finance the remainder for 15 years. His bank would provide the loan, and he would close at the end of the month.

Returning to his small apartment, he stood just inside the entry way and thought as he surveyed his meager belongings, *I will sell most of the contents. With the exception of family photos, nothing in the place means anything to me. Besides, most of it is junk. I sold the best of my parents' beautiful furniture and possessions to raise money for legal fees to pay that bastard lawyer. His advice on how I could get that kid and his no good father was worthless. Thanks to the American justice system and his Daddy's money and position, he's walking around free – and I am alone. But Praise Allah, your Omar will avenge you Mom. Now I have money and position. Someday I will use that position to destroy that sniveling little puke, his rich and powerful Daddy, and every infidel that helped them. Yes, Praise Allah. With the help of my al-Qaeda brothers, they will be brought to their knees and burn in hell.*

That night he drafted a letter to his uncle.

Moscow, Winter 1990

Alexei received a message requiring him to report to the General's office by noon. The weather was typical Moscow – cold and windy. His automobile's heater brought the temperature to just above freezing. Alexei dreamed of owning a Mercedes or BMW. The Germans did know how to build an automobile. Entering the building he took the elevator to the 6th floor. Inside the reception area, the General's secretary Ivana greeted him.

"Good morning Alexei Valek, you just made it on time. The General is expecting you. Go right in."

"Thank you Ivana. How is your beautiful daughter?"

"She is fine, and much too young for you."

"So true, but she is growing up and one day will be as beautiful as her mother."

Ivana laughed. This was a regular exchange. Actually Alexei was more like an uncle to her daughter. Ivana's husband, a major in the regular army, had been killed in Afghanistan in 1983. The General had arranged for her to keep her apartment, where she lived with her daughter, Maria, who was 16. Ivana was still an attractive woman with long dark hair, large hazel eyes and an oval face. Her loyalty to the General was unquestionable.

Alexei entered the General's office and closed the door behind him. "Good afternoon General."

"Good afternoon Alexei Valek, I trust my call did not cause you too much trouble getting here."

"No sir, my only trouble was the poor heater in the Luaz. I kept thinking of how nice it would be to drive a Mercedes."

"Alexei Valek, I think you may make a good Capitalist. The way things are going we may all have to learn how to earn an honest living."

Alexei laughed, "Yes General, and we must start by learning how to earn a good commission."

"That is good Alexei Valek. Speaking of commissions, we have had an inquiry from Saravo concerning orphans. The seller will call our special number at 2 P.M. today. I want you to take the call and evaluate the quality of the orphan. It may be of interest to our Arab collector."

"Thank you sir, I will leave immediately for the 'store' – an unused KGB safe house. It will probably be necessary to travel to Saravo. I will take the train."

"Let Ivana know your schedule, she will arrange for a car when you arrive."

Alexei entered *Volga Antiques* – the KGB safe house under the General's control. At 2:22 P.M. the phone rang. Alexei answered "*Volga Antiques*, Sergey speaking."

"Hello . . . ." the voice was shaky. The caller was very nervous.

"Hello, this is Comrade Sergey. How can I help you?"

"Hello. . . . I was told by a friend that you were interested in locating abandoned items."

"Yes, we are interested in locating certain kinds of high value items. From where are you calling?"

"I am calling from Saravo. Do you know where that is?"

"Yes, I am familiar with the town. I will of course require a detailed description of the item to determine interest. If it meets our requirements, then it will be necessary to see the item and appraise it. Is the item in Saravo?"

"No."

"I understand. Can you provide a detailed description?"

"Yes . . . it is . . . ."

Alexei broke in, "It would be best if you described it to me in person."

"Yes . . . I understand, but I cannot come to Moscow."

"That is all right. I can visit Saravo on Friday. What is your name comrade?"

"My name is Ivan Zeldovich."

"Contact me Friday morning at the Grand Saravo Hotel. My name is Alexei Valek."

"Thank you Comrade Valek. I will contact you at 9 A.M. Good day."

"Good day Comrade."

Alexei called Ivana and requested travel orders, a ticket to Saravo, a hotel room, and a car.

Saravo, January 1991

Alexei Valek arrived at the railroad station in Saravo just before noon on Thursday. Walking across the crowded platform, he entered the station and stood near the ticket office. There he waited for his contact, Boris Glukhih. Boris, the General's agent in Saravo, was responsible for making contacts with scientists and engineers regarding abandoned materials of interest. Looking around, Alexei noticed an overweight man of medium height, about 88 kg, wearing steel rimmed glasses, with close cropped hair, and dressed in a typical Soviet, ill-fitting, gray overcoat. Catching the man's eye, Valek nodded, then walked toward him and asked, "Comrade Glukhih?"

"Yes, I am Boris Glukhih, you must be Comrade Colonel Alexei Valek," Glukhih said offering his hand.

"Yes, comrade. Thank you for meeting me," Valek said taking the offered hand and shaking it.

"It is always a pleasure to meet one of the General's staff. How may I be of service?"

"I am hungry. Let us go to my hotel; then we will go to a quite place where we can dine and have a private conversation."

Glukhih picked up Valek's bag and they walked from the train station to a black Zil automobile. "This automobile has been assigned to you while you are here. Will you require a driver?"

"No, however, I wish for you to drive at this time."

After checking in at the Grand Saravo Hotel, Glukhih and Alexei proceeded to a small restaurant, where they would be able to have a confidential discussion. Small talk over, Alexei proceeded to the reason for his visit.

"Comrade Glukhih, we have received an inquiry regarding orphans from an Ivan Zeldovich. Is he one of your contacts?"

"No Comrade Colonel Valek, I have not heard the name. When we return to the office I will see what the file has to say about him."

"Good, I must know about him and how he came to know about our interest in orphans. I have a meeting scheduled with him at 9 A.M. tomorrow."

"At your hotel?"

"Yes. I will talk with him and make an initial evaluation. Be in your office tomorrow until I call you. When I obtain his source, I will call to confirm that you have the source on your contact list."

"I will wait for your call comrade."

"Comrade Glukhih, we must be very discreet in these matters. You understand that. . . . Yes?"

"Absolutely, Comrade Colonel."

"Good, let us finish our meal and check out your files on Comrade Ivan Zeldovich."

Later, in Glukhih's office the two men sat reviewing Glukhih's files. "Comrade Colonel, our records show Ivan Zeldovich was a member of the Bureau-11 staff and traveled frequently to the Semipalatinsk Test Site in Kazakhstan. This means that he may have knowledge about items we are seeking; however, he is not on my contact list."

"Good comrade, is there anything else that I can use?"

"Ah, yes, it appears that he retired three years ago at a low pay grade. He is living with his Russian wife here in one of the old apartment buildings – very run down. Most likely his retirement stipend is several months behind."

"That is good for us," Alexei said, taking the file with him, as he rose and walked out side. Glukhih followed, smiling and nodding as the Colonel complimented him and gave him further instructions, "Good work Comrade Glukhih. I will call you tomorrow. If he turns out to be useful I will need a safe place to debrief him. A house outside of town would be best. Arrange for a non-Russian speaking cook to have a good meal prepared around 4 P.M. I suspect he has not had a decent meal in sometime. Feeding him some good meat and vodka will put him in a talkative mood. Please have such a place available tomorrow afternoon."

"Will you want me to assist you, Comrade Colonel?"

"No, if I decide to proceed after the morning meeting, I will want you to show me the meeting place. I intend to limit Ivan Zeldovich's knowledge of us to as few people as possible."

"I understand Comrade Colonel."

Alexei returned to his hotel, parking the Zil in the parking lot. After a dinner, he planned to study Ivan Zeldovich's file.

Ivan Zeldovich entered the hotel lobby at 9 A.M. the next day. Approaching the desk, he asked the clerk for Comrade Valek. After calling Comrade Valek, the clerk told Zeldovich that Comrade Valek had directed him to come to his room. The clerk watched as Zeldovich turned and walked to the elevator; then, as he had been directed, the clerk phoned Valek's room again to inform him that Comrade Zeldovich was on his way up. Ivan approached the door with trepidation. *What am I getting myself into?* he thought – *too late now for second thoughts. He knows my name.* After a pause, Ivan knocked on the door.

"Come in," a voice from inside beckoned.

Ivan grasped the door knob turned it slowly and gently eased the door open. Except for a table lamp beside an overstuffed chair the light inside the room was dim. A neatly dressed man wearing sharply creased slacks and a bulky wool sweater sat in the chair.

"Comrade Valek?" Ivan asked.

"Yes, and you are Comrade Ivan Zeldovich, . . . yes?" Valek asked and gestured for Ivan to enter. Closing the door behind him, Ivan stood speechless waiting for further instructions. Gesturing again for Ivan to come forward, Valek spoke again. This time his voice was more authoritative. "Have a seat comrade, there in the chair directly in front of me," Valek ordered.

Ivan, who was already terrified and could hardly move, began to slowly shuffle forward. Afraid to look directly at Valek, Ivan looked instead at the chair; and upon reaching it took off his cap, brushed back his hair and sat down. Only then did he cautiously peer over his spectacles at the imposing figure in front of him. All the while Valek, who was sipping a cup of tea when Ivan entered, continued drinking while studying the image of his visitor.

Shabbily dressed in a well-worn topcoat with tattered trousers and battered shoes, this stooped old man was a sorry sight. With his unkempt gray hair hanging to his shoulders, his half closed eyes down cast and staring at his limp karakul wool cap, he appeared to be nothing more than a drunkard looking for another shot of vodka. *He is so thin and so weak. He must not weigh more than 65 kg. What can this old fellow possibly know that is worth anything?* Valek thought.

Just then the old man spoke in answer to Valek's question, and when he did he looked Valek right in the eye, "Yes sir, my name is Ivan

Zeldovich," Ivan said and thought, as if to give himself courage, *and I am proud of it too; for it is a also the name of a great Russian scientist.*

Though his voice shook when he spoke and it was obvious he was nervous Valek was taken aback at the direct way the old fellow eyed him, and now that he could see Ivan's face at his overall look of intelligence.

Ah, he is scared to death, and well he should be, but from the look in his eye I can tell he is a sharp one, thought Valek. It will be good to keep him scared – just enough to keep him off balance, but not scare him away. Maybe he knows something worth hearing after all, Valek thought and refilled his cup of tea, but offered none to Ivan. "I have a limited time to spend here. Tell me, how did you hear about our interests in orphans?"

A bit more relaxed now that he was sitting down Ivan answered promptly. "Thank you Comrade Valek for taking time to see me. An old friend told me about inquires regarding misplaced components, which he called "orphans." He was able to obtain your telephone number for me."

"What is your friend's name?"

"Comrade, I do not wish to cause him any trouble."

"That is not your concern. Now, his name!"

"Comrade, I think I have made a mistake in coming here, please excuse me, I will go now," Ivan said as he stood up and turned toward the door.

"Sit back down Comrade Zeldovich, it is good to be cautious and not be quick to betray a confidence. Would you care for a cup of tea?"

Sitting back down, Ivan tried to control his shaking hands. He did not know who this mysterious Comrade Sergey Valek was, but he clearly was used to giving orders.

Again Ivan thought, *What am I doing here? Well I am here, so it is best to be cooperative and take the tea.*

"Thank you comrade, I would very much like a cup of tea."

Alexei studied Zeldovich for a long minute; then said, "Can you tell me how you come to know about the orphan you mentioned on the phone."

"Yes comrade, I was an engineer with Installation No. 558, and later with Design Bureau-11. Much of my work was conducted at the Semipalatinsk test range in Kazakhstan. I was assigned to the team developing a nuclear bomb like the one the Americans dropped on Hiroshima, Japan."

"Yes, we tested one like it in 1949."

"No comrade that was a different type of atomic bomb – an implosion bomb using plutonium. The one I was working on was a gun-type atomic bomb that used uranium."

Alexei paused to consider this. He had a general knowledge of nuclear weapons, their size and purpose, but not design details. *What is a gun-type atomic bomb?* he wondered.

"Well, if our first atomic bomb was an implosion bomb, when was this gun-type atomic bomb tested?" Valek asked.

"It was not tested comrade. We conducted two development tests at Semipalatinsk in 1947 and 1948. But First Lighting, the implosion bomb was detonated before we could test our final design. After that, all effort was directed toward the implosion design, which is much more efficient. My team was disbanded, and the lower level personnel like myself were reassigned. As far as I know, all records were destroyed."

"What are you telling me? That you worked on a bomb development project that was not completed. I thought you understood that we are seeking lost or misplaced items, orphans, not designs or drawings."

"Yes comrade that is why I am here."

"But you said the . . . what did you call it? The gun-type device was not tested. I do not understand."

"Comrade, the gun-type device was never tested, but it was built."

"Built but not tested? It *still* exists?"

"This I am not sure of . . . but I think yes, it still exists."

"At the Semipalatinsk test range? And you think it will still work – *detonate*?"

"Yes, it is a very simple design. Just like the one the Americans called 'Little Boy.' They never tested their design – just dropped it on Hiroshima."

"The Americans ran a test before they dropped the bomb on Japan. Comrade Stalin was informed of the American's test before he attended the Potsdam conference. He was amused at the new American President Truman's cocky attitude during the conference."

"The American test was of their implosion plutonium bomb, 'Fat Man,' which was much like our First Lighting."

Alexei paused to consider this. A functioning atomic bomb might exist at the Semipalatinsk test site. After filling both teacups he continued, "Comrade Zeldovich, I must consider these things and investigate this gun-type design. Can you return tomorrow afternoon?"

"Yes comrade, it would be my pleasure."

"You will mention this to no one. Have you told anyone else that there may be an atomic bomb at Semipalatinsk?"

"No, Comrade Valek, not even my wife. And, there may be five devices there."

"*Five!* Five of these gun-type bombs?"

"Yes, but they are test devices, not bombs you can drop from a plane."

"Could they be moved and then assembled?"

"Yes," Ivan said. Relaxed now, having overcome his nervousness, he was feeling confident talking about things he understood. Valek was obviously interested, and that was good.

"We will discuss this in more detail tomorrow. Be here at 3 P.M. Now, you must tell me your friend's name. I assure you that I will not cause him any trouble; nor for that matter, even speak with him. However, I must verify his existence and position."

"His name is Georgi Akademii. He was an engineer on the First Lighting team."

"Thank you Comrade Zeldovich," Alexei said as the stood up, indicating that the meeting was over.

Ivan rose too, and nodding slightly at Alexei in a half bow of respect, turned and shuffled out of the room. He worried as he rode down in the elevator, *I hoped I have not made a terrible mistake – too late to change things now. I must be careful not to tell Anya too much. What about Georgi Akademii? Best not to mention anything about my meeting with Valek to anyone.*

After Ivan Zeldovich left, Alexei called Glukhih, gave him Georgi Akademii's name and told him that he would need the house at 4 P.M. tomorrow – instead of today. He also told Glukhih that he would need a secure line to call the General. When Alexei arrived at the local KGB office, Glukhih told him that the General was expecting his call.

"Thank you Comrade Glukhih. What about this Georgi Akademii?"

"He checks out comrade, he is one of the scientists that I spoke with."

"Very good. I will call the General now."

Entering the secure room containing encrypted telephone equipment, Alexei placed a call to the General.

"Good afternoon sir, we may have found our first antiques."

"Antiques you say. More than one?"

"Yes sir, possibly five."

"In Saravo?"

"No sir, at the Semipalatinsk test range. They date back to a 1948 test program, and may have been left there. I plan to meet with the contact, Ivan Zeldovich, again tomorrow at 3 P.M. and fully debrief him at our safe house."

"How could five atomic bombs have been left at Semipalatinsk? I know our scientists were careless with their leftovers, but we are not rich like the Americans. Even they did not abandon atomic bombs at their test site in Nevada."

"Yes General, I agree, but stranger things have happened. I wish to proceed. If this information is true, we have some extremely rare antiques. I need some details regarding the design of atomic bombs."

What do you require?"

"Zeldovich said that the bombs at Semipalatinsk were gun-type bombs; that he was a member of a team developing a gun-type bomb as a backup to the implosion bomb. He said that the Americans had dropped a gun-type bomb called the 'Little Boy' on Hiroshima; and that they had never tested this bomb before using it. I need verification."

"Good work Alexei, call me back tomorrow morning."

"Yes sir, good day."

That evening, Glukhih knocked on Alexei's hotel room to deliver a message. The General had arranged a meeting the next morning with Dr. Leonid Fedotov, a nuclear weapons physicist. Dr. Fedotov would brief Alexei on the American Little Boy bomb.

Alexei awoke early the next morning. He was excited at the prospects he had discovered. *Yes, a black Mercedes, the S class would do nicely – a 400 series.* After shaving, he had breakfast in the hotel dining room. At 8 A.M. he arrived at the main gate of the All-Russian Scientific Research Institute of Experimental Physics (VNIIEF), had his identity checked, and proceeded to Building 503, the main administrative building. The original nuclear weapons laboratories had been set up in the buildings of the Sarovskaya Pustyn monastery.

"Good morning Comrade Valek," Dr. Fedotov said in greeting. Alexei extended his hand to a short heavyset man with a dark beard and hair. On his nose sat a pair of round steel rimmed glasses with lens so thick that they magnified the doctor's eyes to enormous proportions. The arms of his glasses were so ill fitting that they pulled the doctor's ears straight out.

"Good morning Comrade doctor." *A true scholastic about 55 years of age*, Valek thought as he followed the doctor into a small conference room, *but how do I keep from laughing, he looks for all the world like a big chimpanzee.* Valek fought to control his penchant for humor as he followed the doctor into small conference room in the main administrative building.

"I hope you do not object to my pipe," The doctor asked.

"No, please smoke all you want," replied Valek – again suppressing his urge to laugh. "Thank you for seeing me on such short notice."

"I am always happy to be of service to the state. I understand that you are interested in the American Little Boy atomic bomb."

"Yes, I require basic information on this type of atomic bomb. I have some knowledge of implosion bombs. However, my present duties require me to become knowledgeable of the gun-type bomb. Until recently, I had never encountered the term."

"I am not surprised, this type of nuclear warhead is very inefficient, produces unpredictable yields with excessive fallout, and is limited to yields in the 10 KT to 25 KT range."

"Can you tell me how it functions, in simple terms?"

"I will try. Are you familiar with the concept of critical mass and supercritical mass?"

"As I recall, a critical mass will sustain a nuclear chain reaction, and a supercritical mass will produce an atomic explosion."

"In very simple terms, that is correct."

Valek continued, "The basic concept is that when an atom of plutonium or uranium splits, it releases neutrons that cause another atom to split. In a nuclear bomb, one fission produces two or more, which then produces more fissions."

"That is a good starting point Comrade Valek. Unfortunately it is much more complicated than that. Let me try to explain in, as you say, simple terms."

"Thank you comrade doctor."

"Plutonium and uranium have isotopes that will fission. Do you know what an isotope is?" the doctor asked.

"Yes, an element has the same number of protons in its nucleus, but the number of neutrons can vary. The variations are called isotopes," Valek responded and following the doctor's hand motion to sit down, tried to listen intently as the doctor proceeded with a lecture that proved to be anything but simple.

"Correct! Uranium always has 92 protons." Turning to the chalk board, Dr. Fedotov began writing as he continued, "Uranium-235, the isotope used in a nuclear bomb is written like so, $^{235}_{92}U$. It has 92 protons, 143 neutrons and 92 electrons in orbit. The atomic mass number is the total number of protons and neutrons in the nucleus of the atom, in this case 235 atomic mass units. Fission is caused by the nucleus absorbing or capturing a free neutron: which makes the atom unstable, causing it to divide into two new atoms. When this happens neutrons are released, sometimes two and sometimes three or more. Let me show you the fission equation for uranium-235," Dr. Fedotov said, continuing to write on the chalkboard. "$^{1}_{0}n$, this is the way we write a neutron, $+ \ ^{235}_{92}U \rightarrow 2$ fission products $+ 2.43 \ ^{1}_{0}n +$ energy. Typical fission product pairs are $^{94}_{38}Sr$ and $^{140}_{54}Xe$, or $^{96}_{40}Zr$ and $^{138}_{52}Te$. In reality there are hundreds of fission products. The average is 2.43 neutrons per fission. These neutrons fly off in various directions, collide with the nuclei of other uranium atoms, and if captured, cause that atom to split, releasing more neutrons. This is an oversimplified description. The energy of the neutron controls its ability to cause a uranium or plutonium atom to fission."

Valek, who had been madly writing in a spiral bound notebook raised his hand to stop the doctor and gave him a look of confusion.

"To understand this concept, think of cue ball on a billiard table striking a group of balls. If the cue ball is moving very slowly, it will not cause the other balls it hits to go very far, and the cue ball will stop after a short distance. On the other hand, if the cue ball is moving very fast it will cause the balls it hits to go farther, some striking other balls. In both cases the weight of the balls are the same, but the speed of the cue ball is different. In other words, the cue ball has more energy when it is going faster. Or to be more precise, the cue ball has a higher energy.

"This type of energy is called kinetic energy (KE) and is calculated by the formula $KE = 1/2mv^2$ where **m** is the mass of the object, and **v** is its velocity. Using the cue ball example, the cue ball has less energy after it collides with another ball: while the other ball now has more energy, because it is moving and has a velocity. Energy is used up by friction, which causes the balls to stop rolling. Nuclear reactions are described by the energy of the particle – not its velocity. The unit of measurement is the electron volt (ev). Nuclear physics is about energy. When particles or gamma rays collide with atoms they interact and energy is gained or lost. A free neutron has energy: which is measured in electron volts, for low energy; and million electron volts (Mev), for high energy. If the neutron has too much energy, for example 10 Mev, it is called a 'fast neutron.' Fast neutrons will collide with an atom and bounce off, much like balls on a billiard table. Each time the neutron collides with an atom it will lose some energy. Slowing down neutrons is called 'moderating.'

"The best materials for moderating neutrons are atoms with low atomic mass, for example hydrogen. Plastics are good moderators. When the neutron has lost sufficient energy it will be captured by the nucleus of a fissionable atom, thereby causing another fission. A neutron going at the proper speed to be captured is called a 'thermal neutron' and has an energy of 1/40 ev - 1/30 ev. In order to have a chain reaction the released neutrons from fission must bounce around until they slow down and become thermal neutrons. If they leave the uranium mass they are lost. Two things must be considered: first, reflecting the neutrons back into the uranium so that they will continue to bounce around and slow down to thermal speed; and second, and the distance between the atoms of uranium-235."

Again Valek stopped writing, shook his head and gave the doctor a quizzical look.

"Think about a tennis court. If you place ten tennis balls at random all over the court and then roll one ball down the middle of the court it probably will not strike another ball. To increase the probability that it will hit at least one ball, you have to either put many more balls on court, or put all ten balls very close together and then roll the ball into them. An implosion nuclear bomb brings the balls closer together – compresses the atoms closer together with explosives. The gun-type nuclear bomb adds more balls – increases the amount of uranium-235."

Again Valek stopped writing and gave the doctor a quizzical look as he sighed, "You said you would make this simple."

Taking two puffs on his pipe while vigorously scratching his right ear the doctor adjusted the rims of his glasses and squinted at Valek, who again stifled his desire to laugh and tried to concentrate.

"Ok," . . . the doctor continued, "The amount of 100 percent pure uranium-235 in the shape of a sphere, required to create a supercritical reaction – a nuclear explosion – is 55 kg. A plutonium-239 sphere only requires 18 kg. Obtaining pure uranium-235 is extremely difficult; and the uranium-235 used in a nuclear bomb must be very pure – at least 89 percent. Thus much more uranium-235 is required for a gun-type bomb than the amount of plutonium-239 required for an implosion nuclear bomb.

"In an implosion bomb, the sub critical mass of plutonium-239 is surrounded by specially designed high explosives called, 'explosive lens,' which focus the detonation wave into the center. Think of a soccer ball. Each section on the surface of the ball would be the outside of the explosive lens. When viewing the outside of the explosive sphere, you can see the outline of each explosive lens. The pattern on the sphere is similar to the one on the outside of a soccer ball. A detonator must be placed in the exact center of each lens. A sphere of plutonium-239, about the size of a grapefruit, must be placed in the *exact* center of the soccer ball. The sphere of plutonium is called the 'pit,' because the configuration reminded the scientists of a peach. Now picture the grapefruit sized pit. When all of the explosive lens are detonated at exactly the same time, the force of the explosives will reach the outside surface of the pit at exactly the same time, and squeeze the pit down to the size of a golf ball. This brings the atoms closer together, increasing the density, causing the neutrons to collide with more atoms and loose energy. When the neutrons have lost sufficient energy, they become thermal neutrons (energy less than 1/30 electron volt), and can be captured by the nucleus of plutonium-239: thereby causing the atoms to fission. Neutrons that leave the pit are said to have 'leaked.' Some escaping neutrons can be reflected back into the pit by surrounding it with a layer of tungsten or uranium which is called the *tamper*."

"I do not understand. Why don't the explosives destroy the pit before it has time to fission?" Valek asked.

"Good question. Explosives detonate at about 7,600 meters per second. This sounds fast, but consider this. Comparing the detonation velocity of high explosives to the speed of a nuclear chain reaction is like comparing a man running to the speed of a mach 2 jet fighter. Nuclear reactions take place in nanoseconds. A nanosecond is 1 billionth of a second."

"Ok, an implosion bomb squeezes the atoms together; so that the neutrons have a better probability of hitting atoms and slowing down so they can be captured. The sub critical pit is compressed into a supercritical mass by the explosives. How does a gun-type weapon work?" asked Valek.

"The other method of achieving a supercritical mass is by increasing the amount of uranium-235 or plutonium-239, called 'fissile material,' until the supercritical mass is achieved. Of course, the problem is that the fizzle material will start a chain reaction when critical mass is achieve, and melt or vaporize before it can reach the supercritical configuration. To prevent this, the supercritical mass must be divided into parts, and put together very quickly. One effective way to do this is to use a gun to shoot the sub critical components together."

"Do you mean, Doctor, that a sub critical component is fired like a pistol bullet at another bullet?"

"Close. You are interested in the American Little Boy weapon. The Americans started with a cylindrical geometry. Think of a solid cylinder like a large wooden post. Next, drill a hole down the centerline of the post. Make the hole about one third of the diameter of the post. In effect you have cored the post or cylinder leaving the center hollow. If the cylinder is made from highly enriched uranium-235 it would be a supercritical mass. Since the center is hollow, it is a sub critical mass. The Little Boy consisted of two main components, a hollow cylinder and a smaller cylinder that was the size of the hollowed-out center of the first cylinder. If these cylinders were made of steel, you would be able to slide the small one into the larger one. If they are made of uranium-235, the little cylinder must be inserted into the larger hollow cylinder very quickly; because the nuclear fission reaction will begin as the small cylinder approaches the larger cylinder."

"Don't you want the nuclear fission reaction to begin as the cylinders come together?"

"Yes and no. Yes, a fission reaction is required to produce the detonation. No, if it starts too soon the two cylinders will melt before joining. The trick is to insert the small cylinder into the large one as fast as possible. Even then complete assembly will not be achieved. Uranium is a very dense metal; thus a cylinder made from uranium will be much heaver than a cylinder made from steel or lead. The only practical way to join the two cylinders is by shooting the small one into the larger one with a gun. This is how the Little Boy worked. The Americans called the small cylinder the 'projectile,' and the larger cylinder the 'target.' The large cylinder or target was cut into slices, which formed rings, thus the target became 'target rings.' Natural fission will occur in uranium-235. Dividing the target into rings reduces the probability of one fission producing another fission while the rings were in storage – a safety precaution that made the bomb easier to assemble."

"So, the Americans used a gun to fire the projectile into the target rings?" Valek asked.

"Yes, in fact they used a three inch naval gun tube; because very high chamber pressure is required to accelerate the dense uranium projectile. Their scientists overcame incomplete assembly by increasing the amount of fissile material; so that even partial assembly would produce a nuclear detonation. The bomb they dropped on Hiroshima was designated 'Model 1850.'"

"This appears to be a wasteful design. I do not see the advantage of a gun-type nuclear bomb," Valek said.

"You are correct Comrade Valek. However, it does have one large advantage – simplicity. Large gun tubes are available, along with propellant and firing mechanisms. All that is required is enough fissile material to fabricate the projectile and target. Also, a gun-type nuclear bomb will not deteriorate in storage like an implosion bomb does. Propellant is easily replaced. As long as the nuclear components are not stored closely together, radiation can be contained with shielding."

"In other words, a gun-type weapon does not make a good military weapon. It does appear to be easy to make – a poor man's nuclear bomb," Valek concluded.

"Yes, unfortunately that is true. The madman in Iraq is trying to build one now," the Doctor said, scratching his left ear this time, before adjusting his glasses.

"Thank you Dr. Fedotov. I apologize for all my interruptions, but what you were explaining was difficult for me to grasp; however, I now think that I have a better understanding of the principal of the gun-type weapon. I am curious about one final thing. When we were catching up with the Americans – after they detonated their first bombs – did our atomic bomb project build a gun-type weapon?"

"No, we had the advantage of learning from the American's mistakes and successes and decided that there was no reason to pursue a flawed design. They had to win a war, we did not."

"Again, thank you Dr. Fedotov, you have helped me to understand my task. I must be on my way. Good morning."

After leaving the building, Colonel Valek pondered over the doctor's lecture as he drove back to the hotel. Fedotov's explanation agreed with

Ivan Zeldovich's statements. The nuclear components would not deteriorate, and there was no record of the 1946 – 49 Soviet gun-type programs.

If those devices, as Ivan calls them, are still in the bunker, I may have, as the nursery rhyme says, found the "Goose That Laid the Golden Eggs," Alexei thought and letting his imagination wander he just knew he could smell the leather upholstery of his new Mercedes. With those thoughts in his mind, along with the image of the doctor scratching his ears Valek could no longer contain his laughter – and laugh heartily he did, on and off, all the way back to the hotel.

Reaching the hotel a few minutes before 2 PM, he went to his room to freshen up before Zeldovich arrived.

Ivan Zeldovich arrived at the hotel at precisely 3 P.M. Again he considered the danger of dealing with a man like Valek. *To late to back out now, he knows who I am*, Ivan thought before knocking on Comrade Valek's door.

"Come in," the Colonel responded.

Opening the door, Ivan found Valek standing in the center of the room putting on a heavy coat. *It would be nice to have such a warm coat*, Ivan though.

"Good afternoon Comrade Valek."

"Good afternoon Comrade Zeldovich. We will be going to a more comfortable place for our chat. Come with me."

Ivan followed Valek down the stairs and out the hotel's back door to a black Zil automobile. Valek had no driver. He opened the door, got in and reached across to unlock the other door for Ivan. Starting the engine, Valek drove out of the town taking a road into the countryside.

"It will be warm soon, comrade. The heater in this car is more than adequate." *Not like my old car,* Valek thought. "May I inquire as to Anya's health?"

Startled at the mention of Anya's name, Ivan flinched and quickly turned to look at Valek. *Good*, Valek thought, *it is good to keep him off balance.*

"My wife Anya is not well comrade. She needs medical attention and our apartment's heating system is inadequate."

"Perhaps something can be done about that comrade. We will see."

"I would be very grateful for any assistance Comrade Valek."

Of course you would, thought Valek. *I think you can be bought for a small price.* Valek turned into a road leading to a small cottage. Smoke was rising from the chimney.

"I have arranged for a quite place for us to meet; where our discussion will not attract unwanted attention," explained Valek. "A good meal has been prepared, and we will not be disturbed."

Entering the house, Ivan found a large warm kitchen with a stone fireplace and an oak table set for two. A woman smiled a silent greeting to them. Valek explained that she would serve them, and then retire to another room until needed. The aroma of the hot food made Ivan's mouth water. He had not smelled such good food for many years.

"Do I smell roast beef?" Ivan asked.

"I see that you are hungry, comrade. Good, come, sit, let us enjoy this good meal we have before us. There on the table was a steaming tureen of borsht, a bowl of winter salad, a platter of thick slices of roast beef and pilaf, and a large loaf of freshly baked crusty bread.

Ivan took his seat and starred in silence as the woman sliced the bread, placed the breadboard and rich creamery butter in front of them, then served them two large, steaming hot bowls of borsht. Once she was satisfied that they were settled she nodded to Valek, who said in a different language, "That will be all, I will call you if we require anything else." The woman nodded and left the kitchen for another part of the house. After she had closed the door, Valek turned to Ivan.

"Eat my friend. We will serve ourselves from these dishes on the table, and we can talk while we eat. Will you join me in some wine?" He asked as he poured a hearty portion of red burgundy into his goblet.

"Just water, thank you. I want to enjoy the taste of all this wonderful food," Ivan responded.

"Good! Now let us discuss your orphans in detail. You can speak freely. This place is secure. Tell me about the five gun-type atomic devices that you think may be at the Semipalatinsk test range. How do you know they were ever there? Where they might be stored, and why no one has found them?"

Ivan, who had been enjoying the good food and warm room, paused to consider his position. How much could he tell this KGB man without loosing the value of his secret? No mention of a reward had been made. If he told too much, there would be no need to pay him a reward. *Yes, I must be careful.*

"Thank you comrade for the very good meal. The best I have had in a very long time. I only wish my wife could have shared it."

"She knows nothing of our meeting I presume."

"Of course not comrade. I told her I was meeting an old friend from my work. She knows not to ask questions about my past work."

"Good."

"Comrade Valek, my friend, Georgi Akademii, mentioned rewards for helping to find what you call orphans."

Valek almost laughed. He had been wondering how long it would take Zeldovich to get to the proposed reward. *Well,* he thought, *if what he has is real, and if Mohammed al-Mihdar was correct that this bin Laden had access to the funding sources he had mentioned, then these atomic bombs would be worth a king's ransom each. Zeldovich would be more than satisfied with crumbs from the table. Best not to offer very much, let Zeldovich make the first offer.*

"Well comrade, if the devices are where you can find them; and they are what you say they are, then you should receive a proper reward. What do you think it should be?"

Now Ivan was at a loss. *I had hoped to get him to establish the level of value. I have no idea what to ask for. Best to do a little fishing,* Ivan thought. "Comrade, my first concern is my wife. She is not well and the climate does not agree with her. Her family is in Leningrad, where she has a younger sister. Perhaps a visit could be arranged, and funds for her trip and comfort. It would be best if she could stay there. As for myself, I would like for us to live in a warm climate with enough money to spend the remaining years of our lives in modest comfort."

Just as I suspected, thought Valek. *He has no idea of the value of his little secret. His request is simple, easy to fulfill. In fact, it would set a good example and encourage others to assist our work. Rumors would spread that Ivan Zeldovich had found something, received a reward and was gone. Yes, good for business. It would be a simple matter to arrange for Zeldovich and his wife to go to Cuba, and it would not cost very much to grant him the lifestyle he had requested. In fact, this would simplify everything. It will be necessary to take Zeldovich to Semipalatinsk in order to find the bunker and to check out the bombs. After that, he could be sent to Leningrad, and then on to Cuba; where he and his wife would be located in the Russian community and could be watched – eliminated if necessary.* "This is a reasonable request. If things are as you say, it will be granted."

Ivan was astounded at how quickly Valek had agreed. *Maybe I have not asked for enough. No, be satisfied! What more do I really require? Medical attention . . . yes, medical attention.* "One more thing comrade. We will require medical attention, access to doctors."

Valek breathed a sigh of relief. At first he had expected Zeldovich to increase his demand.

"Of course you will be provided medical attention. Cuba has fine doctors. The warm climate will be good for both of you. Now, please answer my questions."

"Yes Comrade Valek, it will be my pleasure to do so. Each of the devices is based upon the Little Boy design, and each has a different improvement. We determined that the Americans used a naval gun tube to shoot a small cylinder of HEU, highly enriched uranium, into a larger hollow cylinder. The small cylinder was the projectile, and the large hollow cylinder was the target. The target was actually made up of rings. The problem was that as the projectile approached the target rings it first created a chain reaction; then a prompt critical reaction, and finally, a supercritical reaction: before it could completely enter the target. The result was a reduced yield and much of the HEU was wasted."

As Ivan explained, Valek looked at him intently, chewed his food slowly, and nodded at the end of each long explanatory phrase.

"We had conducted a test by dividing a critical mass in the shape of a sphere into two parts and propelling them together," Ivan continued. "Our test identified the pre-initiation problem. Instead of a cylinder being inserted into a cylinder, our first design was to make the first half of the projectile in the shape of a cone, or point. The target was shaped to accept the pointed projectile; so that the projectile would be able to enter further into the target before initiating the nuclear reaction. Three variations of this design were made. All would produce a larger yield than the Little Boy. Our last two designs were similar, but the projectile was machined in a series of increasing diameters. Starting at the nose of the projectile, the first diameter would be 2 cm and 3 cm wide. The next diameter would be 4 cm, followed by 6 cm. The target rings would be sized to mate with the projectile. Quite simple, yes?"

"Very clever. You are sure that they will detonate?"

"If they are still where I left them, they will function."

"Where you left them?"

"Yes, I was responsible for receiving them and placing them into storage. There was one more component, but I do not think it will be useful now."

"What was that?" Valek asked in a concerned voice.

"Our scientists had developed a neutron source for the implosion bomb. We had incorporated it into our design. If neutrons can be introduced as the projectile enters the target, the yield will increase, because the number of initial fissions will be increased."

"Why do you think this neutron source will not be useful now?"

"This is complicated. Do you have a piece of paper and a pencil? It will be much easier if I can write the formula so you can see it."

"Yes, you can use a page in my notebook," Valek said, turning to a blank page and handing the notebook and a pencil to Ivan.

Taking the notebook and pencil, Ivan continued, "The neutron source was constructed by combining polonium-210, written like so, ${}^{210}_{84}\text{Po}$, and beryllium-9, ${}^{9}_{4}\text{Be}$. Polonium-210 is radioactive and decays by emitting an alpha particle, ${}^{210}_{84}\text{Po} \rightarrow {}^{206}_{82}\text{Pb} + {}^{4}_{2}\alpha + \text{energy}$. The alpha particle reacts with the beryllium to release neutrons and the beryllium decays and becomes carbon, like so: ${}^{4}_{2}\alpha + {}^{9}_{4}\text{Be} \rightarrow {}^{12}_{6}\text{C} + {}^{1}_{0}\text{n}$. Polonium-210 has a half-life of 138 days, which means that half of the polonium will decay in 138 days, half again in the next 138 days. By now, the polonium will have no value."

"I see, but it would be possible to replace the polonium?"

"Yes, we can produce it by bombarding Bismuth-209 with fast neutrons in a nuclear reactor. A very small amount is required, but polonium is a very difficult and dangerous material to handle."

"How much polonium would be required to repair the neutron initiator?"

"Only a few centigrams for each initiator. A small container of polonium would be attached to the nose of the projectile; and a second small container of beryllium attached to one of the target rings: so that they would be combined as the projectile entered the target."

"It would only be necessary to replace the containers of polonium?"

"Yes, that is correct."

"What about the uranium, will it have decayed also? Will it still be usable?"

"The half-life of uranium-235 is 800,000,000 years. Plutonium-239 is, I think, around 24,000 years. The loss of uranium-235 will be undetectable."

"Good. Are all of these atomic bombs the same size?"

"Physically yes. The yields are expected to vary between 20 KT to 30 KT depending upon the effectiveness of the polonium-beryllium neutron source."

"I think a drink is called for, yes?"

"Yes, thank you comrade, vodka would be very nice."

Valek rose and thought to himself as he walked to the kitchen sideboard to get a bottle of vodka. Finding Zeldovich was indeed good fortune. *The man is brilliant. What a memory he has at his age. Recalling those formulas alone would challenge even the youngest of men.* Valek was becoming more excited as the interview progressed. *If these bombs exist, Zeldovich keeps referring to them as devices; and he can find them, well the possibilities were astounding. I will require a large dacha with a large garage in which to store my Mercedes. . . . Back to business.*

"To your health comrade," Valek said before downing his glass of vodka.

"Thank you comrade," Ivan said as he downed his glass.

"To orphans," Valek said as he downed a second toast.

It was time to conclude today's business. He would return to Moscow in the morning and brief the General.

"Ivan Zeldovich, you have provided me with much valuable information. Information, however, that has little value if the five devices cannot be located. How can they be found?"

"Comrade Valek, I have given much thought to this since our first meeting. The only way will be to go to the test range and look for them. This cannot be done in the winter. I am certain I can find the bunker entrance, if I have enough time and the ability to drive over the test range. The location was not recorded on the range maps. The entrance is not obvious. I do not know how long it will take, and I do not have the means to go there."

"Yes, I have had similar thoughts. I can make arrangements for your trip. We will plan to go together in May."

"May would be a good time, but I have the problem of leaving Anya alone."

"We will find a solution to your problem. Perhaps she should go to visit her sister in Leningrad. Yes, that should solve your problem."

"I will need an explanation to give her."

"We will prepare a proper story for her and your neighbors. Do not tell her, but she will not return to Saravo. That will be your surprise for her after we find your orphans."

"Thank you comrade. I look forward to our trip."

"Prepare sketches of each of the five devices showing the projectile and the target; so that I can visualize what you have told me. Do not use any words that would identify what they are – such as uranium or nuclear or atomic. Just refer to them by number: target 1, target 2, projectile 1, and projectile 3. Do you understand?"

"Yes."

"Good, how long will it take to produce these sketches? They do not have to be drawings, just something you can do on plain paper with a ruler."

"Comrade, I can produce the shape of each component, but I do not remember the exact dimensions."

"That will suffice. Place them in a sealed envelope and give them to Comrade Boris Glukhih. He will come for them tomorrow afternoon and forward them to me. It is time for you to return home."

Valek and Zeldovich rose and left the cottage. Both were lost in their thoughts as Valek drove back to Saravo. Valek let Ivan out near his apartment.

"I will be in touch, Ivan Zeldovich. Speak of these things with no one, including my agent here, Comrade Glukhih. I will use him to deliver messages to you, and you may give him your reply, but use general terms and no locations. Do you understand?"

"Yes Comrade Valek. I will speak to no one, including Comrade Glukhih," Ivan said as he stood shivering in the cold on the curb in front of his building.

"Good, but if you require anything, he will assist you. In fact, I will instruct him to get information about Anya's sister from you. Goodbye."

"Goodbye comrade," Ivan said closing the car door, and taking great care as he did so to keep his gloved hand positioned over the bulge in his coat pocket: inside which was a napkin stuffed with some of the good food Ivan had purloined from the table while Valek was pouring the vodka. *I just could not eat all that delicious food and not save some for my Anya.* Ivan thought as he climbed the stairs to his drafty apartment.

Valek returned to the local KGB office, called the General's office and left word with the duty officer that he would be returning the next day. Next he turned in the Zil and requested to be driven back to his hotel. After a light dinner and several more vodkas Alexei went to bed. There would be plenty of time to frame a report on the train the next day. His last thoughts before sleep were that maybe he should get a 500 series Mercedes.

The next morning Glukhih arrived to drive Valek to the railroad station.

"Good morning Comrade Colonel. Did you have a good meeting?"

"Yes Comrade Glukhih, I think my time was well spent. I want you to keep an eye on Comrade Zeldovich and his wife. They may prove to be useful. In fact, get him a good coat, a military field jacket should do. Also, some meat and vegetables, and arrange for medical treatment for his wife. When you deliver the coat and food, obtain the name and address of his wife's sister. She lives in Leningrad. He will give you an envelope. When he does send it by courier to me."

"Very good Comrade Colonel. The coat and food will cause talk."

"Yes, word will get around that Zeldovich is assisting you and being rewarded. This should encourage others to come forward. Get them some coal for their fireplace too."

"Excellent idea comrade, I had not thought of that."

And that is why I am a colonel and you are not. "Keep Ivan Zeldovich under light surveillance. Nothing obvious. Contact me immediately if anything out of the ordinary occurs. I expect that I will have to return for another interview with him. Now I must board the train. You have done good work."

"Thank you Comrade Colonel Valek. It will be as you directed."

On the train, Alexei made himself as comfortable as possible and chuckled to himself as he thought, *I had best not include a description of the doctor's ears in my oral report to the General. He does not always appreciate my sense of humor.* Before taking a much-needed nap, Valek mentally composed his report; carefully omitting what had been to him the best part of a deadly boring experience.

The next morning Alexei entered the General's office and greeted Ivana, "Good morning Ivana."

"Good morning Alexei Valek, would you care for a cup of tea?"

"Yes, thank you."

"The General has a visitor and asked that you wait in the conference room until he sends for you."

Alexei accepted the cup of tea, picked up his briefcase, left Ivana's outer office, turned right and walked down the hall to the conference room. Alexei reviewed his planned report and the need for additional information from Ivan Zeldovich. On the train he had realized that he had not questioned Zeldovich about the specifics of the assembly mechanism. They must be transportable, because it was planned to move them to the test site for detonation. How heavy? . . . How long? . . . How many components? These questions required answers. After the meeting with the General there would be more. Another meeting with Ivan Zeldovich would be required, maybe more than one.

"Comrade Valek, the General is ready to see you," Ivana said.

Lost in thought, Alexei had not heard her open the door. Picking up his briefcase Alexei said, "Thank you," as he stood to follow her back to the General's office.

"Go right in, he is waiting for you."

Alexei entered the General's office and stood at attention. The General stood, walked around his desk and offered his hand to Alexei. "At ease Colonel. Was your trip successful?"

"Yes sir," Alexei answered and remaining perfectly straight-faced continued, "Thank you for arranging the briefing with Dr. Leonid Fedotov. He explained the principal of gun-type weapons, which allowed me to understand what Ivan Zeldovich had to say."

"And just what did Ivan Zeldovich have to tell us?"

"Sir, are you acquainted with a gun-type atomic bomb?"

"Of course." The General had arranged for his own briefing.

"Sir, Dr. Fedotov told me that no gun-type atomic bombs had been developed at the beginning of our atomic bomb development program. He said that we had no reason to pursue a flawed inefficient design when we knew how to build an implosion bomb. This confirmed Zeldovich's statement that all records had been destroyed. In other words, you can't misplace what you never had."

"Yes, that is possible."

"Ivan Zeldovich said he was responsible for accepting and storing the components for the five gun-type test devices. They were placed in an underground bunker complex in a remote area of the test range. He thinks that he can find the entrance."

"That will mean a trip to Semipalatinsk."

"Yes. With your permission, I plan to take him there in May when the snow is gone."

"Please continue with your report."

"Ivan Zeldovich is an old man with a sick wife. She is Russian and her sister lives in Leningrad. I asked him what he wished for a reward. His request is, as I expected, very simple – medical care, and enough money for a comfortable life in a warm climate. My plan is to send his wife to her sister in Leningrad, and to take Zeldovich with me to Semipalatinsk. If the bombs are there, we must be prepared to move them immediately. If things go as planned, Zeldovich will return to Leningrad to join his wife and then both of them will be sent to Cuba."

"He will be content with that?"

"Yes sir, I think he will be completely satisfied with that reward. I have instructed Boris Glukhih to provide for Zeldovich and his wife. Word will get around that he is helping and receiving rewards. This should encourage others to come forward. Who knows what else is out there."

"Cuba is a good idea. We will have no problem keeping an eye on them, and if necessary. . . . "

"Yes sir, my thoughts exactly."

"Proceed Alexei."

"Yes sir, each of the five devices used a different configuration for the projectile and target. Three are variations of a cone and two have a stepped face projectile. I have instructed Zeldovich to prepare sketches of each."

"Details are not important to me. Will they still function?"

"Ivan Zeldovich says that the stored nuclear components will not be affected by time. The propellant for the guns is readily available. The only component that must be replaced is part of the neutron source. The polonium will have to be replaced. If not, the yield will be reduced, but the bombs will still function."

"Can the polonium be replaced?"

"It may be available. Only a few centigrams are needed."

"I will look into it. I do not believe that we still use this type of neutron source."

"Sir, I overlooked asking Zeldovich one thing. It did not occur to me until I was on the train this morning."

Alexei had been dreading this portion of the briefing. Better to bring it up rather than having the General note the omission. There is no doubt he would ask.

"What is that Alexei Valek?"

"Sir, I did not obtain information as to the number of containers nor their weight."

"Yes, that would be useful information. I trust you will obtain it." The General was having a hard time keeping from smiling. It was obvious that Alexei was very embarrassed by his omission; however, it was understandable considering the enormity of the information he was receiving. *I bet he has already picked out his Mercedes.*

"You are correct, Alexei, we must be prepared to move the antiques if they check out. We do not want to keep them in our possession any longer than necessary. I think it will be best to have a customer ready to accept delivery. What do you think of al-Qaeda?"

"This is something that they would want. It will also let us determine if they really do have access to unlimited funds. Do you have a price in mind?"

"I have given this quite a lot of thought since your telephone call – $50 million U.S. dollars each. There is no established market price. Do you concur?"

"Yes sir, but why American dollars?"

"I suspect that soon the Americans will be crawling all over Russia and our states. American dollars can be spent anywhere, and we may have to leave Russia. Besides Alexei, the Germans will be glad to sell you a Mercedes for dollars."

Alexei laughed. General Yatchenko liked to tease him about his love of German automobiles.

The General continued, "Set up a meeting with al-Mihdar and find out if they are truly high value collectors. If they are, plan to remove the bombs as soon as you find them and arrange for delivery as soon as they can be transported to a safe delivery site. We do not want to be caught with them in our possession, nor do we want to leave any fingerprints on the transaction. I will provide you with banking instructions for payment and all required orders and requisitions. We must move quickly, for I think we may loose our control over Kazakhstan within the year."

"Yes sir. I will let you know when the meeting is set. I will also return to Saravo and obtain the missing information."

"Keep me posted on your progress."

"Yes sir."

Alexei knew he had been dismissed and left the office. Ivana smiled and asked, "Any more trips Alexei?"

'Yes, I will have to return to Saravo, and then Cairo."

"I would love to go to Cairo. When are you going to take me?"

Ivana was not bad looking for a 40-year-old widow with a teen age daughter. She loved to tease Alexei, and sometimes he wondered if she was serious.

"I do not think you would like Cairo, Ivana. Wait until I am going to Paris."

"In your dreams, Alexei, the General is the only one who goes to Paris."

"Goodbye Ivana," Alexei said as he walked out the door.

Returning to his small cramped windowless office, Alexei began to prepare a message to Mohammed al-Mihdar. This was a complicated situation, not like selling mortars or SA-7 shoulder launched anti-aircraft missiles. The fact that al-Mihdar had an advanced degree in physics would help. *Still,* Alexei thought, *I do not know how much practical experience al-Mihdar has. There were several problems. First, he could not be sure they had atomic bombs, he preferred to think of them as bombs rather than devices, until they found the bunker and looked inside. If the bombs were there they must be removed quickly. How many trucks would be needed? How many men? Where to make delivery?* After considering these questions, Alexei decided it would be best to first determine if they had a buyer. Alexei picked up a pencil and started to draft a message.

> To: Ahmed al-Hijazi.
> From: Volga Antiques.
>
> Have located five extremely rare antiques of great value. Suggest we meet at same location in two weeks to discuss your interest. Sergey

Yes, Alexei thought, this will do nicely. I will send it today.

The next afternoon Glukhih knocked on Ivan Zeldovich's door. Out of breath from climbing the stairs to Ivan's fifth floor apartment, Glukhih was sweating and somewhat disgruntled. He hated stairs. Ivan opened the door to find a portly, red-faced, unknown man wearing a heavy wool coat over a gray suit.

"Good afternoon Comrade Zeldovich, I am Boris Glukhih. Comrade Colonel Valek instructed me to get an envelope from you."

"Good afternoon Comrade Glukhih, please come in."

"No, I am in a hurry. Just get the envelope for me."

"As you wish Comrade, it will only take a minute," Ivan said, turning and walking over to the table to pick up the envelope. Handing the envelope to Glukhih, Ivan said, "Please thank the Colonel for his hospitality."

Mohammed al-Mihdar received a signal that he had a message from *Volga Antiques*. Returning to al-Qaeda headquarters in a mosque on the outskirts of Riyadh he read the telex from Alexei Valek. *Very interesting* he thought. *I hope high value means nuclear warheads. If so, they were definitely high value. I must contact the council to discuss this.* He told his assistant to arrange a trip to Peshawar and to signal for a council meeting.

Four days later the council met at one of the safe houses in Peshawar. In attendance were: Usama bin Laden; Mohammed Atef, al-Qaeda's military chief; Ayman al-Zawahri; and Mohammed al-Mihdar.

"Praise be to Allah, for our cause is truly blessed," Usama said opening the discussion.

"Allah be praised for our successes," Ayman al-Zawahri said.

"Allah has truly blessed us and given us great success," added Mohammed Atef.

"In the name of Allah, the great, the merciful, I am pleased to report that we have received word from our antique broker, Alexei Valek, that he has five antiques of great value," Mohammed al-Mihdar said. "He has requested a meeting in Cairo next week."

"Praise Allah the merciful, for he surely has blessed our cause," al-Zawahri said. "Was there anything else in the message?"

"No," answered al-Mihdar, "but I am inclined to think that he is referring to nuclear war heads."

"Praise be to Allah," commented bin Laden. "If that is so we are truly blessed. You must meet with this infidel Russian Valek as soon as possible."

"Allah be praised, that is my thought, but I wished to have your concurrence before meeting with the infidel," replied al-Mihdar.

Always the practical one, Mohammed Atef said, "If this is so, Allah has truly blessed us and our cause. You said the message referred to extremely valuable antiques. We must decide how much we should pay these Russian dogs for their antiques."

"Thanks be to Allah," said bin Laden. "There is no established value for a nuclear warhead. The Russian dogs can ask any amount for one. From the message we must assume they have more than one," commented bin Laden. "Perhaps as much as $100 million dollars each. If these antiques are nuclear warheads we can make plans to kill tens of thousands of the

Americans on their own soil – among their sons, and next to their soldiers and intelligence agencies. We are planning to soon kill them outside their country. Praise to Allah, and with atomic bombs, someday we will kill them by the tens of thousands on their own soil."

"Do we have the funds to pay $100 million dollars per nuclear warhead?" Atef asked.

"Allah be praised, our Saudi and Iranian supporters can provide this amount and much more," answered bin Laden. "Mohammed will proceed with meeting the Russian infidel and determine what he has. Does anyone else have questions or comments?"

There were none, and the meeting proceeded to other subjects. Upon returning to Riyadh, Mohammed sent a reply to Sergey at Volga Antiques in Moscow. A meeting would be scheduled for Wednesday of the following week. Next, he mailed a letter to Dr. Eid advising him that his cousin Ali would soon be visiting the United States.

Boris Glukhih knocked on Ivan Zeldovich's door. It had been three days since Alexei Valek had interviewed Zeldovich. Out of breath from climbing the five floors to Ivan's apartment Glukhih was sweating and somewhat ill humored. He hated stairs. In his arms he carried several packages; and tucked inside the breast pocket of his heavy overcoat was an envelope containing instructions for Zeldovich from Alexei. Ivan opened the door to find a red-faced decidedly out of breath Comrade Glukhih.

"Good morning Comrade Zeldovich, Comrade Colonel Valek asked me to provide you with some items and deliver a message. May I come in?" The latter was more of a command than a question.

"Comrade Glukhih, yes please come in. I can only offer you some tea. We have little else."

"Thank you comrade," Glukhih said as he entered the small cold apartment. *Yes, Valek was correct, Zeldovich and his wife will be very grateful for my simple presents.* Setting four of the packages down, Glukhih lifted a bag, handing it to Ivan. "Some food, including meat. I will arrange for you to obtain ration coupons so that you can purchase what you need."

Ivan was stunned. He had not expected much until he had made the trip to the Semipalatinsk test range. "Thank you and Colonel Valek. My wife will certainly enjoy a good meal."

Glukhih smiled. *It is so easy to impress and control even educated people. Well, let us give him the rest.* "Here are two more bags of food." Opening the last bag, Glukhih took out a new Army parka and said, "You will need this for your trip."

Ivan took the parka and tried it on. It was a little too large, but a sweater would help fill it out. "Thank you, I really needed a new coat." *Colonel Valek was certainly keeping his promises.*

Next, Glukhih took a large envelope from his coat pocket and handed it to Ivan, "The Colonel has some additional questions. Please provide me with your replies tomorrow. I will return at the same time. Now let us have a drink," he said as he removed a vodka bottle from his other coat pocket.

Ivan went to the kitchen and returned with two glasses. Glukhih filled both and offered a toast, "To your success." Their glasses emptied, Glukhih left the bottle on the table, rose and walked to the door. "Good day comrade. Until tomorrow." Ivan nodded and closed the door. *I am still not sure what I have gotten into, but at least our life is improving.*

"Who was that dear?" asked Anya, who was standing in the bedroom door. She had a blanket wrapped around her to keep warm. Then she noticed the bags on the table and the new parka draped over a chair. "Where did this come from?" she asked, pointing at the bags and parka.

"Anya dear, do you remember me telling you about Georgi Akademii's story about a man looking for abandoned items. Well, I contacted the man and told him that I remembered where some test equipment had been left at the test range. He is interested in finding the equipment and I am providing him with my recollections as to what instruments were left. He brought us some food and the parka as a reward. He requested that I answer some questions by tomorrow. Why don't you take the packages containing food and go into the kitchen and fix us a good meal, while I start on the questions? If he likes my answers, he may bring us more food. He gave me ration coupons, but we do not have many rubles to buy food."

"Ivan, this is wonderful. I hope you can tell him enough so that he brings more food. I will fix us a good meal." Noticing the vodka bottle on the table she asked, "Did he leave the vodka too?"

"Yes dear, let us have a little drink," Ivan said as he filled his glass and got a clean one for Anya. "To lost instruments," he said before downing the vodka. Anya joined him in the toast, then walked into the kitchen carrying the packages.

Ivan waited until she left the room to open the envelope. He gasped at what he found inside: one thousand rubles, along with a list of questions. A note told him to answer the questions, place the answers in the envelope, reseal the envelope and return it to Boris Glukhih. Still shaken at the sight of so much money, he nervously looked over his shoulder at the kitchen door. *What would Anya think?* he wondered, as he tried to calm his racing heart. *What makes this information worth so much? Am I doing something against the law? Well, I guess I should just be grateful and not ask questions. I certainly cannot complain about Colonel Valek not keeping his word. I will have the answers ready for Comrade Glukhih when he returns in the morning.*

The questions dealt with the number, type and weight of containers. Necessary information, if he planned to move the "orphans," as he preferred to call the devices. The last questions dealt with the type of gun used, the caliber, length, and gun carriage. Ivan began to write answers to the questions, as the aroma from the kitchen made his mouth water.

The next morning Glukhih, again red-faced, puffing and grumbling, arrived at the same time. Ivan opened the door and invited him in. Anya was in the room. "Anya, this is Comrade Boris Glukhih. Comrade Glukhih, this is my wife, Anya."

Glukhih made a slight bow and said, "It is a pleasure to meet you."

"The pleasure is all mine, Comrade Glukhih. Thank you for your gifts."

"You are entirely welcome. I am pleased to be able to help, in fact, I have arranged for you to have priority medical treatment at the clinic."

"That is most kind," Ivan said.

"This afternoon," Glukhih continued, "one of my men will deliver a basket of coal for your fireplace. Now, if you will excuse us Anya, I need to review Ivan's answers."

"Again, we thank you Comrade Glukhih," Anya said as she turned, went into the bedroom and closed the door behind her.

Ivan offered Glukhih a chair at the table and joined him. Next, he gave Glukhih the sealed envelope containing the questions and his answers. Glukhih took the envelope, fingered the seal and gave Ivan a questioning look. "The envelope is sealed according to the Colonel's instructions," Ivan answered in response.

Glukhih shrugged, then said, "I require the name and address of Anya's sister in Leningrad. We will arrange for Anya to leave when you leave in early May. She will take the train from Moscow to Leningrad. You will tell your neighbors and friends that you both are going to visit her sick sister. Do not tell Anya about the trip until a week before you are scheduled to leave. She must think that you both will be returning. If things go well you will join her in Leningrad, and then both of you will board a ship for Cuba. A house and funds will be provided for you; so that you will be able to live a comfortable life. Cuba has excellent doctors, and the care is free."

Ivan was overwhelmed. Everything was going so fast. *All that I have asked for has been provided. If I can find the devices, I will have everything I want,* he thought. "Comrade Glukhih, my friends will notice our improved state. What should I tell them?"

"Very good comrade, tell them you are working for me. This will encourage them to assist me in finding other items. Yes? Now, what shall we tell them we are looking for?"

"I understand. I have told Anya that we are looking for abandoned test instruments. That should be sufficient to answer questions."

"Yes, that will do nicely. Test instruments are expensive and hard to get in today's economy. Let us have a drink before I go," Glukhih said, producing a liter bottle of good vodka from the pocket of his bulky coat. After the toast, Glukhih stood, left the bottle on the table and turned toward the door. "Expect a visit from the Colonel. He plans to come here soon. I will let you know when," Glukhih said at the door, then stepped into the hall and walked toward the dreaded stairs. "Damn I hate stairs," he muttered to himself.

Colonel Alexei Valek received a call from Ivana. He had been working on a routine investigation concerning the loyalty of a bureaucrat in the Ministry of Trade. *The Soviet Union is disintegrating, and we are worrying about the party loyalty of a trade negotiator.* He was looking at a photo taken in Uzbekistan when the phone rang. "Good morning Ivana, it is always a pleasure to hear your voice."

"Thank you Alexei, the feeling is mutual. Please come to the General's office immediately."

"Anything important brewing?"

"You know I cannot divulge state secrets to you. Anyway, Comrade Gorbachev does not tell me everything," joked Ivana.

"On my way." Alexei hung up the phone, took the classified files on his desk and placed them into his file cabinet, then secured the locking bar with a padlock. Leaving his office in the basement of the building, he took the elevator to the 6th floor, exited, turned right and walked past the conference room to the General's office.

Ivana smiled as Alexei came in. "Go right in," she said motioning him toward the General's door.

Entering the room, Alexei found Lt. General Valrie Yatchenko busily working on a desk full of official papers. Without looking up the General said, "Please close the door and take a seat." Alexei walked to the couch and sat down, and waited for the General to speak.

"Alexei, Volga Antiques has just received a message stating that Ahmed al-Hijazi, contingent upon authentication of the information by his expert, is interested in acquiring all of the rare antiques – provided our terms are acceptable. This is very good news. We must accelerate our timetable and find these items as quickly as possible. My sense is that the end of our Soviet Republic is very near."

"Is it really that bad sir?"

"Yes Alexei, it is. How quickly can you get started?"

"I have a couple of reports to complete and two on-going investigations."

"You can complete the reports as a secondary task. I will have your investigations assigned to some other officer. From now on, antiques are your only priority."

"Yes sir, I understand."

"Good, start preparing a plan. As soon as you have a good draft, bring it to me. I must acquire the necessary resources while they still exist. Have you given any consideration to the number of vehicles and men required for this project?"

"Sir, I planned to visit Ivan Zeldovich and review his answers. Based upon his answers, I estimate that we will require two light trucks, five 6x6 trucks, and at least two additional ones for back-up. We will also need two fuel trailers and a mechanic with parts. As to men, we will require guards and drivers. We may need a crane to remove the components from the bunker. I will be able to refine my plan after I meet with Zeldovich."

"Very good Alexei, meet with Zeldovich as soon as possible. Plan to move up your visit to Semipalatinsk. Time is not on our side. We must hurry. Funding has been made available for any off-the-book activities you may require. See Ivana on your way out, about cutting travel orders for your departure to Saravo tomorrow."

"Yes sir, I will make arrangements immediately."

"Very well, report to me upon your return."

Back in his office, Alexei placed a call to Glukhih advising him to prepare the cottage for a meeting in two days. Next he organized his files for on-going investigations in preparation for their transfer. Finally he drafted a reply to Ahmed al-Hijazi. "Received your statement of interest in the five rare antiques. Taking all necessary steps to expedite delivery. Will advise you of delivery schedule." *Yes, that should be sufficient. I will have it sent immediately.*

Early the next morning Alexei called Glukhih, and instructed him to inform Ivan Zeldovich that he would pick him up for the meeting in the same place at noon the following day. Alexei also instructed Glukhih to meet him at the train station at 6 P.M.

After receiving instructions from Colonel Valek, Glukhih drove to Ivan Zeldovich's apartment building; where he climbed the damnable five flights of stairs and knocked on the door. Ivan opened the door to find a flushed Boris Glukhih in his usual breathless state. "Come in Comrade, have a seat here at the table. Can I get you anything?"

Glukhih immediately noticed that the temperature in the apartment was comfortable. "The coal for the fire place has improved your living conditions I see," he said as he sat down, unbuttoned his coat, and pulled a bottle of vodka from his pocket. Glukhih was also aware of a marked change in Ivan's appearance. The old man's long hair had been cut short and neatly trimmed. His eyes appeared less sunken, his color more robust, and his posture less stooped. *Ah, a little nourishing food and some snips of the scissors have made you a new man Ivan Zeldovich,* Glukhih thought.

"Yes, thank you. Your men deliver a basket of coal every day. We are quite warm and Anya is improving thanks to the medical care."

"Excellent! Comrade Colonel Valek will arrive this afternoon and will pick you up in front of your building tomorrow at noon. You will be taken to the same location."

"I will be waiting on the sidewalk at noon tomorrow. Does the Colonel want me to bring anything?"

"Not that I am aware of," he said as he handed Ivan the bottle of vodka, " Let us have a toast and I will be on my way." Ivan poured two glasses, set the bottle on the table, and said, "To Mother Russia."

"To Mother Russia," Glukhih responded, draining his glass. "Keep the bottle. I must be on my way. Good day," Glukhih said as he rose and left the apartment.

Anya entered the room and inquired, "Was that Comrade Glukhih?"

"Yes my dear. I have to attend a meeting tomorrow. I will be picked up at noon. I do not know how long I will be gone. If I am not back by dinner time, prepare a meal for yourself."

"Does this have to do with the test instruments?"

"Yes. It is best if you ask no more questions at this time."

Anya had grown accustomed to not asking questions about Ivan's work. Whatever was going on, it had improved their life and that was all she needed to know.

That evening, Colonel Valek stepped off the train at Saravo into the frigid night air. Entering the station, he spotted Glukhih sitting on a bench reading a copy of *Pravda*. "Good evening Comrade Boris Glukhih," Alexei said as he hurried in from the cold. "Anything new in the headlines?"

"Good evening Comrade Colonel. No nothing of interest. Did you have a pleasant trip?"

"Yes, as good as can be expected in a poorly heated railroad car. Let us get to the car. I'm chilled to the bone and in need of a drink and a hot meal."

Glukhih picked up the Colonel's bag, and the two started for the exit to the parking lot. This time the automobile was a black Volga. After opening the door for the Colonel, Glukhih placed the bag in the trunk, got in and started the engine.

"Does the heater work?" Valek asked.

"Yes, but not as well as it could."

"One day I hope Russia will learn how to build an automobile with a good heater. We can launch men into space, but we still do not know how to build a good automobile with a good heater," Valek huffed, voicing his usual complaint.

"Where do you wish to go Colonel?"

"To the hotel where it's warm. We can talk in my room."

After checking in, Alexei and Glukhih entered the room. "Do you have any Vodka?" Alexei asked as he hung up his coat.

"Yes, of course," Glukhih replied, produced a bottle from his coat, and poured two glasses.

Downing his glass, Alexei shuddered slightly and asked, "How is Ivan Zeldovich?"

"He is doing well. His hair has been cut and he looks much healthier. Yesterday, when I delivered your message about the meeting, he thanked me for assistance. I think he is impressed with your authority and power and will do whatever you require of him."

"Good, that is precisely what I wanted," Alexei said as lifted his glass for a refill. "Have you prepared the cottage for our meeting?"

"Yes. I hired a different cook."

"Very good Boris Glukhih, we would not want anyone to become curious about our activities. The timetable must be moved up. Do you have all of the required information regarding Anya's sister?"

"Yes, I have a report with all of the required information," Glukhih said, handing Alexei an envelope."

Alexei opened the envelope and read the report. "Excellent, you have covered everything that I require. When the time comes, you will collect Anya and take her to the train station. My agent will meet her in Moscow and make certain she boards the train to Leningrad. When she arrives in Leningrad, she will be met and taken to her sister. Ivan knows that she will not return; however, she will not be told until later."

"What about Ivan Zeldovich?"

"As soon as Anya has left, Ivan Zeldovich will proceed to Moscow the next day, where I will meet him. If all goes well, you are certain to receive a generous bonus."

"Thank you, I shall look forward to it. As to the additional antiques, I have received two inquires. Unfortunately neither of them had any value."

"Keep at it, another good lead will appear. When we are ready to implement the Zeldovich's travel plans, a message will be sent to Anya

Zeldovich telling her that her sister is ill, and she should come. Ivan will tell her that he can make arrangements for her trip. That is all she needs to know."

"When do you expect that to happen?"

"Sometime in April. The weather must start to clear. I will give you ample warning. Now, let us go to your office."

Both men left the hotel room and drove to Glukhih's office. Alexei had to be seen in order to prevent questions regarding his presence in Saravo. He spent a half and hour reviewing files and speaking with another agent, then returned to his hotel when the agent left.

The next morning, Alexei had hot coffee and an early breakfast in the dining room before returning to the KGB office. After spending an hour discussing current assignments with local agents, Alexei decided it was time to check out the cottage prior to his meeting with Zeldovich. Satisfied with Glukhih's arrangements, he drove the Volga back to his hotel. At precisely 11:45 AM, he started the Volga's engine for the drive to Ivan Zeldovich's apartment. Ivan was standing at the same place Alexei had let him out after their last meeting. Pulling the Volga to the curb, Alexei waited for Zeldovich to open the door and get in. Alexei noted that Zeldovich had on the new parka and smiled. *So much good will for such a small investment,* he thought. "Good morning Comrade Zeldovich."

"Good morning Comrade Colonel," Ivan said as he entered the Volga.

"Yes it is a good morning – no *snow*, and the sun is shining. The temperature may get above zero. How are you getting along? I trust Comrade Glukhih is taking good care of you."

"Yes, thank you Colonel. The food and coal for our fireplace have made life much better for both of us, and the parka keeps me warm."

"Has any of this new found wealth attracted attention?"

"Yes, some of the neighbors have asked Anya about this; and she told them I had obtained a job helping identify lost test equipment. My friend Georgi Akademii noticed the parka and became curious. I told him basically the same story, except that I told him I was working for the orphan hunter locating valuable test equipment."

"Good."

"My friend Georgi Akademii is talking to his friends; and they are all trying to remember where anything of value might be."

"Excellent, just what we want. Good work Comrade. It may be necessary to move up the trip to the test range. Do you think we can start our search in April?"

"I will be ready to assist you at any time. The weather in April may pose a problem, making the search more difficult, but there is no reason why we cannot start then."

Colonel Valek turned into the road to the cottage. Ivan hoped they would have more good food. The last meal had been wonderful. Valek parked the car in the same place, and led the way to the cottage. Ivan noted that a different woman was present. Valek addressed her in what sounded like a Polish dialect. Turning to Ivan he said, "She does not speak Russian. A precaution to ensure that our conversation will not be overheard."

After serving ample helpings of lamb curry, the woman departed through the same door used by the previous woman. The room was warm and the aroma of the meal inviting. Valek said to Ivan, "Let us enjoy the meal, then get down to business. How is Anya's health? Is she able to travel to Leningrad?"

"Anya is improving, thanks to the medical treatment you provided her. She would like to thank you; and yes, she is well enough for the trip."

"It is best that Anya never meets me. However, you may tell her that I am pleased that her health has improved. You have not mentioned a trip to Leningrad have you?"

"No sir, I have followed your instructions in all things."

I see you still understand the need for security and how to follow orders. *If you continue to follow orders, it may not be necessary to eliminate you later. I have come to like this Ivan Zeldovich and would prefer that he retired to Cuba and lived out his life there. He reminds me of my uncle. Am I getting soft? I had best not allow myself to become like the sentimental Americans,* Alexei thought. "Good Comrade Zeldovich. Your future depends upon your discretion," *I hope he gets my meaning.*

"Comrade Colonel, I have lived with secrecy most of my life. I have seen what happened to people who violated security. One of my comrades and his family just disappeared after his wife talked about a classified project to another wife. Anya knows not to ask about my work and understands the consequences of doing so."

"Excellent, then we should have no problems. About two weeks before you are scheduled to leave with me, Anya will receive a message from her sister telling her that she is ill and asking her to come. When she starts worrying about how to make the trip, you will tell her that you will ask Comrade Glukhih for assistance. You must not tell her that you will be leaving the next day, nor tell her she will not be returning. Make sure that she takes any personal items such as photographs or papers with her. Tell her that her sister will want to see them. If you cannot arrange this, you must take them with you. We do not want to have a problem with her later when she learns that she is not going to return."

"I had not thought of this. Yes, personal items and photographs are very important to a woman, and wanting to return for them would cause a problem. It will be as you say."

"Good, now I will call the woman back to clean the table and prepare coffee and tea. Have you tried coffee?"

"Yes comrade, but it was not very good."

"I have brought some Columbian coffee. When it is brewed strong it is quite good. I will instruct her to make tea in case you do not like the coffee."

Valek rose, walked to the door, opened it and gave the woman instructions. Little was said as she removed the dishes from the table, started a Krupp coffee maker, and brewed a pot of tea. When her task was completed, Valek dismissed her and she retired to another room in the cottage.

"Let us get down to business. I must obtain detailed descriptions of each of the devices, in order to plan how to move them. Please describe one of the devices in detail. Include all of the components as they will be found and their dimensions and weights."

"I expected this question. It has been a very long time. So the best I can provide is approximate dimensions. Of course we can measure them when we find them."

"Approximate dimensions will have to do. Transportation vehicles will be standing by. It will be too late to redo the calculations." Alexei opened his notebook and waited for Ivan to begin.

"The largest and heaviest component is the gun assembly. Actually the gun assembly consists of the breech and barrel of a D-10S, 100 mm high velocity gun. All other components of the gun were removed. The barrel length was cut down to 2 meters. A steel box, designed to accept the 4 target rings, and called the 'target assembly container,' was welded on the end of the barrel. The box was lined with 15 mm of depleted uranium: designed to act as a reflector for the neutrons, and also a radiation shield for gamma radiation released from spontaneous fissions. A handle was attached to the top of the box; so that it could be lifted off to insert the target rings. The top was secured by a series of bolts. The gun assembly was contained in a wooden crate, approximately 60 cm, by 100 cm, by 2.5 meters long. I do not know the weight, but a small crane was used to lift the crate from the truck and lower it onto a dolly in the bunker. The gun assemblies were all the same. Smooth bore test gun tubes from the discarding sabot projectile project were used. Each gun assembly was mounted in a steel frame that formed a stand. The stand containing the gun could be lifted and set down on the test platform."

"I do not recognize this gun. What do you know about it?"

"It came from a tank destroyer, and was selected because it had high muzzle velocity."

"Please continue."

"The gun uses fixed ammunition: the cartridge case, propellant, igniter and projectile are all one item called the 'complete round,' which looks like a large rifle cartridge. As you may know, a discarding sabot anti-tank round was under development. Accuracy was the main problem that kept it out of production; however, our project did not require accuracy: so the sabot technology was adapted to meet our requirements. The principal behind the discarding sabot is that firing a smaller projectile from a larger gun tube allows the projectile to achieve very high velocities. The sabot separates from the projectile after it leaves the gun tube. Standard armor piercing rounds were 100 mm solid steel projectiles, and depended upon kinetic energy to penetrate armor. The formula is $KE = 1/2mv^2$. Reducing the projectile's diameter, which reduces its mass, causes an increase in the projectile's the velocity. Much more energy is created. Our design required the 76.2 mm uranium-235 projectile to have high velocity. The density of uranium is much greater than steel, so the 76.2 mm uranium projectile would weigh more than the standard 100 mm steel projectile. Muzzle velocity of the DS-10S gun with the standard steel projectile was about 860 meters/second. We expected to achieve 600 meters/second, because of the shorter tube length and the increased mass of the uranium projectile. The complete round was placed in a wooden crate about 30 cm x 30 cm x 90 cm, with a combined weight of approximately 30 kg."

"Are all of the gun assemblies the same? In other words, does it matter which gun assembly is used?"

"No, any of the five gun assemblies can be used. They are all the same."

"Very well." Valek stood up and walked to the kitchen counter. Selecting one of the cups, he turned and asked Ivan, "Would you like to try the coffee or would you prefer tea?"

"I will try your coffee, thank you comrade."

"Cream and sugar?"

Not knowing very much about coffee, Ivan decided to follow Valek's lead. "I will take it the same way you do."

Alexei smiled. *My new friend Ivan knows how to get along, that is good,* he thought as he added a small amount of cream and one spoon of sugar to each cup and stirred both. Alexei carried the two cups to the table and stood waiting for Ivan's reaction as he took a sip.

"This is quite good. Nothing like the only other coffee I have tasted."

"I'm glad you like it. You will enjoy the coffee in Cuba. There the beans are dark and have a rich flavor – just one of the many pleasures, besides a warm climate, that the island has to offer. This brew is very strong with caffeine and will keep us awake while we continue our discussion."

"Now, back to the guns. Can more than one of the gun assemblies and projectiles be placed on the same truck?"

"Yes, as many as the weight limitations of the truck. The projectiles should be placed as far apart as possible."

"Please continue."

"The other major components are the target rings. There are 4 target rings for each device. Each target ring was packaged in a separate aluminum container that had a lead sheet on both sides of the ring to act as shielding. As I remember, the container was a cube, measuring about 30 cm on each side, and weighing approximately 50 kg. The container had 2 handles – one on each side. Each container was marked to show the test series and ring number."

"Is this information included as part of some type of serial number?"

"Yes."

"Then the rings and projectile containers *could* get mixed up. Will this be a problem?"

"Yes, I had not thought of that. Each set of rings is designed to mate with a specific projectile, and the rings must be placed in the target assembly box in the proper sequence. If the rings were mixed up, the projectile will not mate properly."

"Please continue Comrade Zeldovich. We will find a solution to this problem later." *Our clients will not be able to read Russian. We must develop a simple coding system for them.*

"Yes, and there are also two additional small containers: one holds the five polonium initiator components; and the other the beryllium components."

"Can all of the ring components be transported on one truck?"

"Yes, as long as the ring components are kept separated to prevent any reactions between them. This also will reduce any radiation which could be detected or injure the men."

"How close together can the ring containers be placed?"

"A minimum of 40 cm should be sufficient. Do not stack one container on top of another one, unless is it absolutely necessary."

"Would it be possible to place the ring containers in a row down the side of a large military truck, if each container was separated by a minimum of 40 cm? Could a second row of containers be placed down the middle; and a third row on the other side of the truck: as long as filler packing material was used to prevent the containers from moving?"

"Yes, empty crates could be used to hold the aluminum containers in place. That should reduce the probability of a neutrons produced by spontaneous fission being captured by a uranium-235 atoms in a different ring. The result would be a slight increase in gamma radiation."

"How would I know if there was a danger?"

"The best way is to monitor gamma radiation as the target ring containers are being loaded onto the truck. Walk around the truck with low level and high-level gamma meters. If the count starts to increase, stop loading: and increase the distance between the containers on the truck."

"Can we do this while we are loading?"

"Yes."

"Will the radiation harm us?" Valek had no intentions of obtaining a harmful dose of radiation.

"No comrade, if the containers are placed on the truck one at a time, and the radiation measured each time: no harm will come to any of us. We are not in danger of causing a critical mass. There will be a slight increase in radiation in the cargo area, but it will not cause a harmful dose: unless a man stayed in the cargo area for a long period of time. When a device is assembled for use, the four target rings are placed next to each other – without causing a self-sustaining chain reaction. However, gamma radiation will increase. Once the top of the target ring container is installed, the radiation will be contained by the depleted uranium liner."

"Why not install the target rings in the ring container assembly of the gun? That way they are shielded."

"In a bomb, that is how they would be placed. We are talking about a test device, and the target assembly container is not designed for transportation. No provisions have been made for vibration or shock associated with transportation by a truck. The weight of the rings could cause the target assembly container to deform or fracture, changing the alignment of the gun tube and target assembly container."

Alexei sat quietly for a few seconds while he considered this information. "Comrade Ivan Zeldovich, you are doing very well. Would you like another cup of coffee?"

Ivan immediately noticed that Valek, addressing him in a more informal manner, had included his first name. *This must mean that he is pleased with what I am telling him.* "Yes, Comrade Colonel, I would like another cup. A little more sugar please."

Alexei stood up, picked up both coffee cups and walked to the counter to fill the cups. "Let us enjoy our coffee while I think about what you have told me." Alexei sat down in his seat and reviewed his notes while Ivan sat in silence, trying to remember more details about the test devices. After a few minutes, Alexei said, "According to my notes, there will be five large, heavy crates containing the gun assemblies, five medium size wooden crates containing the complete rounds, twenty small aluminum containers containing rings, and two small containers for the neutron initiator components."

"Yes, that is correct."

"Tell me about the bunker."

"The only direct access to the bunker is by means of stairs that lead down into the bunker. A small cement structure, just large enough to have a door, is the only part of the bunker visible above ground. The back of the structure is tapered down at an angle that matches the stairs. There is an over-hang above the steel door to protect it from the elements. After opening the door, there is a landing just large enough for two men stand on; and then the stairs start down into the bunker.

"Equipment and components can be lowered by means of a crane or hoist into the bunker through an access shaft: located a short distance from the bunker door. There is no freight elevator. Two flat steel doors cover the access shaft. When the doors are closed, they are level with the ground. At present they are most likely covered over with sand and dirt. Once they are located, the doors can be opened by swinging them through 180 degrees. The components can be removed by positioning a crane on one side of the shaft and a cargo truck on the other. The floor of the bunker is approximately six meters below ground level. A corridor extends from the shaft. One large chamber and ten smaller ones open into the corridor.

"The gun assembly containers were stored in the large chamber, and the components for the five test devices were stored in the other chambers. Each chamber was secured with a lock. The door to the stairs and the loading door were also secured with locks. I do not have keys for any of the locks."

"What kind of locks?"

"Special padlocks with a metal shield protecting the hasp to prevent cutting them off. The door to the stairs also has a standard door lock."

"I think you said that the gun assembly containers were placed on dollies. Were they left on the dollies?"

"Yes, but I do not think the dolly wheels will still function. Even in the test site's dry climate the bearings will have rusted and frozen."

"Will it be possible to lower a small fork lift down the shaft and use it to move the gun assembly crates?"

"The access shaft is large enough. A small forklift may be able to maneuver in the corridor and large chamber, and will be able to move the crates to the access shaft. The only problem is the length of the forklift blades. All other components can be carried to the shaft and placed on a lifting pallet."

"Good, I will plan on bringing a small fork lift with the blades shortened to one meter. I will also bring a lifting pallet."

"Lifting straps and cables will be required for the gun assembly crates. It will be a simple matter to lift them out one at a time." Ivan suddenly realized how excited he was becoming as the planning progressed. For the first time in many years he felt enthusiasm, pride in his work. It was a good feeling – good to be useful again.

Alexei had noticed Ivan's growing enthusiasm. The old man is really getting with the program. *He is going to be much more help that I expected. This is good, because the removal and transportation of the devices is much more complicated than I first thought. Yes, Ivan has much more value than I had assigned to him. I may need him to explain the devices to al-Mihdar. No, if Ivan meets al-Mihdar he will have to be killed. I do not wish to do this unless it is absolutely necessary.*

"Let us discuss our plans for searching for the bunker location. You know its general location. I will provide a suitable vehicle that has adequate ground clearance so that we can travel anywhere on the test range. How long do you think it will require to find the entrance?"

"We must assume several hours of travel just to go to and return from the general area where the bunker is located. It could take several days. If luck is with us, we will find it the first day."

"I understand. Once we find the door, I will have tools to open it. What equipment will we need?"

"Good lights. The air will be stale, so we will have to leave the door open. Two hand-held Geiger counters; one that measures high level gamma radiation; and one that measures low-level gamma radiation in mil-roentgens; and an alpha particle detector. We will also need hand tools to open the containers to inspect some of the items to determine their condition. I will need several hours for the inspection."

"Why do we need radiation detection equipment?"

"The condition of the components is unknown. I think I was the last person to be in the bunker, but it could have been found and looted. Worse, if someone got in who did not know what they were doing, they could have opened containers and placed components together: thus starting a chain reaction. To be safe, we will approach the bunker with high-level gamma instruments; so that we do not receive a large dose of radiation should there be a problem. If we find high level readings, we will know that the bunker has been contaminated and it is dangerous."

"O.K., but why the low level instruments?"

"We can expect to find slightly elevated levels of radiation above background. Some natural radiation will always be present. We call this background radiation. First I will determine background radiation near the bunker, and then monitor increases as we enter the bunker. Low-level radiation will not be a problem, because we will not be exposed to it for very long. Alpha particle radiation is expected from natural decay of the radioactive uranium isotopes. The alpha detector will record this type of radiation when the probe is placed very close to the uranium. This will serve to verify that the item is uranium."

"We do not wish to attract attention. After we have completed our inspection, I will secure the door and we will return to our base of operations. The extraction team will be in position and ready to go. They will open the bunker and remove the items as quickly as possible."

"I do not wish to pry into your business Comrade Colonel, but I do not understand the rush to find and empty the bunker."

"Yes Ivan, you have been very good about not asking questions. I will answer your question; however, you must treat this as secret, need to know information. Do you understand?"

Yes, Comrade Colonel, I do."

"Good, so far you have proven to be trustworthy, so I will tell you. The Soviet Union may break up. If it does, some of our republics such as Kazakhstan will become independent. We must recover items such as your devices as quickly as possible without anyone knowing what we are doing. If anyone discovered that atomic devices had been left at the test range there would be serious trouble. Mother Russia could suffer serious embarrassment at the United Nations. This is why we started the orphan hunt. We must find and remove all such items as quickly as possible." *I hope Ivan accepts this explanation.*

"Thank you Comrade Colonel. Now I understand the rush, and will do all in my power to assist you."

"Good Ivan Zeldovich, I am sure that you will. Let us now develop a simple marking system that I can remember; and more important, be able to explain to my General. I have been thinking about this and have an idea. You know how to interpret the current markings. So, using different color paint, you can mark each container belonging to a device with the same color. For example, the first device will be red; therefore, you will mark the projectile container with a red P; and the four target ring containers with a red R1, R2, R3, and R4. Make sure that the numbers are in the correct sequence, starting with the ring closest to the gun tube as R1."

"That is a good idea. It is a fast, simple and effective marking system."

"Can you think of anything else that I should know about?"

"No Colonel, I think that we have discussed everything. If I think of anything else I will send you the information through Comrade Glukhih."

"Very good. I am very pleased with your assistance Ivan Zeldovich. Tell Comrade Glukhih of your needs, and he will take care of them. Be prepared to leave in April as soon as the weather permits. Comrade Glukhih will take you to the train station, and I will meet you in Moscow. From there we will travel together to Semipalatinsk. Once your task is completed, transportation to Leningrad will be provided. From there you and Anya will travel to Cuba by ship. I will give you all of the details before you leave. You will, I hope, think of me fondly each time you sit in the warm sun and enjoy that rich Cuban coffee. You will also discover another Cuban delicacy – rum," the Colonel said with a smile. "Now, I regret to say, it is time for us to go out into the cold."

The trip back to Saravo was uneventful. Neither man spoke. Both were considering what they had to do to prepare for the search. In front of Ivan's apartment building Alexei pulled the car to the curb, smiled, and turned to hand Ivan a thick envelope. "This will provide you with funds until it is time to leave." Then speaking in a more commanding tone the Colonel cautioned, "Remember you must be discreet in all things." Reaching over to open the door, he bid Ivan farewell, and as the old man stepped from the car solemnly said, "I will see you in Moscow."

Ivan tucked the envelope into the pocket of his parka as he bent down to say farewell. "Thank you Comrade Colonel. I look forward to our trip." Turning, Ivan walked to the apartment building door and entered the lobby. From there he watched as the Volga moved off into the traffic. Only then did he open the envelope to find a thick sheaf of currency. More rubles than he had ever had at one time. *Yes, I have found a good sponsor, who rewards good work and loyalty. I am very fortunate indeed.*

The following afternoon, Colonel Alexei Valek made his verbal report to the General, and following the General's orders, prepared a detailed list of containers: including size and weight, and a list of tools and equipment required. No mention of the contents of the containers nor their location was included. The General would arrange for the necessary trucks, equipment and personnel to be available when required.

Gamaa Islamiya Safe House, Cairo, Egypt, February 1991

Alexei Valek had arrived at the Cairo International Airport Wednesday morning and cleared customs with no problem. Soviet visitors rarely had problems in Egypt. After collecting his bag he exited the main building and stopped to light a cigarette. A young Egyptian whom he had met on his last trip approached him and used the proper identification code. Following the young man to an old car, Alexei put his bag in the back seat and got in. As the car eased slowly into the traffic, Alexei turned to look anxiously behind them; where he checked the traffic for several minutes to see if they were followed. Neither man spoke. Finally satisfied all was well, Alexei relaxed a bit, sat back and watched the bustling crowds as his driver took a circuitous route to a house on the outskirts of Cairo.

Familiar with the house from a previous meeting, Alexei knew the routine when he entered, and stood waiting to be shown into the garden. *I wonder if it is safe to meet twice in the same place,* he thought. This time he noted several guards posted up and down the street, and there were additional men in the house. He assumed, rightly so, that the adjoining houses were under Gamaa Islamiya control.

In the garden Alexei found Mohammed sitting, as he had been at their previous meeting, drinking tea.

Walking forward Alexei greeted Mohammed al-Mihdar, "Good afternoon."

"Good afternoon. Allah be praised, for surely he has blessed your safe arrival," answered al-Mihdar. "We were most pleased with the contents of your message. Come, sit, please join me in the shade and have some tea."

"Thank you my friend. It feels good to be in a warm climate. Moscow is not my favorite place this time of the year. A cup of tea would be most welcome."

"Thanks be to Allah, for the climate in Afghanistan is also unpleasant. I much prefer the Saudi desert."

Valek and al-Mihdar waited for the servant to withdraw. Alexei was still concerned about meeting in the same location – even though considerable time had passed. Al-Mihdar, observing Valek looking around, understood why he was nervous.

"Do not be concerned about our safety and privacy. This house has not been used in several months; and we have eyes and ears everywhere in the neighborhood. Provisions have been made to quickly leave this place should the need arise."

Alexei shrugged and nodded his head in agreement. "I am sure you have taken proper precautions, but it is my nature to worry about such things. Perhaps that is why I am still alive."

"Praise be to Allah, you are correct, one cannot be too careful. Tell me about these rare antiques you have found."

"Mohammed, how much do you know about atomic bombs? I know you are an educated man and understand physics much better than I do. Specifically, do you understand that there are two types of atomic bombs?"

"Allah be praised. Allah has smiled upon us if you have found an atomic bomb. I am familiar with the concept of implosion, and how it is used to produce an atomic explosion. We have been seeking technical information on the process."

"I see, but do you know about the other type, called a 'gun-type atomic bomb?'"

"I have heard the term. From what I have read it is inefficient and requires a great amount of fissionable uranium. Is this what you have brought to us?"

The tone of al-Mihdar's voice told Alexei to be careful. These Islamic fanatics had volatile tempers. He could not afford to loose the Arab's attention. Alexei decided to proceed with caution.

"You are correct, but the gun-type bomb also has advantages that you will find attractive. The nuclear components can be easily separated into several pieces for transportation: thereby reducing the risk of detection. In fact, if they were discovered, very few would be able recognize the components as atomic bomb parts. The design is simple, and the components can be stored for long periods of time without affecting the explosive yield. The same is not true for an implosion bomb, which has a very complicated arming and firing mechanism. For example, an implosion bomb requires a great amount of electricity to charge capacitor banks required to function their special detonators. As you may know, implosion bombs have many detonators. Some even have over 250.

"Implosion nuclear warhead detonators do not function like an electric blasting cap or bomb fuse. In such conventional devices, the bridge wire is heated red hot by a low voltage electrical current that causes a primary explosive to detonate; which then detonates the booster charge in the cap or fuse; which detonates the main charge. This arrangement is called the 'explosive train.' In a conventional bomb fuse, part of the explosive train is out-of-line with the booster; so that if the primary explosive detonates, the bomb will not. Such an arrangement is not possible in a nuclear warhead.

"A conventional bomb or artillery shell uses available energy to cause a metal disk to rotate the out-of-line component of the explosive train in line with the rest of the explosive train. This energy comes from the spinning of the shell, or a propeller type device on a bomb that uses air to turn it – much like a windmill.

"Nuclear weapon detonators have no primary explosives so a hot bridge wire will not set off the explosive train. Nuclear weapon's detonators use an exploding bridge wire and are called 'EBW' detonators. Large capacitors are charged; and then the charge is dumped into the wires leading to each detonator at exactly the same time. The voltage and current is sufficient to vaporize the bridge wire; which produces enough energy to detonate the secondary explosive; which detonates the main lens charge."

"I understand the principal."

"O.K., thermal batteries are used to produce current to drive an electric motor, which drives a generator that charges the capacitor bank. Thermal batteries have a shelf life and must be constantly checked. The same is true of the capacitors. The fusing and firing circuits are complex, and the components are subject to all types of failures. The warhead cannot be disassembled for shipment and then reassembled."

"Ah, . . . tell me about the gun-type bomb."

"You understand critical and supercritical reactions?"

"Yes."

"Uranium must be enriched in the uranium-235 isotope to at least 89%. This is the difficult part. Once highly enriched uranium (HEU) is obtained, the rest is very simple. The supercritical mass is divided into components, and then very quickly assembled. As the components come together the fission reaction begins. The trick is getting the components together before they melt. If that is done, then you have an atomic explosion."

"This has been done?"

"Yes, the American's first atomic bomb dropped on Hiroshima was a gun-type bomb called the Little Boy. They did not test the design before using it."

"May Allah punish the arrogant American infidels. . . . Go on."

"A gun-type weapon is referred to as a 'poor man's atomic bomb': which is very easy to make, if you can obtain enough highly enriched uranium-235. Getting the HEU is the problem. Once you have it making the bomb is simple."

"Praise be to Allah, our brother Saddam Hussein is trying to produce HEU. It is very difficult to do. Please continue."

"The Soviet Union was developing both types of atomic bombs. We were successful in testing our implosion bomb before the gun-type. The reason we failed to test the gun-type bomb lay in the fact that the chief project scientist was waiting until he had enough HEU for several bombs. He wanted to test several component designs, in order to select the best one. He was two months away from his test when the implosion bomb was detonated. Had his bomb been tested first, he would have been a Hero of Socialist Labor."

"Yes, yes, this is very interesting, but how does this concern us?" Mohammed rejoined, and waved his hand as if to say get on with it. *What do we care if the man was a hero? Our only concern is whether these bombs even exist; and if so, their usefulness in blowing the Americans to hell,* he thought, *get on with it. Do you have them?*

Aware now that Mohammed was irritated, Alexei quickly responded.

"The five test bombs were built, but never tested. We think they are still in storage at the test site." While he was speaking Alexei had opened his brief case and withdrawn an envelope. "This envelope contains sketches of the nuclear components, projectiles and targets for each device."

"*You think*! You do not *know*?" Mohammed said in a disgusted voice and sat forward as if to rise.

"Our information is that they were left in a remote area and forgotten, " Alexei said quickly.

Mohammed raised a questioning eyebrow and eased back in his chair.

"Yes, this is possible, because the team responsible for them was punished for not being first. All records of the team were destroyed; and as you have already said, their designs are inefficient. Also, Joseph Stalin was set on having a thermonuclear bomb. To verify their actual existence we must go to the test site and find them."

Mohammed made no reply. Instead he sat with his eyes closed obviously thinking and toying with his teacup, *So the Russian pigs have something after all, but how great a something and what will they want for it? Nuclear weapons!* He reveled in the thought, *Allah's answer to our prayers. Usama will be jubilant. I must not appear too anxious . . . show casual indifference in my response.*

"When are you thinking of doing this?" Mohammed asked as he slowly reached for more tea, watching Alexei out of the corner of his eye for signs that the Russian sensed his growing excitement.

"Depending upon your interest and ability to purchase one or more of the bombs, I will go in May." *The Arab goat herder is pretending not to be interested,* Alexei thought and laughed to himself, *but he is hooked and just doesn't want me to see it. Give him a reason to pretend more interest by speeding up the timetable just a bit.* "If we find them, they must be moved quickly. Our great Soviet Union is coming apart. This will make removing them easier. We can truck them to the Uzbekistan border near Termez; where you can take possession of them."

"You actually believe they will still function, after being abandoned for so long?"

"Yes, a standard artillery piece is used to shoot the smaller piece into the larger one. We will supply fresh propellant for the guns."

Fingering his beard Mohammed continued his feigned indifference. "You say there are five of these atomic bombs?"

"Yes, but understand that while they are complete atomic bombs, they are also test devices designed to be installed and then detonated. They are not bombs designed to be dropped from an airplane."

The pompous ass, he must know we have no capability to drop a bomb from an airplane, Mohammed thought and almost sneered his next reply. Instead he unassumingly replied, "Allah the great has not provided us with bombers. You said these bombs, or devices as you call them, can be easily disassembled and moved as components."

"Yes. This will also reduce the chance that they can be detected by radiation detectors."

Allah be praised, nuclear, portable, undetectable: that makes them even more interesting – and priceless. Even though Usama has said we have unlimited funds, I refuse to let this greedy Russia know how eager we are to have so great a prize as these bombs. Devices, keep using the word devices that devalues them somewhat. "What are you thinking of asking for these devices?"

"The price will be $50 million U.S. dollars each." Alexei watched al-Mihdar carefully. This was the crucial point of the conversation. If they had the money, things were about to get very interesting.

Mohammed was pleased with the price. He decided to be silent for a while and pretend to consider the offer. For Usama that is cheep at half the price. *Let the pig sweat while I pretend to contemplate how we poor goat herders can pay so great a price.* Signaling to one of the guards, he said, "Ali, I think it is time for our meal." Turning back to Valek, he said, "Let us enjoy a meal while I consider your proposal."

Valek was anxious, but knew Mohammed was playing him with a feigned bargaining strategy. *He wants this deal so bad he can taste it,* Valek thought and decided to play his own game – *he who speaks first losses.* "Mohammed, the lamb is excellent. Thank you for this fine meal." *It would be much better with a glass of vodka.*

"Allah be praised, I am glad that you are enjoying it," Mohammed said while thinking, *You gluttonous swine.* "How is our friend Kamal?" he asked with a smile.

"I have not spoken with him for some time. As you know, officially things are going badly between the withdrawing Soviet army and Pakistan."

"Yes, Allah the merciful has granted us victory over your army. I am glad that you do not take this defeat personally," Mohammed said and thought, *You are no better than an American capitalist pig – greedy like those stinking devils.*

"Business is business," Valek said, confirming Mohammed's thoughts.

During the pause in the conversation that followed, the two enjoyed their meal, but Mohammed silently calculated his next move while complaining to himself. *How I would like to end this irritating meeting and get rid of this Russian pig; however, I must be patient, there is much to be learned and decided. Allah the Great is blessing us; and I am anxious to share this promising news with my beloved brother Usama. Get on with it! Let him know you are ready to deal, but take care to keep him off guard. . .*

.

Deliberately acting to unnerve Valek, Mohammed abruptly pushed his chair back from the table, and broke the silence by gruffly saying, "With Allah's blessing, I will discuss your antiques with my brothers. . . . Your price is extremely high," he added and intentionally avoided looking at Valek. Instead he jerked his chair back up to the table, stared at his food, and sat quietly shaking his head and stroking his beard for the longest time before continuing, "*If* we are interested, when and where do you think you can make your delivery?" he asked.

Got them! thought Valek, who was well aware of Mohammed's trading tactics. *But wait,* he told himself, *Do not reply.* Instead he played Mohammed's game and sat for a while pretending to be enjoying his meal.

"I plan to start the search in May." *Give him some more details to stir his interest.* "When we find them, we will have a convoy of trucks available to remove them. I suggest that we make delivery near Termez in Uzbekistan. From there you will be able to get them into Afghanistan. Assuming that you are able to meet our price, it will take approximately two weeks to move the antiques from their location to Termez."

"How many trucks will be in the convoy?"

"The exact number has not been determined, but the minimum is five – plus two as back-ups."

"The trucks will be included in the purchase?"

"We had not planned on that, but if you purchase all five antiques I see no problem. We will only require one for our men to return in."

"Will you be present at the point of delivery?"

Alexei had not considered this. But now that the subject had come up, he was sure that the General would require him to command the convoy. "Yes, I will be there to ensure that all goes well."

"Allah be praised. If my brothers approve of this purchase, I will meet you there. I am curious as to why you have not offered these items to Saddam Hussein?"

"There are several reasons, first we have intelligence to the effect that Saddam Hussein plans to invade Kuwait. If he does, he will force the Americans to confront him. It is possible that they will invade Iraq, and then we would be exposed. Second, too many bureaucrats would be privy to the purchase, and it could be traced back to us. Third, we have respect for your accomplishments – especially your security. We must be sure that these items, which do not exist in our records, are not traced back to us. If you have the funds for this purchase, we will be able to do more business."

"Thanks be to Allah. Yes, we understand that there are plans to seize the oil fields in Kuwait. Saddam is very strong and powerful. He will throw the Americans back into the sea if they invade. Iran was not able to defeat his army."

"While I detest the Americans, I do not underestimate their military. The Iraqi army has not fought a battle against first-rate troops. No, with the current president, the American military will squash Saddam's army. If they were fighting us it would be a different matter."

Yes, your army did so well against our Mujahedeen. "Allah will provide our brother Saddam the means and will to destroy the Great Satan's army if they come."

There is no point in continuing this discussion. It is amazing how an otherwise intelligent man can ignore facts if they contradict his religious beliefs, Alexei thought. "It will be as you say. The important thing is that these bombs must never be traced back to us. My country knows nothing about this and has no record of the devices. If you are able to use one or more of them, there must be no way to trace their origin. If my government ever found out they would hunt all of us down and kill us. Make no mistake about that. If one or more of these devices is used in America, you will have stirred up a nest of killer bees that will pursue you as long as you live. Never underestimate the fury and resolve of angry Americans."

"Allah will protect the righteous, which are doing his work. However, what you say has truth. Muslim governments would be forced to help find us to appease the west. We will limit the knowledge of their origin to a small group of my brothers."

"Good. Secrecy is our best ally. Please inform us of your interest by sending me a message to Volga Antiques. If our terms are acceptable, simply say you wish to purchase so many of the antiques. Do not mention the price. We will acknowledge with banking instructions. When we find the items, we will message you with an approximate delivery date. No location will be specified. You will provide contact details without mentioning the location. Payment will be half upon receipt of our delivery message, and the remainder after you have inspected the items. The items will be released to you upon receipt of final payment."

"It will be necessary for us to verify that the antiques are authentic."

"Yes, I understand that. Actually, if we were to deliver a fake, all you would have to do is report us to our government. This is your best insurance."

"May Allah be praised, for he has brought us the means to bring the Great Satan to his knees. One of my brothers will take you to your destination. Allah bless you."

"And may Allah bless you and your brothers," Alexei said as the stood up to leave.

The same young Egyptian drove Alexei to his hotel – where he immediately took a shower. God he hated dealing with Arabs. *So much flowery talk to settle something so simple*, he thought as he toweled off and drank a shot of vodka. *The only thing pleasant here is the weather. I will enjoy this vodka and the warmth of the evening. Tomorrow morning I must fly back to frigid Moscow and brief the General.*

With the Russian out of his way Mohammed al-Mihdar smiled to himself and whispered a silent prayer, *Allah be praised, bless this miserable Russian in his quest for our holy bombs,* and with that he entered the house to prepare a telex to bin Laden's headquarters in Peshawar. "Antiques are what we are seeking. Price reasonable. Half of your estimate. Suggest meeting in Riyadh. Returning to Riyadh tomorrow."

Rancho Nuevo, February 1991

Ralph Edi rose early on Saturday morning. After completing his 5-kilometer morning run, he shaved and showered. He had been taught in Afghanistan that a beard attracted attention. In keeping with his usual Saturday routine, he had a light breakfast consisting of orange juice and cold cereal, while reading the *San Francisco Chronicle* on the patio. After eating he finished reading the newspaper and sat looking out over the valley. *A beautiful view,* he thought, *too bad it was populated by ungodly infidels. One day the heathens will know the true faith. I hope I will be part of Allah's plan.* Next came his normal Saturday chores, cleaning, laundry and washing the car, followed by a light lunch.

It was now 1 PM, time to go. On Saturdays Eid drove to Oakland and check his mailbox at Mail Boxes *Etc.* After that he planned to attend prayer service at a Mosque in San Francisco. Following the instructions he had received at the al-Qaeda training camp, Ralph kept a low profile and did nothing to call attention to his religion. The only time that he attended prayer services was on Saturday, and then he went to different Mosques in San Francisco, Oakland, Concord, San Jose and sometimes Pleasant Hill or Stockton. When invited to return he explained that he was just visiting the area.

Time to leave, he thought as he entered the garage, and started his new black Ford Mustang convertible. I really wanted a Mercedes, but that would definitely attract attention. No one would notice a young bachelor with a good job driving a Ford. Backing out of the garage onto the street, Ralph stopped to lower the top and thought, *Such a beautiful clear afternoon. Why not enjoy it?*

The drive to Oakland was uneventful. At Jack London Square, Ralph parked near Mail Boxes, *Etc.*, entered the lobby and silently began reciting a verse from the Quran to calm his nerves, *"God is the best protector and He is the most merciful. Do not hearts become tranquil in remembering Him?"* He turned right and made his way through the crowd to his mailbox. At the box he relaxed and retrieved his mail without attracting attention. *Praise Allah, He is The Hearing, The Knowing*, he thought and smiled when he recognized a letter from Uncle Saleh, who was in reality Mohammed al-Mihdar.

Outside the mail center, Ralph, despite his delight at hearing from his uncle, walked slowly back to the parked Mustang. Only when he was safely inside the car did he dare open the envelope; and allow himself to become excited over learning that he should soon expect a visit from his Cousin Ali – who was also Mohammed al-Mihdar. *My prayers are being answered. I may be getting an assignment.*

Prayer services at the Al Noor Mosque were over, and the beautiful day had lengthened into a balmy afternoon. *Too soon to drive home*, Ralph thought as he put the Mustang in gear, *How about an early dinner at Fisherman's Wharf, and a visit to some of the singles bars? I do despise the decadence of western women, but on the other hand, "Allah does not charge a soul with more than it can bear. . . ."* and, why not take advantage of such women as long as they were available?

Riyadh, Saudi Arabia, February 1991

It was a clear, cool morning, ideal weather for Saudi Arabia – four days after Mohammed's meeting with Colonel Valek in Cairo. Usama bin Laden was in a meeting with Mohammed al-Mihdar at one of bin Laden's companies. Bin Laden had just returned from Khartoum, Sudan; where he was in the process of establishing a foothold for al-Qaeda, and starting a new business. "May Allah bless you Mohammed, I am anxious to hear what the Russian dog had to offer."

"Allah is great, for he has provided us the means to inflict a mortal wound on the Great Satan. If the Russian infidel can deliver what he has promised, we shall have the wrath of Allah to unleash on the godless Americans," Mohamed replied.

"Allah be praised, tell me what you have learned."

"Allah, in his wisdom, allowed the Soviets to attempt to duplicate the American atomic bomb program in the 1940s. They formed two teams of scientists and engineers. One to duplicate each type of atomic bomb – the gun-type and the implosion type. It was a race to see which team would detonate its bomb first. The implosion team won in 1949, and got the credit. Lavrenti Beria was in charge and did not want a failure recorded; so he simply abolished the other team and destroyed all records of its existence. According to Valek, he has reason to believe that five gun-type atomic bombs were delivered to the Soviet's test range, and stored in an underground bunker complex. When the command to abolish the gun-type team came, everyone was ordered to stop work and to immediately return to Russia. If so, the five atomic bombs were left in the bunkers, and they may still be there."

"Allah be praised for his wisdom. He is allowing the infidels to provide the means for their own destruction. Please continue."

"Valek requires a statement of interest from us, including the number of bombs we wish to purchase at $50 million U.S. dollars each. Once he has received word from us that we wish to purchase some or all of the bombs, Valek will proceed to the test range and attempt to find them. If he is successful, he will send me a message specifying a delivery date. He suggested that we accept delivery at Termez, Uzbekistan. I concur with this location, because it is under the control of our brother Juma Namangani: with whom we must arrange for safe passage for the Soviet convoy" – Juma Namangani would eventually become the leader of the Islamic Movement of Uzbekistan, the IMU.

"Thanks be to Allah. This appears to be reasonable. What terms did the Russian dog ask for?"

"Once we receive a message that the rare antiques are ready for shipment, half of the purchase price is to be transferred according to instructions. The second half must be transferred after we inspect the bombs. When payment is received, the bombs and the transport vehicles will be turned over to us."

"Allah be praised. How long will it take to transport the bombs to Termez?

"Valek estimated two weeks."

"Yes, that is probably a good estimate. What will prevent us from simply taking the bombs away from Valek at Termez?"

"I have considered that possibility. If I were Valek, I would have the bombs protected with a self-destruct charge. We must assume this to be the case. Besides, Valek may be able to provide us with more of the items we are seeking. He expects the Soviet Union to come apart and sees opportunities to acquire many things."

"Thanks be to Allah. Your advice is sound. You may signal Valek that we wish to acquire all of the rare antiques, and that the terms are acceptable. How do you plan to proceed?"

"Allah is great. Do you remember Ralph Eid, the Egyptian, who is an American citizen?"

"Yes, we discussed him at our meeting at Zawar Kili. He was going to return to America and finish his Ph.D. in nuclear physics. You hoped that he would be able to obtain employment at the American nuclear weapons lab."

Mohammed was again awed by Usama's memory. *Did he ever forget anything?* "Yes, by the grace of Allah, he has succeeded and is now employed at the American nuclear weapons Livermore Laboratories in the state of California."

"Thanks be to Allah. I thought the American's nuclear weapons laboratory was in the state of New Mexico at a place called Los Alamos."

"The Americans have several such laboratories. The two main ones are: Laurence Livermore Laboratories in Livermore, California; and Los Alamos in New Mexico. Both are operated by the University of California. I have sent Eid an alert that I will be visiting him soon. With your approval, I will travel to California and meet with Dr. Eid. He has followed our instructions to become a member of the local community and purchase a house. If he has been successful in getting into the nuclear weapons program, he will be able to evaluate the Russian's information on gun-type weapons. If Eid verifies what Valek has told me, I will send the message confirming our intent to purchase the rare antiques. Once I am satisfied with Eid and his progress, I may wish to place him in charge of importing and hiding the components of the five bombs."

"This is a sound approach. Proceed with your plans. Funds are available to you for use in America. Consider purchasing a business that will provide cover for our project. Also consider a name for this project. May Allah bless you."

"With Allah's blessing I will succeed."

The meeting was over and Mohammed left the building. It was a beautiful day. His driver was waiting and he instructed him to go to the al-Jawf travel agency; where he would purchase round trip, first class tickets to San Francisco, California, returning via Chicago. Mohammed al-Mihdar was a frequent traveler to the United States and had a current entry visa.

For a moment Mohammed had considered going to visit his parents before leaving the city. It had been over two years since his last visit. His father was opposed to his involvement with Usama bin Laden, whom he considered to be a radical extremists and a threat to the royal family. No, a visit would only invite unwanted questions. His family was content that he had completed advanced studies, and hoped that one day he would come to his senses and join the family businesses. His older brother, Saad, was now running the businesses and Mohammed and Saad did not get along.

Next, he mailed a letter to Ralph Eid's Mail Boxes, *Etc.* address. The letter informed Ralph that his cousin Ali would arrive in San Francisco on the third Saturday of the month, at 1:13 PM, on TWA Flight 11, from New York's Kennedy Airport. In spite of himself, Mohammed was looking forward to visiting America. Like many Moslems, he had acquired a taste for fine foods and wine. *Too bad I cannot bring back a case of Stag's*

Leap, Cabernet Sauvignon. Time to switch to my American persona. I must shave off my beard, and think and act like an American to avoid unwanted attention.

San Francisco International Airport, March 1991

Mohammed al-Mihdar unbuckled his seat belt, stood and retrieved his briefcase from the overhead compartment. It had been a pleasant flight from Kennedy. Leaving the Saturday *New York Times* on the seat, he was the fourth person to deplane. Walking through the terminal, he looked like any other tourist with his clean-shaven face and western attire. The signs to baggage clam led him to his agreed meeting place with Ralph Eid. Descending the stairs, he located the baggage carrousel for his flight. As he walked toward the carrousel, Ralph Eid approached him. "Good afternoon, Mohammed, I hope your flight was pleasant."

The two men shook hands in the western manner of greeting and Mohammed replied, "Good afternoon, Ralph. Yes, I had a most enjoyable flight."

Mohammed enjoyed using his American persona. Flowery phrases and hugs in greeting so common in the Arabic world were not used in America. *English is a better language for communicating information. It is unfortunate that our people judge a leader by the quality of his poetic speech. Reality is often obscured by rhetoric and bravado. Events from the past are mixed with current events in such a way that all appear to have just occurred. Arabs spend much too much time posturing.*

"You are looking fit, Dr. Eid," Mohammed said to Ralph Eid, who was casually dressed in a golf shirt, khaki Dockers and Nike running shoes. Mohammed was pleased with Ralph's appearance. Standing six feet one inch, and weighing 180 pounds, Ralph Eid was a good looking man of twenty-eight years. Ralph had no immediate family in America. His older sister was married and lived in al-Qantarah, a small town near the Suez Canal. She had never visited America, and Ralph barely remembered her. Since his parent's death, Ralph had become a dedicated follower of the Prophet and had been recruited into al-Qaeda through a local mosque.

Pleased that he was making a good impression, Ralph responded, "Thank you, I try to keep in shape."

Mohammed and Ralph continued with small talk while they waited for Mohammed's suitcase. Finally, bag in hand Ralph directed Mohammed to follow him across the pedestrian bridge that lead to the short-term parking lot.

At the Mustang, Ralph took Mohammed's brief case and bag and placed them in the trunk. "Be sure to fasten you seat belt," he cautioned

Mohammed as they entered the car. "No need to get a ticket and draw undue attention to ourselves." Snapping his own seatbelt in place, Ralph backed out of the parking place, drove out of the garage and paid the parking lot fee.

"New car?" Mohammed asked as he noticed the smell of the Mustang's leather upholstery.

"Yes," Ralph responded, somewhat embarrassed at having this decadent, sporty car. "I needed something in keeping with my new status as an up-and-coming scientist," he explained, and changing the subject asked, "Are you hungry? Would you like to go into the city for a meal, or go directly to my house and eat later?"

"Let us go to your house, if you consider it to be a safe place to talk. I had a fairly good lunch on the plane," Mohammed responded and settled back to enjoy the ride in this beautiful American automobile. *Yes,* he thought, *I do enjoy my western persona, and almost envy this young man Allah's rich blessings. But as Muslim brothers, we are cautioned, "Covet not the advantage which God has given to some over others." Praise Allah for his wisdom!*

Ralph took the San Jose exit onto the 101 Expressway. Driving south toward the San Mateo Bridge Ralph said, "I have two large rib-eye steaks that I can prepare on the grill, if you like beef." Ralph who had little personal contact with Mohammed, was unsure how to proceed.

"Grilled steak sounds wonderful," replied Mohammed. "Do not forget that I spent many years here as a student. I developed a fondness for western food. A bottle of wine would be nice. Do you have any red wine?"

Ralph was surprised, and it must have shown. "No, I do not drink alcohol," *The Quran forbids drinking alcohol,* Ralph instinctively thought, *but I'd better not mention that. Do as he wishes and offer to purchase one.* "But if you like, I can stop and purchase a bottle on the way."

"Good, let us do so. Now, tell me about your social life and the Livermore area."

Ralph told him of his associates at work and the mosques he attended as he drove across the San Mateo Bridge, and turned north on I-880. At the next exit, which led to Southland Mall, he left the interstate and quickly located a wine and beverage store. Ralph parked the Mustang in front of the store. The two men entered the store, and Ralph listened intently as Mohammed spoke of the wonders of wine making while he perused the wine racks. Mohammed settled on two bottles of 1985 Beaulieu Vineyard's estate bottled, private reserve *Cabernet Sauvignon.* "Not my favorite vintage, but this will do," he said as the cashier packaged the bottles in two separate brown paper bags.

"I see I have much to learn about wines," Ralph remarked when they returned to the Mustang. "It's such a beautiful afternoon. We have a distance to go, and the drive is lovely. Would you like me to put the top down?"

"Yes, that would be most enjoyable."

Ralph returned to I-880 and continued north to I-238, which connected to I-580 east. He continued east on I-580, past the exit for San Rio, and Tassajara roads. A little while later, he pointed to the right in the direction of Livermore Labs. "That is where I work, Mohammed. I cannot take you in unless I get permission, and that will entail identification and questions."

"It is best that I do not call attention to myself. Thank you for showing me your work place. It is much larger than I expected."

Taking the next exit, Ralph reversed directions and entered I-580 west bound, and headed for his house. Turning into Rancho Nuevo, Ralph waived to a neighbor, proceeded to the end of the street, clicked the garage door opener, and pulled into the garage. Mohammed got out of the car and took his briefcase from the trunk. Ralph picked up the suitcase and preceded Mohammed into the house through the laundry room. Walking through the kitchen, he led Mohammed down the hall to a large bedroom on the left. "I hope you will be comfortable here. The bathroom is across the hall. As soon as you are ready, I will show you the rest of the house."

While Mohammed unpacked, Ralph returned to the car and brought the two bottles of wine to the kitchen. *I wonder if I should put them in the refrigerator. Best I leave them out for Mohammed.* Ralph took two water glasses from the cabinet and waited for Mohammed to return. After a few minutes Mohammed came in. "Would you like the wine now or a Coke or Pepsi? I also have ice tea."

"A Pepsi will be fine."

Ralph poured two glasses and handed one to Mohammed. "Let me show you around the house." Walking down the hall, Ralph showed Mohammed the master bedroom, his office located in the third bedroom, and then returned to the living room, the adjoining dining room and large family room. Next, he opened the sliding glass doors and stepped out onto the patio. Come enjoy the view," he said and motioned right and left with his arm out toward the valley.

"You have a fine house, and the view is grand," Mohammed said.

"Thank you, I would not have it without your funds. We have privacy here. No one can look down onto us. My office and the family room face toward the valley, which makes monitoring conversations very difficult. This was a model home, and I purchased it with the furniture."

Mohammed nodded and said, "Clever, very clever," as he sat down on one of the patio chairs. "Tell me about your duties at the lab. Are you involved with nuclear weapons?"

Sitting down, Ralph replied, "Not directly. I am assigned to a group working on methods of disposal of radioactive waste. We are evaluating various packaging and encapsulation technologies. I am concentrating on isotopes from medical treatment."

"Medical treatment?"

"Yes, low level isotopes, which have short half lives are used in medical treatment. Usually they are injected into the blood stream; so that instruments can track them through the body, and take pictures of organs. Very energetic high-level isotopes that emit gamma radiation are also used to treat cancer – for example cobalt-60. I have become quite knowledgeable about this subject."

"But not nuclear weapons," Mohammed said, feeling somewhat disconcerted.

"No, not yet." It was getting late and soon the temperature would start to drop. "Let me put the steaks on, and we can continue this conversation inside while we eat dinner."

Mohammed nodded his approval; and thought as he watched Ralph light the gas grill, and go into the house to prepare the salad and potatoes, *I had hoped to be able to report that Ralph was directly involved with the nuclear weapons program. Usama will not be pleased.*

Returning in a few minutes with the steaks, Ralph asked, "How do you like your steak cooked?"

"Medium. They look like nice ones. I am going to open the wine. Would you care for a glass?"

Ralph was not sure how to answer. *Perhaps I should try a glass*, he thought. *It would not be proper to let my superior drink alone.* A set of four wine glasses came with the house. "Yes, I would like to try a glass. I know nothing about wine, but I guess I should learn in order to fit in at work. As you know, the famous Napa Valley is not far from here; and my colleagues like to talk about wine."

Both men entered the house. Mohammed picked up one of the wine bottles and said, "In that case, you must learn more about wine. If we had time, we would visit the Napa Valley and tour some of the wineries. Do you have a cork screw?"

Ralph remembered that a corkscrew had also come with the house and began looking for it. Finding it in the back of a drawer, he took two wine glasses from the cabinet, set them in front of Mohammed, and watched as Mohammed deftly uncorked the bottle, poured the wine and sniffed the red liquid in the glass before taking a sip.

"Not bad," Mohammed said, "Now it's your turn. First you sniff the bouquet and then you taste. Wine should not smell nor taste vinegary."

Ralph sniffed the wine, tasted it and remarked, "It smells and tastes slightly woody, like oak, but the overall flavor is very good. I have never tasted wine before."

"I am glad you like it. *Cabernet Sauvignon* is my favorite type. *Beaulieu* Vineyards is one of my preferred vintners; however, my favorite is *Stags Leap*. Both are in Napa Valley. Enjoying a good bottle of wine is one of the few forbidden pleasures in which I indulge when I am in America."

Ralph nodded, set his glass down, and left to put the steaks on the grill. Mohammed took a seat inside at the attractively set table with its view of the sparkling valley lights below and sipped his wine. Soon Ralph returned with the steaks, put the salad and potatoes on the table and they sat down to eat.

"Your table looks most inviting," Mohammed remarked as he tasted his salad and jokingly asked, "You are quite the accomplished chef."

"I'll wait until you have tasted the steak, before I accept you complement," Ralph smiled as he responded.

Both men continued eating and exchanging small talk about the pleasures of living in America. Ralph rose to clear the table and asked, "Would you like coffee or should I open the other bottle of wine?"

"Coffee for me," responded Mohammed, "We need to have clear heads to discuss the business at hand. You say you have not been able to gain information about nuclear weapons?"

"No, not as part of my duties. Current nuclear weapons design information requires a top-secret clearance and special clearance, called a Q clearance. I only have a secret clearance. However, once you are a member of the staff, and have a security clearance, it is possible to learn a great deal. I have followed your instructions, and have used every opportunity to learn about them. The scientists at the lab do not pay a great deal of attention to the concept of 'need to know.' They have assumed that my curiosity is normal and answer my questions.

"The library is full of reports, and documents that deal with the history of nuclear weapons – even current designs. I have read many of the Manhattan Project documents, which have been reduced in classification or declassified, and reviewed the design information on the early atomic bombs. The history of the Manhattan Project is fascinating. The first atomic bomb detonated, actually a device, was named 'Gadget.' It was a prototype of the Fat Man, plutonium implosion bomb. It was detonated at 5:29:45 A.M. mountain wartime, on July 16, 1945, at Trinity Site in the Alamogordo Test Range, in the *Jornada del Muerto* (Journey of Death) desert, in New Mexico. After testing, Gadget was weaponized, and became the Fat Man atomic bomb dropped on Nagasaki at 11:02 AM, the morning of August 9, 1945. The other atomic bomb was a uranium bomb, named the Little Boy, and was the first atomic bomb used in war. It was dropped on Hiroshima on August 6, 1945. There was only enough uranium-235 available for one bomb, so the first atomic bomb dropped was an untested design."

"So you are familiar with the designs of the first generation of atomic bombs. The ones developed in the 1940s. Do you know what a gun-type atomic bomb is?"

"Yes. That was the type of atom bomb dropped on Hiroshima – the Little Boy. It was constructed from uranium-235. A three inch naval gun was used to shoot the projectile into the target rings."

You have seen drawings and photographs of this type of weapon?"

"Yes."

"Good, I have something to show you after coffee. The steak was delicious. You *are* quite the chef," Mohammed said and both men laughed as they sat enjoying yet another western pleasure – ice cream for dessert.

With coffee and dessert finished, Mohammed went to his bedroom to get his briefcase; while Ralph cleared the table and put the dishes into the dishwasher.

So he can gain access to nuclear weapons information. This is good! Mohammed thought as he returned and joined Ralph at the table. Opening his briefcase, he removed several sheets of paper and placed them on the table. "These are supposed to be sketches of gun-type atomic test devices. See what you think of them," Mohammed said as he handed Ralph the first sheet showing a cone shaped projectile.

Ralph studied one of the drawings for a couple of minutes. "Very interesting. The cone shape of the projectile should allow it to enter the target; at least get very close to complete entry before the bomb functions. That was the problem with the Little Boy. You might call it premature detonation. The yield was less than expected."

"So you think that this is a valid design for a gun-type atomic device?"

"Yes, I do," Ralph said, pointing to the drawing with a pencil, "These are the target rings. The target is composed of rings, just like the Little Boy."

Mohammed gave a sigh of relief. *So, the Russian dog was telling the truth. They may have what they claim to have. Allah be praised.* Mohammed handed Ralph the next sketch showing the projectile with machined steps, "And this one?"

Again, Ralph studied the sketch. "This is a different design, and may be better – produce a more consistent yield. I have never seen these designs. Can you tell me where you got them?"

Mohammed ignored the question and handed Ralph the remaining three sketches. "And these?" he asked.

Ralph Eid was puzzled. Why was he being shown these designs? He was sure that they were not American. Then he realized that Mohammed al-Mihdar had journeyed from Saudi Arabia to show them to him and ask for his opinion. This meant that Mohammed and other senior al-Qaeda members, maybe even Usama, had a high opinion of him; and that he was being trusted with very sensitive information. *I must be worthy of the task Allah is about to give me,* he thought.

Taking the remaining sketches, Ralph studied them one at a time. Finally, he said, "These are five different designs of a gun-type atomic device. I have never seen these designs before, but they are practical and should work. Do you have any information about the uranium, and the actual gun that will fire the projectile?"

Mohammed was very pleased as he thought, *I was correct in my judgment of Ralph Eid. He has followed my instructions and gained the information we need. He may be the man to take responsibility for this project. Usama asked me to name the project. I must do so by the time I return. I must also determine Ralph's commitment to the jihad.* "The projectile and rings are fabricated from highly enriched uranium, ninety percent uranium-235. The gun is from a 100 mm anti-tank cannon."

"Do you know the muzzle velocity of the gun?"

"Yes, it is estimated to be 600 meters per second."

"That's much faster than the Little Boy's gun . . . and the diameter of the projectile?"

"76.2mm. A discarding sabot projectile is used to fit the smaller projectile into the lager gun tube." Mohammed paused to allow Ralph to absorb the information. "Let us assume that these devices were constructed in the late 1940s, and have been in storage ever since. Do you think that they will still function?

1940s vintage weapons . . . yes, that would explain the design. All modern nuclear weapons were implosion types. The small ones are linear implosion. They are not American designs. Who else? British, maybe . . . German, perhaps . . . Russian! Yes, Russia would have had the capability to produce HEU. But why would Russia have kept these antiques? The HEU has other uses. Should I ask? Better to wait for Mohammed to tell me, Ralph thought. "If the major components are intact, they should function. The half-life of uranium-235 is over 25,000 years; so it should be as good as the day it was produced. The gun itself could have rusted and become non-functional. Also, the propellant charge for the gun may have deteriorated."

"How can the HEU components be tested to verify that they are real HEU – not EU or depleted uranium?"

"Any nuclear laboratory could analyze the metal and determine the isotope and purity. Of course, you would have to take the sample from the actual components."

"Assuming that taking samples from the actual components . . . say at a remote location, with only simple instruments . . . is impractical. How can I quickly determine if the components are real?"

Ralph thought about this for a couple of minutes, and then decided to ask for more information. "Mohammed, I understand security and restricting information. But, I must know more if I am to provide answers. Can you tell me more about where the testing will take place?"

"Assume that the transfer of the components will take place in a remote desert, and that the verification must be made without delay."

"This is a serious problem. Please allow me to think about it for a while."

"I understand," Mohammed said backing off the subject. *I must control my enthusiasm and give him time to reflect.* Changing the subject Mohammed decided to question Ralph about the seriousness of his commitment to their cause.

"Are you having any trouble with your faith, being alone and not being able to participate in the Islamic community?" he asked.

"No, my faith is strong; however, I do miss being able to be active in the Muslim community. Only there was I able to express my true contempt for the establishment, and vent my anger at the loss of my parents. There I felt safe and secure – among brothers who are like- minded. I tire of my associates at the lab, who are devoted to obtaining material things. At least I am comforted by the fact that I can use the knowledge I am gaining to destroy what I hate."

"So you still believe strongly that America must be converted to Islam and be ruled by *sharia*."

"Yes, only the words of the Prophet can provide true meaning to these godless infidels."

"Do you believe that it is necessary to destroy the current government to do so?"

"Yes, there is no other way."

Mohammed was satisfied with Ralph's answer, and decided that enough had been accomplished for one day. "It is getting late. We can continue tomorrow. I would like you to think about one other issue. If al-Qaeda were able to obtain devices similar to the ones shown in the sketches, how could they be brought into the United States? How could they be hidden? How could they be assembled for use? Let us discuss these issues in the morning."

Ralph agreed and both men retired to their bedrooms.

The next morning Ralph woke at dawn. His mind was full of the things Mohammed had told him. Somehow al-Qaeda had found old WWII vintage atomic bombs and was planning to acquire them. The fact that Mohammed was willing to tell him the details meant that perhaps he was going to be put in charge of the project. This was more responsibility than he had ever dreamed about. *I must be worthy. Mohammed will expect answers to his questions. I must think about this carefully.* After shaving and showering, Ralph went into the kitchen and brewed a strong pot of Columbian coffee. Pouring a cup of the black brew, he walked out onto the patio and gazed into the valley below.

Two hours later, Mohammed awoke, shaved, showered and joined Ralph on the patio. "Good morning, Ralph. You are an early riser."

Startled, Ralph turned to greet Mohammed. "Good morning Mohammed. Sorry, but I am used to living alone. You startled me. Would you like a cup of coffee or juice?"

"Yes, thank you, both."

"Do you want cream and sugar?"

"Just sugar, thank you."

Ralph entered the house and poured a glass of orange juice and a cup of coffee. Returning to the patio, he placed the juice and coffee on the table. "Did you sleep well?"

"Yes, the bed is most comfortable."

Sitting down at the table, Ralph continued, "I have been thinking about your questions. I am sure that I will have better ideas later, but I can offer the following answers now."

"Your answers and ideas are most welcome."

"I have thought of one simple method to validate the components. It is very dangerous and may cause harm to the individual performing the test. I got the idea from an experiment conducted at the Los Alamos laboratory while they were developing the Little Boy. Assemble the target rings, and then have one of your men pick up the projectile and start walking very slowly toward the rings from a distance of several meters. Use a Geiger counter to measure gamma radiation. If the components are made from HEU, the readings will increase as the projectile approaches the rings. The man carrying the projectile must move very slowly, and must stop when you tell him. If not, you could cause a critical reaction, and he could receive a very dangerous dose of radiation – even a fatal dose. This is a very crude test method."

"Yes, I understand the principal. I would not have thought of it. You are correct, it is a dangerous, but effective test. What are your thoughts on the other issues?"

"I will be happy to share my thoughts with you; but first, would you like something to eat?"

"Yes, thank you Ralph. My body still thinks it is in Saudi Arabia. Something light will be fine.

"I usually have cold cereal for breakfast. Would you care for some?"

"Yes, cold cereal will be fine. Do you have *Grape Nuts*?"

"Yes, I will get us both a bowl," Ralph replied as he turned and went into the house. Returning with two bowls, a box of *Grape Nuts* and a pitcher of milk on a tray, Ralph set the tray on the table.

After Mohammed and Ralph had prepared their cereal, Mohammed bowed his head and prayed, "In the name of Allah, the Compassionate, the Merciful we are thankful for the food we are about to eat, and pray for divine guidance and protection in the mission we are about to undertake."

Getting back to the subject, Ralph continued, "There is an old saying to the effect that the best place to hide something is in plain sight. I think this saying can be used as a guide. How can the components be detected? By the emitted radiation. Where is radiation expected? Several places: a cancer treatment facility; a medical facility that uses radioactive isotopes; and a radioactive waste storage site."

Mohammed was impressed. This scheme had never occurred to him. *It was brilliant,* he thought. *Only Allah could have inspired such a thought.* "Ralph, I am very pleased with your ideas. Let us develop a plan to implement them."

"When will the components be available?"

"Allah willing, by May of this year. They will be stored in a safe place until we are ready to ship them to America. I am going to suggest to Usama that you be placed in charge of the project in America. Only Usama, you and I will know the details."

"You honor me with your trust. I will pray to Allah for strength and guidance."

"I am sure you are worthy or Allah would not have brought you to us. Remember, al-Qaeda has many true believers in America, with many skills. You must start developing a plan. Funds will be made available. Perhaps we should acquire a business that uses radioactive isotopes or collects radioactive waste – perhaps both. Think in large terms. Also, we must decide upon targets for our devices. My thoughts are Washington, New York, Chicago, Atlanta, and one of the following: Denver, Boston, San Francisco or Dallas. I will value your thoughts. We will meet again after we have acquired the devices. By then, you must have a plan."

"I will. Do you have information regarding the expected yield?"

"25 KT each. Oh yes, that reminds me of another item. The devices incorporated a beryllium-polonium neutron source. The polonium-210 will have decayed and must be replaced. This may cause a problem. Do you have any ideas?"

"I will look into it. Beryllium-polonium is not used in current nuclear weapons. I think neutron sources are available from commercial sources for use in logging oil wells. I will look into it and let you know."

"This is important. If you can find a commercial replacement, send your uncle a message saying that . . . uh . . . that you have purchased a new Rolex watch. I will need this information as soon as possible. Now, let us go to Fisherman's Warf and enjoy the afternoon. We can have an early dinner, and you can drop me at the Airport Hilton on your way back."

The next morning, carrying an overcoat, Mohammed boarded a TWA flight for Chicago. He had other business to take care of in the United States. Looking out the window, sipping a glass of champagne, he considered the project. *Ralph Eid is the best brother to be put in charge of this project. I will recommend him to Usama. His idea for testing the components was brilliant, likewise his ideas for hiding the components. I look forward to receiving his final plans. Projectiles, guns and rings. Rings, yes rings. Usama wants a name for the project. Allah's Rings. Yes, I shall suggest "Allah's Rings" as the name for this most holy project.*

April 1991, The Search

Glukhih received a call from Colonel Valek telling him *the game was afoot.* Anya Zeldovich was about to receive a letter from her ailing sister requesting her to come to Leningrad to help her recover. Ivan Zeldovich would contact Glukhih and request assistance. Glukhih would tell Anya that he would attempt to obtain travel permits, but it would require at least two weeks. She should be ready to leave as soon as the permit was obtained. Ivan Zeldovich understood that he would leave to meet Colonel Valek in Moscow the day after Anya departed.

Later the same day, Ivan Zeldovich returned to the apartment after purchasing groceries to find Anya sitting at the table crying. "What is wrong my dear," Ivan asked.

Looking up, Anya said between sobs, "My sister is sick and needs me to come. What am I to do? Such a trip is not allowed. We do not have the funds, even if it was possible."

"Be calm my love, I may be able to find a way for you to go." *So it begins at last.*

"How can you possibly get permission for me to go to Leningrad?"

"Our friend Boris Glukhih may be able to help us. He has been able to do many things for us."

"Do you think he will help?"

"I do not know, but we can ask him the next time he comes."

Boris Glukhih had established a pattern of stopping by the apartment twice a week. If he kept the pattern, he would come the next day.

"Please ask him for help. I have not seen my sister since she was a young girl. It would be good to return to Leningrad after all these years."

Ivan, seeing an opportunity said, "Would you like to stay in Leningrad and not return?"

"Oh yes, I would, but only if you could come with me."

"Let me ask Comrade Glukhih if such a thing is possible."

The next afternoon Glukhih climbed the five flights of stairs to Ivan Zeldovich's apartment. *Thank God I will not have to do this too many more times.* Knocking on the door, he waited for Ivan or Anya to open it. This time Ivan opened the door and nodded to Glukhih, indicating that the letter had been received, and that the game was on. "Good afternoon Comrade Boris Glukhih," Ivan said.

"Good afternoon, Ivan Zeldovich, and good afternoon Anya," Glukhih said, noticing Anya sitting at the table with tears in her eyes and a red puffy face. "What is wrong, Anya?"

"Oh Comrade Glukhih, I have received a letter from my sister telling me that she is ill and asking me to come."

"I am very sorry for you. Is there anything I can do to help you?"

"I am sure Comrade Glukhih is much to busy to be bothered with our problems," Ivan said.

"Nonsense, Ivan, you have provided great assistance to the State, and if we can return the favor we should. Where does you sister live?" Glukhih asked turning to Anya.

"Leningrad," replied Anya.

"Leningrad, that will not be a major problem," replied Glukhih. "I will look into it and let you know what can be arranged. Travel permits usually require a minimum of two weeks, so you should be prepared to leave at that time."

"Comrade Glukhih, do you think it would be possible for me to accompany Anya, and for us to remain in Leningrad?" Ivan asked standing behind Anya and winking at Glukhih.

This is a change of plans from the script. I must consult with Colonel Valek. It will simplify the plan. Yes, I will tell them that it may be possible, Glukhih decided, "This is a much more difficult request. I will look into it, however, the visit should not be difficult to arrange. Now, I must be on my way."

Ivan walked Glukhih to the door and followed him into the hall. "This was Anya's idea, and it does simplify the plan. She will pack all of our important things and take them with her. I hope I have not caused a problem."

"No, it may be better, but I will have to discuss it with Colonel Valek."

"Of course, thank you comrade," Ivan said as he turned and reentered the apartment.

Two days later, Glukhih returned to Ivan's apartment. Smiling as he entered, he said, "I have good news. A travel permit and a temporary relocation permit can be obtained for both of you; however, Ivan will not be able to accompany you, Anya. We have not been able to locate all of the test equipment at the Semipalatinsk Test Range. Ivan must go there with us to help find the missing equipment. Ivan can join you after he has completed his task."

Anya appeared confused. "Anya dear," Ivan interjected, "I have been expecting this request. Actually, it will be for the best, because I was worried about leaving you alone. This way, you will be with your family, and I can join you after I have completed my tasks."

"Yes, what you say makes sense, but I am afraid."

"Of what are you afraid, my dear?"

"I have never made a long trip by myself. I do not know what is required of me."

"Do not worry, Anya," Glukhih said, "I will arrange for someone to meet you at the train station in Moscow and make sure you get on the train to Leningrad. I will arrange for you to have a sleeper compartment, and food is available on the train."

"Thank you Comrade Glukhih, but Ivan, can we afford such a trip?"

"Ivan will be well paid for his assistance at the Semipalatinsk Test Range. Do not concern yourself about funds. You should be prepared to leave in two weeks. Pack your belongings into no more than two large trunks. Ivan, pack your belongings in the same manner, but leave them with me. I will arrange for you to get them after you complete your assignment."

"Thank you Comrade Glukhih, you are truly a friend," Anya said, starting to cry again.

"Please excuse me Anya, but I must leave. I will have the permits and travel authorizations delivered to you. After you have been in Leningrad for several months, your temporary relocation can be made permanent," Glukhih said, getting up and walking to the door. At the door he motioned Ivan to follow him into the hall. "Ivan, be prepared to leave the morning following Anya's departure. You may leave your belongings in the apartment, and my men will retrieve them. They will be delivered to you later at Anya's sisters after you have arrived there. Comrade Colonel Valek will meet your train, and then both of you will travel to Semipalatinsk. Quarters have been arranged for you at the senior officer's barracks. If you have any questions call me at my office."

"Again, thank you Comrade Boris Glukhih. I will be ready, in fact I am looking forward to it."

Glukhih departed and Ivan returned to the apartment. "Anya, this is wonderful. I am looking forward to living in Leningrad. Let us begin to select what we will take with us."

Two weeks later, Glukhih, accompanied by two men, knocked on the Zeldovich's apartment door. "Good morning Ivan Zeldovich. Is Anya ready to leave?"

"Good morning Comrade Boris Glukhih. Yes, I will get her."

"Is that her trunk and suitcase? Asked Glukhih.

"Yes."

Glukhih turned to the two men and said, "Take them to the car. We will be along shortly."

Anya came into the room, looked around with a sad expression and said, "It is very hard to leave our home." She began to cry. Ivan put his arms around her.

"There, there, my love. You know your sister needs you. You must go now or you will miss your train," Ivan said as he walked her to the door. Ivan and Anya followed Glukhih down the stairs and out to the waiting Volga.

Glukhih turned to Ivan and said, "You should say goodbye here. We do not want to attract attention at the train station. I will make sure Anya boards the train. She will be met in Moscow. One of my men will take her to the Leningrad train and help her find her compartment. Does she have sufficient funds?"

"Yes Comrade Glukhih, Ivan has given me more than enough rubles for the trip," replied Anya. She embraced Ivan, then got into the front seat of the Volga. Glukhih said goodbye to Ivan, opened the driver's door, got in and drove away. Ivan watched the white Volga until it was out of site, then returned to the apartment to pack. Tomorrow it would be his turn to leave. Ivan felt his excitement rising, *Life is strange. After all these years, I am going back to Semipalatinsk, but this time I will leave with my head held high and rubles in my pocket.*

The next morning a much younger looking Ivan Zeldovich stood waiting for Glukhih in the lobby of the apartment building. He was neatly dressed in his only suit. Before leaving Anya had starched and ironed his one white shirt and pressed a sharp crease in his pants. She had also carefully trimmed his thick gray hair, which he had painstakingly brushed in place. Beside him on the floor lay his one suitcase and a duffel bag.

Anya had made arrangements with her friends to take the furniture and any remaining items. There had been many questions; and Ivan had stuck with the story that he had been called back to work to help locate test equipment. Because he would have to travel, it had been arranged for Anya to return to Leningrad and her family. Everyone knew not to ask too many questions.

As soon as the white Volga stopped in front of the apartment, Ivan walked out carrying the duffel bag and suitcase. Opening the trunk, Glukhih greeted Ivan, "Ready to go I see. You are looking quite well this morning."

"Good morning Comrade Boris Glukhih. Yes, thank you I am ready and anxious to get started."

"Very good, Colonel Valek is also anxious to get started. He will meet your train. Have you had breakfast?"

"Yes, I prepared my last meal here early this morning."

Glukhih gestured for Ivan to get in as he walked to the driver's door. As soon as Ivan got in, he pulled away from the curb and drove to the train station. "Here is you ticket and travel orders to Moscow. The train will depart in thirty minutes," Glukhih said and handed Ivan an envelope, "and here is some travel money. Good luck. I do not think we will meet again."

"Thank you Comrade Boris Glukhih, for all you have done for us. Anya will pray for you. She is still a Christian. I hope you do not mind."

"You are welcome. Please thank Anya for her prayers. Have a good trip. I hope you find what you are looking for. Goodbye Ivan Zeldovich."

Ivan removed his bags from the Volga and walked into the train station. The train had just arrived, and he boarded and found a seat. *I am about to begin the biggest adventure of my life.*

Colonel Alexei Valek was standing on the platform of Kursk Station when Ivan's train arrived in Moscow five hours later. "Good afternoon Ivan Zeldovich."

"Good afternoon Colonel Valek. Thank you for meeting me."

"Come, let us have lunch, and I will tell you about our travel plans. Get Comrade Zeldovich's bags," Valek said to a man standing near him. Leaving the main station, Alexei and Ivan followed the man carrying Ivan's bags to a black Volga. Alexei did a quick appraisal of Ivan's appearance while they waited for the driver to put Ivan's luggage in the trunk. *My God, what a change in the man. It's not just the haircut. His whole expression and demeanor has changed. There is a spring to his step.*

He is standing erect. It is as though his is ten years younger, he thought as the driver opened the rear door for the Colonel to enter.

The Colonel indicated for Ivan to get in first, then entered, turned and said, "Ivan, you must be hungry, we will have a late lunch; while I fill you in on our plans." Turning to the driver, Valek said, "Take us to *Etazherka.*"

"Serge," Valek said to Ivan, indicating the driver, "met Anya yesterday and got her settled in a sleeper compartment on the train to Leningrad. I will receive word when she arrives and will let you know. Everything is going according to plan."

Colonel Valek and Ivan entered *Etazherka,* a Russian bar and restaurant near the Lubyanka metro station. Sitting down at a table in the rear, Valek said, "Tomorrow we will fly to *Semey,* Kazakhstan. Our flight departs at 7 A.M. I will pick you up at your hotel at 6 A.M. I have arranged for you to stay at the *Arbat* hotel near the airport. Your room is paid for. You may charge dinner to the room. Do you have good boots and clothes suitable for the test range?"

"I will be ready at 6 A.M. Thank you for making these arrangements for me. Except for my parka, my clothes are old and worn. I do not have boots, but my shoes will do."

"I should have thought of clothes before now. After we finish our lunch, Serge will take me to my office, then he will take you to the GUM department store to obtain suitable clothes and boots. When you have the required items, he will take you to your hotel."

The next day, the flight to Semey – the Kazakh word for Semipalatinsk – was uneventful, but long. It was a military flight with three stops. They arrived late in the afternoon and despite the change in his appearance Valek could see that Ivan was very tired. He was concerned about Ivan's ability to keep up. *He will need some rest. Best to let him sleep in tomorrow, while I meet with my team and get things organized.*

Entering the terminal building, Colonel Valek was met by Captain Yury Kyrillov, a heavyset officer of 29 years, standing 183 centimeters, and weighing 83 kilograms.

"Good afternoon Colonel. I am Captain Yury Kyrillov. Everything is arranged in accordance with your orders," Kyrillov said saluting.

"Good afternoon Captain, this is Comrade Ivan Zeldovich, our technical expert."

"Good afternoon, Comrade Ivan Zeldovich. Colonel, I have a car waiting outside. Do you have any more luggage on the plane?"

"No Captain just my bag and Comrade Zeldovich's two bags. We are ready to go. Please lead the way to the car. How far is it to *Kurchatov*?"

"150 kilometers, sir. It will take us approximately two hours to get there."

Kurchatov was a small town west of Semey – also known as Semipalatinsk-21 – located on the northern edge of the Semipalatinsk test range on the bank of the *Irtysh* River. The town had been a base camp established to service the test range. The Semipalatinsk test range covered an area of 18,500 square kilometers (7,143 square miles). Kurchatov provided housing for employees, and all required support functions necessary to operate the test range. The central, and most secret, portion of the test range – a 200 square kilometers area known as the "Polygon" – was the local control center for nuclear testing. There were no fences around the perimeter of Semipalatinsk test range.

A cover story had been arranged. Colonel Valek was in charge of a special KGB team: charged with locating special test equipment and radioactive sources left at various locations throughout the test site. Such items, when located, were to be removed by the Colonel's team. Colonel Valek, Captain Yury Kyrillov, Lieutenant Anatoly Borisov, and Ivan Zeldovich would be quartered in the officer's barracks at the test site. The enlisted men would be quartered in the enlisted barracks. Captain Kyrillov, Lieutenant Borisov, and Senior Sergeant Umov were aware of the true mission and destination of the unit. The other sergeants and men had been on other secret missions for the KGB. They knew not to ask questions. All would be rewarded upon the successful completion of the mission.

Arriving at a large warehouse size building, the driver, Captain Kyrillov, stopped the car and announced that they had reached their destination. Ivan, who had slept during most of the two-hour trip, woke up and seem a little disoriented.

"Captain, Comrade Zeldovich is tired. Have one of your men take him and his baggage to his quarters and help him get settled. Make sure they show him where the officer's mess is."

"Yes sir."

"Ivan, you are tired from traveling. I will not need you until tomorrow afternoon. Have a good dinner and get as much sleep as possible. You will need your strength when we start our search."

Captain Kyrillov turned to a senior sergeant, who had approached the car, and said, "Sergeant Umov, you heard the Colonel's order. Please take Comrade Zeldovich to his quarters."

"I will meet you at noon tomorrow in the officer's mess, Ivan," Colonel Valek said.

Ivan and the sergeant left, and Colonel Valek turned to the Captain. "I would like to meet the troops and inspect our gear."

"Yes sir, please come with me," said the Captain, who then turned to a junior sergeant and ordered, "Sergeant Vanin, take the Colonel's baggage to his quarters, then return to our building."

"Sir, we have been assigned this building that is suitable for storing our equipment. The troops are waiting for you inside."

When Colonel Valek and Captain Kyrillov entered the building, Lieutenant Anatoly Borisov called the troops to attention.

"Sir, Sergeants Umov and Vanin will be joining us as quickly as possible," Captain Kyrillov said, "Tell your men to stand at ease, Captain. Please provide a breakdown by assignment."

"Yes sir, in addition to myself, Lieutenant Anatoly Borisov, and Sergeants Umov and Vanin, there are two squads of seven combat infantry men, and one mechanic. All of us are qualified to drive the vehicles, and Sergeant Vanin is a qualified heavy equipment operator. The Sergeant will operate the off-road crane. All of us have AK-74s. The officers and noncommissioned officers also have side arms. Five of the trucks have RPK-74[*] light machine guns. In addition we also have four *Dragunov* (SVD) sniper rifles."

"Very good, Capitan, now the vehicles."

"Sir, our vehicles consist of seven URAL-375D trucks, two GAZ-3934[**] *Siams*, and a fuel trailer. The fork lift and an off-road mobile crane belong to the local garrison."

"Have the blades of the fork lift been shortened?"

"Yes sir."

"Very well. Tomorrow morning I will inspect the equipment and interview each of you. In the afternoon, Captain, you will accompany Comrade Zeldovich and me on a reconnaissance of the test range."

Turning back to the troops, Colonel Valek addressed the assembly, "We are on a highly classified mission. Our purpose is to locate test equipment and items that may have been abandoned in the late 1940s. Semipalatinsk is a nuclear weapons testing site, and the materials we seek may be radioactive. As soon as I locate the items, our assignment will be to recover the items from the storage site, place them on the trucks, and

---

[*] Introduced in 1974, the Kalashnikov AK-74 light weight assault rifle, and the RPK light machine gun are chambered for a 5.45 mm high velocity cartridge. The U.S. M-16 rifle, introduced in 1964, is chambered for a 5.56 mm high velocity cartridge.

[**] The URAL-375 is a diesel powered 6 x 6 military truck, capable of hauling 3,200 kilograms off road; and is similar in appearance to the U.S. M35A3 2 1/2 ton general-purpose military truck. The GAZ-3934 *Siam* is a 125 HP diesel enclosed 4 x 4 personnel carrier that has 3 + 8 seating (three in the front, plus 8 in the rear). Designed for off-road travel, the Siam has a payload capacity of 1,500 kilograms and a top speed of 95 kilometers per hour. Even though it does not resemble an American "Hummer" in looks, it serves the same purpose.

remove them from the test site as quickly as possible. There is political unrest here in Kazakhstan, and the test site may be closed in the near future. My orders are to move the items to a safe place. Once we leave the test range, your major responsibility will be security. None of you will *ever* speak of our mission to *anyone* outside of this unit. Do you understand?"

A chorus of "Yes sirs" followed. "That is all, Captain, you may dismiss the men."

"Yes sir, Lieutenant, dismiss the men."

"Captain, please accompany me to my quarters. I will brief you on my plans."

The next morning, Colonel Valek inspected the equipment and interviewed the men. Selecting one of the Siams, Valek directed that two of each type of radiation monitoring instrument, and tools and equipment necessary to open shielded padlocks be placed in the Siam.

"Captain, please meet me in the officers' mess at noon. Bring a map of the test range. Plan on making a reconnaissance drive this afternoon with Comrade Zeldovich. It has been a long time since he was here; and he is the only one who knows where to look."

"Yes sir."

Colonel Valek found Ivan sitting at a table in the officers' mess. Sitting down, he greeted Ivan, "Good afternoon Ivan Zeldovich, you look rested. Are you ready to get started?"

"Good afternoon Colonel. Yes, I am ready, in fact quite anxious. When do we start?"

Colonel Valek laughed. "Very good, Ivan. We will start as soon as Captain Kyrillov joins us, and we have eaten. Captain Kyrillov is aware of our real mission, but do not speak of it here."

Before Ivan could reply, Captain Kyrillov joined them, and a mess steward took their order.

"Good afternoon Comrade Zeldovich, you look much better today," Captain Kyrillov said.

"Thank you, Captain. Yes, I feel rested, and I am ready to get started."

"Captain, do you have the map?" Colonel Valek asked.

"Yes," replied Captain Kyrillov, spreading the map out on the table. "There are three main testing areas: *Murzhik*, sometimes referred to as Ground Zero, where the atmospheric bomb tests were performed; the *Degelen* mountains, where more than 200 underground nuclear explosions occurred; and the *Balapan* area, which had 123 underground explosions, and one excavation leading to the 'Atomic Lake.' Between 1949 and 1963 a total of 456 nuclear explosions have occurred, including 111 atmospheric events (86 air bursts and 25 surface bursts). After the Limited Test Ban

Treaty was signed in 1963, the tests at the test range were restricted to underground shafts and tunnels; except for four cratering events carried out within the framework of the program of peaceful uses of nuclear energy between 1965 and 1968, one of which created the Atomic Lake. The last underground test event conducted was on October 19, 1989."

Ivan studied the map until the steward brought their meal, and he continued studying it while they ate. There were no other personnel within earshot. Finally, Ivan said, "I think the area we are looking for is located in a small valley that runs north and south between the Balapan and Degelen test areas. There are several large canyons in the mountains to the east and west. The site we are seeking is in one of them. The test range was very primitive in those days. Kurchatov was a simple village. Our teams were in competition with each other. My team was based in the village of *Znamenka*, located on the east side of the test range," Ivan said, pointing to a small village on the map. "Our test area was located in the area of the bunker. The other team was based in *Kurchatov*. Its test area was the *Murzhik* area."

"Can you describe what we are looking for?" asked the Captain.

"Yes, the only above ground structure is a small cement building. It is actually nothing more than a door that opens to a staircase leading down into the bunker. There was no road leading into the canyon; however, the heavy equipment and trucks had made a trail. The ruts were quite deep and may still be there."

Studying the map, Captain Kyrillov said, "It appears that the site is located over 100 kilometers south of here. It will take at least 2 hours to get to the area."

"Let us take one of the Siams and explore the roads leading to the general area. We will return before dark. Tomorrow we will leave at dawn and make our first attempt to find the bunker. Captain, ask Sergeant Umov to join us tomorrow morning," Valek said.

Two hours later traveling south from Kurchatov they reached a fork in the main road. The right fork led southwest to the Murzhik area; and the left fork led southeast toward the Degelen test area. Ivan said, "Much has changed since my last visit. We should take the left road. I remember the valley we are seeking is to the east. I hope the valley has not been totally changed."

Colonel Valek said, "Let's go a little farther, then turn around. We will loose the light soon."

That evening, Colonel Valek ate dinner with Ivan. "I was surprised at how little snow is on the ground. The salt flats are mostly bare. Finding your road should be possible. We will have breakfast here at 5:30 AM, and then leave on our expedition. It should be light by the time we reach the point where we turned around yesterday. Get a good night's sleep. Tomorrow will be a long day."

After dinner, Ivan retired and Colonel Valek drafted a short message to the General.

> To: Lieutenant General Valrie Yatchenko, KGB, Moscow
> From: Colonel Alexei Valek
>
> Arrived yesterday. Everything is in proper order. Completed initial reconnaissance today. Will start early tomorrow."

The next morning, Colonel Valek, Captain Kyrillov, Sergeant Umov and Ivan Zeldovich had just passed yesterday's turnaround point. Ivan was sitting in the front seat. It had been light for the last hour, and Ivan was attempting to orientate himself. The Degelen Mountains were passing on the right side. Soon the entrance to a large valley began to appear.

"This is the valley," Ivan said pointing to the right, "Now I must look for the road."

A few minutes later a well-used road appeared. "Is this the road? asked Sergeant Umov, who was driving.

"No, this road is too close to the mountain. The road we are seeking has to be further," replied Ivan.

Within the next two kilometers, two more roads showing signs of recent use were encountered. Ivan rejected both. After another five kilometers, they began to approach the mountains on the east side of the valley entrance.

"We have gone too far," Ivan said. "We must turn around. The road we seek probably has not been used for many years and will be very difficult to find. Please drive more slowly."

After driving back for approximately three kilometers, Captain Kyrillov told the driver to stop. Getting out he walked across the road and into the open salt flat desert beyond. After walking for about one hundred meters, he returned and observed, "I think this is the trace of an old road leading south into the valley. The trace becomes more visible once you get away from this road. Sergeant, did you see where I turned around?"

"Yes sir."

"Good, then drive on past that point for another kilometer, then turn south into the desert for a half a kilometer. Make several loops, drive further south and make some more loops, and then head back using the same path. After that, turn around and drive back again using the same path. We want it to look like someone went exploring for a short distance and then returned. This time, after the second set of loops, slowly turn east so that we will cross the road trace. This way, we have not marked the location of the old road."

"Very good, Captain," Colonel Valek said.

After finally finding the road trace – barely visible through the patches of snow and clumps of grass and bushes – they turned south to follow it into the valley. Ivan requested that they stop several times so that he could get out and study the terrain. Finally they stopped for lunch. After lunch, Ivan pointed toward the west. "I think that is the way."

After proceeding for more than two kilometers without any sign of a road trace, Ivan had to declare a mistake. After two more false starts, Ivan suddenly saw something that triggered a memory. "That way," Ivan pointed, "That seems familiar. It is the way to the bunker."

Turning southwest, a faint road trace reappeared. This time Sergeant Umov saw the trace and turned right to follow it. "How much farther, Comrade Zeldovich?" Sergeant Umov asked.

"About a kilometer. The road should lead to the bunker entrance," replied Ivan.

Ten minutes later Ivan cried out, "There it is!" and pointed to a low structure just ahead of the vehicle. "Stop here. I must take radiation readings."

Selecting a high range gamma meter from their test equipment, Ivan got out of the Siam, turned on the meter, and pointed it away from the bunker. After allowing the meter to warm-up and pressing the test button, he carefully studied the needle on the meter for a response, as he slowly turned toward the bunker – there was no response. Ivan continued to point the meter toward the bunker and slowly walked to the entrance to the structure. Then pointing the gamma meter probe toward the ground, he continued walking around the entrance.

Returning to the vehicle, he picked up a low-level gamma meter and repeated the warm-up procedure. He then obtained a "background radiation" reading by taking measurements in several directions away from the bunker. Next, while still carrying the high-level meter, he used the low-lever meter and repeated the same approach procedure.

"What does the meter measure?" Sergeant Umov asked.

"It measures the presence of X-rays and gamma radiation in roentgens per hour – the larger the number the more ionizing radiation. Smaller amounts of ionizing radiation are measured in mill roentgens. There is always some ionizing radiation present, called 'background radiation,'" Ivan said, demonstrating this by pointing his low level meter away from the bunker. "The meter continues to click, indicating that there is ionizing radiation in the desert."

"How much radiation is dangerous to us?" Sergeant Umov said.

"A simple answer is an exposure over 50 roentgens. If the meter shows 50 roentgens per hour, you would have to stand still for one hour to receive a dose of 50 roentgens. The amount of radiation we will be exposed to is mill roentgens – one thousandth of a roentgen. Uranium will produce additional small amounts of radiation, because of spontaneous fissions. The amount of radiation in the bunker should be only slightly higher than background. Actually, damage to the human body depends upon how much ionizing radiation is absorbed by the body. Some radiation may pass through the body without causing damage. Absorbed radiation is measured in *rads*, 'radiation absorbed dose.' The correct unit of measurement for damage to the body is the *rem*, which stands for 'roentgen equivalent mammal.'" Ivan replied.

"Is it safe for us to approach?" Colonel Valek asked.

"Yes, I am reading a very slight increase in gamma radiation over the bunker with the low level meter. This is just as it should be."

"Are you sure this is the bunker?"

"Yes Colonel, this is the bunker. There is no doubt."

"Do you think the items are still here?"

"Yes, the door is intact, just as I left it. There is no sign of forced entry, and the gamma readings are what I expected to find."

Colonel Valek stood still for a while, staring at the bunker entrance and thinking. *I have done it. We have done it. No . . . still too early to count your fortunes. The bunker must be opened and the devices inspected. That will take all day tomorrow. Too late today to get started.*

"It is getting late, and it will be dark soon. Best we leave now and return early tomorrow. Now that we know the way, it will only take about three hours to get here. I do not want to have to drive out or here with our lights on. That would attract attention," the Colonel concluded.

Early the next morning, Colonel Valek, Captain Kyrillov, Sergeant Umov and Ivan left Kurchatov and drove south. Retracing their route from the previous day, they arrived at the bunker at 9 A.M. Ivan again took radiation readings. Satisfied that the bunker was not emitting harmful amounts of radiation, Ivan signaled for the rest of the party to approach.

As the others looked on Sergeant Umov approached the bunker door and applied penetrating oil on the door hinges and in the key slot. Then using a small acetylene torch, he cut the padlock shield and padlock. Ivan and the Colonel moved forward anxiously waiting while the oil did its work; and the Sergeant sorted through a ring of keys he planned to use on the door lock. After several tries he finally succeeded in finding the right key that turned in the rusty old lock; then forcefully pulling the door handle, the Sergeant made several attempts to free the rusted door hinges – to no avail. Finally he stopped pulling and in frustration sputtered, "Colonel, I think they need more oil," then added more lubricant. After waiting several more minutes, he once again set about jerking on the handle. Then suddenly after one mighty heave from the Sergeant, the hinges gave way with a nerve-wracking shriek and the door sprang open. A rush of dank, fetid smelling air assailed the men as they stood staring into the dark, cobweb covered stairwell.

Grimacing at the smell, Ivan turned away and told them, "Let the bunker air out."

"And Captain clean away those cobwebs," the Colonel ordered, shuddering slightly as he thought how he hated spiders. Then turning to follow Ivan, who was walking away from the door, the Colonel nodded at the Sergeant as Ivan said, "Now, let us look for the access shaft doors. They should be over there," he said, pointing to a spot on the ground.

Sergeant Umov retrieved a shovel from the vehicle and started to dig where Ivan had pointed. When after several minutes of digging Umov found no doors. Ivan walked to a spot three meters from where the Sergeant was digging and said, "Try over here."

This time after another couple of minutes of digging, the shovel struck metal.

"Colonel, I have found the door. Do you want me to uncover it?" the Sergeant asked.

"Yes, but do not cut the lock. Pour penetrating oil on the hinges and leave a rag soaked with the oil on each hinge. "Ivan, do you think it is safe to enter the bunker?"

"Yes, Colonel, but to be sure, I will get the radiation instruments and take measurements."

Ivan returned to the entrance carrying both gamma meters – one in each hand. After ensuring that both were working properly, Ivan first pointed the high level meter down the stairs. Motioning Captain Kyrillov, who had knocked down most of the cobwebs inside the entry with a shovel, to lead the way down, Ivan entered the door. Holding a powerful flashlight in one hand and the shovel in the other, the Captain proceed down the steps. Ivan cautiously followed, taking one step at a time and listening to the clicks from the low level Geiger counter; while watching the meter on the high level instrument. The clicking of the Geiger counter so close to his ear was making Captain Kyrillov extremely nervous. Turning to Ivan, he asked, "Is the radiation level safe?"

"Yes, Captain, the readings are what I expected. We would have to stay down here for several years to receive a dangerous dose of radiation. There is no danger."

The Captain continued down the steps, clearing the hanging cobwebs as he descended. At the bottom of the stairs the Captain turned slightly and swung the light in an ark around him to ensure the way was clear for the Colonel's decent. As he turned back toward the stairs Ivan spoke, "It is safe to proceed."

"Colonel," the Captain called out as he shone the light on the stairs, "It is safe for you to come down."

Outside the bunker Colonel Valek ordered the Sergeant, "Stay here on watch. Let me know if you see anyone or anything out of the ordinary."

Picking up another light the Colonel anxiously descended the stairs. Ivan and Captain Kyrillov were waiting for him. Together, they moved down a short hall into what appeared to be the main chamber. The bright lights revealed the access shaft in the ceiling at the far corner of the chamber; and in the center, five large dust covered wooden crates resting on dollies – just as Ivan had described. Cursory inspection of the crates revealed that all were intact. "They are just as I left them," Ivan said with glee and smiled at the Colonel.

Then struggling hard to contain his excitement, Ivan directed them to proceed down a corridor to the left of the access shaft. There they found a series of locked doors. All of the locks were intact. At each door Ivan paused and pointed the high-level gamma meter probe in order to note the reading. "It appears that everything is as I left it," Ivan said, "but it will be necessary to open each chamber and inspect the items to be sure."

"Let us get started," Colonel Valek said. "Captain, relieve the Sergeant and send him down to open the chambers."

"Yes sir," Captain Kyrillov said, and happily left the bunker.

As soon as the first chamber was opened, Ivan took a reading in the corridor with the low level meter; then watching the meter he and Colonel Valek entered. "This chamber should contain three of the complete rounds in wooden crates," Ivan said as he continued reading the low level meter and walking toward the crates. As the clicking increased Ivan spoke to assure the Colonel, "Everything appears to be in order. The increased readings indicate the projectiles are still in the crates. In order to be sure, we must open them and take measurements with the alpha meter. I must return to the vehicle and get the meter and hand tools."

Leaving the Colonel below, Ivan slowly ascended. He did not remember the stairs being so steep. Outside the temperature was still well below freezing, and the wind had picked up. Ivan was glad that Colonel

Valek had arranged for him to acquire warm clothes and boots. Working down in the bunker would be preferable to standing outside in the cold.

Collecting the alpha meter and hand tools, Ivan returned to the projectile chamber: where Sergeant Umov took the wire cutters from Ivan, cut the steel bands on the first crate, and removed the lid. Inside was what appeared to be a complete anti-tank round. A plastic sabot partially covered the projectile; leaving only the projectile's nose exposed. After turning on and testing the alpha meter, Ivan took a reading on the floor near the crate. He then held the probe and slowly brought it toward the exposed nose of the projectile – the reading dramatically increased.

"Colonel, this *is an HEU projectile*. Shall we open the other crates?" Ivan asked.

"Yes, but first let us get the paint; so that you can mark the crates and rounds as you inspect them." Then, raising his voice to the Sergeant, who was unlocking the other chambers, Valek called out, "Sergeant, get the paint cans and brushes from the vehicle."

When Sergeant Umov returned with the paint cans, Valek called him aside and said, "Be sure to remove or paint over *all Russian markings and signs* on the crates and the projectiles. There must be no visible information left on anything to indicate their origin. Now open the remaining crates for inspection."

While the sergeant carried out Colonel Valek's order, Ivan set about choosing the paint colors and placing the cans and brushes by the crates. He repeated the inspection process on the other two crates. Then picking up a brush loaded with paint, he began marking the first of the three rounds, then stopped and asked, "Colonel, will paint on the brass cartridge case of the round cause a problem after the gun is fired?"

Laughing, Colonel Valek replied, "Very good Ivan. Yes, the paint may create some difficulty when ejecting the brass case, but I do not think that will be a problem."

Embarrassed by making such a foolish statement, Ivan winced and somewhat sheepishly replied "No Colonel, removing the cartridge case will not be a problem – if the devise has functioned. I was not thinking."

"No, Ivan," Valek chuckled, "you *were* thinking. Keep on doing so. It is altogether too easy to miss an important point. It is much better to call attention to small or non-issues than to miss an important one."

While the Colonel watched, Sergeant Umov and Ivan opened the remaining crates in the second chamber; so that the rounds could be inspected and properly marked. Assisted by Sergeant Umov, who opened the aluminum ring containers, Ivan proceeded with his inspections after a lunch break. As Ivan completed his inspection of each ring, Sergeant Umov repackaged it; then painted the proper code on each of the ring's aluminum containers. By 3 P.M. all of the projectiles and thirteen of the rings had been inspected.

"It is time to start back. Leave everything here. Sergeant, secure the door," ordered Colonel Valek, "We will return tomorrow with the entire unit and start removal. It will require more than one day, so we will camp here tomorrow. Unless someone follows our tracks, our camp will not be visible."

On the return trip, Colonel Valek issued instructions for the next day's operations to Captain Kyrillov and Sergeant Umov. The unit would deploy in elements – to avoid attracting attention. Ivan and Lieutenant Borisov would leave first in the Siam with six of the men: followed by the mobile crane, and a truck carrying the forklift and auxiliary generator. Two hours later, Sergeant Umov would lead a convoy of four trucks; followed two hours later by Colonel Valek and Captain Kyrillov in the other Siam, and the remaining two trucks. Upon arrival, Lieutenant Borisov's men would open the access shaft, and lower the forklift into the bunker. The auxiliary generator would be hooked up, and heaters and lights installed in the bunker. Next the camp would be set up. During this time, Ivan and Sergeant Umov would begin their final inspection of the remaining seven ring containers. Two of the men, who were ordnance experts, would inspect the five guns to determine if they were operable.

That night Colonel Valek sent a coded message to the General stating that the test equipment had been located and appeared to be in working order. Recovery would be completed in two days. On the third day, according to the plan, the unit would leave the test range and proceed east – then south to *Georgiyevka*.

Kazakhstan coal miners had begun a general strike. Political unrest was spreading. A rumor was circulating that the Semipalatinsk test range would be closed. Equipment was being removed and personnel were leaving. No one would pay any attention to Colonel Valek's convoy. When the unit reached Georgiyevka, Colonel Valek planned to contact the General, who was attempting to obtain railroad cars, and a train to take the unit and its vehicles to *Shymkent* – or even on to *Tashkent* in Uzbekistan. A train should be available, because there was no coal to haul. The train would reduce the travel time; and also reduce the chance of breakdowns or other problems that could be encountered on a long road trip.

The next day things went according to plan. Ivan, Lieutenant Borisov and the unit departed Kurchatov at 6 AM, arriving at the bunker at 9:45 A.M. By 4 P.M. all elements of the unit had arrived, a base camp had been established, the bunker shaft opened, lights installed, and the forklift lowered into the bunker. Ivan had completed inspection of the final seven containers.

Colonel Valek decided to start removal activities at 7:30 A.M. the following morning. Captain Kyrillov instructed Lieutenant Borisov to post guards. Mess was served from a simple field kitchen – the unit was prepared to spend many nights camping near the road as they traveled across Kazakhstan. After eating dinner, Ivan, who was exhausted, retired to his heated tent and fell into a deep sleep.

Colonel Valek directed Captain Kyrillov and Lieutenant Borisov to let Ivan sleep in the following morning. "We will not need him until we start to load the containers from the first two chambers marked with 'Ps.' He has worked very hard for us, and I do not want him to get completely exhausted."

The following morning, the first URAL-375 truck, its canvas removed from the cargo area, was positioned next to the shaft. The crane was already in position, with its cable lowered into the access shaft. Using the forklift, the first gun assembly crate was lifted from its dolly and moved to the access shaft. Lifting straps were secured, and the crate was raised up the shaft and swung over the bed of the truck. The process was repeated two more times. Then a lifting pallet was lowered into the shaft. Ivan, who had finished a cold breakfast and hot cup of tea, entered the bunker to supervise loading of the complete round crates. Ivan requested that Sergeant Vanin have one of the complete round containers placed on the pallet, then the next one brought toward the pallet while he monitored the movement with the low and high range gamma instruments. The clicker function had been turned off to avoid scaring the men. Ivan decided to remove the projectile containers one at a time.

Ivan climbed the stairs and took up a position near the truck where he could monitor the loading of the second projectile container on the truck. "I think we can place the third container on the truck. Place it at the rear behind the large crates," he said.

The third complete round container was placed as Ivan had directed, and the truck was moved away from the shaft; so the canvas covering the containers could be replaced. A second truck was pulled up next to the shaft; and the final two gun assembly crates and projectile containers were loaded onto it.

Next came the target ring containers which would be loaded on the third truck. Starting near the cab, the first four containers marked with Green R1, R2, R3, and R4 were loaded down the right side of the truck – the side furthest from the shaft. Each ring container was separated by an empty wooden box 40 cm by 35 cm by 35 cm high. Next came containers marked with a yellow R1, R2, and R3 which completed the first row of containers. A second row of empty wooden boxes 40 cm wide was added.

Ivan, who had been monitoring the loading, signaled to Colonel Valek and Captain Kyrillov to continue. The next container, yellow R4, was removed from the bunker and placed next to the row of empty wooden crates near the cab. Ivan kept both gamma meters pointed at the truck while the yellow R4 container was loaded. After it was in place, Ivan walked around the truck keeping both meters pointed at the cargo area. Satisfied that there was no radiation problem, Ivan signaled to continue the loading. All of the ring containers could be loaded onto the third truck.

Ivan was cold and tired. He had been outside most of the day. Captain Kyrillov noticed Ivan's condition and pointed it out to the Colonel, who immediately walked over to Ivan, and said, "You look tired. You have completed your duties. In fact, you have done an outstanding job. Go to your tent and get warm; a hot meal will be brought to you later. I received word this morning that Anya arrived safely and is with her sister. Apparently there was some mix up. Her sister was not sick," he said with a smile and a wink.

Both men laughed, and Ivan smiled and nodded his thanks to the Colonel.

Turning, to Sergeant Umov, Colonel Valek said, "Sergeant, have the heater in Comrade Zeldovich's tent lit. Ivan, I will come by later to check on you."

"Captain, thank you for watching out for Ivan. Get Lieutenant Borisov and meet me in my tent."

"Yes sir."

Captain Kyrillov and Lieutenant Borisov entered the Colonel's tent. Colonel Valek had a map spread out on the table.

"Gentlemen, we are completing this portion of our mission. Tomorrow we will depart the bunker and proceed to our next destination. Have the forklift placed on one of the remaining trucks and seal the bunker. Cover the access doors with sand. You will break camp and leave at first light tomorrow. The command will be split into two elements to avoid attracting attention.

"Captain, you will command the first element of trucks with our special cargo. Lieutenant Borisov will command the second element. Captain, when you reach the main road, turn east and proceed to Znamenka, then north to Semey, then proceed 79 kilometers southeast to the rail siding at *Suyqbula*," Colonel Valek said, pointing to a small town on the map.

"Lieutenant, you will return to Kurchatov; where you will leave the crane and the truck with the forklift at the warehouse, and pick up the fuel trailer. After that, you will proceed to the rendezvous point at the railroad siding in the town of Suyqbula. I will take Comrade Ivan Zeldovich back to Kurchatov today. Tomorrow I will leave him at the airport in Semey, and then join you in Suyzbula. By then, I will know if we have a train. Any questions?"

"Sir, why not load on a train in Kurchatov?" The lieutenant asked.

"To avoid any record of our departure. Anything else?"

"Yes sir. Do you want to deploy the drag?" Captain Kyrillov asked.

"Yes, have it attached to the last truck. The driver will detach it before he reaches the main road. Be sure it cannot be seen from the road."

A heavy metal rectangle had been fabricated with disk wheels and bars containing teeth. Its purpose was to obscure the vehicle tracks. The device was similar to a disk and drag used by farmers to smooth a plowed field. The trail to the bunker would soon be covered by sand and disappear.

Satisfied that everything was under control, Colonel Valek entered Ivan's tent. "Are you able to make the drive back to Kurchatov with me? If so, we will leave right away."

"Yes Colonel, I am ready."

"Good, you can rest on the way. Tonight we will stay in our quarters in Kurchatov. Tomorrow, I will take you to the airport in Semey where you will board a flight to Moscow. I will provide you all the details and proper travel orders and permits tomorrow. Let us be on our way."

After a hot meal with Ivan at the officers' mess, Valek saw the old man to his room, where he said, "Good night Ivan Zeldovich. Sleep well. I will meet you for a late breakfast at 8 A.M. tomorrow morning; and then see you on your way to a new life." Valek watched as Ivan closed his door, then returned to the communications center.

Upon arrival in Kurchatov the Colonel had sent a coded message to the General.

> All test equipment removed and stowed on vehicles. Equipment will depart tomorrow for first checkpoint. Consultant will return according to schedule. Advise if transportation available."

After dinner, Colonel Valek returned to the communication center and received his reply from the duty sergeant. Returning to his room, he decoded the massage.

> Congratulations. Good job. Transportation will be available tomorrow afternoon. Expect to arrive at the primary destination, Qarshi, Uzbekistan, in three days. Will make other notifications and request guide to meet you at primary destination. Consultant has earned bonus.

Colonel Valek smiled, and poured himself a glass of vodka. Tomorrow he could sleep until 7 A.M. – a luxury.

The next morning, after breakfast, Ivan and Valek took the Siam and drove to the Semey airport. Colonel Valek parked the vehicle near the terminal and turned to Ivan. "You have done an outstanding job for us. Here are your travel documents. You will be met in Moscow and taken to the same hotel. The next day you will board a train for Leningrad; where you will be met and taken to Anya. Approximately two months later you will receive a message to return to Saravo. Three days after you receive the message, one of my agents will come for you. He will take both of you to the harbor where you will board a ship for Cuba. Another of my agents will meet you in Cuba and make sure you are settled in your new home. You and Anya will be given passports and identity papers with a new name and a history to match your new name. You must never tell anyone, including Anya, about our business. If Anya wishes to correspond with her sister, you will give the letters to my agent who meets you in Cuba. The letters will be mailed from Saravo. Return mail will follow the same route.

"Do you have any questions?"

"Just one . . . will I ever see you again?"

"I do not know. If you have any problems, any kind of problems, contact my agent in Cuba." Valek took another envelope from his briefcase. "Ivan, this is part of your bonus and travel money. A bank account with the remainder of your bonus will be established in your new name in Cuba. I am sure you and Anya will enjoy Cuba. There is a Russian community there. They will accept you without questioning your background. Most of them will be like you and will not talk about their past. Now it is time to say goodbye."

"Thank you Colonel Valek for all you have done for us. Maybe sometime you will visit us in Cuba," Ivan said as he shook hands with Valek; then he picked up his bags and entered the terminal building. He had two hours to wait before his plane arrived. Inside the terminal he turned and watched as Valek merged the Siam into the traffic and the vehicle was out of sight. For quite some time he just stood there holding his bags and allowing other passengers to jostle around him; then abruptly turning, he walked to the ticket counter and presented his travel papers. *Soon,* he thought, *I will be leaving the miserable cold of Kazakhstan for the last time and enter a new life in a wonderfully warm new country.*

Colonel Valek left the terminal and drove southeast to Suyqbula. Locating the railroad terminal, he entered the main building and sought out the stationmaster. After identifying himself, he was told that a passenger car with sleeper compartments and three flat cars were assigned to him. Both elements had arrived and the trucks had been loaded on the flat cars. A train was scheduled to arrive at 7 P.M. His passenger and flat cars would be added to the train and switched to a new train in Almaty that would continue on to Tashkent, Uzbekistan. There the cars would be switched to another train destined for Qarshi, Uzbekistan, their primary destination where the vehicles would be unloaded.

From Qarshi, Valek estimated that it would take two days to reach Termiz. Mohammed al-Mihdar was supposed to have a representative meet them in Qarshi. The last two days would be the most dangerous.

Livermore, California, March, 1991

Ralph Eid was excited, more excited than he had ever been. After dropping Mohammed al-Mihdar at his hotel, Ralph had returned to his home in Rancho Nuevo. The magnitude of the possibilities associated with Mohammed's project was immense. The fact that he was to be entrusted with planning and implementing the project was both frightening and stimulating. Ralph hardly slept that night. The next day he would start research and planning. *What is the most important thing to do,* Ralph wondered, *finding a replacement for the old beryllium-polonium neutron source?*

The next morning, Monday, Ralph sat at his desk and wondered how to proceed. One of his colleagues was working on an explosive detection technology, using neutrons to excite the atoms of elements found in explosives. Excited atoms emitted a specific kind of measurable beta or gamma ray, which provided a method for detection. Such equipment required a neutron source. Similar technology was also being used to interrogate the soil surrounding oil well casings – a process known as "oil well logging." Ralph decided to initiate a casual conversation with Tom Roberts to see what he could learn about neutron generators.

That afternoon, Ralph knocked on the Dr. Robert's office door. Looking up, Dr. Roberts waived for Ralph to come in. "What can I do for you, Ralph?"

Dr. Tomas P. Roberts was a slightly over weight, thirty-eight year old, balding scientist, with a full beard. Like most of the Livermore scientists, the Doctor wore an open collar blue dress shirt, tan slacks and brown loafers. He was the principal investigator for explosive detection technology.

"Just visiting," replied Ralph. "I was curious about your project. You never know when someone else's work will give you an idea for your own project."

"Yes, we call it 'cross pollenization.' What are you interested in?"

"Neutrons. Their use in detection, and their possible use in medical diagnostics," Ralph replied.

"Neutrons can be produced by a number of techniques including: isotopic sources; small deuterium-tritium neutron generators; and large accelerators. Isotopic neutron sources produce continuous fluxes of neutrons. The most common isotopic source of neutrons is from spontaneous fission of californium-252, which has a half-life of 2.3 years. The average energy of neutrons from californium-252 is 2.3 Mev (million electron volts). Neutrons may also be produced by mixing an isotope, which emits alpha particles: polonium-210 for example, with beryllium-9. Isotopic neutron sources have long useful lives and produce a relatively constant flux of neutrons. Unfortunately, isotopic sources have disadvantages. They cannot be turned off, and they require bulky shielding at all times. Isotopic neutron sources cannot be pulsed. The energy spectrum of the emitted neutrons is broad and peaks at energies below the threshold for some important reactions."

"What about deuterium-tritium neutron generators?"

"Small neutron generators can be pulsed and use the deuterium (^{2}H) - tritium (^{3}H) reaction. Neutrons are produced by creating deuterium ions, and accelerating these ions into a tritium target: thereby producing high energy 14.2 Mev neutrons that are emitted isotropicly – uniformly in all directions. Lower energy 2.5 Mev neutrons can be produced by using a deuterium - deuterium reaction. The deuterium - deuterium reaction produces fewer neutrons, and the neutron flux is peaked along the axis of the deuterium ion beam."

"Do you mean that the beam is focused?"

"No, but more neutrons are emitted in one direction. In both cases, the helium nucleus – which is an alpha particle – is emitted in the exact opposite direction of the neutron."

"So, if I understand correctly, the deuterium - deuterium neutron source provides a more directable neutron flux of low energy neutrons. In other words, the beam of neutrons can be – to a small degree – pointed."

"Yes, I guess you could say that. My project requires the 14.2 Mev neutrons. The equipment must have a lot of dense shielding to protect the operator. I have not used the deuterium - deuterium source. I am curious as to the application you have in mind."

"I do not yet have an application, just an idea. I am wondering if neutrons can be used as a tool for medical diagnostics. Do you know of a source for a deuterium - deuterium (D-D) neutron generator?" asked Ralph.

"My supplier, General Neutron, Inc., produces both types for oil well logging. My neutron generator is a special design, and produces a larger neutron flux." Picking up a pen and note pad, Dr. Roberts wrote down the name and phone number of his contact. "They are always willing to support a Livermore project, because it may lead to a new product. When you have time, I will show you my unit."

"Thank you Tom. If my idea shows any merit, I will be back to see it," Ralph said, getting up and walking out of Tom's office.

Returning to his office, Ralph placed a call to General Neutron and spoke with Bob Johnson, Dr. Roberts' contact. Ralph discussed his possible requirements and requested information. Johnson gave him some ideas and offered to fax Dr. Eid a sketch of a D-D 2.5 Mev neutron generator that could be used to direct a beam of neutrons. After receiving the fax, Ralph considered how the D-D neutron generator could be adapted to Mohammed's devices. On the drive back to his house that evening, it occurred to him that, *The gun could be disguised as a large medical diagnostic instrument. The package could be designed so that the neutron generator – generators . . . why not use two! – could be installed later. No shielding would be required because the neutron generators would only be used one time; however the weight of the instrument could be explained as shielding.* After thinking about the concept for a while, Ralph decided it would work.

As soon as he arrived home, Ralph booted his PC and started a letter to Uncle Saleh.

Dear Uncle Saleh,

My new position is very rewarding. I am becoming very interested in medical diagnostic equipment. I have an idea for a new instrument that uses neutrons instead of X-Rays. I have established contact with a supplier of neutron generators, and hope to be able to design a prototype instrument. My concern is the instrument's length and height and weight.

I enjoyed Cousin Ali's visit. It was a pleasure to be in the company of relatives again.

Sincerely,

Ralph.

P.S. I purchased a Rolex Watch similar to Ali's.

After reading the letter, Ralph printed it out, signed it and placed it into an envelope. He would mail the letter on his way to work in the morning.

In the following weeks, Ralph made inquires pertaining to medical diagnostic equipment, radiological treatment equipment and clinics. Radioactive isotope diagnostics was a profitable field – as was cancer treatment. He began to draft a business plan for forming a treatment and diagnostic medical business, a business that could be located in any city. A prime requirement would be that the treatment center must be located in a tall building – the higher the better. The effectiveness of a 25 KT blast increases with the burst height. By the end of May, Ralph had completed a draft business plan, which he sent to Uncle Saleh with a letter suggesting that such a business would be a good investment for the family.

Mohammed al-Mihdar was delighted with Ralph's *Uncle Saleh letter*. What a brilliant idea! He would provide Ralph the exact dimensions of the gun assemblies as soon as they were safely stored in Afghanistan. A medical instrument supply company would be formed in Karachi, Pakistan – with a branch in Newark, New Jersey. It would be a simple matter to enclose the gun assembly in a shell converting it into a radiological diagnostic instrument, which would then be crated and shipped to the New Jersey branch. Ralph's company would purchase the instrument, and another al-Qaeda company would install it. *Allah be praised. Yes, we have a plan, now if the Russian dogs deliver the bombs, we will implement it,* Mohammed thought.

A week later, al-Mihdar received a message from Volga Antiques.

To: Ahmed al-Hijazi.
From: Volga Antiques.

All five antiques obtained. They are in very good condition. Delivery will be made as agreed. Request you meet our agent, Sergey, in Qarshi, Uzbekistan on May 9th. He will be arriving by train from Tashkent. Please acknowledge.

Allah be praised. I will notify Usama, but first I must acknowledge the message, Mohammed said to himself, and sent his reply.

> To: Volga Antiques.
> From: Ahmed al-Hijazi.
>
> I will meet Sergey at the train station in Qarshi on May 9th.

His telex on the way, Mohammed began mulling over plans for his next move, *I must be in Qarshi at least one day early. Train schedules vary. They could be early or late. I must assume they will have vehicles on a flat car, so it will be easy to identify them from a distance. Now, to inform Usama. Fortunately he is here in Riyadh. After that I will fly to Dushanbe; then take a local flight or charter a plane to get to Qarshi. I will select a remote area south of the village of Sayrab to do the inspection and test. This will also be a good place to camp for the night. If the test proves the items are HEU, then I will send a message to Usama from Termiz and final payment will be wired to the Russian's bank in Geneva. As soon as confirmation has been received, the items will be mine. I will have our men meet the convoy at the campsite. It will be best if they keep a distance, and not join us until I signal them after the payment has been received.*

With his plans mentally in order, Mohammed picked up the telephone and called Usama.

Qarshi, May 9, 1991

The convoy's boarder crossing into Uzbekistan had been uneventful. The KGB border guards had received orders to pass them without questions. The four cars belonging to Colonel Valek had been switched to his train in Tashkent. The train would reach Qarshi at 9 A.M. It was time for him to talk to the men.

Colonel Valek stood up and signaled Sergeant Umov to call the men to attention; then motioned for Captain Kyrillov and Lieutenant Borisov to join him. When they had, he addressed the assembled group.

"At ease. For the past two days things have been easy. Soon we will reach the train station in Qarshi, where our vehicles will be off-loaded. From this point on we must consider ourselves in hostile territory. I expect to be met by a Saudi, who is supposed to provide safe passage to Termiz. We cannot count on this. Be prepared for an ambush. Termiz is 275 kilometers southeast of Qarshi. Be on guard for an attack the moment we disembark. After this briefing, Sergeant Vanin and his team will install the explosive devices on all of the containers. Captain Kyrillov, Lieutenant Borisov and I will each have remote detonators. If things go according to plan our cargo will be turned over to the Saudi at Termiz. We will return to Qarshi and re-board this car for the return trip to Tashkent. From Tashkent you will proceed to your next assignment, and each of you will receive your bonus. If things do not go according to plan we may have to fight. We will not be able to relax until we are once again in this car on the way back to Tashkent. Are there any questions?" There were none.

Captain Kyrillov stood and said, "Load your rifles, but keep then lowered. We do not want to appear to be on guard and attract attention. The light machineguns will not be mounted, but will be kept ready under cover. We must plan on two days travel to reach Termiz. Guards will be posted as soon as we make camp."

Sergeant Umov began making assignments. Eight of the men were assigned guard duty on the flat cars. Duffel bags were made ready for transfer to the unit's cargo truck. All weapons were checked.

Upon arrival at Qarshi, the four cars were shunted onto a siding, where the trucks could be unloaded. Lieutenant Borisov was in charge, and Captain Kyrillov kept the operation under observation. Colonel Valek walked around the area then entered the train station. After visiting the restroom, he walked out of the station and started in the direction of the town. As he entered the edge of the town proper, an Uzbek man stepped out of a shop behind him.

"Good morning Sergey," the man said.

Startled, Colonel Valek turned to see Mohammed standing behind him, dressed as a local Uzbek. "Good morning Ahmed al-Hijazi. I did not expect you to meet us. Let us walk so that I can brief you on our antiques."

"Allah be praised. I am most anxious to hear about the antiques."

"Everything is in very good condition – with one exception. We have not been able to replace the polonium-210. To do so will entail great risks and could jeopardize the entire project. New containers of propellant for the rounds are included in the shipment. The proper charge is 5.5 kg. I assume you will have the capability to replace the propellant."

"Praise be to Allah. The polonium is not a problem. Yes, we can replace the propellant in each round, and had planned to do so. Having the proper type will be a blessing. What is the condition of the guns?"

"My ordnance expert inspected each one. All were packed in preservatives at the factory, and are in working order."

"Allah be praised."

"Mohammed, listen carefully, this is important. Each device consists of one round with a HEU projectile, and four target rings, which must not be mixed with rounds or rings from another device. Each is a set and must be kept together. The rings must be installed in the box mounted on the end of the gun tube in the proper order."

"This presents a major problem. How are we to know which is which?" Mohammed asked.

"We have found a simple solution to this problem. Each set is marked with a different color. Device one is coded with the color red. The projectile container is marked with a red P. Each of the target rings is marked in red. The numbers start at the gun tube. For device one, you must install the ring in the container marked with a red R1 next to the end of the gun tube: followed by red R2, then red R3, and last with the red R4."

"Yes, this is a simple system. Simple systems always are the best. Allah be praised, you have provided a very simple and reliable solution."

"When do you wish to inspect the items?"

"Some place along the road. I will select a suitable place. We should be able to reach the village of Sayrab before dark. I assume that you will pitch a camp for the night."

"Yes, sometime before dark."

"If possible I will stay in a local village. If not, I will have to stay at your camp. I will inspect the items in the morning. It will be necessary to open several of the containers. I must verify that the items are HEU. After I have verified the authenticity of the items, we will proceed to Termiz and I will authorize final payment. As soon as you receive verification of payment, we will return."

"Very good. That is what we will do. When will your men join us?"

"My men are waiting at Sayrab; however, I plan to keep them at a distance until payment has been made. At that time, your men will depart and mine will take possession of the vehicles."

"That is an acceptable plan. The cargo is on three of the trucks, and the fourth has the propellant and vehicle spare parts. You may also keep the truck towing the fuel trailer. We will keep the two Siams and the fifth truck," Colonel Valek said.

"Allah be praised. This is as we agreed."

"Mohammed, my main concern is being ambushed by Mujaheddin."

"Do not be concerned. Usama bin Laden has arranged safe passage for our journey and your return. I will collect my bag and meet you outside of town. Allah be with you," Mohammed said, as he turned and walked away.

Colonel Valek returned to find most of the vehicles off-loaded. One truck remained, and it would be off-loaded within the half hour. The men, who appeared at first glance to be loafing, were actually in positions to guard and protect the vehicles. As soon as the last truck was off-loaded, Captain Kyrillov signaled for the men to mount their vehicles; and the convoy, heading south, departed for Qarshi. Colonel Valek's Siam brought up the rear. At the edge of town, he signaled for it to stop and pick up an Uzbek, who was standing beside the road holding a bag.

The convoy made good time and reached the small village of Sayrab by 4:30 P.M. Colonel Valek's vehicle was now in the lead. Ten kilometers south of the village, Mohammed told the Colonel to look for a man on a horse. He would mark a road running off to the west. A few minutes later the man on the horse came into view. As the convoy passed he waived. Colonel Valek told the driver to turn right onto a road leading off to the west. The convoy proceeded 2 kilometers into the desert; then turned south into the desert for half a kilometer, where they found a suitable campsite.

"I will stay in your camp tonight," Mohammed said to the Colonel.

The next morning Mohammed requested that he be allowed to select several containers for inspection. The containers would be removed from the truck and placed some distance away in the desert. Colonel Valek told Mohammed that each container had an explosive charge attached to it for security purposes. *Just as I expected*, thought Mohammed.

"I do not understand Mohammed, why you wish to take the containers 100 meters into the desert," Colonel Valek said.

Captain Kyrillov nodded his head in agreement. The Captain was concerned about an attempt to seize the cargo by Mohammed's men, bandits, or other Mujaheddin.

"Colonel, it is necessary for me to verify that the components are HEU fizzle material. It is not practical to take samples and send them off to a laboratory for analysis. The determination must be made here and now. After much thought, we have devised a simple way to conduct a test," Mohammed replied.

Captain Kyrillov appeared nervous. It was apparent that he was not accepting Mohammed's explanation. Colonel Valek gave the Captain a slight shake of his head, then turned back to Mohammed, "Please explain your test."

"I will select one of the ring sets, and a projectile from a different set. The ring containers will be opened; and the rings removed and stacked together just as they would be in the device. The projectile container, which will be positioned 15 meters from the rings, will be opened and the complete round removed. I have instructed one of my men to come to the camp. He should be arriving shortly. When he arrives, he will pick up the complete round and start to walk toward the rings. I will monitor the rings with low level and high-level gamma meters. If the components are fizzle material, the meters will show increasing gamma radiation as the man carrying the round approaches. When I am satisfied, I will signal the man to return to the starting point."

"I do not understand," said Captain Kyrillov.

"I do," said Colonel Valek. "This is a very dangerous test. The principal, Captain, is that the projectile will interact with the target rings by creating fissions in the uranium. Fissions produce gamma radiation. I am concerned that we will receive a dangerous dose of radiation if the man carrying the projectile gets too close to the target rings. In any case, the man will receive a dangerous dose. Gamma radiation is similar to visible light in that it decreases as a function of square of the distance. To a man standing directly under a 100-watt light bulb hanging on a cord in the center of a large room, the light will appear to be bright. If the man moves ten meters away, the light will appear to be dim, because the light spreads in all directions. The man carrying the projectile is like the man standing directly under the light bulb; while the men taking the radiation readings are like the man standing thirty feet away. In other words the amount of light available ten meters from the bulb would be the amount of light at the bulb divided by the distance squared. I this case 10 x 10 = 100."

"You are correct, Colonel. That is why I am not asking one of your men to carry the round," Mohammed said.

In other words, Captain Kyrillov thought as he looked at the Colonel, *this Arab is willing to sacrifice his man for the test. I wonder if the man knows what his fate is going to be.* The Colonel, reading the Captain's thoughts, gave a very slight grimace.

"Very well. We will conduct the test as you requested. Do you have radiation meters?" Colonel Valek asked.

"Yes, I have brought two meters."

"I will also monitor the radiation from a distance. You must instruct your man to stop if I call out to him. If not, he will be shot. If the projectile gets too close to the rings, the radiation will be so great that it will be impossible to retrieve it without loosing another man. In fact, the radiation could be so severe that it would be necessary to leave the projectile and rings. This is not an acceptable option. The worse case would occur if the man got close enough to cause a critical reaction. The radiation would kill all of us," Colonel Valek said, establishing the rules for the test. "Mohammed, go with the Captain and make your selections. The explosive charges will then be removed."

An hour later, the four yellow target rings had been removed from their containers and stacked on top of each other. Mohammed had selected the blue projectile and the case was positioned 100 meters from the camp and 15 meters from the rings. Mohammed's man had arrived and Mohammed was giving him instructions. Four of the KGB troops – one with a sniper rifle – were in position to shoot the man upon command.

Colonel Valek and Captain Kyrillov had radiation meters and had established the count emitting from the target rings. Sergeant Umov was watching the two officers for a signal to shoot the man, who would soon be carrying the round toward the rings. Mohammed left the man and went to a spot near the Captain and the Colonel. Picking up his radiation meters, Mohammed obtained readings from the stack of rings. Next he raised one arm, signaling the man to start walking toward the rings.

Turning toward the Colonel, Mohammed said, "I have told him to slowly proceed ten steps, then stop. I will then signal him to take a small step. He will only advance one small step at a time until I see an increase in radiation. When the first increase is obtained I will signal him to advance by the length of his foot. Each time I signal him he will move one foot closer to the rings until I signal him to go back."

All three watched their meters as the man slowly advanced. As the man took the tenth step . . . the meters remained the same.

The man waited, watching Mohammed, who raised his arm, signaling him to advance one more step. The meters registered no change. The process was repeated several more times until a slight increase registered on the Captain's low-level meter. "Getting a slight increase Colonel," the Captain said.

Mohammed raised his arm, signaling him to advance one foot, then another foot.

"Reading up to 100 milliroentgens, Colonel," the Captain called out, as the man completed his last movement.

Mohammed also noted the increased reading on his low level meter. Again he raised his arm and the man advanced another foot. This time the reading showed a noticeable increase.

"400 milliroentgens," the Captain called out.

Mohammed signaled for another foot.

"1 roentgen," the Captain called out, this time his voice showed tension.

"That is close enough, tell the man to go back," Colonel Valek ordered.

Mohammed, who was considering signaling for one more foot, heard the tone of the Colonel's voice and decided to comply. Setting down his instruments, Mohammed raised both arms. The man turned and started back toward the projectile container. Captain Kyrillov visibly relaxed as the reading on his meter quickly dropped back to the original level.

Sergeant Umov ordered the four shooters to stand down. Next he led a party out to the target rings and began repackaging them in their containers. Mohammed's man had placed the round back in its container. After securing the four rings, the round was properly secured in its container and all five containers returned to the trucks.

Mohammed instructed the man to return to the village and await his call. He then joined Colonel Valek in one of the Siams, and the two left for Termiz, a town very close to the Afghan border. A road from Termiz led directly to Mazar-E Sharif. At Termiz, Colonel Valek let Mohamed out at the largest bank in the town. He then proceeded to the KGB office; where he sent a coded message to the General indicating that final payment was being authorized. Colonel Valek left the office and found a café where he had a long lunch. Returning to the KGB office, he found a message from the General indicating payment had been made and acknowledged. Getting into the Siam, Valek drove past a café where Mohammed was seated at an outdoor table. A block past the Café, Valek stopped waited for Mohammed to join him.

"Everything is in order. Payment has been received?" Mohamed asked as he got in.

"Yes, congratulations, you have purchased the antiques. To celebrate properly, we should drink a toast with vodka. Since you do not drink alcohol I must wait to toast with my men."

"Allah be praised. Thank you Colonel, I am tempted. I would like to take possession as soon as we arrive at the camp."

"No problem. Captain Kyrillov had orders to break camp and load all of our equipment onto one truck."

"Please drive into Sayrab so that I can alert my men to come. They will remain a kilometer away until you have departed the camp site."

Upon return to the campsite, Colonel Valek and Mohammed found that everything was as the Colonel had ordered. Mohammed inspected his trucks and cargo, then the Russian's truck and Siams to be sure that all of the components had been left on his newly acquired vehicles. Satisfied, he turned to Colonel Valek and said, "Everything is in order. I will ride with you until we reach my men on the road. Allah be with you."

Mohammed joined his men and returned to the campsite and the Russian trucks. "It is late, we will camp here tonight, cross the border tomorrow and continue on to Mazar-E Sharif. It was time for evening prayers. Prayer rugs were spread and all faced southwest toward Mecca. *Praise be to Allah, the Compassionate, the Merciful. You have provided us the means to bring death and destruction to the Great Satan, to destroy the decadent infidels, to bring sharia to that godless land,* Mohammed silently prayed. Once more a deity was called upon to sanction and justify man's inhumane acts. History does indeed repeat itself.

Colonel Valek's return trip to Qarshi was without incident. The remaining vehicles were loaded onto one of the flat cars. That evening the two cars were attached to a train for the return trip to Tashkent, where Colonel Valek took a plane back to Moscow.

Looking out the window of the plane into the dark sky, a troubled Colonel Valek wondered if he had opened the gates and loosed the hounds of hell. *What have we done?*

Part II

REM Investments, Inc.

Riyadh, Saudi Arabia, June, 1991

Mohammed al-Mihdar entered the conference room of "Al Hijra," Usama bin Laden's construction company, and took a seat at the table to await Usama's arrival. The last three weeks had been hectic. After crossing the Afghan border using a smuggler's road west of the main road to Mazar-E Sharif, the convoy of Russian trucks had stopped; while Mujahedeen symbols had been painted over the Russian ones. The convoy had then proceeded southeast through Baghlan to Dowshi, and turned east into the mountains where the components of the five atomic devices had been hidden in caves. One of the gun assemblies had been uncrated so that it could be photographed and measured. Arrangements were made for the projectile containers, holding the complete rounds, to be sent one at a time to the al-Qaeda ordnance facility located near Konduz; where the propellant and electric squibs were to be replaced.

Several days later Mohammed, traveling as Ali al-Libi, made his way to Peshawar, and from there by plane to Karachi. In Karachi, a suitable building had been found for the new company that would manufacture and export surgical instruments, medical equipment, and radiation diagnostic equipment. It was time to return to Riyadh and report to Usama.

Usama entered the conference room, and greeted Mohammed, "Allah be praised. You have returned. Please recount everything that has transpired."

For the next three hours, Mohammed told Usama every detail. Usama asked many questions, and was especially inquisitive regarding details of the location of the components. Finally satisfied, Usama turned the discussion to the problem of moving the atomic bombs to America.

"I have reviewed Dr. Eid's preliminary plan to form radiological diagnostic centers and found it to be workable," Mohammed said. "On my return trip, I stopped in Karachi to evaluate the feasibility of forming a company to produce and export medical equipment and radiological diagnostic equipment. Facilities for such a company are available, and the plan is sound. The gun assemblies can be concealed in a metal shell that appears to be a diagnostic instrument."

"Allah the Merciful has shown us the way. You have done well with your project. Here is the number of a bank account at the Bank of Credit and Commerce International in Pakistan. Sufficient funds will be placed into the account to fund the project. Only you and I shall know all of the details. Have you found a name for the project?" asked Usama.

"Yes," replied Mohammed. "Allah's Rings."

"Allah's Rings. Praise be to Allah. An appropriate name, Allah's Rings will never be spoken of with anyone but you, Ralph Eid, and myself," Usama said.

"Allah be praised. It shall be as you say. I plan to return to America to meet with Ralph Eid to accomplish two things: first, to design an instrument suitable for concealing the gun assembly; and second, to initiate acquiring or starting a company to import the first instrument and install it in the first target city."

"Praise be to Allah. I will have a company formed in Pakistan to manufacture and export medical diagnostic equipment and medical instruments. One of our Pakistani brothers will be the manager, others will be the workers. The company will be a legitimate business. When you return from the land of the Great Satan, the company will have been formed. The next step should be purchasing or forming an American company. Perhaps you will be able to do so while you are there."

"Has the American war with Saddam interfered with our plans?" Mohammed asked.

"Allah be praised. No. I have no reason to believe that al-Qaeda has been detected; or if it has, it has not been recognized as a threat. There are many lessons for us to learn from this war. The Americans are extremely gullible. They have a loud and vocal minority of liberal extremists, who provide grist for the mill of the American press. The American press is like a school of sharks. They will attack anything for any reason in order to satisfy their need for attention that feeds their egos. The press has no concept of loyalty to country. It is astounding that the Americans have allowed Saddam to remain in power. Even more astounding that Saddam was able to outsmart them by retaining control of his helicopters, which he used to crush the Kurds in the north and the Shiites in the south. Saddam will continue to be the center of attention, deflecting attention from us and providing us time to grow and establish cells throughout the world."

"Saddam was very foolish to mistreat the Kuwaitis. They are Muslims, even if they were becoming decadent," Mohammed observed.

"That is minor compared to his mistake in invading Kuwait before he had a working atomic bomb. He was very close to having one. Calutrons at al-Tarmiya and the centrifuge enrichment facilities at Tuwaitha and al-Furat were starting to produce HEU from his EU feedstock.[*] He could have built a simple gun-type nuclear bomb. He had the plans for one. His ego demanded an implosion bomb; and he thought intimidation would

---

[*] Additional information can be found in *Iraq's Programs to Make Highly Enriched Uranium and Plutonium for Nuclear Weapons Prior to the Gulf War*, prepared by David Albright, U.S. weapons inspector, in 1997 and revised in October, 2002.

force his scientists to make one faster than they were able to. Instead of producing a bomb, his facility was bombed. Now his country is to be inspected and his weapons destroyed. What can we learn from this?"

"By Allah's blessing, we can learn patience. We can also learn to be subtle and not strut like a peacock before the world, puffing out our chest like a carnival wrestler. We must plan well and execute our plans before the enemy knows we are there," replied Mohammed.

"Praise be to Allah. We have also learned that the liberal American press seems to control the government. Most American politicians are puppets being manipulated by the liberal controlled news media. Liberals support the Democratic Party no matter what it does. Saddam was saved by America's liberal press, which pressured their president to stop the war, thereby allowing Saddam to remain in power. Some in the American press consider themselves to be the real government. They try to use their power to sway public opinion to their cause. We must also learn to use the press to our advantage; to manipulate it to help elect weak leaders we can easily overthrow. I pray that Allah will replace the current American president with a weak liberal. With Allah's blessing, we will be able to build al-Qaeda into a mighty instrument for Allah under such a weak liberal president."

"Allah be praised. Al-Qaeda will not make the same mistake. Our atomic bombs will be in place without anyone in the Great Satan knowing of their existence. When Allah wills it, we will bring the Great Satan to its knees without warning. Once America is an Islamic state, we will have no use for their press and they will be eliminated. People who place themselves above their government can never be trusted," Mohammed said.

"Allah's blessings be with you Mohammed," Usama said, ending the meeting.

Ralph Eid's mailbox held a letter from Uncle Saleh. According to the letter the family was interested in his business plan, Cousin Ali would arrive in two weeks. *Time to begin serious planning. I may have to resign my position at the Lab*, Ralph thought. On the way back to his house, Ralph decided it was time to start looking for a business to purchase. On Monday he would contact business brokers in Chicago, New York, and Atlanta.

Two weeks later Ralph again greeted Mohammed in the San Francisco International Airport. This time they proceeded directly to Ralph's home. Anticipating a longer meeting, Ralph had arranged to take Monday off.

After unpacking Mohammed joined Ralph on the patio. Opening a large manila envelope, Mohammed extracted several photographs and a sheet of paper with measurements written on it.

"These are photographs of the gun assembly and its measurements. You must create a detailed sketch for an instrument that will convert the gun assembly into a large instrument. Do you have any ideas?" Mohammed asked.

"Yes, my current thinking is that the instrument will be a *Neutron Induced Gamma Spectrometer*: an analytical research instrument that can be used to analyze samples. Neutron generators can be purchased and installed in the unit. A simple computer, a PC, will be included as part of the instrumentation. The computer will have the firing program as an invisible file on its hard drive. Gamma detection instruments will be part of the instrument. The gun will be hidden in plain sight."

"Excellent! But can a simple computer be programmed to detonate a nuclear device?"

"Yes. The gun-type weapon does not require a sophisticated firing control like an implosion warhead. The firing device for an implosion bomb is called an X-Unit. Unlike the implosion warhead that has multiple exploding bridge wire detonators, the gun-type has no detonators. The only thing required to set it off is an electric squib that ignites the propellant charge in the round. The electric squib serves the same purpose as a primer in a rifle cartridge or shotgun shell. Once the propellant is ignited, the projectile starts its journey to the target rings. The PC's firing program will be set to initiate the two neutron generators a few thousands of a second later."

"Indeed, is it really that simple?" Mohammed asked.

"*Yes, that simple.* I must perform come calculations to estimate the delay time for the neutron generators. I have chosen the deuterium - deuterium or D-D generator, because it produces 2.5 MeV neutrons that can be directed into forming the supercritical mass. The 2.5 MeV neutrons will slow faster than the 14 MeV neutrons produced by the tritium - deuterium generator. It will be necessary to drill two holes into the target assembly container so that the neutrons produced by the generators will not be reflected by the depleted uranium liner."

"You plan to use two neutron generators? That should increase the yield."

"Yes, the yield should be increased. In fact, a third neutron generator could be added. Each of the generators mounted at ninety degree intervals. I had planned to place one on each side of the target assembly container at 90 and 270 degrees. The third one could be placed on the bottom of the target assembly. This way, a beam of neutrons would be introduced into the assembling supercritical mass at 90, 180, and 270 degrees."

"How much will the yield be increased?" asked an excited al-Mihdar.

"I have no way of making a scientific estimate without running tests or having access to a computer simulation model. A guess would be twenty-five to fifty percent. It could be more."

Mohammed sat quietly, contemplating this information. *By the grace of Allah, we truly have been given the means to bring the Great Satan to its knees. Praise be to Allah!* Turning back to Ralph, Mohammed continued, "You have given me much to think about. Let us have dinner and discuss other things. Do you have any more of those delicious steaks? The last ones were very good."

"I hoped you would ask me that," Ralph said as he rose to light the gas grill. "I had the butcher cut two a little thicker than the last ones. Sit and enjoy the view while I put our meal together."

Gazing into the valley, Mohammed sat on the patio lost in thought until Ralph startled him with the call, "Dinner is ready."

"Excellent, I am very hungry," Mohammed said and entered the dining room to take his seat at the table. Ralph joined him and set a bottle of 1983 estate bottled private reserve Stags Leap, *Cabernet Sauvignon* on the table for Mohammed's inspection.

"You remembered. This is one of my favorites," Mohammed said with a smile.

After removing the cork, Ralph poured a small portion into Mohammed's glass and waited while the vintage was sampled.

"Excellent bouquet. Thank you," Mohammed said, indicating for Ralph to fill his glass.

"You are welcome. I have read a couple of books on wine since your last visit and spent one day touring the Napa Valley. That is where I purchased this wine. I bought a case. The cellar master recommended this vintage."

The rest of the evening was devoted to bringing Ralph up to speed on events in the Middle East and Central Asia.

The next morning Mohammed, looking rested and refreshed, joined Ralph on the patio.

"Good morning Mohammed, would you like breakfast?"

"Good morning, coffee, juice, some cold cereal and milk, thank you."

After breakfast Mohammed made a serious announcement, "Ralph I spent last evening before dinner thinking about how to proceed with the project. It is time to begin to implement our plan. The devices have been obtained and are in storage. We have reviewed you preliminary business plan, and funding is available to implement it. To do so, it will be necessary for you to take charge of the American operations on a full time basis. How much more time do you require in your laboratory position before you feel ready to assume your new assignment?"

"I have given much thought to this issue. I have learned all I need to know at this time. However, it will be useful for me to keep my contacts here. To do so will require a reason for leaving that will also allow me to keep in touch with my associates."

"Do you have any ideas as to how to do this?"

"Yes. My uncle could die and leave me a large amount of money. This would provide a reason for returning to Egypt. The inheritance would provide me the means to purchase a business. This way there will be no questions about my leaving; and I could maintain contact with associates in order to obtain any additional technical advice I may require."

"Good. I will arrange for your uncle's demise as soon as I return home. Have you identified any potential business yet?"

"I have made preliminary inquiries with business brokers in Chicago, New York and Atlanta. I will need a medical doctor as a partner or senior director."

"Usama will locate a suitable medical doctor to be your partner. We have many faithful brothers here. We should be able to find a suitable professor at one of the universities. He will be a director, but not the manager. No one but you will know what the Neutron Induced Gamma Spectrometer is."

"A university professor of medicine would be an asset. The spectrometer can be explained as a test instrument, part of a research project."

"Let us proceed as follows. Once you receive notice of your uncle's death, you will request leave and fly to Cairo. I will meet you there. From there we will continue on to Riyadh, Saudi Arabia. Bring final sketches for the Neutron Spectrometer, and specifications for the neutron generator. After a few days, you will contact your boss. Tell him that you have very complicated family affairs to settle and request to be placed on indefinite leave without pay. Will that present a problem?"

"No, I do not think so. Tuesday, when I return to work I will tell my friends that my cousin informed me of my uncle's failing health. I can imply that he is very wealthy; that I may inherit a lot of money."

"That should set the stage," Mohammed said. "From Riyadh we will travel to Karachi. By then we will have formed a company to produce medical diagnostic instruments. Your sketch will be used to produce drawings for the cover panels for the first Neutron Induced Gamma Spectrometer. After that, you will concentrate on forming your American diagnostic company. Usama is arranging for the formation of a Delaware corporation that will be the source of funding. You will become its CEO."

"Things are moving very quickly. It is obvious that I must sever my employment with Livermore Labs," Ralph said, showing his excitement. "Do you wish me to sell this house and move to a northern city?"

"No, this location provides a safe meeting place, and will allow you to keep up your contacts with Lab personnel. I think we have completed our business. You have done very well. Your plan is brilliant. It is important for you to be free to travel. The sooner we complete your separation the better. I had planned to spend another day here, but now I think it best for me to return and set our plan in motion. I will change my flight schedule, then we can go into the city for dinner. You can drop me off at a hotel on the way back."

Mohammed called the airline, rescheduled his flights and thought as he was packing, *We were fortunate to complete our transactions with the Russians. The Soviet Union is falling apart. Kazakhstan is trying to force the Soviets to close the test range. If we had waited much longer it would have been very difficult to remove the bombs. I think that no one except the key players know about them. With Allah's blessing, when we finally use them, it will be impossible to find their source. It will be best if all records of Eid's companies, and Eid himself, are located near one of the devices when they are detonated. We must complete our plans and install the devices in America before al-Qaeda becomes operational and is identified as a threat by western intelligence. Yes, we must move quickly.*

Five days later, Mohammed again met Usama in the same conference room in Riyadh.

"May Allah's blessing be upon you," Usama said in the way of a greeting.

"Allah has truly blessed us," a smiling Mohammed replied.

"Please tell me about your visit and your plans."

Mohammed relayed all of his discussions with Eid to Usama.

"You are correct, Allah's Rings must be placed in a safe place in the land of the Great Satan as quickly as possible. Al-Qaeda must soon begin to act. Allah's Rings must be safely placed before we act. When do you plan to bring Ralph Eid here?"

"A telegram has been sent to Dr. Ralph Eid from Cairo informing him of his uncle's failing health. A week later he will be informed of his uncle's death. He will request leave and immediately fly to Cairo, where I will meet him. Two days later we will fly here, where Eid will assume control of his inheritance. He will resign from his positions upon his return to California."

"Allah be praised. Indus Instruments, a medical equipment company has been formed in Pakistan. Hamayun Junaid, Professor of Radiology, Rawalpindi Medical College, will be the technical director. Omar Mumtaz, an engineer and one of our al-Qaeda brothers, will be the general manager in Karachi. An office and warehouse is being secured in Newark, New Jersey that will act as the distribution point for equipment being exported to America."

"Praise be to Allah. An American corporation, a holding company, is required to provide a mechanism for Dr. Eid to acquire or form the nuclear diagnostic business in America. He will also require a medical doctor to be on his board as the technical director."

"What do you suggest?" Usama asked.

"A Delaware corporation, with Egyptian and Saudi stockholders – the corporation will be a holding company that owns and operates the various diagnostic centers."

"Have our New York attorneys form the corporation. Funding will be provided from the Al-Shamal Islamic Bank accounts. Funds will be transferred to our Pakistani friend's Bank of Credit and Commerce International (BCCI) that has a branch in America. As soon as the new company is formed, it should establish banking with one of the large American banks. How much funding will you require?"

"I would like to establish sufficient funds now; so that no additional funds will have to be transferred later. Once the devices are detonated the Americans will begin an investigation. The first place they will look is at recent money transfers. This way there will be no current money trail when the investigations begin. However, I do not wish to stress al-Qaeda's funds unnecessarily."

"May Allah bless you Mohammed for your concern. Many of our ventures are beginning to produce cash. Funds from donations and charities are increasing. Our friend the General is using Russian criminals to import heroin. Our fee for providing the drug is fifteen percent, and I expect the trade to increase to over one billion dollars per year. We are also establishing al-Qaeda groups in the Balkans. My experts tell me we can grow poppies there. Of course, we are still receiving major funding from our Saudi brothers and Iran," Usama continued.

"Allah be praised. We must also thank Allah for the American President, Jimmy Carter. If Reagan or Bush had been the president, Ayatollah Khomeini would still be in Paris or perhaps dead – and we would not have Iranian friends who provide funds. I would like to fund the new American holding company with thirty million dollars. Dr. Eid will be the CEO, if you approve."

"The fund will be made available. Allah be with you," Usama said, standing up to indicate the end of the meeting.

After the meeting, Mohammed sent instructions to a law firm in New York to form REM Investments, Inc., a Saudi owned Delaware holding company. The usual Saudi names would be the stockholders, and Dr. Ralph Eid would be the CEO and a major stockholder. Banking would be established with Citibank of New York City. Arthur Anderson would be the accounting firm. Initially one of the Arthur Anderson accountants would keep the company's books.

The following week Dr. Eid received a telegram at his office informing him of his Uncle's death, and that he had inherited his Uncle's estate and businesses. His immediate presence was requested in Cairo. Ralph shared the news with his friends, associates, and his boss, Dr. Jameson. Dr. Jameson approved Ralph's vacation request, and after further discussions with Ralph, understood that additional leave may be required. Depending upon the extent of Ralph's inheritance, Ralph may have to quit the Laboratory to manage his business interests. Word soon spread throughout the Lab that Ralph was now a millionaire. Pleased with his charade, Ralph returned to his office to put things in order and to place a call to Bob Johnson at General Neutron.

"Hello Bob, this is Dr. Eid at Livermore Labs."

"Hello Dr. Eid. What can I do for you?"

"Bob, I have reviewed you sketch, and it looks like something I may be able to use. My project requires low energy neutrons. Is it possible to get a generator that can concentrate a low energy neutron flux . . . say a ninety degree beam?"

"Do you wish to irradiate a small area with neutrons?

"Yes, I am thinking in terms of a cubical chamber, of say thirty centimeters. I would like to irradiate it from three directions, let's say 90°, 180°, and 270°. Can you make a generator that can do that?"

"It is possible. I do not see why not. We make a single tube neutron generator, the Mk 37 that could be modified to excite three tubes instead of one. As you know, the neutrons are produced by creating deuterium ions, and by accelerating these ions into a tritium or deuterium target. The target is a thin film of a metal, such as titanium, scandium, or zirconium that is deposited on a copper or molybdenum substrate. When combined with hydrogen or its two isotopes deuterium and tritium, titanium, scandium, and zirconium form stable chemical compounds called 'metal hydrides.' For your requirement, the metal hydride would be deuterium. A magnetic field, produced by a permanent magnet oriented parallel to the source axis, directs the ion beam to the target. Maximum neutron flux can be delivered to a sample by grounding the target and keeping the source at a high positive potential."

"Will the neutron generator tubes be sealed?" Ralph asked.

"Yes."

"I may want to rapidly mix my sample – especially if it is liquid or gas. To do this I will need something to initiate a mixing mechanism before the neutron tubes are fired. I am thinking of using an electric squib as the energy source to cause the mixing. Can you provide a computer that is programmed to send a 12 volt current to a squib and incorporate a settable delay for firing the neutron tubes?"

"Yes, that will not be a problem."

"I would also like to be able to set a delay time; so that the operator will have time to get behind shielding.

"No Problem."

"Can you incorporate a sensitive gamma detector that will record the exact energy level of the gamma radiation produced?"

"Yes, we have done so for Dr. Roberts. The results can be displayed on the screen as a table and as a graph."

"Please do some preliminary engineering on this concept. I am working with an instrument company and will have them get in touch with you. We may want to order a unit in the next couple of months."

"I will have a preliminary design and cost estimate in the next two weeks. Thank you for your interest," Bob said in closing.

His conversation with Bob Johnson completed, Ralph began putting his office in order. He carefully packed his personal items and arranged for all files to be transferred to his boss. Alice the group secretary came in.

"Ralph, it looks like you do not plan to return," she said.

"I don't know. I am taking a week's vacation so that I can travel to Cairo to evaluate what I have inherited. I will probably have to go to Saudi Arabia since much of the business is there. I have arranged with Dr. Jameson to be placed on unpaid leave if required, and I expect that it will be. Therefore, I am cleaning out my office so that someone else can use it. If I return, I will get a different office."

"We are going to miss you. Send me a post card. I have never been to the Middle East."

"I will Alice. I will miss you and the others too. In any event, I plan to keep my house, so I will be able to come by for a visit once in a while. Can you contact the utility companies and tell them I had to leave the country for an emergency?"

"When will you leave?"

"I will fly to New York's Kennedy airport tomorrow. I should be able to get a direct flight to Cairo from Kennedy. Watch out for my post card and thank you for being such a good secretary and friend."

"I will. Thank you Ralph. Have a pleasant flight and don't forget to stop mail delivery," Alice said, as she turned to leave.

Ralph held similar conversations with his co-workers. Before leaving, he paid a visit to Dr. Roberts. Upon reaching Dr. Roberts' office, Ralph saw that he was on the telephone and stood outside of the door. Looking up, Roberts saw Ralph and motioned him to come in. Pointing to a chair Dr. Roberts indicated for Ralph to take a seat. Concluding his conversation and placing the phone in its cradle, Dr. Roberts said with a broad smile, "I hear you are a millionaire."

"I see the grapevine is in good working order," Ralph replied, laughing. "I really don't know – probably won't for some time. I have to go to Egypt and Saudi Arabia to find out."

"How long will you be gone?"

"At least a week, more likely a month. I have arranged for an indefinite unpaid leave. I will call my boss by the end of my one week's leave to let him know if I should be placed on indefinite status."

"So, you are going to leave your work behind and become a business man."

"Yes and no. If I really do inherit a lot of money, I would like to continue developing radiological diagnostic instruments. With sufficient funds, I hope to form a company and become an entrepreneur. I think the neutron activation technology you are working on has a place in medicine. If such is the case, I would like to stay in touch with you."

"I would seriously consider a high paying job in your new company," Dr. Roberts said smiling. "Of course I will be happy to keep in touch and provide any assistance I can."

"Thank you, Tom. I will let you know my plans when I return," Ralph said, standing up and shaking hands. "Good-bye for now."

"Have a safe trip."

It was time to leave the Laboratory. Returning to his office, Ralph picked up the box containing his personnel effects and walked out to his car. At home Ralph finished packing, made sure the house was safe to leave for an extended period of time, and dropped a stop mail notice in his mailbox.

Early the next morning, the limousine picked him up for the trip to San Francisco Airport. The next phase of his life had begun.

Cairo, Egypt July, 1991

Ralph Eid cleared customs and, as planned, met Mohammed al-Mihdar by the baggage carousel.

"Allah's blessing be upon you," Mohammed said.

"And Allah's blessings upon you too," Ralph replied.

"I have a car waiting. You have a room reserved at The Mena House. Tomorrow, we will visit some government buildings and one of our attorneys. The visits are to establish your identity and the purpose of your travel. The next day we will fly to Riyadh. There we will begin our real business. Use the rest of the day to adjust to the time change."

Ralph was grateful for the time to rest. Mohammed dropped him at the hotel.

"I will meet you here in the morning. We can have breakfast and then proceed on our rounds. I will call your room around 9 A.M. It would be a good idea if you took a taxi to the American Embassy and registered with them," Mohammed said before driving off.

Ralph checked in, selected several post cards from the lobby rack, and proceeded to his room to unpack and shower. Next he followed Mohammed's advice and registered with the American Embassy. Returning to the hotel, he decided to visit the swimming pool, and then have dinner in the hotel restaurant. Back in his room, Ralph wrote notes on the postcards in preparation for mailing them the next day, then retired.

The next morning Mohammed dialed Ralph's room from the lobby and agreed to meet him in the restaurant. Spotting Mohammed, Ralph walked over to his table.

"Good morning Mohammed," Ralph said.

"Good morning, you look rested. I hope you slept well," Mohammed responded, standing up and greeting Ralph in the Arabic fashion, except the embrace was tighter and lasted longer than usual.

Breaking the embrace, Ralph replied, somewhat nervously, "Yes, after visiting the Embassy, I went swimming and had dinner here."

"When we have finished breakfast, we will visit our solicitor. An inheritance has been arranged for you. It is important for you to establish a verifiable trail. The security people at Livermore may check. Once a plausible reason for your presence here has been established, we will visit a couple of government agencies to update records. Then your cover story becomes real."

"What does my inheritance consist of?"

"Ownership in various companies and businesses. All located in the Middle East – most in Saudi Arabia. Of course you will want to visit some of them, so we will fly to Riyadh tomorrow."

"I am not sure I am following your thoughts," Ralph said, shaking his head.

"Your tasks are in America. We do not want you to become involved in businesses in the Mideast. So, after you have acquainted yourself with your new holdings, you will arrange for them to be liquidated. You will have the funds transferred into a new American corporation, which is being formed – REM Investments, Inc. You will be a major stockholder and CEO of REM."

"Now I understand. REM will be the vehicle to acquire and operate radiation diagnostic centers."

"Yes, REM will also provide you with a salary and travel expenses. The total funding for REM will be thirty million U.S. dollars. We want you to start immediately."

"Thirty million U.S. dollars! That is a lot of money," Ralph exclaimed. "I will prove myself worthy to you, Usama bin Laden, and most of all Allah."

Smiling, Mohammed continued, "Before you return to America, we will fly to Karachi, Pakistan. While you are in Riyadh, you should call your boss and tell him you wish to be placed on unpaid leave until you return and resign."

"That should not be a problem. I discussed this possibility with my boss, and I do not think he expects me to return to the Lab. Has the instrument company been formed in Karachi?" Ralph asked. *I cannot believe my good fortune, to be given this much responsibility. I must dedicate myself totally to the cause. I will prove myself worthy,* he thought.

"Yes. Our brother and manager, Omar Mumtaz, is ready to start the cabinet shell design. We will have the first unit ready to ship by September. We hope you will have a location by then."

"There is much to be done. I will spend as much time as required in Karachi. I have contacted an American company, General Neutron, and requested they quote a neutron generator that has three neutron tubes. I will have to decide whether to have the neutron generator installed in Karachi, or purchase it and install it myself. Do you have any suggestions, Mohammed?"

"I think it would be better to purchase a complete instrument. That way you will not leave a paper trail that leads back to you. When you complete your work in Karachi, you must stop in New York City and sign the documents for REM. After that, you are free to go about completing your mission. You will communicate with me as Cousin Ali. Usama has directed that our special project, code name 'Allah's Rings,' be run as an independent operation with only the three of us knowing its purpose or name. Usama has also made it clear that you are to spend whatever is required to accomplish your tasks. Do not be afraid to purchase businesses, land, vehicles, anything that you need. You are not expected to make a profit, but you probably will. It is important that you become a businessman, operating successful diagnostic treatment centers until you receive the signal to activate Allah's Rings. The signal's code words will be disclosed to you after the first device is in place. The signal can only be given by Usama or me."

"I understand, however, I do not have a working knowledge of the devices you have acquired," Ralph said.

"True, and it is for that very reason we will journey to the storage location of one of the devices. There in a secure out-of-the-way place, you will be able to familiarize yourself with how to assemble and detonate the device. All of the devices are in Afghanistan. We do not wish to have a record of your entrance to the country on your passport. When we reach Riyadh you will be provided a set of new identity papers for our trip to Afghanistan. We will then fly to Kabul, Afghanistan and drive to the storage location. Once there, we will practice assembly of the device. When I am satisfied that we are both competent to assemble and function the device, we will return to Riyadh. After that, we will proceed, using our real names and passports, to Karachi, Pakistan. Do not forget to register with the American Embassy while you are in Riyadh and Karachi."

Later that night as Ralph prepared for bed he recalled the events of the day and Mohammed's reference to the code name for their project. *"Allah's Rings," what a perfect name for this plan; and I will be one of only three to know its name and purpose. No, I will be more than that. I will be the key to making the plan work. One day I will meet Usama himself, but for now I must be satisfied to let Mohammed be the intermediary. Allah be praised,* he prayed as he drifted to sleep.

Leningrad, July 1991

Valya Golovko, Anya's sister answered the knock on the front door and found a nondescript man in a wrinkled gray suit standing there. "Good morning comrade," she said.

"Good morning comrade, I have a message for Ivan Zeldovich. I understand that he is visiting at this address," the man said, making no effort to introduce himself.

"Yes, Ivan Zeldovich is here, please come in."

"That will not be necessary, please ask Comrade Zeldovich to step out here. I am in a hurry."

Valya turned and walked to the kitchen where Ivan was sitting. "Ivan, there is a man who wishes to speak with you at the front door. He did not identify himself nor provide any additional information. He looks like a KGB man. Are you in trouble?" Valya asked in a hushed tone.

"No Valya, I am not in trouble. It probably concerns my work. As I told you, I have been working on a State project. I may be needed again," Ivan replied. *If everything is going according to plan, this should be the beginning of our trip to Cuba.* Ivan walked out the front door, closing it behind him. Greeting the man he said, "I am Ivan Zeldovich."

"Comrade Ivan Zeldovich, I have a message and instructions for you from Colonel Alexei Valek," the man said handing Ivan a thick envelope. "I was instructed to tell you that I will come for you and your wife next Wednesday at 8 A.M. I am to take you to the pier to board a ship. You will tell your relatives that you have been recalled to Saravo as part of your work. That is the extent of my instructions."

"Thank you Comrade. We will be ready Wednesday morning. We will have two large trunks and four suitcases," Ivan said, and then he turned and entered the house.

"What is it?" Anya asked in a concerned voice.

"A message and instructions concerning my work. I will know more after I read the information in the envelope," Ivan said before turning and walking into their bedroom.

Ivan sat down on the bed and opened the large thick envelope. Inside he found two passports in the names of Nicholas Karpov and Maria Karpov; and a five-page document providing background information for their new identity. There was also an unsigned letter from the Colonel telling Nicholas that he had done well; and providing information regarding the sea voyage, the location of their new house, contacts in Cuba, and a bank account in Nicholas Karpov's name. The ship's captain would have funds for Nicholas when they boarded. Ivan was elated, but now he faced the task of explaining everything to Anya . . . *no to Maria.*

Returning to the kitchen, Ivan sat down to tell Anya and Valya he had been recalled to Saravo on State business. "My work has become more important and I have been recalled. In fact, I may be assigned to a different location in the future. Anya is to return with me. Do not worry about us Valya. My new assignment will provide for us. A car will call for us next Wednesday morning."

Ivan waited three more days before telling Anya about their new life. At first she was frightened and confused, then accepted her new situation. The hardest part was not being able to tell her sister. The following Wednesday Nicholas and Maria Karpov boarded a freighter bound for Havana, Cuba, with several port calls on the way. The voyage was for both of them a dream come true: at its end would be a wonderful new way of life on an island in paradise – paradise for a Russian.

Kabul, Afghanistan July 1991

Mohammed al-Mihdar, now Ali al-Libi, and Ralph Eid, now Saif Abdullah, left the Kabul airport and obtained a Toyota 4x4 Land Cruiser. With Saif driving they started north on Route A76, the main highway to Mazar-E Sharif. The roads were in poor condition, but passable. Approximately 80 kilometers north of Kabul they entered the Salang Tunnel to pass through the Hindu Kush Mountains. On the far side of the mountains, just before the town of Dowshi, they crossed a road leading almost due east to the village of Andarab, where they spent the night. Early the next morning they proceeded east back into the Hindu Kush Mountains, toward the location of one of the atomic devices. The road was nothing more than a two-lane gravel path that switched back and forth up the face of the mountain. Ralph, who was unused to traveling in such rugged terrain, was glad they had a four-wheel drive vehicle; because, even with the added traction the wheels spun, throwing gravel in a plume beside and behind the vehicle. He was more than relieved when later that morning they reached the cave complex, which was guarded by al-Qaeda fighters. Recognizing Mohammed, the leader welcomed the pair.

"Thanks be to Allah, you have returned Ali," said the commander.

"May Allah bless you, Abdul," replied Ali. "This is our brother Saif who has come to inspect our treasure."

"May Allah's blessing be upon you, Saif," Abdul said.

"And upon you also," Saif replied.

Addressing Abdul, Ali asked, "Have all of the five containers and adequate mechanic's tools been brought to the cave?"

"By Allah's will, everything is as you requested," Abdul replied.

"Thanks be to Allah. Saif and I will be working in the storage chamber for the rest of the day. No one is to enter. No exceptions," Ali said to Abdul. "Thank you for making all of the arrangements."

While Mohammed and Ralph were talking to Abdul, other fighters were covering the Toyota with camouflage netting. Ralph followed Mohammed into the cave entrance that was concealed under an overhanging rock: obscuring the entrance from view – either from the road or from above. Once inside the entrance, they followed a long passageway that curved to the left. Deep ruts in the ground indicated the recent movement of heavy equipment along the passageway. As they neared the end of the passageway, they came upon the entrance to a large cavern that had been modified to create a storage chamber. On the far side of the chamber, sat a large crate and four cubical containers arranged along the wall to its right. Several meters to the left of the crate a rectangular container sat on the ground. The cavern was brightly illuminated with a string of light bulbs and portable lamps. Warmth from the lights provided some relief from the frigid temperature in the cave that was located high in the mountains where the air was thin and cold.

"We have an arduous task ahead of us. Thin air and the cold will slow our progress. Be prepared to pace yourself and to take frequent breaks. Our task here is too important to make mistakes; and we need precise measurements to ensure proper fabrication of the medical instrument shell. Much thought must be given to ensure proper design and fabrication of the shell. You and I will assemble all the components of the device together; so that both of us will be knowledgeable of the procedure," Mohammed said to Ralph.

Working together the two men set about the task of removing the top of the crate containing the gun assembly. After removing the screws holding the top in place, the wooden top of the crate was set to the side, and the packing material removed and bagged for reuse. Inside the crate they saw the exposed top of the cannon barrel and target assembly container attached to the end of the barrel.

"We have to completely break down this crate to gain working access to entire device," Mohammed said as they proceeded to unscrew the sides of the crate. With all sides of the crate removed they were now able to view the device in its entirety.

The thin air was tiring both men, but Ralph was too excited to feel fatigued. Instead he felt a serge of adrenalin as he brushed away the remaining packing material and stood back to get a better view of the device sitting there on the floor of the crate. *This will do nicely*, he thought, *nicely indeed to bring the great Satan to its knees and make them feel the full wrath of Allah.* Ralph smiled as he looked at Mohammed and said, "Allah be Praised."

There before them stood the 100 mm cannon. A rectangular steel box, the target assembly container that would house Allah's Rings, was attached to the end of the cannon's barrel with steel bars, and supported by a steel frame. A gap of about 8 cm separated the box from the end of the barrel. On the face of the box there was a hole approximately 76 mm in diameter that had to be perfectly aligned with the centerline of the barrel. On the opposite end there was a 50 mm vent hole. The cannon assembly was mounted in a steel frame base that provided rigid support for the barrel and the target assembly container. This support was required to maintain alignment of the barrel and center axis of the target assembly; so that when the cannon was fired the projectile would enter the target rings directly through the hole without binding. There was no need for a recoil mechanism, because the cannon would be destroyed by the atomic detonation when the first round was fired. Later the steel frame would serve another purpose when it provided attachment points for the aluminum framework that would support the instrument façade: concealing the cannon assembly and converting the weapon into a Neutron Induced Gamma Spectrometer.

From the supply of mechanic's tools assembled in chests along one wall of the chamber, Mohammed located a socket wrench with a 16 mm socket. *Abdul has done well,* he thought as he handed the socket wrench to Ralph, and said, "The first step is to remove the lid of the target assembly container."

Six bolts were welded to the outside walls of the target assembly container. The lid extended over the container's walls and formed a flange with holes that aligned with the six bolts. Six nuts secured the lid in place. Once the nuts were removed, the handle attached to the container's top could be used for removal. After Ralph had removed all of the nuts, he grasped the handle with one hand and attempted to lift the top. "Ugh, this is heavier than it looks," he said and rested a moment before exerting more effort. On his next attempt he was able to successfully remove the top and clear the six bolts, by grasping the handle with both hands and lifting the lid straight up.

This is a far more difficult task than I anticipated, Ralph thought, as he turned and set the heavy metal lid on a tarp placed on the ground beside the cannon. Remembering Mohammed's instructions, he took a few moments to rest and to reflect on the modifications he had theorized. Properly placing the neutron generator tubes would definitely increase the yield and killing efficiency of the weapon.

He is savoring the moment of the great Satan's ultimate destruction, thought Mohammed, studying Ralph's face as they both took time to rest.

With the top removed both men were now able to look down into the target assembly container, and see that the bottom of the container was contoured to match the shape of the rings. Mohammed watched as Ralph took a small metal tape measure from his pocket, carefully measured the outside and inside of the exposed target assembly container, and wrote the dimensions in his notebook. Ralph continued to study the container in silence for several minutes before turning to Mohammed, "These measurements are critical to the weapon modification I have been considering. I think that I will use three neutron generator tubes, and offset them so that they will introduce the neutrons at different locations. I will place them here, here, and here," he said pointing to three locations on the container.

"Aha, an excellent idea! It will greatly increase the number of first generation fissions," replied Mohammed, smiling. *Yes, I did pick the right man for this task. He has a mujahedeen's soul.*

"Now let us install the rings – Allah's Rings." Walking to the row of small cubical containers, Mohammed pointed to the green markings on each of the containers. "As you know, each device has a different configuration. Each device is color coded to prevent mixing the components. If the components were mixed, the device may not function." Gesturing to the row of containers, Mohammed continued, "These are the ring containers. Note the Green R1, R2, R3, and R4 markings. R1 is placed next to the barrel of the cannon, R2 next to R1, and so forth. The matching projectile will be marked with a green P. Let us open R1 and install it."

Ralph released the catches on the R1 container and removed the top. Inside they found and removed a layer of packing material, beneath which lay a lead sheet that proved difficult to remove; because it was almost the exact dimensions of the inside of the container. Using a screwdriver to lift one side, they removed the lead sheet by simultaneously lifting all four sides. Beneath the sheet lay the first of Allah's uranium rings. Looking much like a large dull black washer, the ring had a hole in the center that measured 76.2 mm in diameter. Ralph quickly determined that the ring would be very heavy for one man to lift. Turning to Mohammed, he said, "One never truly appreciates density until he tries to pick up uranium. If this ring was made of lead it would only weigh about half as much."

"Yes, and this is the lightest one. R4 has a smaller center hole," Mohammed replied. "It will take both of us to lift this one into the container."

When the third ring had been installed, Ralph turned to Mohammed and said, "If we install the last ring, how will we remove it?"

"You are correct, once the ring is in the container there is no way to grasp it. We will not install it. We have two problems that neither of us had anticipated. I had not considered how heavy the rings would be. It never occurred to me that the rings could not be removed. Let us take a break before removing the three rings and think about it." *Either the Russian dogs never thought of this problem, or they never anticipated the need to disassemble the device. That must mean there is no danger in leaving the four rings in the assembly container. This must be so, because the Little Boy must have had the rings installed when the bomb was assembled.*

Mohammed and Ralph sat on two of the empty ring containers. Both were out of breath from their exertion and the altitude. Ralph took a minute to consider the problem before concluding, "It appears that two people are required to install the rings. It may be possible to install a lifting eye into each ring, but that would require drilling into the uranium, which requires an oil bath. The shavings and dust must be kept in oil. Let us place the lid back on the target assembly container and take a reading to see how much radiation is emitted. We may be able to install the rings in the container and leave them there."

Together they replaced the top of the ring assembly container. Then Mohammed walked over to a bag he had carried into the chamber. Removing a low-level gamma meter and performing the proper start-up procedure, he pointed the instrument at the device. After looking at the reading, he repeated the procedure from several different positions. Turning to Ralph, he said, "The readings are about the same as the background reading I took in the desert. The container has a lining of depleted uranium that is an excellent shielding material. You are correct, it will be possible to install all of the rings when the device is setup at its final location. Now, let us remove the rings and then reinstall them, this time we will leave out R1 and install R4. If the readings are the same, we have solved the problem."

Two hours later, Mohammed and Ralph had completed the second assembly procedure and determined that emitted radiation would not be a problem. After another break, they removed the three rings and replaced them into their respective cases.

"Now it is time to complete the training by installing the round into the breech of the cannon," Mohammed said. "Let us uncrate the cannon round with the uranium projectile."

They opened the wooden crate with a green P painted on it and removed the packing material. Inside lay the complete round that looked like a giant rifle cartridge: and, like a rifle cartridge, the brass case was larger in diameter than the bullet. In this case, the bullet was the uranium projectile. Covering most of the projectile was a molded plastic sleeve that increased its various diameters to a uniform 100 mm: so that the sleeve would make contact with the insides of the gun barrel, and maintain proper alignment of the projectile. Only the nose of the projectile was exposed. Pointing to the plastic sleeve, Ralph said, "This must be the sabot. It acts as a pressure washer keeping the hot propellant gases from passing around the projectile while it is being propelled down the barrel. Some of the sabot material will enter the target rings, and because it contains hydrogen atoms it will act as a moderator for the neutrons. The rest will be extruded through the 8 cm gap with the propellant gasses."

"Yes, and the 50 mm hole on the other end of the ring container is there to vent the air inside the center of the target rings that otherwise would be compressed as the projectile enters the target rings," Mohammed commented.

The nose of the uranium projectile was dull black in color – the color of oxidized uranium. This time the weight of the round did not surprise Ralph. A small green P was painted on the side of the brass shell case.

Mohammed pointed to the base of the cartridge case where a primer would be located on a rifle cartridge, and said, "See the two metal rings. These are the electrical contact points for the electric squibs. The cannon was modified with two contact pins that will touch the rings when the breech is closed. This provides a method to electrically fire the round by igniting the squibs. It also provides a method to check the continuity of the firing circuit to ensure the bridge wire is intact. For reliability there are two squibs wired in parallel. Either squib is sufficient to ignite the propellant. The original squibs and propellant have been replaced. Now let us load the round and close the breech."

A simple lever was used to unlock the breech and to swing it open. The breech was coated with heavy grease. Two small spring-loaded pins protruded from the face of the breechblock. A copper cap or shunt covered both of the pins connecting them together, so the electrical circuit could be tested for continuity.

"Remove the shunt and use a rag to remove the grease. I have a container of similar grease that we will use to replace it after we have completed our practice run," Mohammed said. "The grease is a preservative against rust during storage. When the time comes to load the round for use, you will have to wipe the grease off again."

Following Mohammed's instructions, Ralph removed the shunt, wiped the grease from the cannon's breech, lifted the round, slid it into the open breech, and pushed it to ensure that it was properly seated. Next he swung the breech back into position and rotated the lever to lock the breech. An electrical firing cable was secured to the side of the cannon.

From his bag, Mohammed retrieved a blasting galvanometer to test the bridge wire and circuit continuity. The blasting galvanometer – about the size of a small cassette tape player – was contained in a leather case and equipped with an exposed meter scale and pointer. On one end were two round metal posts. A special battery was used to ensure that the voltage and current was less than one tenth of the amount required to function the blasting cap or squib. To use the meter, the operator touched the two lead wires from the squib or blasting cap to the two metal posts on the blasting galvanometer. If the circuit was complete, the pointer on the meter would indicate a small flow of current by moving across the scale on the meter. Thus indicating that the bridge wire and circuit was intact.

In order to function a squib or blasting cap, a larger current passes through the circuit. The larger current causes the bridge wire to become red hot – like an electric heater. Heat from the bridge wire then causes the surrounding sensitive compound to ignite – if it is a squib, or detonate – if it is a blasting cap. Then the metal tube containing the bridge wire and sensitive compound ruptures, and either ignites the propellant or detonates the explosives.

Mohammed handed the blasting galvanometer to Ralph and instructed him to test the firing circuit. Taking the meter, Ralph placed one of the firing leads on a terminal post of the meter and held it in place with one finger. Next he picked up the other firing cable lead and touched it to the other post of the meter. Watching to see if the pointer moved, which it did, Ralph smiled and replaced the cable leads in their position on the cannon.

"The firing cable can be connected to the computer that will control the detonation sequence: first by igniting the squib, causing the projectile to be propelled down the cannon barrel and into the target rings; and then by triggering the neutron generator. I have performed calculations for timing and will program the computer accordingly. This timing will be simple, because we are only dealing in thousands of a second – not the billionths of a second required for a supercritical nuclear reaction," Ralph commented.

"Yes, the timing is based upon how long it will take the projectile to reach the target rings after the squib fires," Mohammed said, nodding his head.

Ralph then removed the complete round by reversing the procedure. The round was returned to its container and the container sealed.

"It is late and we are tired. Help me cover the gun assembly with this tarp, and we can finish our tasks tomorrow," Mohammed said. "Tonight we will sleep here in the cave complex."

Another chamber in the cave served as barracks and mess hall. The evening meal was simple and nourishing. After the meal and evening prayers, both men fell into a deep sleep.

The next morning, following breakfast and morning prayers, Mohammed and Ralph returned to the chamber and removed the tarp from the gun assembly. Mohammed handed Ralph a container of grease and said, "You must replace the electrical shunt, and the preservative grease in the breech and on the outside of the cannon. When you have finished, I will help you reassemble the crate."

Two hours later the crate had been reassembled, and all of the other containers properly closed and sealed. It was time to leave.

Mohammed, in the person of Ali, gave instructions to Abdul, "Upon receipt of orders from me, the large crate is to be sent to a specified destination in Kabul. The other containers are to be returned to their storage locations until you receive my directions to ship them – one at a time – to the location in Kabul. You have done very well in securing and organizing this storage installation. Our work here is almost complete. I will be certain to commend your diligent service to al-Qaeda to our glorious leader Usama bin Laden. Allah be praised for brothers like you."

Ali al-Libi and Saif Abdullah departed the cave complex and returned to Kabul, where they spent the night. The next morning Ali and Saif caught a direct flight to Riyadh and promptly assumed their real identities.

The following day Mohammed al-Mihdar and Ralph Eid flew to Karachi, Pakistan.

Karachi, Pakistan August, 1991

Dr. Mohammed al-Mihdar and Dr. Ralph Eid were met at the entrance to Indus Instruments by the company's General Manager, Omar Mumtaz. Mumtaz had been told he was to design and fabricate the aluminum framework and outer cabinet shell for a new instrument that would act as a façade to camouflage a cannon. The cannon barrel had a strange box attached to its end and was supported by the steel frame. The new instrument, a Neutron Induced Gamma Spectrometer, would be purchased by REM Investments, Inc., an American corporation headed by Dr. Eid. Omar Mumtaz had strict orders that he was to follow Dr. Eid's instructions, and to ask no questions beyond those required to perform his task.

"Allah be praised. I am Omar Mumtaz, General Manger. I am pleased to meet you and to welcome you to Indus Instruments," Mumtaz said in the way of a greeting.

"By Allah's blessings, we are pleased to be here and to meet you," Mohammed answered. "I am Dr. Mohammed al-Mihdar, a Director of REM, and this is Dr. Ralph Eid, REM's CEO. Dr. Eid is a resident and citizen of America."

"Allah bless you," Dr. Eid said to Omar Mumtaz.

"Please follow me, the conference room has been prepared for your visit," Mumtaz said, as he lead the way through the lobby and down a carpeted, oak paneled hall. At the end of the hall, he turned right and entered a well-appointed room containing a large conference table and ten chairs. A large bulletin board had been placed on one wall, and several sketches were attached to it. Photographs and a sheet of paper containing measurements were placed in front of three of the chairs.

"Coffee, tea and pastries are available," Mumtaz said, pointing to a side table. "Would you care for anything?"

"Yes, thank you, we will both have coffee," Dr. Eid replied. "Mine with cream and sugar and the other with sugar only."

"Cream and sugar, you truly are from America," Mumtaz said with a smile.

Mohammed began the meeting by saying, "REM is establishing diagnostic imaging centers in America and will purchase a Neutron Induced Gamma Spectrometer and other items from you. REM will take delivery at your warehouse in Newark, New Jersey."

"Praise be to Allah. That is my understanding. Sketches of the instrument have been prepared; however, I know nothing of neutrons, nor how to obtain them," Mumtaz said.

Mohammed could not help but chuckle. "Dr. Eid will review your sketches and explain the neutron source. Once you have completed the concept sketches, you will start fabrication of the aluminum framework and cabinet shell. When both are completed, the main component of the instrument will be delivered. It is very important that the main component not be uncrated until you are ready to install the framework and shell. Only your most trusted workers will be involved in this operation. No one else should know of it."

For the next three hours, Ralph and Mohammed reviewed Omar Mumtaz's sketches and suggested changes. By the end of the meeting designs for the framework and instrument shell had been agreed to.

Ralph provided Mumtaz with a copy of the General Neutron, Inc. brochure and Bob Johnson's name and phone number. Then he explained how and where the three neutron tubes were to be attached to the target assembly container. The Mk 37's computer would become part of the control panel for the instrument. The completed Indus Instruments' Neutron Induced Gamma Spectrometer would appear to be what the name implied and would fool anyone other than an expert in the field. The price for the instrument would be $385,000.00, FOB Newark, NJ.

Following lunch, Mumtaz sent a fax to Bob Johnson from Omar Mumtaz of Indus Instruments requesting: a quotation; two sets of drawings and specifications; a delivery schedule for a modified Mk 37 Neutron Generator with three neutron tubes; and a dummy modified Mk 37 Neutron Generator with three empty neutron tubes. The dummy modified Mk 37 was to be sent to Indus Instruments in Karachi to be used to build a Neutron Induced Gamma Spectrometer that was to be shipped to America. The real modified Mk 37 would be shipped to the Indus Instrument facility in Newark, New Jersey; where it would be installed to replace the dummy Mk 37. Shipping the real modified Mk 37 to New Jersey would not require an export license, and General Neutron would not be required to notify the government. The fax cover page authenticated the request by referencing conversations held between Dr. Ralph Eid, Livermore Labs, and Bob Johnson regarding the design of the modified Mk 37.

The meeting was concluded, and it was time for Ralph and Mohammed to leave.

"Allah bless you Omar Mumtaz," Ralph said at the door. "Notify both of us as soon as you have a reply from General Neutron. One set of the drawings and specifications are to be forwarded to me at this address. When the framework and shell are completed, and the dummy Mk 37 is received, you are to notify both of us. Upon your notification, the main component of the instrument will be shipped to you. I will return and assist in assembling the first instrument. If possible, the two of us will perform the task alone. Then your workers can package it for shipment to New Jersey."

"Allah be praised. It will be as you say," replied Mumtaz.

Ralph and Mohammed returned to Riyadh that evening. Both were well satisfied with their progress and accomplishments.

"It is time for you to return to America and become the CEO of REM," Mohammed said to Ralph. "You have much to accomplish. It is important that you find a location for the first diagnostic center, and take delivery of the first instrument. It is imperative that all five devices are positioned in America before al-Qaeda becomes recognized as a true instrument of the jihad. We have arranged for Dr. Umair Bhatti, Professor of Radiology at Harvard and a well-known medical doctor, to be your Chief Medical Officer. Call upon him whenever you need assistance. His name will provide credibility for REM."

"I assume that Dr. Bhatti does not know of our purpose or of Allah's Rings."

"That is correct. He is a brother Muslim and a strong sympathizer with our cause, and he will not ask embarrassing questions," Mohammed replied.

"Good, I will arrange a trip to Boston to meet him at a later date. When I get to New York I will call him and request that he prepare a list of recommended personnel and diagnostic equipment for our centers."

Changing the subject, Mohammed said, "I am concerned about the American president. He has proven that he has teeth and will use them. If he or his lackeys detect al-Qaeda and recognize our potential, our plan could be foiled."

"The Americans, like the British, are a fickle people. President Kennedy once said 'Ask not what your country can do for you; ask what you can do for your country.' A more apt saying would be, 'Don't tell me what you did for the country – tell me what you are going to do for me.' It is entirely possible the Americans will not reelect the current president, just as the British did not reelect Winston Churchill after WWII."

"Who do you think they might elect?" Mohammed asked.

"Perot is running as an independent. I do not think he can possibly win, but he can get enough votes to defeat Bush and allow a Democrat to win. My colleagues at Livermore are very liberal, and they like a man named Clinton. All I know about him is that he was Governor of Arkansas," replied Ralph.

"I will watch this Clinton, and research his history. If he is liberal, it will make al-Qaeda's work easier. Let us pray to Allah to make it so."

The next morning Ralph flew to New York City. On Monday morning he met with the attorneys, and became the CEO and major stockholder of REM, Inc. Back in his hotel room, he placed a call to the Chicago business broker, Samuel Rossman, who informed Ralph he had located a small business that might meet his requirements. The business, Erie Diagnostics, had an unimposing office in a suburb of Chicago. Erie Diagnostics was under capitalized, but had a good reputation and all the required permits and licenses. Ralph decided to stop in Chicago on his way to California. Arrangements were made for Rossman to meet Ralph at O'Hare airport the following day. Then Ralph called Bob Johnson at General Neutron and told him of his good fortune: his intentions to leave Livermore Labs; and that he had become CEO of his own company, REM Investments. Bob congratulated Ralph and told him that he had an inquiry from Indus Instruments. Ralph replied that he planned to purchase the Spectrometer for his new company, and requested a copy of the proposal and drawings. Ralph knew that Bob Johnson would mention the order to Dr. Roberts at Livermore, who would then say that he knew Ralph was interested in developing such an instrument for medical diagnostics. The net result was that no questions or red flags would be raised regarding the Indus' order.

Chicago, August 1991

Samuel Rossman was waiting at the gate for Dr. Eid. Walking through the doorway from the boarding ramp into the waiting area, Ralph Eid looked around and noticed a large, heavyset man with a swarthy complexion, who was watching the deplaning passengers. Walking over to the man, Ralph asked, "Mr. Rossman?"

"Yes, and you are Dr. Eid?"

"Yes, thank you for meeting me. I have reservations at the airport Hilton hotel. We can talk in my room if that is agreeable with you," Ralph said.

"That will be fine. Do you have baggage?"

"Yes, two bags."

The two walked to the baggage area and waited for Eid's bags to come down the chute. Retrieving the bags, they crossed the vehicle lanes, entered the hotel lobby and Ralph checked in. An elevator took them to the ninth floor and proceeded to Ralph's room.

"Excuse me while I use the bathroom," Ralph said.

Rossman opened his briefcase and removed a folder marked Erie Diagnostics. Taking a seat at the table, he waited for Dr. Eid to return. Ralph closed the bathroom door and walked over to the table, where Rossman handed him the Erie Diagnostics folder containing a business plan, and income statements for the last three quarters. It took Ralph ten minutes to read through all of the material and ask questions.

"This looks like something I am interested in. Is it possible to visit the facility this afternoon?"

"Yes, I made arrangements for a visit in case you so desired," Rossman replied, as he picked up the phone. "I will let them know we are coming. Have you had lunch?"

"No."

"We can have a late lunch at an Italian restaurant near the facility. I can ask Dr. Arlington to join us if you like. He is the Director of Erie Diagnostics."

"Yes, that would speed things up. I assume Dr. Arlington is a medical doctor?"

"Yes, Dr. Arlington is also on the staff of Mercy Medical Center," Rossman said.

Inside the restaurant, Rossman surveyed the room and remarked, "That's him," as he waved to a man seated at a corner table. Ralph followed Rossman as he walked toward the doctor, who stood as they approached. Dr. Arlington was a tall man, about 45 years old, with a receding hairline.

Gesturing for Ralph to go ahead of him, Rossman stepped aside and politely began the introduction, "Dr. Arlington, this is Dr. Eid."

"It is a pleasure to meet you, Dr. Eid," Dr. Arlington said as he shook Ralph's hand. "Please call me Steve."

The three took their seats and gave the waitress their drink orders. Ralph and Dr. Arlington ordered ice tea. Rossman ordered a glass of white wine.

"The luncheon special is usually good, and the veal scaloppini is my favorite," Dr. Arlington said.

The waitress returned with the drinks, and announced that the day's special was Chicken Parmesan. Ralph and Dr. Arlington ordered Veal Scaloppini, and Rossman chose the special.

"I have had a chance to briefly look at your business plan and your last three quarter's operating results," Ralph said, opening the conversation. "It appears that you are not growing, and only turning a small profit. Is that why you wish to sell the business?"

"I have two partners who are demanding increased profits, but who do not wish to invest additional capital in the business. In order to grow, the treatment center should be relocated to provide additional space for treatment rooms and new diagnostic equipment," Dr. Arlington replied. "Are you a medical doctor?"

"No, I am a physicist, and a business man," Ralph replied – shocking himself. *Yes, now I am a businessman,* he thought, and realized for the first time the full import of his new position. "I am the CEO of an investment company that has identified a business opportunity in the emerging field of radioactive diagnostics."

"You are correct, however, I hope you realize the technology is constantly changing and this is a capital intensive business. The life of a diagnostic instrument is short, it must be amortized over a couple of years."

Ralph was impressed with Arlington's candor. *He is not trying to snow me. This man can be useful, at least for a time.* During this exchange, Rossman remained quiet and watched Dr. Eid, who appeared to be interested. Rossman would not enter the conversation until he was needed.

"Tell me what you would like to do with Erie Diagnostics," Ralph said to Dr. Arlington.

"First, find a new location near the major hospitals with sufficient room to expand the treatment area. A location near major hospitals will result in referrals, a better class of patients, and increased fees. Since instruments have a short useable life, their use must be maximized. Therein lies our problem. We do not have sufficient business to allow us to amortize our equipment and replace it with the most current model. Also, as new instruments are designed they must be added; if we are to provide the best of services, and qualify as a first class diagnostic and treatment center."

"Do you have a location in mind?" Ralph asked.

"No, but it must have parking facilities and be in an upscale building. Unfortunately, people judge you by your location and decor," Arlington replied.

The waitress returned with their lunch, and the conversation ceased.

"Steve, this veal is excellent," Ralph said.

"Thank you. How is the chicken, Sam?" Dr. Arlington asked Rossman.

"Good as always," Rossman replied.

"Tell me, Steve," Ralph continued, "If you sell Erie, what are your plans?"

"I plan to return to the hospital as a staff physician."

"If my company, REM, were to purchase Erie, I would require your services for a period of time. How long could you stay?"

"As long as you would require, within reason, say six months to a year."

"Let us assume that I am interested in acquiring Erie. What are you looking for?" Ralph said.

It was now time for Rossman to earn his commission. Opening his briefcase, he extracted a balance sheet for The Erie Partnership. "As you can see, the partners have invested $100,000 each. There is a bank note for another $100,000, with a balance of $25,000. The equipment is leased, and over half the leases will expire within five months. This is good, because the equipment is outdated and new equipment can be leased."

"As I recall from looking at the income statements, Erie is doing about $2,250,000 in sales and is earning about $180,000. Sales appear to be decreasing each quarter," Ralph replied.

"Correct, revenue is decreasing, because we do not have the latest equipment. My partners do not want to commit to leasing more expensive equipment when the current leases expire," Arlington responded.

"How about the building lease. When does that expire?" Ralph asked.

"The building lease will expire in six months. We have an option to renew, but the rate will increase," Rossman replied. "The timing is good if you wish to relocate the clinic."

"What has been the profit history of the partnership?" Ralph asked.

"Erie was formed eleven years ago. Revenue and profits were very good for the first five years. They began to decline last year," Arlington said.

"How much has each partner earned during the life of the partnership?" Ralph asked.

"I do not know the exact amount. I would have to ask our accountant," Arlington replied.

"Has the return exceeded the investment?" Ralph persisted.

"Yes, we have all earned more than our initial investment, approximately three times the investment," Arlington replied.

They finished their meal, and Dr. Arlington paid the bill.

"Shall we have a look at the clinic?" Rossman asked.

"Yes," Ralph replied. "Thank you for a fine lunch."

As they left the restaurant, Rossman said to Dr. Arlington, "We will meet you there."

Erie Diagnostics was located in a strip mall that also contained a dentist and a chiropractor. Ralph and Rossman followed Dr. Arlington into the lobby where several older patients were seated.

"Good afternoon Doctor. Hi Sam," the receptionists said.

"Good afternoon Judy," Dr. Arlington said, returning the greeting. "This is Dr. Eid."

"Hello Judy," Ralph said.

"You have several messages, one is urgent," Judy said, handing several pink message slips to Dr. Arlington.

"Please come with me," Doctor Arlington said to Ralph and Rossman, as they walked through the door and down the hall to his office. "I have to return the urgent call. Sam, you can show Dr. Eid around the office area. I will have to accompany him in the treatment areas."

A short while later, Dr. Arlington returned and took Ralph through the treatment and diagnostic areas of the facility. After completing a tour the three men entered a small conference room. Ralph was very interested in the storage of the radioactive isotopes used in diagnostics. Addressing Dr. Arlington, Ralph said, "You store the unused radioactive isotopes in a lead lined refrigerator or storage cabinet. After use, each vial still contains some of the radioactive isotope. The vials with the residual radioactive isotopes are placed in lead containers called pigs; in order to allow them to decay until the radiation level is below established regulatory limits. By doing this, you avoid having to pay for disposal of radioactive wastes."

"Yes, the vials containing residual liquids can be disposed of as hazardous waste. We have a contractor, who can handle both types of wastes," Dr. Arlington replied.

"Lead shielding is also required in the X-ray room?" Ralph asked.

"Yes, but only to protect the operator. We use a lead apron or bib to shield the patient," Dr. Arlington replied.

"Additional diagnostic equipment will require additional radiation shielding," Ralph said.

"Yes, that is another reason why this location is not suitable for expansion," Dr. Arlington said, agreeing with Dr. Eid's statement.

"I think I have seen enough. I will consider all you have told me on the flight back to California. If I have further interest, I will request that our Chief Medical Officer, Professor Umair Bhatti, call you and discuss specifics for expansion, and the equipment and instruments we will wish to add. Either way, I will let Mr. Rossman know my decision within a week. Thank you for your hospitality and for a very good lunch," Ralph said as he stood up.

"Thank you for coming. I hope that we can work together. You appear to understand the technology and business. With sufficient resources, Erie Diagnostics can provide a needed service and make a good profit," Dr. Arlington said as he walked Rossman and Dr. Eid to the door.

Ralph was quiet for most of the drive back to O'Hare. Finally, turning toward Rossman, he said, "Erie Diagnostics has potential. Steve is correct, the location is bad. I will evaluate the financial data on the plane tomorrow, and then discuss the opportunity with Professor Bhatti. Let us assume that I wish to proceed. That being the case, a suitable location must be found so that the clinic can be relocated by the end of the lease. Can you find a suitable location?"

"Yes, but I will require guidance as to what you are looking for – how many square feet, how much you are willing to spend for space – and most of all on the location."

"I agree with Steve's assessment that the location must be upscale, near major medical facilities. Ease of parking is essential. I am somewhat familiar with Chicago. A downtown location would be preferable. I would like a high-rise building – the higher up the better. The ideal choice would be a building that is under renovation; so that lead shielding and large instruments can be installed before other tenants arrive. Some of the new instruments will emit radiation, so lead shielding in the walls is required. If the shielding is in place before other tenants arrive there will be no questions and concerns."

"I know of two buildings that meet those requirements. One is near the Wrigley Building. I think the forty-second floor is available. How much space would you want?" Rossman asked. *If this guy is for real, I can earn two commissions.*

"I am not sure, but at least twice what Erie currently has. If it is available, have Dr. Arlington take a look, and see if he thinks it is a good location."

"I will check on the availability of the forty-second floor tomorrow. I will have an answer for you when you call me."

"Good. Please do so. Also check on other buildings. I will be in touch with you in the next couple of days," Ralph said, exiting the car at the hotel. *Allah has provided the first location. Erie is just what I was looking for. If Rossman finds a location that will provide a good detonation point, I will have my first city. The next problem is how to hide the Neutron Induced Gamma Spectrometer so that the staff will not have the opportunity to discover it is a fake. I am sure Allah will provide the answer.*

The next morning Ralph called Professor Bhatti and introduced himself. Next he explained his intentions to establish state-of-the-art radiological diagnostic centers in several cities, and then discussed Erie Diagnostics. Professor Bhatti was excited and very enthusiast about the venture. He would prepare a list of equipment and instruments, and would be active in staffing the facility and getting it started.

Concluding the conversation with Bhatti, Ralph left for the airport and caught a United Airlines flight to Oakland International. A limo service would meet him and provide transportation to his house. During the flight he reviewed Erie's financial statements. He decided to make an offer as soon as a suitable location was found. First, Erie Diagnostics Partnership would have to convert to a subchapter C corporation. REM Investments would then offer $200,000 in cash for all of the outstanding stock in the new corporation. All of the partner's personal liability, especially their personal guarantees for the leases and loans, would be assumed by the new corporation, Chicago Nuclear Diagnostics, Inc., that would be acquired by REM. Dr. Arlington would be offered a short term employment contract and a long term consulting agreement that would become effective at the end of his employment. A medical facility, architectural and engineering firm would be needed to design the facility.

Exiting the limo in front of his driveway, Ralph paid and tipped the driver, then picked up his two bags and entered the house. The air was stale and he opened the patio sliding doors, then his bedroom and office windows. *Tomorrow will be a busy day. I will have to go to the post office and get my mail. Then drive over to the lab and take care of my resignation. I hope Alice followed through and notified all of the utilities that I had to leave the country for an emergency. I guess she did, the electricity and water are still on. Tomorrow I will have to pay bills. That's another problem. I am going to have to get a secretary – at least a part time one. Perhaps I should open an office.* After unpacking, Ralph decided to go for a run, and then drive into Livermore for dinner. There was no food in the refrigerator.

The next morning Ralph rose early, made coffee and planned the day's activities. First would be a trip to the post office and the grocery store. Then he must pay the important bills. He spent the afternoon visiting friends at the Lab. Dr. Jameson wished him well and asked him to keep in touch. Dr. Roberts had heard from Bob Johnson about the potential order for an Mk 37 neutron generator. Ralph had to explain that he was going to do some experiments using neutrons to activate organic samples in a manner similar to the process used to identify explosives. If certain elements associated with specific medical conditions can be identified, then the instrument would be a valuable diagnostic tool. Dr. Roberts wished him well, and Ralph departed for human resources to resign his position.

After leaving the Labs, Ralph drove to the city of Livermore and located the Office Depot store: where he purchased a fax machine, a laser printer, an answering machine that could be accessed remotely, several reams of paper, envelopes, and miscellaneous office supplies. *I never realized how much Alice did until now. I will have to get a secretary.*

Returning home after eating dinner, Ralph installed his new office equipment in his bedroom office. Tomorrow he would call Rossman.

The following morning after his usual jog, Ralph made breakfast, showered and entered his newly set up home office. First he called Professor Bhatti, who had spoken with Dr. Arlington and was excited about acquiring Erie. Ralph gave the professor his phone number and asked him to fax his list of equipment and instruments. Professor Bhatti was sure the planned diagnostic treatment center would be a success and had already contacted colleagues in Chicago. Obtaining qualified staff and referrals was not going to be a problem. It was time to call Rossman.

"Good morning Sam, this is Ralph Eid."

"Good morning Dr. Eid. I was hoping you would call. I have found two locations for you. The best is the one I told you about. It is in the heart of the city. You can lease five thousand square feet or more for $25.00 dollars per square foot, triple net, five-year term with options to renew. The owner will provide basic hookups. You will be responsible for the build-out."

"What did Dr. Arlington think of the location?"

"He thought it was excellent."

"Sam, I am interested in making an offer for Erie. This is what I have in mind. I would like you to run it up the flagpole for me. If it is acceptable, I will have my New York law firm, Swartz, Kaplan and Goldberg prepare a formal offer," Ralph said. He then went into detail regarding his offer.

"I will set up a meeting with all of the partners as quickly as possible. I will let you know as soon as I have an answer. Will you be able to come back to Chicago to meet with them if necessary?" Rossman asked.

"Yes. I will want to inspect the building and secure the space as soon as the offer is accepted. Call me when you have an answer. Also, have the building agent forward a copy of the lease to my attorneys. You have their address."

Ralph then placed a call to his attorneys and discussed his plans to acquire Erie Partnership. The firm would begin preparing the necessary documents for an offer.

After completing the call, it occurred to Ralph that he must have a California office address. The afternoon was young and he decided to drive into Livermore and look for an office. After looking as several available office spaces – some were too large and others were not in good buildings – he was pleased when he located an office building that provided furnished offices with secretarial and office services for businessmen. Selecting the best office available, he established the corporate office for REM Investments, Inc. Next he called the phone company to arrange for a phone line to be connected. The office secretary, Betty, suggested Sir Speedy Printing for business cards and stationary.

Ralph now had an office with a secretary to take messages and type letters and documents. Betty, a tall dyed blond with an average figure, about 32 years old, would perform general secretarial services. She could also transcribe Ralph's dictation from mini cassettes. Ralph could dictate letters and notes, and when traveling mail her the cassettes. Ralph gave Betty a list of names and addresses and requested that she send a notice to each informing them of his new address and phone numbers. His office problems resolved, Ralph stopped at Sir Speedy, then Office Depot to purchase a mini cassette dictating machine and six cassettes. The last task for the day was to obtain a mobile phone. That evening, Ralph composed a letter to cousin Ali describing his accomplishments, and providing his new office address and phone numbers.

Monday morning Rossman called to tell him that he had met with the partners. The offer would be acceptable with the following changes. REM would pay for all legal costs associated with converting to a subchapter C corporation and the cash price had to be $300,000.00. Ralph accepted. He also instructed Rossman to tell the building agent he wanted the space; and he would instruct his law firm to arrange for an option pending the final acquisition of Erie. Next he called his law firm and instructed them: to prepare a formal offer; to finalize the acquisition as quickly as possible; and to arrange for converting Erie Partners to *Chicago Nuclear Diagnostics, Inc.*

It was now time to contact the consulting firm that would design the facility. LRM Associates had been recommended. The firm specialized in designing medical offices and treatment and diagnostic centers. From his briefcase Ralph removed the business card of Kevin A. Patterson, Senior Vice President, LRM Associates, located in Atlanta Georgia. He then placed a call to LRM and asked to speak to Kevin Patterson.

"Mr. Patterson, I am Dr. Ralph Eid, CEO of REM Investments. REM is entering the radiological diagnostic field and plans to establish diagnostic treatment centers in several cities. We are acquiring an existing diagnostic facility in Chicago, and plan to relocate the facility as quickly as possible. I am interested in obtaining a proposal from you for the design of our new facility."

"Dr. Eid, we would be pleased to prepare a proposal for you. Can you provide specific information?"

"Yes, the new location will be in a high rise building on the forty-second floor. The building is being renovated, and the floor is empty. I plan to visit the location in the next few days. Perhaps you can meet me there. In the mean time, I will have Dr. Arlington, the current director of the facility we are acquiring, call you. I will also have our Medical Director, Professor Umair Bhatti, call you and send you a list of the equipment we plan to install."

"I will be happy to meet you in Chicago. Let me know when."

"Is next Monday O.K.? We can meet for dinner that night and visit the facility the next morning," Ralph responded.

"Monday will be fine. Where will you be staying?"

"I will be staying at the Four Seasons. My secretary will fax you a letter with a list of contacts and phone numbers."

"I will call you when I get in. Dr. Eid, thank you for providing us this opportunity. Good-bye."

Yes, Allah is providing the path. This is beginning to be fun. I find that I like being a businessman, Ralph thought.

The following Monday, Ralph flew to Chicago from Oakland International Airport and checked into the Four Seasons late that afternoon. A message was waiting for him from Kevin Patterson saying that he would arrive around 10 PM; and suggesting that they meet for breakfast in the hotel.

Sam Rossman met Ralph at the airport and took him to see the new site. The building was located one block east of Michigan Avenue. Looking out a window toward the lake, Ralph could see high-rise buildings making a wall from north to south. Changing his view to a window facing south, he could see the top of the Sears tower. The location was ideal. The blast would reflect off the high-rise buildings and boost the shock wave traveling west. The heart of Chicago would cease to exist in a mater of seconds. After carefully inspecting the floor, Ralph had elected to lease half of the floor on the side facing east toward the lake – to the great pleasure of Rossman and the building rental agent. Ralph then informed the agent that he would be returning in the morning with a design consultant; and asked Rossman to drop him at the Four Seasons. On the way to the hotel, Rossman told him the partners had accepted the offer. A date for closing would be set in a couple of weeks: as soon as Erie Partners was converted to Chicago Nuclear Diagnostics, Inc.

The next morning Ralph called Patterson's room and arranged to meet him in the hotel restaurant at 9 A.M. Ralph entered the restaurant at 8:45

and ordered a glass of orange juice and coffee. Kevin Patterson walked up to the hostess a couple of minutes before 9 A.M. and informed her that he was to meet a Dr. Eid. Smiling, she led him to Ralph's table. Ralph watch them approach. Patterson was a man of medium height, a little overweight, wearing a gray suit, stripped tie and light blue shirt. He had a full head of light brown hair and appeared to be in his mid forties.

"Good morning Dr. Eid," Patterson said, "I am Kevin Patterson."

"Good morning Mr. Patterson. Thank you for meeting me. I hope you had a pleasant flight."

"I missed a connection in La Guardia and had to be 'wait listed' on the next flight. Managed to get the last seat, middle row coach. I am just happy to be here. Sorry I was not able to get here in time to take you to dinner."

"No problem. Would you like a cup of coffee or juice?"

Speaking to the hostess, Patterson said, "I will have a glass of orange juice and coffee, thank you."

"Your firm was recommended to me. Can you provide me with some information about LRM Associates?" Ralph asked.

"Certainly, the firm is five years old, formed by Doctors Lamar, Ramas, and Medcalf, all PhD's. Doctors Ramas and Medcalf are architects, and Dr. Lamar is a structural engineer. The firm has three vice presidents, 10 senior associates, 17 associates and me. We have designed three hospitals, two medical facilities and over 20 specialized diagnostic facilities similar to the one you described. We currently have nine major projects underway. I am a mechanical engineer and also have my Ph.D. from Georgia Tech. Are you a medical doctor?"

"No, like you, I have a Ph.D. – in physics. Professor Bhatti and Dr. Arlington are medical doctors," Ralph replied.

Ralph signaled to the waitress. "Let us order breakfast."

Ralph ordered a cheese omelet, and Patterson Eggs Benedict. Over breakfast they continued the discussion regarding LRM. After breakfast, they took a taxi to the building, and then an elevator to the forty-second floor. Ralph showed Patterson the half of the floor that he planned to lease.

"The total area will be 18,000 square feet. You have a list of the instruments and equipment that we plan to install. I assume that you are familiar with all of them," Ralph said.

"Yes, you have enough space so that we can design a first class center. I will obtain building plans from the manager. We should be able to provide you with a preliminary design and proposal within two weeks. It will be best if I can make a presentation. Would you like to have it here or in our office in Atlanta?"

"Let me think about that. I am developing a new type of radiological diagnostic instrument. This is a proprietary project and has nothing to do with the diagnostic center. I would like to install it here, but keep it entirely separate from the main facility. Here is a sketch of the area that I will require. It has the general dimensions for my office, a room that will contain the instrument and a storage room. The instrument and storage rooms will require shielding because radioactive isotopes will be used and stored in this area."

"That will not present a problem. Do you want this area included in the main set of plans, or would you prefer a separate layout?"

"A separate layout. There is no reason for the staff of the diagnostic center to know about this suite. My work is highly confidential – developing a new diagnostic instrument for REM. In fact, let's make it two proposals. The large area will be for Chicago Nuclear Diagnostics, Inc., the new name for Erie; and the small area will be for the parent company, REM Investments, Inc. This will simplify accounting."

"You have told me everything that I require for the proposal. I will need to stay here for a while, and then spend time with the building manager. There is no need for you to stay. I will call you when the proposal is ready and we can decide where to meet," Patterson said.

Ralph took the elevator back to the ground floor, hailed a taxi and returned to the Four Seasons. Before checking out, he placed calls to Dr. Arlington and Professor Bhatti to bring them up to date on the project. He then called his law firm in New York City to review the progress of the acquisition. Next he called the business brokers in Atlanta, Boston, New York, and Washington, D.C. to check on progress. The New York broker had a lead. Ralph requested that financials be faxed to him at the hotel. If the lead looked promising, he would fly to New York the next day to evaluate it. If not he would continue on to California.

After calling his office and speaking to Betty, Ralph decided to take some personal time and visit the Field Museum of Natural History, where he encountered a mob of unruly school children. *Allah give me patience,* Ralph thought as he watched the teachers attempting to maintain some degree of order. Avoiding the children, he completed his tour of the museum and returned to his hotel. Financial statements and a description of the New York business were waiting for him at the front desk. A hospital wanted to spin off its radiological diagnostic facility, which was located in the upper Bronx area. After consulting a map, Ralph decided, that the location was not suitable. Calling the New York business broker, Ralph told him that he wanted a location in Manhattan, preferably below Central Park. With no concrete leads for a New York center forthcoming, Ralph decided to return to California the next day.

At REM's new Livermore office, Ralph collected his messages from Betty; then proceeded to his office. A copy of the General Neutron proposal was on his desk, along with the usual mail to a new office. Ralph spent the next hour reviewing the proposal and drawings. The Mk 38, the new designation for the three tube generator, could be shipped 40 days after receipt of order. The dummy unit would be available in two weeks. Payment terms were acceptable. He noted a few minor changes and included them in a letter to Omar Mumtaz. He instructed Betty to fax the letter to Mumtaz and also to fax a copy to Bob Johnson. The telephone intercom buzzed and Betty told him that Mark Swartz, of Swartz, Kaplan and Goldberg, was holding. Mark Swartz was the son of the general partner of his New York law firm, and the attorney handling the Erie acquisition. Pushing the button on the blinking line, Ralph answered, "Hello Mark."

"Good afternoon Ralph, or should I say good morning? It is still morning in California, isn't it?"

"Yes, it is still morning here. What's up?"

"Your guys in Chicago must really be in a hurry. They want to close in two weeks. How about Monday after next?"

"Good, do you have all the closing documents prepared, and Dr. Arlington's agreements?"

"Yes, do you want to close here or in Chicago?"

"Let's close in Chicago. Can you be there on Monday?"

"Yes, we can use our associate firm's office. They handled Erie's conversion to a C Corp. I already called them and they are available for a 3 P.M. closing."

"O.K., good work, let's do it on Monday at 3 P.M. Fax me the address and phone number of the law firm. I will meet you there. Bring a cashier's check, you have authority to draw down funds from one of REM's bank accounts. I assume that you will fly in that morning."

"Yes, I can get a flight from La Guardia to Midway. See you there," Mark said ending the call. Ralph buzzed Betty and asked her to book a flight to Chicago for Sunday afternoon with an open return, and to reserve a room at the Four Seasons. Office work completed, Ralph left for home where he would draft a letter to cousin Ali.

Friday morning Ralph received a call from Kevin Patterson telling him that the proposal was ready. Ralph decided to fly to Atlanta the following Wednesday. *After the meeting in Atlanta, I can take a copy of the proposal and fly to Boston to meet Professor Bhatti. I need to fill him in on the Erie acquisition.* Ralph placed a call to the professor and confirmed a meeting for next Friday. That decided, Ralph called the travel agent.

Late that night Ralph received a call from Omar Mumtaz in Karachi. Ralph approved the General Neutron order and instructed Omar to call him and Dr. al-Mihdar when the dummy unit arrived. That would trigger the shipment of the gun assembly to Indus Instruments. Ralph would travel to Pakistan as soon as the gun assembly reached Karachi. *Things are moving very quickly. I expect that Mohammed will meet me in Karachi. He will probably accompany the shipment from Kabul. If he does, the three of us can assemble the instrument. That will minimize the number of people who have knowledge of the plan.*

Thursday morning Ralph entered the lobby of a high rise building in the Peach Tree Center. The building directory showed LRM Associates' building address to be suite 920. Taking the elevator to the ninth floor, Ralph quickly located suite 920. Entering, Ralph presented his new business card to the receptionist and told her he had an appointment with Kevin Patterson. She informed him that he was expected and escorted him to a large conference room. "I will tell Kevin you are here. Would you like a cup of coffee?" she asked.

"Yes, thank you, cream and sugar."

A few minutes later Kevin Patterson entered the conference room. "Good morning Dr. Eid, I see you have coffee."

"Good morning Dr. Patterson," Ralph replied. "Please call me Ralph. Doctor is too formal."

"O.K. Ralph, I am Kevin. Two of our associates will be joining us. The one thing we are missing are the specifications for your research instrument," Kevin replied.

"Yes, I did not have the complete specifications when we met. Here they are," Ralph said removing an envelope from his briefcase. "This should provide everything you require."

The two associates entered and the presentation began. A detailed layout of the diagnostic center had been prepared. Two hours were spent reviewing the layout in detail. Finally, Ralph said, "This layout appears to meet our requirements. I will be meeting with Professor Bhatti on Friday, and I will provide him a copy of your proposal and layout. He will contact you directly if he has any changes. I am giving you the authorization to proceed. Our initial payment of $25,000.00 will be sent to you by my attorney. Do you have the plans for the REM office area?"

"Yes, it is a simple three room suite consisting of an office, a storage room and a room for the test instrument," Patterson said, opening a layout drawing and placing it on the table. "I checked with the building manager and an additional 450 square feet are available and have been reserved for you."

Ralph studied the drawing, then said, "There appears to be sufficient space to set my instrument here," he said pointing to spot on the drawing. "I see that the instrument and storage rooms are shielded according to my instructions. The double doors leading to the instrument must be steel and have two separate dead bolt locks with different keys. I do not want some unauthorized person trying to turn the instrument on. They could damage the instrument and injure themselves. You may proceed with both designs. Invoice the Chicago Center to my attorney, Mark Swartz. Here is his card. Please prepare a separate invoice for the small office and bill it to REM at this address," Ralph said, handing Patterson his business card. "Please send me four sets of the final drawings for the center and six for the office. If you don't mind, ask the building agent to forward a separate lease in REM's name for the small office space to my address in California."

Following the meeting, Kevin Patterson invited Ralph to lunch. While sitting at the restaurant table enjoying desert and coffee, Ralph mentioned that he planned to open other diagnostic centers and was looking for a similar location in Atlanta. Patterson, realizing that REM represented a source of continuing fees, offered to assist in finding locations.

"Are you interested in starting a diagnostic facility if you cannot find an acquisition?" Patterson asked.

"Yes, but acquiring an existing business is easier. Do you have any suggestions?"

"I do not know of any diagnostic facilities that are for sale, but I do know of a building that is being renovated near here. We are doing a design for a group of doctors with offices in it. If you are interested, I can show it to you."

"I would like that. Can we go there now?" Ralph asked.

"Yes, we can get a taxi across the street. After that we will return to the office to get your suitcase and the drawings. I will drive you to the airport."

The building was located in the downtown area. Ralph was pleased when Patterson pointed out the Federal Reserve Bank and said, "This is the heart of the financial district. Atlanta is a major financial center, one day it may replace New York."

Not quite, but is certainly is important. It might be if New York disappeared, and we would not want that, Ralph thought. The building turned out to be thirty stories high. Renovation of the first twenty-five floors had been completed, and work was progressing on the next five floors. After a tour of the building, Patterson took Ralph to the building manager's office where they consulted the building's plans. The twenty-ninth floor was available. Having already inspected the twenty-ninth floor, Ralph said, "I like this location, but I do not as yet have a business to install in it; however I am interested in obtaining an option for six months."

"I am sure that can be arranged. I know that they are having a hard time leasing the last two floors. You should be able to obtain a low rate if you commit to a long term lease," Patterson said.

A meeting with the building's leasing agent proved Patterson to be correct. Ralph obtained a six-month option for 17,000 square feet at $22.00 per square foot, with a 10-year term for a fee of $3.000.00. The lease and option would be sent to his attorneys. On the way to the airport, Patterson mentioned that two of the radiologists at one of the major hospitals had been considering opening a radiological diagnostic center, but were having trouble with financing. Ralph asked Patterson to feel them out. "I can form a company, Atlanta Nuclear Diagnostics, Inc. and they could manage it and be stockholders in the new company. If they are interested, show them the Chicago layout. If they think they can start up a similar facility here, have them call Professor Bhatti," Ralph said as they entered Hartsfield International Airport.

Friday morning Professor Bhatti picked up Ralph at the Hyatt Regency Hotel. The professor was a partially bald Pakistani, with a neatly trimmed beard, gold-rimed trifocal glasses, and the beginnings of a potbelly. He was approximately five feet nine inches in height and appeared to weigh about 165 pounds. He was driving a gray Volvo sedan. A naturalized citizen, Professor Bhatti was an associate professor of radiology at Harvard School of Medicine. Entering the professor's office, Ralph found himself in somewhat familiar surroundings.

"It has been several years since I was on the Harvard campus. I received my Masters in Business Administration here, but I have never been in this building before," Ralph said to the professor.

"Yes, I was told you had received a degree here. I understand that you have a doctorate in physics too," the professor replied.

"Actually nuclear physics. I was employed at Livermore Labs, operated by the University of California. My uncle passed away and left me a rather large inheritance. So I decided to join several other Saudi investors and start REM Investments. Our objective is to establish medical diagnostic facilities in five major cities. My degree and work experience has pointed me toward nuclear diagnostics. My associates recommended you as our Chief Medical Officer, and I apologize for not coming here to meet you sooner."

"I understand that you have been very busy. My Saudi friends told me that you were the right person to head the new company – energetic, with the right background and education. Your accomplishments to date certainly bear that out. I am pleased to be on your team."

"Thank you. I have brought you a copy of LRM's proposal for the Chicago facility. Dr. Patterson, with whom you have spoken, showed me a similar location in Atlanta. Unfortunately I have not found an existing center to acquire there. However, Patterson may know a group of doctors, who would like to start a nuclear diagnostic facility on a partnership basis. I am considering forming a separate company, Atlanta Nuclear Diagnostics, Inc., with REM being the major stockholder. Patterson is going to see if they are interested in joining us as stockholders in the Atlanta center. If they are they will contact you. Now, let's review the plans for the new Chicago facility."

"What is the status of the acquisition?"

"We will close Monday afternoon in Chicago. The name of the corporation has been changed to Chicago Nuclear Diagnostics, Inc., and will be a wholly owned subsidiary of REM. Dr. Arlington will stay as director for six months, then he will be a consultant."

"Excellent. I have a colleague in Chicago who will be a suitable director for the facility. He is one of our brothers, and a recognized expert in the field. His reputation will guarantee referrals. Do you wish to interview him?" the professor asked.

"No, medicine and medical staff is your responsibility. Take whatever actions you deem appropriate. I will meet him at the opening of the new facility."

The rest of the morning was spent reviewing the plans prepared by LRM. Several minor changes were made and a call placed to Patterson to review the requested changes. Professor Bhatti then drove Ralph back to his hotel; where he called Betty for messages and told her his schedule. He would spend the weekend in Boston, fly to Chicago Sunday evening and return to Oakland on Wednesday afternoon. Betty adjusted his itinerary and booked him a room at the Chicago Four Seasons. Ralph's second call was to Kevin Patterson to request that a small office and instrument room be added to the Atlanta Center plans.

Next Ralph called a few old friends one of whom was also a former girlfriend. Nancy would meet him for dinner, and they would drive up to Kennebunkport Saturday. She had been such fun when they were last together. *I wonder why I let the relationship slide. My parents' deaths had a lot to do with it. I flipped out I guess and lost interest in everything and everybody. She really was beautiful, and we clearly were good with each other,* he thought as he remembered Nancy's wonderful sense of humor. *She is so bright and could always appeal to the better side of my nature. I need that right now, because I find myself tending to be moody – I am taking everything a little too seriously. Then too, I'd like someone to talk to about REM, who will not ask a lot of dumb questions.* One of the things Ralph truly liked about Nancy was that she was always a very good listener.

Plans for the weekend taken care of, Ralph decided to take a nap before getting ready for dinner. As the time approached for their dinner meeting, he found himself really looking forward to seeing Nancy again. He knew they would have a great time on Saturday. They both loved to stop at one of the lobster trap restaurants along the way; where you could pick out your lobster and sit at an outdoor table while it was being cooked.

Monday morning Ralph visited the new home of Chicago Nuclear Diagnostics, Inc. Taking the elevator to the forty-second floor, he carefully paced off the walls according to the LRM drawing. Satisfied, he took the elevator to the second floor and entered the building manager's office. He informed the agent he expected to close the acquisition that afternoon, and he told him the lease would be executed by the end of the week. Then he requested referrals for contractors to begin work on the new center. After discussing the potential contractors, Ralph asked the agent to schedule appointments for the next day with the two contractors he had selected – one in the morning and the other in the afternoon. Returning to his hotel, Ralph prepared for the afternoon closing.

The closing occurred on schedule. Ralph introduced Mark Swartz to Dr. Steve Arlington. Mark Swartz was a handsome young man of 35, who was six feet tall and weighed 185 pounds – an athlete who worked out regularly. Dr. Arlington's partners, now stockholders, were happy to sell their stock to REM for cash. After the closing, Ralph showed Steve and Mark the plans for the new facility, and said, "I plan to meet with contractors tomorrow to review the drawings and request bids. Mark will finalize the lease and the build-out contract when I have selected the contractor. I want to have the facility ready to start installing equipment as soon as possible."

"Yes, we should be completely moved in before the current lease expires," Dr. Arlington replied.

"Professor Bhatti is in charge of selecting the equipment and medical staff. He told me you are being very helpful. I am depending on the two of you to take care of that end of the business. Keep me informed as to the equipment to be purchased or leased and its delivery schedule. All leases must be reviewed by Mark before they are signed. Thank you for your help and cooperation. Mark, thank you for coming," Ralph said ending the meeting.

That evening Ralph dined alone. Pleased with the days events, his thoughts turned to Nancy and the pleasant weekend they had shared. Nancy had matured, but otherwise looked the same, a beautiful five foot six inch, blue-eyed blond with a to-die-for figure. Ralph had not seen or spoken with Nancy since he had left Boston. Both had been career oriented and had no time for a lasting romance. The two had picked up where they had left off as though no time had passed since their last meeting; although Nancy *had* expressed surprise at Ralph's knowledge of wines.

The next day Ralph met with the two contractors, reviewed the plans and the requirement to install equipment before the final build-out was completed. LRM had designed the facility with large doors so that large diagnostic equipment could be installed and removed. The REM office would be completed once the research instrument was installed. Ralph caught a late afternoon flight to San Francisco International Airport and used the limo service to get home. Bids from the contractors were due Friday.

The next morning Ralph composed a letter to cousin Ali bringing him up to date on his progress. Ralph mailed the letter at the post office on the way to the REM office in Livermore.

"Good morning Betty. Do I have any messages?" Ralph asked.

"Good morning traveler," Betty said smiling. "Here are your messages."

"Thank you," Ralph replied walking over to the reception room coffee pot and pouring a cup.

Sitting at his desk, Ralph reviewed his messages. The most promising one was from Kevin Patterson, "Two physicians are interested in opening a radiological diagnostic center in Atlanta with REM. Call for details." Another message was from Bob Johnson stating that the dummy Mk 38 would be shipped in seven days. That message was two days old. Picking up the telephone, Ralph placed a call to Patterson.

"Good morning Kevin, I received your message."

"Good morning Ralph, yes, I have two eager beavers who want to meet you. When they saw the plans for Chicago they were ready to sign on."

"Excellent, have each of them fax a copy of their *curriculum vitae* to Professor Bhatti. If the good professor likes them, I think we can proceed with the Atlanta facility. Tell them to expect a call from Professor Bhatti."

"Did you close on Erie?"

"Yes, Monday afternoon. I met with contractors Tuesday and expect bids Friday. I asked both of the bidders to send you a copy of their bids."

"Thanks, I will let you know what I think after I review them. Anything else?"

"No, I will talk with you on Monday or Tuesday," Ralph said ending the conversation.

Friday morning Ralph called Professor Bhatti, who was pleased with the two Atlanta doctors. After reviewing their *curriculum vitaes* or CVs, Bhatti had spoken with each of them and checked their references. The Professor recommended that REM proceed with the two doctors and the Atlanta facility. In addition he said more favorable lease terms would be available if a second facility leased the same or similar equipment. The businessman in Ralph appreciated the savings. *I can probably obtain even better rates when we add another center,* he thought.

Next, Ralph called Bob Johnson to check on the Mk 38 and learned that the dummy unit had been sent to shipping that morning. The complete Mk 38 would be ready for shipment to the Indus Instruments' facility in New Jersey in thirty days. Ralph decided that his priorities were: first, starting the Chicago build-out; second, forming Atlanta Nuclear Diagnostics, Inc.; and third, traveling to Karachi to complete the first Neutron Induced Gamma Spectrometer for shipment to New Jersey.

Placing a call to Mark Swartz, Ralph provided the necessary information required to start the incorporation of Atlanta Nuclear Diagnostics, Inc. and explained that two physicians would be minority stockholders. The physicians' names would be provided as soon as Ralph had interviewed them and completed the arrangements.

Ralph then dictated a letter that would be faxed to Omar Mumtaz informing him that the dummy Mk 38 was being shipped today. He also requested that Omar inform the REM Saudi director of the shipment; and arrange a time for both of them to see the completed instrument. *That should tell Omar to alert Mohammed to send the gun assembly to Karachi and set the date for assembly of the Neutron Induced Gamma Spectrometer. I will schedule a week's trip to Karachi as soon as I receive a date from Omar.*

Both of the Chicago contractors called and requested an extension for their bids until Monday; so that they could send them Friday afternoon. Ralph approved both requests and then placed a call to Dr. James Clark, one of the two Atlanta Physicians. Dr. Clark was not available, so Ralph left a message for Clark to return his call to Ralph's home over the weekend.

Saturday afternoon, just as Ralph was completing his chores, the phone rang. It was Dr. Clark.

"Hello," Ralph answered.

"Dr. Eid? My name is Dr. Clark. I received your message requesting that I call you."

"Thank you for calling. I understand that you and Dr. Hornell are interested in our plans to establish a nuclear diagnostic center in Atlanta."

"Yes, Kevin Patterson told us of your desire to start an Atlanta Center and showed us your plans for Chicago. He also told us about the downtown building that you have an option on. We sent our CV's to Professor Bhatti and have had several discussions with him. We are both impressed with your plans and would very much like to become part of the Atlanta Center."

Ralph could hear the enthusiasm in Clark's voice. "I am glad that you both are interested. You understand that the center will require your full time participation."

"Yes, but we still wish to remain on the staff with privileges at Baptist Hospital. Tom and I have discussed the opportunity with our boss and he is supportive. He sees your diagnostic center as an asset to Atlanta and the hospital."

"Very well, I am in the process of forming Atlanta Nuclear Diagnostics, Inc. I am offering each of you the following: a base salary of $75,000; ten percent of the stock; a bonus of fifteen percent of the profits; and an automobile. The stock will be issued when Atlanta Nuclear Diagnostics is incorporated. The rest of the package will become effective one month before the center opens. Between now and then, I will expect you to help plan the layout; supervise installation of equipment; and assist in selecting and hiring staff. You and Dr. Hornell can remain in your current positions during this period. As soon as you accept this offer, I will have my attorney, Mark Swartz, contact you for details. I will probably have to leave the country on business in the near future, so please provide an answer as quickly as possible," Ralph said.

"Thank you. I will discuss it with Tom this afternoon and call you back either this evening or tomorrow, if that is O.K. with you," Dr. Clark enthusiastically replied.

"That will be fine. If I am out, leave a message on my answering machine. I am looking forward to you joining the team and will meet both of you on my next trip to Atlanta," Ralph said ending the conversation.

Pleased with the possibilities that were developing for the Atlanta project, Ralph decided to go Oakland to attend evening prayers – even though his heart was not in it. Afterward he would have dinner at Fisherman's Warf; then hit a few singles bars for desert. Early the next morning on his way home, he thought with disgust about the secretary he had picked up. *She drank too much and was terrible in bed. I doubt that she will remember me in the morning . . . no contest when compared to Nancy.*

Monday morning UPS and FedEx delivered the bid packages from the Chicago contractors. Ralph spent the remainder of the morning reviewing them. Rogers Construction, Inc. had a higher bid than G&K Remodeling, Inc., but proposed to complete the job in a shorter period of time. A few minutes later, Betty buzzed to tell him that Kevin Patterson was on the line. Punching the blinking light on his phone, Ralph said, "Hello Kevin. I was just about to call you. I assume you have the bids."

"Yes, we start three hours earlier than you. I have spoken with both contractors. G&K has the lower bid, but I think Rogers' is the best choice. John Rogers showed more interest in the job, and he has the best schedule."

"Thanks Kevin, I appreciate you assistance. I was leaning toward Rogers' before your call, because of the schedule. Do you think that he can complete the job by November fifteenth?"

"I questioned him about the schedule and he is positive he can."

"Excellent, I will fax him an award letter. I am going to be out of the country for a while, so please keep an eye on the job. I trust you to make any necessary decisions while I am away. Doctors Clark and Hornell have accepted my offer, so Atlanta Nuclear Diagnostics is a go. Please prepare a cost proposal and get started on the design. I want to open the facility as quickly as possible. Mark Swartz will handle your contract and payments."

"Thank you, I will monitor Rogers' progress and start designing the Atlanta Facility using the same concept as Chicago."

"I will let you know when I am leaving the country. By the way, I am looking for a similar site in New York. I would like it to be in lower Manhattan. Thanks for your help," Ralph said ending the call.

Picking up his mini-cassette recorder, Ralph dictated letters to Rogers Construction awarding the contract, and instructing them to invoice Mark Swartz and coordinate with Kevin Patterson. A second letter to Rogers awarded another contract for a small office for REM Investments, Inc. In addition the letter instructed Rogers to complete the outer and internal walls containing shielding by October fifteenth; to provide a temporary access for an instrument 42 inches wide; and to invoice the REM California office. Additional dictation included a rejection letter to G&K Remodeling; letters to Drs. Clark and Hornell welcoming them to the team; and finally a detailed letter to Mark Swartz covering all of the details regarding Chicago and Atlanta. According to the Rogers Construction's schedule, the Neutron Induced Gamma Spectrometer could be installed by the end of October.

That evening Ralph prepared a letter to cousin Ali.

Wednesday morning Ralph found a fax waiting for him from Omar Mumtaz informing him that UPS had delivered the parts for the spectrometer and that notification had been made to the Saudi director. While he was reading Mumtaz's fax, he received an additional fax from Mumtaz suggesting a meeting to approve the spectrometer Sunday after next. Ralph sent a reply informing Mumtaz that he would arrive in Karachi on Saturday and planned to visit the Indus Instruments' New Jersey facility on the way. Next Ralph made travel arrangements that included a stop in Chicago to meet with Rogers Construction; and then a flight to Newark, New Jersey for the visit to the Indus facility. From Newark he would use the helicopter service to Kennedy for his flight to Karachi.

That evening Ralph drafted a letter including his travel schedule to cousin Ali. He had a week to finalize the agreements on the Atlanta Center and coordinate the Chicago project before his trip.

Mohammed al-Mihdar was very pleased when he read the fax from Omar Mumtaz. He immediately sent instructions to Abdul to ship the large item to the Kabul address using one of the Russian trucks. Then Mohammed sent a message to his agent in Kabul to expect a delivery of oranges; a prearranged code that alerted the agent to expect Mohammed; and to have drivers and guards available to drive the truck to Karachi. Next he sent a message to Usama bin Laden informing him that he had selected a ring for his mother's birthday, a prearranged code indicating shipment of the gun assembly. After sending both messages, Mohammed arranged for a flight to Kabul as Ali al-Libi. From there he planned to travel with the truck to Karachi.

Wednesday afternoon of the following week, Ralph flew to Chicago for a Thursday morning meeting with John Rogers to finalize the build-out schedule. Satisfied with Rogers' ability to complete the jobs on time, Ralph continued on to Newark where he would meet Abu al-Aziz, the manager of the New Jersey Indus Instruments facility.

The phone in Ralph's Newark hotel room rang at 8 A.M. the next morning. It was al-Aziz, who was in the lobby. Picking up his suitcases, Ralph took the elevator to the lobby and saw a large bald man with a neatly trimmed beard standing near the reception counter. "Mr. al-Aziz?" Ralph asked.

"Yes, it is a pleasure to meet you Dr. Eid," al-Aziz said. Abu al-Aziz was six feet two inches, and weighed about two hundred and twenty pounds. He was dressed in tan slacks, a blue blazer, white shirt and a paisley tie. "Have you had breakfast?

"Yes, thank you. I have checked out and I am ready to go. How far is your facility from here?"

"About twenty minutes," al-Aziz said, picking up one of Ralph's suitcases. "I understand you are going to our Karachi facility tomorrow."

"No, on Sunday. I am going to help assemble the first Neutron Induced Gamma Spectrometer. After it is assembled it will be shipped to your facility; and I will return to install the final component, which will be sent to you by a company called General Neutron. A dummy component will be installed in Karachi, because the real component is too fragile to be shipped by sea," Ralph said as they exited the hotel parking lot. "Karachi will be shipping several additional containers for me as part of regular shipments. When they arrive please notify me immediately so that I can pick them up. They are very important to my business."

The remainder of the morning was spent touring the Indus facility. Ralph learned that Indus had started exporting surgical instruments to America, and would soon add dental X-ray equipment. Additional items were in the pipeline. Al-Aziz had hired two sales representatives, who were starting to produce orders. Soon Indus Instruments would become a successful business: one that would attract no unwanted attention. It was time for Ralph to return to Newark Airport and catch a helicopter shuttle to Kennedy where he would board a flight to Karachi.

Saturday morning Ralph checked in at the Pearl Continental Hotel, in Karachi, Pakistan. A message saying that Mohammed would call Ralph's room at 5 P.M. was waiting for him. After unpacking, Ralph went to the swimming pool for some much-needed exercise, then had brunch, and finally retired for a nap. Ralph woke at 3 P.M. and dressed for a casual dinner with Mohammed. He met Mohammed in the lobby, and they took a taxi to a small private restaurant where they could catch up on each other's activities. Mohammed related his adventures while riding in one of the Russian trucks from Kabul to Karachi. Ralph provided Mohammed a detailed account of his accomplishments.

"Praise be to Allah. You have done very well. Even better than we could have hoped for," Mohammed said. "Usama will be very pleased."

"Thank you. My accomplishments can all be credited to Allah's guidance."

"Will you be able to ship the first spectrometer to Chicago as soon as you have completed the final assembly in Newark?" Mohammed asked.

"The timing will depend upon when the instrument arrives at the Newark Indus facility. If not immediately, then within a week at the most. I am considering installing three of the rings in the instrument. If the radiation is contained as I expect it will be, then the fourth ring can be installed."

"Where do you plan to store the complete rounds with the projectiles?" asked Mohammed.

"The rounds are a problem. Storing them in one location presents an unacceptable risk. They could be stored next to the gun assembly in a storage room, but that also poses an unacceptable risk. It would take a nuclear weapons expert to recognize that the spectrometer is a gun assembly for a nuclear device; but almost any American would recognize the complete round for what it is – a live artillery round."

"What options have you considered?"

"At first I thought of acquiring or starting a low level nuclear waste storage area. Storage areas require special permits from the state and the Nuclear Regulatory Agency, which means inspectors and records. The risk of discovery is too high, so I dropped that idea. Another idea was to acquire a ranch or farm in a remote area where the rounds could be hidden. The last alternative is viable, however I do not want to put all our eggs in one basket. A short-term solution is to rent storage rooms in different locations. The major risk would be the storage facility going out of business and the round being discovered."

"Allah be praised. Your reasoning is sound. The storage rooms may be the best short-term solution, if you can locate storage facilities owned by a national company. That way the round is located close to the gun, which is a big advantage," Mohammed said after giving the matter some serious thought.

"I would like the crates containing each of the rounds to be shielded with lead: then placed into a larger crate with markings indicating some type of instrument or equipment. The lead will prevent the projectile from triggering a Customs or Department of Transportation (DOT) radiation detector. The rings are already shielded. As far as I know, there are no neutron detectors in use by either Customs or DOT."

"That is a good idea. I will make the necessary arrangements," Mohammed said.

After leaving the small restaurant, the two men took a taxi to the hotel. "Let us meet for breakfast at 7 AM," Mohammed said as they parted.

The next morning Omar Mumtaz met them in a small café near the Indus' facility. Both were dressed in a work shirts, blue jeans, and boots. "Allah be praised. The crate has been placed in a separate locked room," Mumtaz told them. No one will be allowed to enter the room without permission. I assume that the three of us will assemble the instrument."

"Allah bless you Omar. That is correct. We will go directly to the facility from here. Is there a private way to enter so that we will not be seen?" Mohammed asked.

"You can enter through a rear service door. I will send the two employees in that area out on an errand, so that you will not be seen."

"Good, it is time to go," Mohammed said, getting up from the table.

In the small assembly room the three men put on coveralls, and began the task of opening the crate. Once the crate was disassembled, they used a power drill to drill three holes in the target assembly container. Dummy neutron tubes would be installed through the holes. A large pan placed under the target assembly container caught the metal shavings and oil used to cool the drill bit. All three men wore a respirator during the drilling operation. Each of them took turns operating the drill. Three different size drill bits were used to drill each hole. It was hard work. The bottom hole was the most difficult to drill because the cutting oil and metal shavings ran down the drill onto the operator's hands. By the time the third hole was drilled, it was noon. Collected oil and metal shavings were placed into a drum for disposal. Mumtaz commented that the drill would have to be disassembled for proper cleaning. Ralph replied by saying, "The drill has served its purpose, place it in the drum; and then put all of the contaminated rags, our coveralls, and other cleanup materials on top of it. It will be best if there is no residue nor contaminated tools left here when we have completed our task."

"I agree. Now let us take a break for lunch," Mohammed said.

After a late lunch the three resumed the arduous task of assembling the materials and panels needed to create REM's first Neutron Induced Gamma Spectrometer. They began by tack welding the three metal mounting tubes for the Mk 38 Neutron Generator tubes to the steel outer shell of the target assembly container. Then they installed the three dummy Mk 38 tubes: taking care to ensure the tubes did not extend past the depleted uranium liner; where they could be damaged when the uranium-235 target rings were installed. Routing conduit was installed from the neutron tubes to the future location of the power supply; so that the neutron tube's connector wires could be pulled through when they were installed. Ralph decided to install pull cords in each conduit to avoid having to fish the connector wires through when the real tubes with cables were installed.

Before proceeding it was necessary to remove the heavy gun assembly from the wooden crate bottom it was sitting on. They accomplished this by attaching the device to an overhead crane and lifting it several centimeters. To allow for the larger size of the completed spectrometer, the wooden bottom was removed and replaced by a steel base that was wider and slightly longer than the wooden crate bottom. For ease in handling, the new steel base had been fabricated with channels designed to accept the blades of a forklift or pallet jack.

With the gun assembly now firmly positioned and attached to the steel base, they were able to begin the process of building the framework for the instrument's façade and concealing the weapon's barrel with sheets of insulation. To create the façade they constructed an aluminum frame, which they attached to the steel base and gun assembly frame. The completed frame enclosed the entire gun assembly, and measured five feet high from the breech end of the gun to the end of the barrel: there it stepped down to three and a half feet over the target assembly container. With the framework in place, they proceeded to carefully wrap the entire gun assembly in layers of fiberglass insulation. When completed, only the end of the mounting tubes supporting the neutron tubes and conduit were visible.

Attaching the frame had been tiring work. It was early evening when they finished installing the insulation. "Let us quit for the day and cover the frame with a tarp. Tomorrow we will get an early start and use these attachment points on the frame to construct the instrument shell," Mohammed said. With the tarp in place, they secured the room and left to have dinner and a good night's rest.

The next morning they began the final phase of building the instrument façade around the weapon. Using fasteners that could only be removed with a special tool, they installed the back and side panels and the top to the aluminum frame. The back panel had an access cover mounted on the frame to allow entry into the main electrical power junction box.

The top section of the three and a half foot high instrument had a door marked, "Sample Chamber," that was ostensibly to be used to place "samples" in the instrument. In reality, the door was there to allow Ralph to remove the top of the target assembly container and insert the weapon's uranium-235 target rings.

To complete the façade they connected an inner and outer panel to the front of the frame. The inner panel contained switches, connector boxes and the dummy computer for the Mk 38. A recessed area on the outer front panel contained the keyboard and CRT display. The firing cable from the cannon's breech had been secured to the gun assembly frame and terminated in one of the connector boxes: where a cable from the real computer would be connected at a later date.

Installation of the outer front panel – that was fitted with doors to allow operator access to the instrument's controls – completed construction of what appeared to be a large blue-gray rectangular box shaped device with "Indus Instruments, Neutron Induced Gamma

Spectrometer" stenciled on the front in gold letters. Directly below the name was a radiation-warning symbol and caution sign advising that the instrument should only be serviced and operated by trained individuals. Each panel had similar warning labels. The complete instrument measured 36 inches wide, by 100 inches long, by 48 inches high; and weighed over 1,500 pounds.

"It certainly looks like an expensive test instrument," Ralph said with pride.

"Allah be praised. It certainly does," Omar Mumtaz said, *I do not know the real purpose of the device, but I can be proud of my work.*

"By the grace of Allah, we have done it," Mohammed said with reverence. Turning to Mumtaz he said, "I will tell Usama of your valuable assistance. Have the instrument properly crated and shipped by sea in a standard shipping container to your Newark facility. Dr. Eid is to be notified as soon as it arrives. I will have four small aluminum containers delivered to you – one at a time. Each is to be placed in a standard Indus Instrument's box and placed in the middle of a shipment of similar boxes being shipped to Newark. Dr. Eid is to be notified when each of the items is shipped, so that he can be in Newark to receive them. Later there will be a larger crate to be handled in the same manner. May Allah bless you and your family."

Mohammed and Ralph returned to the hotel. The next day, Wednesday, Mohammed flew back to Kabul, so that Ali al-Libi could return to Saudi Arabia. Ralph flew to Kennedy International Airport; where he had dinner with Mark Swartz and spent the night at the Four Seasons. Swartz had much to report. Atlanta Nuclear Diagnostics was being incorporated. Leases for the Chicago and Atlanta buildings were being finalized, and employment contracts for Doctors Clark and Hornell had been sent for their review. Ralph was pleased with the progress.

The next morning, while working out in the hotel's health club, Ralph mentally reviewed his project. It was time, he realized, to deal with the storage facility problem. Storage rooms could not be rented in REM's name. Returning to his room, Ralph called Mark Swartz and asked him to establish fictitious name identities for REM Investments, Inc. in Illinois, Georgia, New Jersey, Maryland and Massachusetts. Each fictitious name was to have a separate Wells Fargo bank account with an initial deposit of $10,000. All were to use the REM, Inc. California address. After a late breakfast, Ralph took a limo to Newark Airport, flew to San Francisco International Airport, and went home in another limo. Friday was spent opening mail, returning phone calls and paying bills.

The following week was devoted to organizational matters. By week's end Ralph had received a Fed-X package from Mark Swartz containing signature cards, five checks for each of the new bank accounts, and copies of the applications made to each of the states requesting fictitious names. Also enclosed were copies of the required announcements that Swartz would be sending to local newspapers. Having completed all of his necessary business at home, Ralph decided to fly to Chicago the following Monday.

In his Sheraton hotel room near O-Hare Airport, Ralph opened the Yellow Pages phone book and searched under storage. He limited his interest to national companies and found two that appeared to meet his requirements: Aunt Lil's Self Storage and Walnut Mini Storage. Both had several locations in the greater Chicago area. After selecting four potential locations, Ralph called each and determined that both had space available.

The next morning, dressed in a short sleeve plaid shirt, blue jeans and Rebooks, Ralph entered his rented van and set out to visit each storage facility location. The third location met his requirements. Walnut Mini Storage had an electronic gate, twenty-four hour guards, and storage rooms inside a locked building. Ralph rented a six-foot by ten-foot room, under the fictitious name "Lake Instruments," and paid in advance for one year. Next he visited several used equipment and office furniture dealers; where he purchased several items that he placed in the rented storage room. The next day he met Rogers at the high rise and reviewed the status of the project. Satisfied that all was progressing as planned, Ralph turned in the van and flew to Newark the following morning.

At the airport Ralph rented an automobile and drove to the area where the Indus Instruments' facility was located. Several industrial parks were located in the area, and Ralph began to drive through them. He was seeking a building with a rollup door that would allow him to park a truck inside. A loading dock would be a plus.

In the fourth industrial park he found what he was looking for. An end bay held a company that was being evicted. The tenant had gone bankrupt, and the landlord was willing to make an attractive lease to a company that paid cash in advance. Ralph made an offer to lease the building for five years and to purchase all of the existing furniture, fixtures, and equipment. He completed the lease under the fictitious name "Hudson Instruments," and showed the old tenant the items they could take. The building did not have a loading dock, but it did have a forklift. Ralph explained to the landlord that the building would be used for storage, and that there would be no full time employees. The building had a good security alarm, which sounded a loud horn, called the alarm company and flashed the outside lights. Ralph now had a base of operations near Indus Instruments, where he could store items and vehicles. *Now I can import and store the remaining Neutron Induced Gamma Spectrometers. In fact, I can install the neutron generators here. No point in letting Abu al-Aziz know any more than is necessary.*

The next day Ralph notified the alarm company that he was the new owner, arranged for a locksmith to change the locks and hired a local cleaning company to clean the building. Business completed, Ralph flew back to California secure in the knowledge that his storage problems were solved. During the flight Ralph thought about the future. *The Hudson Instruments building will be an asset. I can use it for several purposes. Tomorrow I must transfer $100,000 from the reserve account into the Hudson Instruments' account.*

The following Tuesday Ralph flew to Atlanta to sign contracts and to inspect the progress on the new diagnostic center. While he was there he located and rented a storage room, this time at Aunt Lil's under the name, "Marietta Instrument Repairs," and purchased a couple of used items to place in the storage room. He now had established two storage locations for the uranium rings and complete rounds – one in Chicago and another in Atlanta. On Thursday morning Ralph received a call from al-Aziz saying that the spectrometer had been shipped and would arrive in ten days. That evening during his return flight home to California, Ralph reviewed his accomplishments in preparation for a letter to cousin Ali. *Allah be praised. So far so good*, he thought, *but I think it is now time to start looking for additional sites.*

Sitting at his computer, Ralph composed his letter to Mohammed.

Dear Ali,

My business ventures are doing very well. I expect to open the Chicago Center on time. The Atlanta Center is on schedule.

I have also established a storage building in Newark; where instruments can be kept prior to shipment to the diagnostic centers.

My main problem is finding a reliable driver to transport components from Newark to the centers.

Sincerely,

Ralph

Five days later, Ralph received a call from Bob Johnson informing him that the Mk 38 was ready for shipment. Ralph gave verbal approval for shipment to Indus Instruments, Inc., Newark, New Jersey, and scheduled a trip to Newark for the following week.

That weekend Ralph received a letter from cousin Ali congratulating him on his success; and mentioning a deserving Saudi living in America, who worked as a truck driver and was seeking additional part time employment. Ali stated that the man, Abdul Khalifa, lived in East Orange, New Jersey, was reliable, and could be trusted to deliver components. Abdul's phone number was included. Ralph decided to call Abdul. After five rings the phone was answered.

"Hello," a female voice said.

"This is Dr. Eid. I wish to speak with Abdul," Ralph said.

"Just a minute, I will get him."

A short time later a man answered, "Hello, this is Abdul."

"Allah be praised. My name is Dr. Eid. My cousin Ali in Saudi told me that you might be available for part time work as a delivery driver."

"May Allah bless you, Dr. Eid. Yes, I am available for part time delivery work. What would be required of me?" Abdul said.

"Picking up an instrument container, driving it to another city, and placing it in a storage facility. Can you provide such a service?" Ralph asked.

"Yes, but I do not have a vehicle suitable for such a task. Can such deliveries be made on weekends?"

"I will provide the vehicle, and weekend deliveries are acceptable. You will be paid $300 per trip plus all expenses."

"Allah be praised. That is most generous. I will be available whenever you need me."

"Good. I will be in Newark next week. Plan on meeting me at the Newark Airport Marriot after work next Wednesday. Ask for Dr. Eid at the front desk," Ralph said ending the call.

Monday morning Ralph placed a call to Rogers to determine the status of the REM office. Rogers assured him that his instrument could be installed anytime after Friday. A forklift, pallet jacks, and other handling equipment was available in the building. Arrangements for a weekend delivery could be made.

Ralph arrived in Newark the following day and rented a car. During his first visit Ralph had noticed a large Ford dealership on the way to the Indus' facility. He decided to go there and purchase a delivery van. At the dealership, he was directed to the new truck manager. After discussing his requirements, the manager suggested an Aerostar delivery van. A white one was in stock. Ralph purchased it and arranged for a local sign company to place "Hudson Instruments" on it in blue letters. The van would be registered to Hudson Instruments at the Newark address.

"When the van is ready, a gentleman named Abdul Khalifa, will be picking it up," Ralph told the new truck manager, "Mr. Khalifa is our driver. I will bring him by tomorrow evening to introduce him. Thank you for your assistance it has been a pleasure doing business with you," he said as he shook hands with the manager and left the dealership to return to the Marriott.

The next morning Ralph called Tom Braggs at Arthur Anderson. Braggs was acting as REM's accounting manager until a permanent comptroller was needed. Ralph inquired about insurance for the company and company vehicles. Braggs recommended a local insurance agent. Ralph called the agent and discussed insurance for the leased building and new van. Pleased with the agent's answers and attitude, Ralph made arrangements to meet him at the Newark building at 3 P.M. After completing several more calls, Ralph left the motel and drove to the Indus facility.

Abu al-Aziz greeted Ralph at the door. "Good morning Dr. Eid."

"Good morning Abu," Ralph replied.

"Your instrument arrived on Monday. It has been placed in the rear of the warehouse, and a screen has been placed around it according to your instructions. The three packages from General Neutron have been placed next to the large crate. Follow me and I will show them to you," al-Aziz said as he led the way down a corridor leading to the warehouse area.

"Thank you. I will require your workers to uncrate the instrument so that I will have access to the front and rear. Once I have completed the installation of the components, the instrument is to be re-crated and prepared for shipment to Chicago," Ralph said.

"I have made arrangements with a custom freight shipper to pick up the instrument and deliver it to your Chicago address. They will place the instrument in your private office suite and uncrate it."

"Tell them they are to provide me with the delivery date. I will meet them at the building and supervise the installation."

"When do you wish to install the components?" al-Aziz asked.

"Tomorrow. The workings of the instrument are proprietary. I do not want your employees involved. If I require assistance I will call upon you for it. There is a box with special tools inside the crate. Instruct your workers to leave the box next to the instrument. I will be back tomorrow morning to install the components. You have done well Abu, thank you," Ralph said, and left to find a local restaurant for a quiet lunch.

After lunch, Ralph drove to the Hudson Instruments building located in the North Star Industrial Park. Opening the door he found mail on the floor. The building was hot and smelled musty so he turned on the air conditioning. While sorting the mail, Ralph decided that he could use the office when he was in the area. *I had better install a telephone . . . at least one line with an answering service. That will solve one problem, but someone must collect the mail,* he thought. At 3 P.M. the insurance agent arrived and surveyed the building. Ralph instructed him to prepare a policy for the contents and the van, and to send the invoice to his California office. After returning to the Marriott, Ralph called the telephone company and arranged for a telephone line to be connected at the Hudson Instruments office.

At 6:12 P.M. Ralph's phone rang.

"Hello, is this Dr. Eid?"

"Yes, this is Dr. Eid."

"Allah be praised. This is Abdul Khalifa. I am in the lobby."

"I will be down in a few minutes. We will have dinner here."

Exiting the elevator into the lobby area, Ralph saw a short, stocky, clean-shaven Middle Eastern man, who appeared to be in his late thirties. He was neatly dressed in a work shirt, jeans, and engineer's boots. Walking up to him Ralph inquired, "Abdul?"

"Yes, I am pleased to meet you Dr. Eid."

"Come, let us get a table in the restaurant," Ralph said, heading toward the entrance to the restaurant.

Once they were seated Ralph asked Abdul to provide some background about himself. Abdul began to explain that he was in the country with a work permit and had a green card. He was currently working for a local company four days per week as a delivery truck driver. Some times he worked a fifth day. He did other part time work when it was available. The waiter arrived and Ralph and Abdul ordered steaks.

"I have a commercial driver's license and live with two other Saudi men. One of our brothers sent word to me to provide you with assistance," Abdul said, letting Ralph know that he understood the need to be discreet.

Ralph nodded and replied, "My company, Hudson Instruments, has a warehouse in the North Star Industrial Park. I will require you to pick up boxes containing instrument components and deliver them to storage facilities in different cities. The first city will be Chicago. Deliveries can be made on Saturday or Sunday. I expect that you will need to make at least five trips to each city."

"I can leave on Friday and return on Sunday. . . ." Abdul said ending in mid sentence when the waiter arrived with their dinner.

When the waiter left, Ralph continued, "Good. After dinner, we will drive over to the building and I will show you around. On the way we will stop at the Ford dealership. I have purchased a delivery van; and I will want you to pick it up when it is ready and park it in the building. Keys, pass codes, and a map for each of the storage rooms will be in the office area. They are to be returned after each trip."

After dinner, Ralph and Abdul stopped at the Ford dealership and made arrangements for Abdul to take delivery of the van. From there they went to the Hudson Instruments building, and Ralph showed Abdul where the boxes he was to deliver were to be located. In the office area, Ralph pointed out the desk where the information for each storage facility would be kept. "Place the keys and paper work for the van in the same place after each delivery," Ralph said. "Can you stop by the building once a week to collect the mail and forward it to me at this address? Ralph asked, handing Abdul a Hudson Instruments business card with a Livermore, California address that was in reality a postal box at Mail Boxes, *Etc.*

"Yes, I will be happy to do so," Abdul replied.

When they returned to the Marriott, Ralph gave Abdul a key to the building, $500 for expenses, and said, "I will call you when the first delivery is ready. It should be some time in the next month," Ralph said.

The next morning Ralph returned to the Indus Instruments building. He found the spectrometer partially uncrated according to his instructions. Opening the special tools box he used one of the tools to remove the back and front panels. Next he opened the first General Neutron package, and extracted the three sealed neutron tubes. Starting at the rear, Ralph removed the first dummy tube and replaced it with the real one. Then he attached the electrical cable from the real neutron tube to a pull wire in the conduit that had been installed in Karachi; so that the cable could be pulled through from the other side. He repeated the process for the bottom tube. Returning to the front, Ralph opened one of the access doors, and removed and replaced the final dummy neutron tube. Next he carefully pulled through the cables from the first two neutron tubes. Now all three neutron tube cables were ready to be connected to the power supply.

The final item in the first package was the "scintillation tube" that measured gamma radiation. In a real instrument, neutrons would "excite" certain atoms in the sample, "inducing" or causing them to emit gamma rays. The scintillation tube would measure the gamma radiation emitted by the sample. Measured energy of the gamma rays would provide information about the material in the sample chamber. The tube was placed on a bracket near the target assembly container, and its lead cable routed to the dummy computer. When the instrument was completed, the scintillation tube would measure gamma radiation from the target assembly container and normal background radiation, which could be displayed on the screen. After the unranium-235 rings had been installed, actual gamma radiation from the target assembly container could be measured.

Ralph then removed the dummy power supply for the neutron tubes and replaced it with the real power supply. This entailed connecting the three 240 volt wires to the power supply. Next, he threaded the control cable from the power supply up to the computer location.

Connections completed, Ralph opened the second General Neutron package and removed the computer. Six hex head bolts held the mounting bracket of the dummy computer in place. After unscrewing the bolts, he pulled the assembly forward and removed the dummy computer. It was a simple task to remove the mounting screws and the dummy computer from the mounting bracket. Installing the real computer required reversing the processes. Once the computer was attached to the mounting brackets, he connected the computer's power cord, the firing lead for the squibs, and the power supply's control cable to the proper terminals on the computer; then bolted the computer back into place.

The final step was to insert the real CRT tube. Exchanging the dummy tube required removing ten screws, and the bracket securing the tube to the frame. Once free, the tube could be pulled forward. The replacement tube, which had been shipped in the third General Neutron package, was easily set in place; with the ten screws tightened the installation was complete. Ralph then opened the door on top of the instrument labeled "Sample Chamber," and exposed the top of the target ring's assembly container. After removing the nuts holding the top in place and lifting off the top, Ralph carefully inspected the three holes to make sure that none of the neutron tubes protruded into the chamber: where they could be damaged when the heavy uranium-235 rings were installed. Satisfied that the tubes were properly positioned, Ralph replaced the top, secured it with the bolts and closed the access panel.

In preparation for running a diagnostic test, Ralph had connected a 240 volt extension cord to the power cord located on the back of the instrument. From one of the General Neutron packages, he removed the operating manual, and the key to the computer: which he inserted in the key slot on the front control panel and turned to boot the computer. Following instructions in the operating manual, Ralph carefully proceeded through the startup and diagnostic steps. The pre-event triggering circuit – the technical term assigned to the firing circuit – showed a closed circuit. When the round was installed, the shunt would be removed and the diagnostic test would check the squib's bridge wires. The diagnostic program continued testing each of the three sealed neutron tubes to determine if: the filaments were heating; the magnetic field was being generated; and the ion beam was ready to be generated, which would cause the tubes to discharge neutrons. The tubes would not be discharged; because the neutron flux being generated would cause substantial ionizing radiation damage to Ralph's body – and any other person in the general vicinity of the discharge.

When he was satisfied that all was in proper working order, Ralph shut down the computer, disconnected the power, replaced the panels, and returned the special panel removal tools to their box. The Neutron Induced Gamma Spectrometer was ready for shipment. *Oops, the scintillation tube will not be able to measure the gamma radiation produced by the uranium-235 in the target ring container when the gun is fired – the pulse will be too strong,* Ralph thought laughing to himself.

Ralph's final chores were to place the dummy components in the General Neutron packages, so that they could be returned to Karachi; and to repack the special panel removing tool box: which he picked up and carried with him to al-Aziz's office. "I have finished the installation. Please see that all the leftover packaging materials from the three General Neutron shipments are properly disposed of. The instrument is ready to be re-crated for shipment to Chicago. This box containing the special tools *must* be placed with the instrument inside the crate. Please call the freight company and arrange for immediate shipment. I will call you tomorrow for the pickup and delivery dates. Also, I am expecting additional containers from Karachi. Let me know when each arrives. I will tell Omar what a fine job you have done," Ralph said to al-Aziz, and then returned to the Marriott.

The next morning Ralph received a call from al-Aziz, who told him that the instrument would be picked up that afternoon and delivered on the following Tuesday afternoon. "Allah be praised. Excellent Abu. Tell the freight company I will meet them in the building manager's office Tuesday afternoon. Good work. Thank you," Ralph said, ending the call. *Well, I can go back to California, which doesn't make sense . . . or I can call Nancy and see if she is free for the weekend. We certainly had a good time on my last trip to Boston. Yes, we can go to Cape Cod. I can meet with Professor Bhatti on Monday to discuss progress.* Ralph placed a call to Nancy at her office and arranged for her to pick him up at Logan airport. Nancy had friends that owned a cottage at the Cape and they would be able to use it. After making additional calls, Ralph, who was looking forward to an enjoyable weekend, caught a flight from Newark to Boston.

Tuesday afternoon, Ralph met the shipping company's driver at the Chicago office building and showed him where to place the instrument. A forklift was used to unload the crated instrument and place it on metal plate dollies, so that it could be rolled onto the freight elevator. Pallet jacks were used to lift the instrument off the dollies after it was properly positioned in the instrument room. After the instrument was uncrated, Ralph signed the shipping manifest, and the driver departed. Ralph locked the outer door to the suite, entered the large instrument room, and turned the deadbolt locks on the inside of the instrument room's steel doors. After connecting the instrument to the 240-volt electrical outlet, Ralph booted the computer and ran diagnostic tests. All tests were positive. *Praise Allah. As soon as the rings and complete round with the projectile arrived, the first of Allah's instruments of destruction would be ready for use,* Ralph thought. *Now I need to purchase office furniture for the front office.* After shutting down the instrument, Ralph used his keys to lock the two separately keyed "Best" deadbolt locks, mounted in the heavy steel double doors leading to the instrument and storage rooms. As he closed the temporary outer door he used a third key to lock the outer door's deadbolt.

Returning to the building manager's office Ralph called John Rogers and told him to complete the REM office by installing a regular office door. Only the room number was to be placed on the door. *I will purchase office furniture and have it delivered during my next visit,* Ralph thought. It was time to return to California and send a report to the REM Investments, Inc.'s board of directors – Mohammed al-Mihdar.

Mohammed received Ralph's CEO report to the REM Board of Directors the following Tuesday. The CEO recommended that four additional Neutron Induced Gamma Spectrometers be ordered from Indus Instruments. One instrument would be installed in the Atlanta office as soon as the building was ready. The remaining three would be stored in the Hudson Instruments building in Newark, where additional modifications could be made. A delivery van had been acquired, and a driver hired; so that instrument components could be shipped to the various centers as required. Maximum effort was being made to site additional diagnostic centers in Boston, Washington, DC, and New York City. After reading the report, Mohammed forwarded a copy to Usama, who was in Al-Khurtum, Sudan. *This is truly good news. Usama is beginning to attract too much attention. He has been forced to leave Saudi Arabia, because of his criticism of the Royal family. The sooner we move the devices and components to America the better. I must speed up the movements of the green and red device components. Ralph is correct. All of the instrument-guns can be sent one at a time. After he has installed the neutron generators in Newark, the instruments can be dispersed into storage facilities in other areas. So far he has placed one instrument in its final location and should have a second placed in the next three months. That leaves three in storage. No reason why the components cannot be pre-*

positioned in the target cities at several storage sites. I will notify Omar Mumtaz to prepare to convert two more guns into instruments as quickly as possible; and to be prepared to accept delivery of the smaller ring containers that must be repackaged and sent to Newark for REM.

Several hours later in a different time zone, Ralph received a phone call in his Livermore office from Kevin Patterson. After providing a project status report for Chicago and Atlanta, Patterson said, "While we were working on a project to expand a major New York City hospital, I learned two things that should interest you. First, one of the radiologists at the hospital told me about a radiological diagnostic center on Long Island, whose owners want to reorganize and move into the city. The partners are not getting along. Three of them want to dissolve the partnership and move. Sounds like Erie doesn't it? The second bit of good news came from one of the building's architects. He is involved in renovating a high rise building in downtown Manhattan. The building is looking for medical tenants. Thought you might be interested."

"You bet I am. Thanks Kevin. How do I get in touch with them?"

"I will fax you the contact information in a few minutes."

"Thanks, I plan to visit Atlanta soon and will let you know my schedule. Plan on having dinner with me," Ralph said ending the conversation. *Praise be to Allah, for he is surely guiding me on my path.*

Half an hour later Betty walked in with a fax. "Good morning Ralph," she said handing him the three-page fax. "Did you get one of the blueberry tarts in the coffee room?"

"Yes, I couldn't pass them up. Did you bring them?"

"No, Tom did. Do you have any dictation for me?"

"Not yet, but I probably will by the end of the day."

Betty left and Ralph read the fax. Kevin recommended contacting Dr. Simon Goldberg at Little Neck Radiology Associates. Kevin would make the introductions regarding the building if the acquisition worked out. *Sounds like a plan,* Ralph thought. Checking his watch, he decided to see if Dr. Goldberg was at still at his office. "Little Neck Radiology," a female voice with a Brooklyn accent said.

"This is Dr. Eid calling for Dr. Goldberg," Ralph said.

"Just a minute, Dr. Eid. I will see if he is available," the voice said.

Half a song later, the line clicked, "This is Dr. Goldberg."

"Good afternoon Dr. Goldberg. My name is Dr. Ralph Eid. I am the CEO of REM Investments. My group is setting up state-of-the-art radiological diagnostic centers in several cities. One of my associates, who is designing our centers, heard that your partnership was looking for investors and wanted to move into the city. If that is correct, I am interested in discussing a mutually advantageous arrangement with you."

After a brief pause, Dr. Goldberg responded, "Can you tell me who your associate is?"

"Certainly, he is Kevin Patterson with LRM Associates in Atlanta. His firm is designing our centers in downtown Chicago and downtown Atlanta. We plan to add centers in New York City and Boston."

"I see. Do you have any centers open at the present time?"

Ralph sensed Dr. Goldberg's hesitancy. *He has no idea who I am or if I am a legitimate opportunity. As far as he is concerned I could be a hustler or a con man.* "I appreciate your caution. Our medical director is Professor Umair Bhatti, at the Harvard Medical School. It is my understanding that your partnership may breakup, and that two of the partners want to establish a diagnostic center in the city. If this is correct, please contact Professor Bhatti for details regarding our medical plans, and Kevin Patterson at LRM Associates in Atlanta regarding the design of our centers. Here are their telephone numbers . . . Patterson has a location in downtown Manhattan that I can option. I am prepared to move very quickly."

Dr. Goldberg was taken aback by Dr. Eid's direct approach. "How far along are you with your two centers?"

"Chicago will open in two months. We have leased 18,000 square feet on the forty-second floor of a high-rise that is being renovated. We purchased a partnership and converted it to a C corporation that we own. Professor Bhatti and Dr. Arlington, the current medical center director, are selecting diagnostic equipment and negotiating leases. Dr. Arlington will continue as a consultant."

"My partner and I are not interested in being consultants."

"I understand. Being a consultant was Dr. Arlington's choice – not mine. Our Atlanta facility, Atlanta Nuclear Diagnostics, Inc., is also a C corporation, and the two doctors who will operate it are stockholders in the corporation. If you and your partners are interested, and if Professor Bhatti approves, I am prepared to offer a similar arrangement."

"I will call Professor Bhatti and Mr. Patterson tomorrow. Then I will discuss your call with my partners. I will let you know if we are interested on Friday."

"Good. I will call you on Friday. Remember I am three hours behind of you," Ralph said. Next he called Professor Bhatti to brief him on Dr. Goldberg and the New York opportunity.

Ralph spent the next three days conducting routine business matters, approving staff positions for Chicago, and helping acquire permits and licenses for Atlanta. Abdul called to say that he had picked up the van and parked it in the Hudson Instruments building. He had also sent the mail. Ralph realized that the bill paying for all of the fictitious names and REM offices was going to become a problem. Soon he would have to retain an accounting service to handle the chores.

Friday morning brought a message from the Saudi Director requesting a meeting at Indus Instruments in Karachi the following Friday to discuss the next two instruments. *That means Mohammed is ready to fabricate the next two Neutron Induced Gamma Spectrometers. Good! One will be ready to install in Atlanta and that will leave one in storage. I will schedule my arrival for Thursday.* Ralph dictated a brief acknowledgement to the director informing him that he would arrive Thursday evening.

After lunch Betty notified Ralph that a Dr. Goldberg was on the line. Ralph thanked her, picked up the phone and punched the blinking button. "Good afternoon Dr. Goldberg."

"Good afternoon Dr. Eid. I have talked with my partners and we are interested. Dr. Saul Weiser and I are interested in forming a center with you. My other three partners would like to be bought out."

"All right. I am interested. Please fax me current financial statements. I will review them over the weekend and call you on Monday. My travel plans call for me to go through New York next Wednesday."

"I have the last four quarters, a five year summary and a balance sheet. I will fax them as soon as I hang up. Assuming you like the numbers, how do you want to proceed?"

"Assuming we agree on a price, Little Neck Diagnostics would be converted to a C corporation; then REM would purchase the stock of your three partners. You and Dr. Wiser would be minority stockholders in the new corporation, New York Nuclear Diagnostics, Inc. Salary and bonus to be determined," Ralph answered. "This is how we acquired Erie Diagnostics in Chicago."

"That is acceptable. I will wait for your call on Monday."

"I will call you Monday afternoon your time," Ralph said, ending the call.

Ralph spent the afternoon analyzing Little Neck's financial statements. The situation was similar to Erie. Equipment was old and out-of-date. Most of the leases were about to expire. The center had to reduce the scope of its diagnostics or greatly increase revenue. On the plus side were the permits and licenses. Looking at the five-year profit and loss (P&L) statements, Ralph concluded that the partners had all recouped their initial investments and earned a substantial profit. Unlike Erie, almost none of the book of business would be transferable to a downtown New York location. Ralph decided to make an offer based on the Erie deal.

Monday morning Ralph called Mark Swartz and discussed the acquisition of Little Neck Diagnostics. Next he called Professor Bhatti and had a similar conversation. It was time to call Dr. Goldberg.

"Little Neck Diagnostics," the Brooklyn accented voice said.

"This is Dr. Eid calling for Dr. Goldberg."

"Just a minute Doctor, he is expecting your call."

Less than a minute later the Doctor was on the line, "Good morning Dr. Eid."

"Good afternoon Doctor. I have reviewed your financials and balance sheet. However, I have some questions. When does your lease expire?" Ralph said.

"Our current lease has about ten months left. Our main equipment leases will expire in the next three to five months."

"O.K., that was my next question. My last question is how much of your current book of business can be transferred to the downtown location?"

"I am afraid the answer is not much. We have a few patients who see specialists in Manhattan. I am confident they will follow me. Actually, it will be more convenient for them. On the other hand, there is a need for your type of diagnostic center in the downtown area. I do not think we will have any problem attracting patients."

"You sound positive. Assuming you are going to manage the new center, how will you go about attracting patients?" Ralph asked. *After all, as long as I am CEO our centers are going to make a profit.*

"First, place an opening announcement in the local medical publications. Next, send a letter to the head of radiology at all of the New York City hospitals. Word of mouth will take care of the rest. After all, we are going to have the best radiological diagnostic center in the city."

"All right, I am interested in going forward. It is obvious that your partnership is ending. There is very little to purchase. We will all be betting on the come – how well you and Dr. Weiser can build up the new center. What are your three departing partners looking for?"

"As you know, we were planning to dissolve the partnership. Our license and permits have value, so my three partners expect to cash out."

"What are they looking for?"

"They think they should get $150,000 each."

"That's too much. Way too much."

"Saul and I both told them it was excessive."

"What do you suggest?" Ralph said, thinking *Weiser and Goldberg want the deal. Let them do the heavy lifting. I do not want to appear to be too anxious.*

"I think they would take $100,000 each."

"Still too much. Here's my offer. I will pay for the legal costs of converting Great Neck Partners into a C corporation. My company will acquire the stock of your three partners for $50,000 each. After the acquisition, you and Dr. Weiser will each have: fifteen percent of the new corporation's stock; a sign-on bonus of $100,000 each; a base salary of $100,000; and a bonus of fifteen percent of the centers profits each. You will continue to operate the current center until the new facility is ready for occupancy."

"I will discuss your offer with Saul. If he is agreeable, we will try to sell it to the others."

"I will be in New York Wednesday. Then I will be out of the country for a while. If possible, I would like your answer by Wednesday so that I can get my attorneys moving. I will call you Wednesday when I get in."

"I will try to have an answer for you when you call."

"Until Wednesday," Ralph said ending the call.

Tuesday Ralph flew to Newark. After visiting the Hudson Instruments building and inspecting the van, he stopped by the Indus facility to talk with Abu al-Aziz and alert him to the pending delivery of two more instruments. At the conclusion of his meeting with al-Aziz, Ralph drove into the city where he turned in his rental car, took a taxi to the Four Seasons and checked in. After unpacking his small bag, he called William Cox, the building manager for the Manhattan office building recommended by Kevin Patterson, and arranged to visit the building the next morning.

At 9 A.M. the next day, Ralph exited his taxi at Lexington Avenue and Twenty-sixth Street. He had decided to walk the last four blocks to get a feel for the neighborhood. Entering the building, Ralph took the elevator to the fourth floor and quickly located suite 404. In the office he was greeted by a thin, balding man, who appeared to be in his late fifties. "Good morning. I am Ralph Eid," he said, introducing himself to William Cox.

"Good morning Dr. Eid. I am pleased to meet you. Kevin Patterson has told me of your two diagnostic centers that he is designing; and I think I have just what you are looking for," Cox said.

"I have great faith in Kevin's ability. When he told me about this building, I was confident that it would meet my requirements. I have not contacted you before because I did not have a business. I hope that will change today. I am on a tight time frame, so let's talk while we look at the available area."

"Certainly," Cox said, picking up a roll of blueprints and starting toward the door.

As they entered the elevator, Cox punched the button for the fifty-third floor. We have twenty-one thousand square feet available. The southwest windows have a partial view of Madison Square Park. *This is an ideal location. The detonation will totally eliminate the financial district. This would be a good location to establish REM's corporate office. I will soon need a general manager and an accountant to consolidate the subsidiaries. REM is going to be a moneymaker. When the time comes to use Allah's instrument of destruction, all records will be destroyed. There will be nothing to link me to the blasts. REM will just be one of thousands of corporations that disappear in the fireball,* Ralph thought. After touring the empty fifty-third floor, Ralph indicated that he was interested in 18,000 square feet for New York Nuclear Diagnostics, Inc. Next Ralph selected 500 square feet adjacent to the diagnostic center for a separate REM office. "The lease for this space will be made out to REM Investments at this address," Ralph said handing Cox one of his business cards. "This will be my private office. Just place the room number on the door. I am considering establishing the main REM Investments, Inc. main office in New York. Do you have 2,000 to 3,000 square feet available on a different floor? I do not want the office on the same floor as the center."

"I have 2,500 square feet available on the forty-ninth floor – a corner suite. The tenant who had leased it backed out."

"Let's take a look at it on the way back to your office."

Returning to Cox's office, Ralph indicated that he would decide on the leases by the end of the day. Ralph gave Cox one of Mark Swartz's business cards. "Send Mr. Swartz a copy of your standard lease. He will review it and negotiate any required changes. I am interested in a ten year lease, actually three leases: one for the diagnostic center in the name New York Nuclear Diagnostics, Inc.; a second one for the corporate office in the name REM Investments, Inc.; and a third one for my private office also in REM Investments, Inc.'s name. Depending on today's events, I may be in a position to instruct Mr. Swartz to execute the first two leases before I leave town. Send the third lease for the 500 square foot space to my California office, and I will execute it when I return to California. Otherwise, I am interested in obtaining a six-month option for the space. If you do not receive approval by tomorrow, prepare an option and send it to Mr. Swartz."

"I will send a copy of our standard lease to Mr. Swartz today. We are very interested in obtaining you as a tenant. Word of your center has spread, and we are getting calls from other physicians who want to be in the same building. Based upon a ten year lease, I can offer you a rate of $5.00 per square foot less than our standard rate," Cox said.

So Goldberg is right. There is a need for our service and word certainly does spread. I must acquire Great Neck. "Thank you Mr. Cox. I am sure we are going to be pleased with this location. Mr. Patterson will be our architect for the center, and his associate will design our corporate office. Please prepare a list of contractors. I will interview them when I return to the city," Ralph said, shaking hands with Cox. After leaving Cox's office, Ralph hailed a taxi and returned to the Four Seasons. Time to call Goldberg. Picking up the phone, Ralph placed a call to the Long Island diagnostic center. "Little Neck Diagnostics," the Brooklyn accented voice said.

"Dr. Goldberg please. This is Dr. Eid."

"One moment Dr. Eid." After a minute the voice returned. "Dr. Goldberg is with a patient. He will call you as soon as he is finished. Where can he reach you?"

"I am at the Four Seasons in the city. Room fourteen seventy-five. Thank you," Ralph said, hanging up. Twenty minutes later the phone rang.

"Dr. Eid, this is Simon Goldberg."

"Good afternoon Simon. I have found an excellent location for our center. The building manager told me that he is getting requests for space from doctors, who have heard that we are going to establish a center there. I hope you have good news."

"I hope so too. My partners think that $50,000.00 is not enough."

Ralph could hear voices in the background. *I think they are all in the room.* "Are your partners there?"

"Yes, everyone is here."

Well, that tells me they are ready to deal. I would like to close this deal before I leave. "Why don't you put me on the speaker phone?"

Several clicks and then several voices could be heard, "Dr. Eid, all five partners are here," Dr. Goldberg said.

"Good afternoon gentlemen," Ralph said. "Why don't you tell me what you want, and why you think it is worth more than my offer?"

"Dr. Eid, this is Dr. Steinberg. The three of us who are leaving the partnership believe our fifth is worth more than $50,000."

"I understand. How much do you think your fifth is worth, and how did you arrive at the number?" Ralph asked.

"We think our shares are worth $100,000.00 each. We have an established clientele, permits, and licenses."

"True, however your clientele is declining, your lease is expiring, and your equipment is out-of-date. In fact, you had planned to disband your partnership. I think my offer is generous," Ralph said.

Ralph listened to the babble of voices, while the partners had a heated discussion. Finally, Dr. Steinberg said, "You have made a valid argument. The three of us are willing to take $75,000.00 each. As I understand it, you wish us to convert to a subchapter C Corporation, and then you will purchase our stock."

"$75,000.00 is acceptable. We have a deal. Yes, I want Little Neck Partnership converted to a C corporation with the name New York Nuclear Diagnostics. My attorney will be in touch with Dr. Goldberg. We will provide the conversion."

"Yes, we have a deal," Dr. Goldberg said, with a background of yeses from the other partners. "When can I expect to hear from your attorney?"

"Tomorrow or the next day. I would come out to meet you. Unfortunately, I have to leave town this evening. I will schedule a visit as quickly as possible."

After the conversation ended, Ralph called Mark Swartz; filled him in on the Little Neck Deal; and authorized the leases for the New York building. The last call was to Kevin Patterson. Ralph told Patterson he had closed the Little Neck deal and had selected three spaces at the New York building. Cox knew where they were. LRM was to duplicate the Chicago design on the fifty-second floor, and an adjacent private office suite. A third project was to design REM's corporate office on another floor. Tom Braggs had agreed to be responsible for its planning and to assist in its design. Like Chicago and Atlanta, the small private office was to be invoiced separately to Ralph in California. After completing his call to Patterson, Ralph decided to shower and take a nap. He had a 9 P.M. flight from Kennedy to Karachi.

The next morning an exhausted Ralph checked in at the Pearl Continental Hotel in Karachi. After unpacking, he lay down on the bed to take a nap. Mohammed would contact him later that day. At 5 P.M. the phone woke Ralph. Mohammed suggested dinner at 6:30 P.M. Following Mohammed's instruction, Ralph walked out of the hotel at exactly 6:30 PM, turned right, and continued walking at a slow pace. After going about fifty meters, a nondescript small car pulled up beside him. Mohammed beckoned for him to get in. Later at the restaurant Ralph filled Mohammed in on his activities and accomplishments.

"Allah be praised. You are doing very well. Two cities to go – Boston and Washington, DC," Mohammed said, slapping the table with glee.

"Yes. Allah has provided the way. My workload is increasing. It will be difficult for me to come back until the three centers are opened. When will the first component be shipped?" Ralph asked.

"Yes, I understand. We will complete conversion of the next two instruments while you are here. Perhaps Omar Mumtaz and I can convert the last two without you. It is becoming critical that we get the instruments and components into America as quickly as possible."

"Is there something I should know," Ralph asked. *Mohammed is concerned. I wonder why?*

"There is a lot of pressure for al-Qaeda to do something. Usama has been forced to go to Sudan; because of his outspoken comments against the American troops in Saudi and also against the Royal Family. Nothing has happened yet to alert the Americans, but once they have been hurt they will become more vigilant. We must position our devices before that occurs."

"How much time do we have?"

"I do not know. With Usama in Sudan I am out of the loop. If I go to see him, I will be noticed by several intelligence agencies. As far as I know, I have not been identified by any agency. For us to succeed, both of us must remain above suspicion."

"I understand. What about the components?"

"I did get side tracked. Didn't I? The first components will be shipped while you are here. They will be shipped by color – green being first. You have made arrangements to receive three sets haven't you?"

"Yes, I have decided to install the rings in the instruments once they are in their final location. That leaves the complete round with the uranium projectile to be stored in a local storage facility. Once the centers are operating, I will move the rounds to new storage sites on a random basis."

"I am prepared to come to America if I can be of assistance. I do not want to meet any of REM's employees or contractors; however, I can assist you in moving the components and installing the rings," Mohammed said. *I have to get involved. Sitting around in Riyadh with nothing important to do is driving me crazy. I guess I have become more western than I realized. My brothers are content to sit around and talk and boast. I cannot mention my work, which leaves me with nothing to say. Anyway, I must know all the details of Ralph's operation. If he were to be killed in an accident all would be lost.* "Yes, I will plan to come as soon as you have completed the New York acquisition. I am the only person who can back you up."

After dinner, both returned to the Pearl Continental. "I will meet you at 6 A.M. for an early breakfast," Mohammed said as they parted.

Ralph managed to avoid Mohammed's hug by stepping back and extending his hand.

The next morning Ralph and Mohammed entered the Indus Instruments shop area through the same rear service door. Omar Mumtaz was waiting for them. All were dressed in blue jeans, work shirts, and boots. Two large crates were in the room. Following the procedures established for converting the first gun assembly into an instrument, the work proceeded at a faster pace. This time it was decided to use the dummy components to verify fit. The components would be removed before shipment. Precise installation of the sealed neutron tube holders was critical. The real neutron tubes must fit properly when installed; otherwise they would be damaged when the rings were placed in the target assembly container. It took three and a half days to convert both of the gun assemblies into instruments. After they completed their work at noon on the fourth day, Mohammed showed Ralph one of the ring containers, "This will be placed into an Indus Instruments container marked 'Shielding Rings, Gamma Spectrometer, and Part Number: GS-47291G.' The last number will be the ring number and the letter will be the color. Only one container will be included in a shipment of products to the Indus Instrument facility in Newark. The Neutron Induced Gamma Spectrometers will be shipped separately. The first instrument and the first component should arrive in Newark within ten days," Mohammed said.

"I will send the green components to Chicago. The rings will be placed in the Chicago storage facility. You can meet me in Chicago after the fourth ring is there, and we will install the rings in the instrument. When the round arrives, Abdul will drive it to Chicago. Later I will move it to a different storage room. This way only you and I will know the procedure and the location of the round," Ralph said.

"Do you plan to install the neutron generators at the Indus Newark facility?"

"No, I will have Abdul pick up the crated instruments and deliver them to our Hudson Instruments building. After the neutron generators are installed, I will ship one of the instruments to Atlanta. The next set of rings will be sent there. The other instrument will be stored until the New York Center is ready. How much can I allow Abdul to learn?"

"As little as possible. If you think he has learned too much, let me know and he will be recalled," Mohammed answered. "Abdul will become a danger to us. Once his work is completed I will arrange for him to return to Saudi where we can find a useful and short-term job for him. Usama is seeking martyrs, even unsuspecting ones."

The next morning Ralph flew to New York, checked in at the Four Seasons, and called Mark Swartz to arrange to meet him at the law office the next afternoon.

Entering the law offices of Swartz, Kaplan and Goldberg, Ralph was shown to Mark Swartz's office. "You look tired," Mark said to Ralph.

"Yes, I just got back from Pakistan. Had to meet with one of our key suppliers. The time zones are getting me down," Ralph replied.

"You should think about moving here. New York City is a wonderful place to live for those that can afford it. You could get a flat or condo in the city. After all, most of your business interests are on the east coast."

"I have given the idea some thought. However, I love California. My house is on the side of a small mountain overlooking a valley. The scenery is beautiful and it is very quiet. Nothing like the east coast."

Changing the subject to business, Mark said, "I have started the paperwork to convert Little Neck Partnership into New York Nuclear Diagnostics, Inc. the conversion should be completed by next week. The Atlanta agreements have been modified and sent to Doctors Goldberg and Weiser for review. They are straightforward agreements and I do not expect any delays there. I have reviewed the building lease and requested some minor changes. Cox promised me an answer by the end of the week. All in all, it looks like you have another center."

"Yes, things are moving very fast."

Mark sat back in his chair and looked out of his window at the view of the harbor. Ralph could see the twin towers through the other window that faced south. "Ralph, you should consider hiring a corporate staff. Once your centers open, you are going to be buried in paper work. Tom Braggs will not be able to keep up."

"You're right, Mark. In fact, I plan to lease two separate spaces here. One for the new diagnostic center and the other for a corporate office. I am glad you brought the subject up. What do you think of Tom Braggs? He has experience in the medical treatment field. He could become REM's President."

"Tom would be a good choice. The medical issues will be handled by the medical director of each center and Professor Bhatti. The corporate office would be strictly management and financial. As long as you keep Arthur Andersen as your auditors, they will not object to Tom coming to work for you. In fact, it is a normal occurrence for Andersen accountants to go to work for clients."

"I will offer Tom the job. Have you met Dr. Goldberg or Dr. Weiser?"

"No."

"If you have time, let's go out to Little Neck and meet our new team members. In fact, I will call Tom Braggs and invite him to come. We can make him an offer to join REM on the way," Ralph said.

Ralph placed a call to Dr. Goldberg and arranged for the visit. Mark asked his assistant to get Tom Braggs on the phone. Tom agreed to go. Mark arranged for a limo for the afternoon and the three departed for Little Neck at 1 P.M. On the way Tom agreed to join REM as President and Chief Operating Officer. The meeting at Little Neck Diagnostics was cordial. Tom Braggs would interface with Dr. Goldberg and Professor Bhatti regarding the staffing and relocation to the new center. Ralph would make arrangements for the build-out contractors, and Mark Swartz would handle all legal affairs. On the return trip Braggs agreed to work with the architect designing the corporate office; select furniture and fixtures; and hire the staff. Tom Braggs would establish accounting procedures for each subsidiary diagnostic center; then consolidate them under REM Investments, Inc.

Rem Investments had been established with two bank accounts: the general account with $10 million dollars; and the reserve account with $20 million dollars. All expenses associated with the subsidiary centers were funded from the general account. Ralph drew checks for special projects from the reserve account. Each subsidiary would be provided $500,000 operating capital. In addition to Ralph, Tom Braggs and Mark Swartz were to have signature authority on all REM bank accounts: with the exception of the REM reserve account that was directly controlled by Ralph Eid. Profits would be transferred into the reserve account at the end of each fiscal year. Arthur Anderson would prepare tax returns and un-audited statements. Subsidiaries would be subject to audit. The next day Ralph returned to California.

Kevin Patterson called the following Tuesday to inform Ralph that work was progressing on the Atlanta Center, and that preliminary drawings were almost complete for New York. Ralph requested that a set of the New York Center drawings be sent to Professor Bhatti, Dr. Goldberg, Tom Braggs, and himself. On Wednesday Abu al-Aziz called to tell Ralph that the first instrument would arrive the following Tuesday. A spare part for the instrument was expected by the end of next week. Ralph requested notification when each of them arrived. It was time to call Bob Johnson and prepare him for additional orders.

"Hello Bob, this is Ralph Eid."

"Hello Dr. Eid. I trust our generator is working to your satisfaction."

"Yes, preliminary results have been very positive."

"Can you share any data with me?" Johnson asked.

"Sorry. The application and data are proprietary. We do have interest from other research groups, who want to obtain an instrument. I am working out a modification to our exclusive use contract, which will allow Indus Instruments to sell additional instruments."

"Are these research groups in the United States?"

"Yes. All are reputable organizations interested in medical diagnostic equipment and biotechnology."

"When do you expect to order additional Mk 38's?"

"We are negotiating with two customers. I expect orders in the next two weeks."

"How confident are you in getting the orders?"

Ralph could feel Johnson's excitement. *Johnson really wants an order. I am sure he had a hard time getting the company to spend money modifying the Mk 37 for one order.* "Very confident. In fact, I suggest you start work on two Mk 38's. You should receive the order next week."

"I will get the ball rolling today. Thanks for the heads up," Bob Johnson said, ending the call.

Like taking candy from a baby. American's have no concept of security or fear. The only thing Bob Johnson was worried about was export licenses, Ralph thought. Friday Ralph prepared a fax to Omar Mumtaz using the code phrase that told him to place the order for two Mk 38 neutron generators.

Ralph and Abdul arrived at Indus Instruments the following Thursday. One of the instruments and a shielding ring had been received. Ralph told Abu al-Aziz that the components from General Neutron had been ordered and would be sent to him. Al-Aziz was instructed to notify Ralph when the two Mk 38 neutron generators arrived. They would be installed at a different location when they were available. The large crate and shielding ring box were loaded onto a rented Ryder truck and taken to the Hudson Instruments building in North Star Industrial Park for storage. After unloading the crate with the forklift, Ralph instructed Abdul to drive the box to Chicago and place it in the Walnut mini-storage room. Abdul said he would leave for Chicago after turning in the Ryder truck.

With his business out of the way, Ralph needed to relax. He called Nancy and arranged to spend the weekend with her in New York. There they could catch a current Broadway show and enjoy some fine dining. He would fly to Chicago on Monday and check the storage room to make sure the shielding ring box was there, then continue on to Oakland and home.

When he entered his California office on Tuesday morning, Ralph found a fax in his in box from Indus Instruments, Pakistan alerting him to the shipment of Part number GS-47292G. After taking care of routine matters and paying bills, Ralph opened the drawing tube from LRM Associates and spent the remainder of the day reviewing drawings.

The following morning he called Professor Bhatti, who recommended several changes to the drawings for the New York center. Later that afternoon in a phone conversation with Kevin Patterson, Ralph relayed Bhatti's recommendations and requests for changes. Included in the conversation was a discussion on the layout for REM's corporate office. "Tom Braggs, REM's newly appointed president, will be responsible for that office. I will fax you his address and phone number. Please copy him with the new drawings, along with Bhatti and Dr. Goldberg. If possible I would like to meet you in New York next week to introduce you to Braggs and have a final review of the plans with the three of them. Call me when you set a day for the meeting," Ralph concluded, ending the call.

Ralph's house was becoming a problem. He did not have time to clean it, and constantly having to stop the mail was calling unwanted attention to himself. What he needed was a cleaning service or a cleaning woman, who would take care of the house when he was gone. Ralph mentioned the problem to Betty, who suggested running an ad in the local paper. Betty helped draft an ad and sent it to the local paper in time for the weekend edition. Ralph used his office number to avoid disclosing his name and address. "Single business executive, who travels a great deal, needs reliable person to clean and watch house. References required. Call Monday. . . ."

Ralph devoted the remainder of the week to management activities, correspondence and catching up on personal matters. Ralph had found it difficult to keep up his jogging and was gaining weight.

On Monday Betty screened calls from persons responding to the ad. She talked at length to one caller, who caught her interest. Putting the call on hold, she walked down the hall to Ralph's office to tell him, "There is a lady on the phone about your ad, who sounds interesting. She is a local housewife, who has never done any cleaning except her own house. She said she might be interested, if you were a neat person, who did not smoke. She ended up interviewing me. Do you want to talk to her?" Betty asked.

"What do you think?" Ralph replied.

"Well, the other calls were from women who cleaned houses for a living and wanted to schedule times on a regular basis. I think you need a more flexible person who can adjust to your schedule. This lady sounds educated, and I like her."

"O.K., transfer the call and I will talk to her. What is her name?"

"Joanne, I think she said Hatter or Hatters."

Ralph waited for the call to be transferred, then answered. "Hello Joanne, my name is Ralph Eid. I am sorry, but Betty was not sure of your last name."

"Hello Mr. Eid. My last name is Murphy. I guess I was nervous. I live in Dublin. My husband works for the state. My son is away at college and I have extra time. When I saw your ad I thought, this might be a way to earn some spending money doing what I have been doing for twenty-three years – keeping house."

Ralph had a hard time keeping from laughing. Joanne had not taken one breath during her entire statement. "So this would be the first time you ever cleaned any one's house other than you own."

"Yes"

"Have you any work experience, jobs I mean?"

"No paying jobs, lots of volunteer work, church, school . . . "

"O.K., let me tell you something about myself. I am single, travel a great deal, and consider myself to be a neat person. I do not smoke or drink, as long as you don't count a bottle of wine with my friends. My business may require me to be away for extended periods, up to a month or more."

"Where do you live?"

"I have a three bedroom ranch in Rancho Nuevo. Do you know where that is?"

"Yes, it is very nice area. How many times a week do you want your house cleaned?"

"I never thought of it that way. When I am home I clean and vacuum on Saturdays. What I need is for someone to come by several times a week and check the house. Clean what needs to be cleaned. Empty my mailbox and place the mail on the counter. Check the refrigerator and dispose of any food that is going bad. I recently found a very bad odor in the refrigerator when I returned from a two week trip."

Joanne laughed.

"I need someone who will treat my house like it was theirs. Do what needs to be done."

"Will you need me when you are in town?

"Probably not. Only if I get behind and do not have time to clean up. Another thing I need is for someone to buy some basic food, and put it in the house before I return from a long trip. It's bad to get home late at night and not have anything to eat. I usually use a limo service to and from the airport."

"Buying food would not be a problem."

"Joanne, if you are interested, can you come out the my house this evening. Bring your husband if he can come. I live at the end of the first street, last house on the right."

"You can expect me around 7 P.M. Thank you," Joanne said, hanging up.

Ralph walked down the hall to tell Betty the result of his discussion with Joanne Murphy. "If she looks O.K., I will have her keep in touch with you when I am gone. Will it be all right with you if I leave you a couple of signed checks on my personal account – in case a bill has to be paid?"

"Sure, as long as you don't mind me doing a little shopping on the side," Betty said smiling.

Ralph laughed and returned to his office. That evening Joanne and her husband came by, and Ralph decided Joanne was just what he needed. He agreed to pay Joanne $400 dollars a month, and leave one hundred dollars in a drawer to cover any expenses. Ralph would call and let Joanne know when he was leaving or had left and when he would return. If he was gone for over two weeks Joanne was to take any bills to his office and give them to Betty. Ralph gave Joanne a list of the types of food he liked; and when she was certain she understood everything he needed, she and her husband left. As he closed the door behind them Ralph felt a great sense of relief to have solved another problem.

During his morning jog, Ralph decided that he had to concentrate on getting the Atlanta Center and his special office suite finished; so that he could have the second instrument delivered. Chicago was coming along and would open by December 15th. Abdul had proven that he could deliver the rings. Getting New York started was also important. As soon as his special office suite was ready the third instrument could be installed. Once the three instruments containing the guns were in place, he could concentrate on Boston and Washington, DC. The last two instruments could be stored in the Newark building until their sites were ready.

Friday morning Ralph met Dr. Goldberg, Tom Braggs, and Kevin Patterson at the office building. Plans for the center were reviewed and everyone was in agreement with the LRM design. Dr. Goldberg left, and Braggs, Patterson, and Ralph went down to the forty-ninth floor to review the corporate office layout. Patterson had already selected two contractors to do the build-outs. Ralph and Braggs reviewed the bids and approved Patterson's selection. The New York City Center was started. It should be ready by March. Equipment vendors were delighted to provide leased equipment for a third center. At the conclusion of the meeting, Ralph called the center build-out contractor aside and explained that his small office suite had priority over the center. He was to be called when the instrument room and outer walls with shielding were complete so that he could install equipment. The contractor told him that he should be able to do so in early January.

Feeling pressure to establish a Washington center, Ralph decided to spend the weekend in DC, and caught a late afternoon flight from La Guardia Airport to Washington National. *I can drive around the city and play tourist. Washington is going to be a problem. It does not have tall buildings like New York and Chicago. All the government agencies have security. I will have to be very careful,* he thought as he checked in at the Hamilton Crowne Plaza Hotel located at Franklin Square, four blocks from the White House. *I'll explore the area around the White House and have dinner at Maxims this evening. Then I can start early tomorrow morning with a local driver, who knows the area,* he decided.

Rising early, Ralph had breakfast and obtained a city map, which he took back to his room and spent an hour studying. His main target was a circle centered around the Capitol that encompassed the White House, Crystal City and the Pentagon. Also included were the many other important buildings including the Treasury, FBI, State Department, and all of the Senate and House office buildings. CIA headquarters would be severely damaged by the blast. If properly placed, one of the devices would effectively destroy the entire American Government. The problem was where to place the device. Radiation detection would be a much more serious threat in Washington than in any other city. Crystal City and Roslyn had tall buildings and were in ideal locations; however, they also housed government and military facilities and detection was too great a risk.

The hotel doorman located a cab driver, who had been working the city for many years. Ralph explained that he was looking for a tall building located in the downtown area, suitable for a medial diagnostic center. By the end of the day Ralph was discouraged. The only area that appeared to be suitable was around New York Avenue North East, but the neighborhood was not conducive to the type of centers REM was operating. There were some old warehouse buildings, but there again the neighborhood was the problem. It would not be safe to store one of the instruments there. Ralph rented a car and spent Sunday morning driving around the area with the same results; then turned the car in at Dulles airport and boarded a flight to San Francisco. *Allah will show me the way. He will provide me with the solution.*

The following week Ralph was consumed with details concerning the grand opening of the Chicago Center on December sixteenth. He decided to fly to Newark on Tuesday; and alerted Abdul to rent a truck and meet him at the Hudson Instruments facility Wednesday. They could then pick up the third instrument and second ring at Indus, and move them to the Hudson building. Abdul would deliver the second ring to Chicago on Saturday.

Wednesday afternoon Ralph flew to Chicago to prepare for the open house. Professor Bhatti was also expected to arrive that evening. Tom Braggs and Mark Swartz and Doctors Goldberg and Weiser would arrive on Saturday. Ralph had not met the new center director, Dr. Qaiser Ahmad, a former student of Professor Bhatti. Dr. Ahmad had been the Assistant Chief of Radiology at Northwestern Medical Center. The center's staff would consist of four medical doctors; eight nurse technicians; and an office staff of three. Dr. Ahmad expected a large turnout for the center's opening, including: the heads of most of the area hospital's and medical centers radiology departments; the health commissioner; a senior representative from the Mayor's office; and many physicians. Doctors Clark and Hornell and Kevin Patterson would arrive from Atlanta Sunday morning. All in all, it was going to be quite a party.

Sunday afternoon all of the REM team met at the new center for a tour and briefing. Dr. Ahmad expected to have enough patients by the end of the first two weeks to be at the break-even point and reach profitability by the end of the first month.

Ralph hosted a dinner for the REM group Sunday evening in a small dining room at the Four Seasons hotel. Frank Braggs explained accounting and management procedures, and Professor Bhatti reviewed medical procedures and policies. The center's directors shared experiences and ideas.

The open house for Chicago Nuclear Diagnostics began at noon on Monday. Dr. Ahmad made the opening remarks and introduced the staff and the other REM personnel. Then Dr. Ahmad provided a brief talk on the center's equipment, "Chicago Nuclear has the most advanced scanning and diagnostic equipment available. Let me briefly explain our main types of equipment, beginning with something everybody is familiar with, X-ray radiography. X-rays are high energy electromagnetic radiation that penetrate the body and expose photographic film placed behind the patient.

"Radionuclide imaging is a technique in which small amounts of a radioactive isotope, called a 'tracer' is introduced into the patient's body. The tracer emits gamma rays, which are similar to X-rays that are detected by a 'PET,' or positron emission tomography scanner. The PET uses photomultiplier-scintillation detectors to detect the gamma rays. A nuclear stress test is measured by a 'SPECT,' or single photon emission computed tomography, instrument that uses a gamma camera to detect the energy. Information detected and recorded by both instruments is analyzed and reconstructed by computers to create very clear images of the patient's body.

"Computed Axial Tomography imaging, known as 'CAT scanning' uses a digital computer, together with a rotating X-ray device to create a detailed cross-sectional image or 'slice' of organs and body parts such as the lungs, liver, kidneys, pancreas, pelvis, extremities, brain, spine, and blood vessels.

"The center also has MRI or magnetic resonance imaging scanning instruments. MRI is an advanced way to visualize the contents of the body without the use of X-rays or radiation. Magnetic resonance scans are produced using a large magnet, radio waves, and a computer. They provide extremely detailed images that cannot be seen on conventional X-rays. The patient lies inside a large, cylinder-shaped magnet that is 10,000-30,000 times stronger than the magnetic field of the earth. The human body is composed of atoms. Hydrogen atoms or water make up 95% of the body. Normally, the hydrogen atoms within your body spin around at random; however, when you are placed within a magnet, which has a very strong magnetic field, the hydrogen atoms line up and spin in the same direction. When a radio wave is passed through the body, the hydrogen atoms give off a signal. That signal, with the aid of a computer, becomes the source of MRI information. It produces the images that will assist in making a diagnosis."

Dr. Ahmad's talk was followed by remarks by the Mayor's assistant, who welcomed the new diagnostic center to Chicago and praised its contribution to the city. After the politicos left, Dr. Ahmad and his staff took turns giving tours to a steady stream of doctors. The new state-of-the-art CAT and MRI scanning instruments were the center's main attractions. The doctors were also impressed with the X-ray equipment and ultrasound rooms. The chemotherapy treatment area would open in February. By the end of the day Dr. Ahmad reported that he had been told to expect many referrals starting the next day. The other center directors were elated with the facility and its acceptance by the local medical community. Professor Bhatti and Tom Braggs gave a second dinner party that evening, which capped the celebration of successful opening.

Ralph returned to Livermore on Wednesday. During the flight he reviewed his accomplishments and successes with pride. *If the next two centers are as successful as the Chicago one appears to be, I will have created a very impressive enterprise. Something to be proud of. It will be a shame to destroy it and the cities it serves. Yet that is what I am expected to do . . . I must pray to Allah for guidance.* The drive home from the airport seemed unusually long to Ralph, who despite the euphoria he experienced at the opening, was somehow feeling down and very tired. He was, however, more than pleased when he entered his house to find his mail neatly stacked on the kitchen counter and fresh milk, orange juice and a steak in the refrigerator. *May Allah bless Joanne Murphy.*

The next morning at the office Betty was anxious to hear about the center's opening. Ralph spent the first hour telling her about it. Next came a series of telephone calls from the other center doctors expressing their high opinions of the Chicago Center. Ralph called Kevin Patterson and told him what a great job LRM had done. He was especially complimentary of Kevin's contribution to the project. They discussed the Atlanta and New York Centers, which were on schedule. Then Ralph mentioned that he had been unable to find a suitable area in Washington for a DC center. Kevin replied that most of the major medical facilities were located in the suburbs around Washington, in Maryland and Virginia. However, a complete facility located in the downtown area would provide a convenient location for the thousands of government employees, who could visit the center during the day. "Give me some time," he told Ralph, "and I think I can help you find a good DC location."

With that promise in mind, Ralph ended their call and devoted the afternoon to preparing a report to REM's Board of Directors. As he walked to the employee lounge area on a coffee break he noticed for the first time the Christmas decorations in the reception area. Christmas was next week. For all practical purposes, all business activities would cease until January second. *Well, a week of reduced activity will be good for me. I must honor the infidel's customs and purchase presents, but for whom? Betty, Joanne, Frank Braggs, Mark Swartz, Kevin Patterson . . . and Nancy. What would be appropriate? A simple piece of jewelry for Betty and Joanne. A Rolex watch for the men. What about Nancy? Jewelry . . . Why not? I wonder if she has plans for Christmas. I could meet her – where? I do not want her to learn too much about my business. She is not one to ask too many questions, but women are naturally curious. On the other hand . . . St. Thomas? Yes, we could meet in St. Thomas.* Picking up the phone, Ralph dialed Nancy's Boston office number.

Nancy Hatterson had been borne in Nebraska, the daughter of a farmer. One of four children, she had excelled in school and won a scholarship to the University of Nebraska. After graduating, her parents had sent her to Harvard for her Masters Degree in Business Administration (MBA). Her three brothers, who had stayed in Nebraska with their father, were expanding the family farming business. Between owned and leased land, her family was planting over four thousand acres.

Nancy was now an officer with a small venture capital firm in Boston. While at Harvard they had enjoyed a casual affair that ended after Ralph's parent's death. He had become so involved with the legal aspects surrounding their deaths, and so moody, that both decided it was best to end their relationship – while they were still on friendly terms. They lost touch when he obtained his degree and left for California. Even though years had passed since they had spoken, Ralph still held a special place in Nancy's heart. She had not forgotten their steamy nights together, his laughing eyes, and charming smile. So she was pleased to hear his voice again after so long a time, and delighted with the three weekends they had shared in recent months.

Nancy was a perfectionist, who was dedicated to her career and had no interest in getting married. She did love a good time and knew when she needed to get away from it all. Ralph had become a very pleasant diversion from the self-imposed stress or her workweek. She had just completed her evaluation of a business plan for a biotech company when her phone buzzed. Lifting the receiver she answered, "Nancy Hatterson."

"Hi Nancy, are you busy?" Ralph said.

"Ralph, I was wondering when I would hear from you. Where are you?"

"Looking out of my office window in California. I just discovered that Christmas is next week."

"How observant of you. What tipped you off?" Nancy said laughing.

"Would you believe a Christmas tree in the reception area?" Ralph replied, also laughing. "What are your plans for the holidays?"

"I do appreciate you ability to make long range plans. As it happens, my plans just fell through, and I will probably spend the next week tidying up loose ends at the office. What do you have in mind?"

"Nothing yet. I just wanted to find out if you were free. Let me do some looking around. I will call you back as soon as I have an idea."

"O.K., just think *warm*. It is cold here," Nancy said ending the call.

Ralph left the office, drove to his travel agent, and waited while she looked for available rooms in St. Thomas. She was able to book a villa that had just received a cancellation notice. Airline tickets were more of a problem. A flight from Logan International airport to St. Thomas was available Christmas morning. Ralph booked Nancy first class returning January third. He was able to book the last coach seat on a Christmas Eve red-eye to Atlanta that connected with a flight to St. Thomas. Ralph would arrive an hour before Nancy's flight on Christmas day.

With their travel arrangements completed, Ralph visited Livermore's largest jewelry store where he purchased three Rolex watches and arranged to have them sent directly to Braggs, Swartz and Patterson. Next he purchased a gold pin for Joanne and a pair of earrings for Betty. He decided to take Nancy shopping in downtown Charlotte Amalie, and let her select her own present. Returning to his office, Ralph placed Betty's present under the office tree. He would leave Joanne's in the drawer at home where she would find it the next time she came to the house. In his office, Ralph placed a second call to Nancy. "Is St. Thomas warm enough for you?" He asked.

"Yes. I love St. Thomas. Did you ever learn to scuba dive?"

"Yes, but I will need a refresher course. It has been several years since I made a dive. Getting there is the biggest problem. I have booked you on an early morning direct flight on Christmas Day – returning on January third. Hope that is O.K. with you."

"Sounds great to me. I am surprised you were able to find a room."

"I didn't. But I did find a villa that had just received a cancellation. I am scheduled to arrive from Atlanta an hour before you. In case I am delayed we are staying at Beach Tops Villa at Cowpat Bay. I will meet you at the villa."

"See you in St. Thomas," Nancy said, ending the call.

January, 1992

On the return trip from St. Thomas, Ralph's mind quickly turned to business. He was spending the night in Atlanta so that he could visit the Atlanta Center's site. There he was pleased to discover that the small REM office should be ready to receive the spectrometer by the end of January. Back in his hotel room he checked messages and learned that the third shielding ring had arrived in Newark. He called Abdul and instructed him to take a package to Chicago.

Ralph smiled as he hung up the phone, and sat for a long while thinking. *Everything seems to be going according to schedule. The Atlanta diagnostic center will soon be up and running – making REM lots of money. Mohammed will be pleased with the news. He will say, "We are one step closer to bringing the evil Satan to its knees – our eggs are being planted in their belly, right under their noses." Better still, I will be one step closer to settling an old score. A brilliant plan if I do say so myself. It's almost too easy.*

That night lying in bed before sleep came, Ralph thought of Nancy as he fingered the 18-caret gold neck chain she had given him for Christmas. The villa had been a good idea. After a few days of swimming and relaxing he felt like a new man. Nancy had been thrilled with the ruby and diamond necklace he had bought her the day after of Christmas. Their time together had been special to Ralph, because he discovered that he really missed having companionship. The nature of REM's true purpose dictated that his private life be solitary. While talking with Nancy in St. Thomas, he came to realize that he really needed someone with whom he could relax and be himself.

Always appreciative of Nancy's capacity to listen, Ralph had been delighted to learn from her comments regarding finance that she was also an astute businesswoman. She was certainly not like the average woman. As the week passed, Ralph became less hesitant to discuss his business ventures, and Nancy showed sincere interest in REM Investments' progress. Ralph found that he enjoyed having someone to talk to who appreciated his abilities and accomplishments. More than once, he had to remind himself not to let his ego get the better of him. *Too bad,* he told himself, *she is an infidel.*

Before leaving Atlanta the next afternoon, Ralph paid a visit to his storage room at Aunt Lil's. Pleased to find that everything was in order he proceeded to the airport and his flight to San Francisco. Drifting in and out of sleep in his first class seat on the plane, Ralph's thoughts returned to Nancy and their wonderful holiday.

They had spent eight wonderful day's scuba diving, enjoying the beach and shopping. They rented a motor scooter for transportation that had a cargo basket on the front. Trips to and from the villa were always great fun. They never knew what they would encounter as they traveled along. Once they came upon a short heavy set island woman, who was walking her milking goat with a rope around its neck along the narrow road. With a quick jog to the left and fast brake they missed hitting the woman, but scared the goat. Much to their amusement, the goat took off and jumped a low rock wall. Yelling some unintelligible island oaths and shaking her fist at them, the woman hiked up her dress, hip rolled over the wall, and sprinted in hot pursuit after the goat. Acting like college kids on spring break, they howled with laughter, especially when Ralph drove the scooter at top speed with Nancy seated behind and holding on for dear life. Speeding along the winding roads Ralph deliberately took tight turns so that everything in the overstuffed basket teetered. Nancy, shrieking like a teenager, would let go of Ralph's waist and try to keep the basket contents from spilling. "Save the wine," she would yell.

Back at the villa their evenings began with a sampling Ralph's most recent wine purchase, followed by one of Nancy's fabulous meals. He had been pleased to discover that she was an excellent cook. Most evenings they took long walks on the beach at sunset and enjoyed an occasional late night swim. Returning to the villa they retired to the master bedroom's king sized mahogany four-poster; where they shared their mutual passions for each other. With their ardor spent, they slept lulled by the sounds of ocean, and the gentle Caribbean breeze drifting through their open balcony doors. Ralph delighted in awakening to the pleasure of Nancy's sinuous body pressed against his. Her long silky blonde hair flowing out across him where her head rested in the crook of his arm.

Even now the memory of the feel of her sleepy breath on his chest aroused him. *I'm going to miss her*, he thought. Images of a smiling Nancy emerging from the water, her golden tanned body accentuated by the bright turquoise swim suit flashed across his mind. *She's a definite ten in a bikini . . . and a ten **plus** in bed.* He sighed. *Even better, she understands what I am doing with REM – what I have accomplished – appreciates my ability.* He had surprised himself when he purchased the diamond and ruby necklace for her at Irma's. In spite of himself, he had begun to think of her in terms of more than a casual girlfriend. They seemed to belong together, similar likes and tastes in food, art and music. *I have to be careful, I cannot allow myself to fall in love.*

Arriving home, Ralph checked his answering machine, mail and fax machine for faxes. A fax from Omar Mumtaz in Karachi informed him that Part number GS-47294G had been shipped, and that Part number GS-47291R was expected to be shipped the following week. A second fax informed him that one of the REM directors would be arriving on Saturday in Chicago – two weeks from the coming weekend. *Good, Mohammed is coming to help install the rings. We will do it early Sunday morning. I will go to Chicago and move the rings from Walnut Mini Storage to the REM office storage room on Saturday. Abdul will deliver the fourth ring on Saturday. Best move them one ring at a time.*

The following morning Ralph received a call from Abu al-Aziz telling him that the second and third Mk 38 neutron generators would be shipped to Newark in five days. *Allah be praised, Mohammed can help me install the Mk 38's in the spectrometers in Newark after we complete our task in Chicago. I should be able to ship the spectrometer to Atlanta the following week. The New York suite should be ready to receive the third spectrometer by mid February. I must find a location for the remaining two instruments.*

Additional calls to Tom Braggs and Professor Bhatti brought the welcome news that the Chicago Center was exceeding Dr. Ahmad's expectations. The center was still operating on negative cash flow because of the billing cycle. Insurance companies normally took six to eight weeks before issuing payments. Braggs expected positive cash flow in March. Professor Bhatti was very pleased with the center's performance. Several small glitches had occurred, but that was to be expected. Doctors Clark and Hornell were pushing to get the Atlanta Center going. *I have really created something. REM Investments is going to be a huge success. Nancy suggested going public with an initial public offering, an IPO, as soon as the three centers are operating in the black. She said the stock would go through the roof, and the current stockholders would triple their investment in a couple of weeks. Perhaps I should mention this to Mohammed,* Ralph wondered.

Two weeks later Ralph arrived in Chicago on Saturday morning. This time he was staying at a local Holiday Inn, where a man wearing jeans and a delivery shirt would not attract attention. After renting a minivan from National Car Rentals at the airport, he first drove to the center's building and parked in the underground loading area. Moving to the back of the van, Ralph opened his duffel bag and removed a kaki work shirt with a

"Lake Instruments" patch and "Ralph" embroidered on it. Ralph had ordered several sets of shirts and pants from the mail order company Ware-Guard. After changing, he took the freight elevator to the forty-second floor. The center was closed, but there appeared to be someone in the office.

Returning to the loading area, Ralph drove the van to Walnut Mini Storage. There he used the hand truck that was kept in the storage room to load one of the three packages containing the rings into the van. Abdul would deliver the fourth ring by closing time.

Back at the high rise, Ralph parked the van in the loading area, and using the hand truck wheeled the package into the freight elevator. At the forty-second floor, he cautiously checked the hall before proceeding directly to the door marked 4216. Ralph had previously numbered the keys on his ring to be in sequence to the entrance doors – to facilitate speed and ease of entry. Quickly finding key #1, he unlocked the office door, pushed the hand truck containing the package into the office, and closed and locked the door behind him. No one had seen him. Inside the office Ralph unlocked the instrument room door's two dead bolt locks, and pushed the hand truck through the instrument room to the locked storage room door. Inserting the last numbered key to the storage room, he unlocked the door and placed the package in the room. His task completed, Ralph secured all the doors and returned to the van. During the following five hours, Ralph repeated the procedure two more times.

After the last trip he returned the hand truck to the Walnut Mini Storage room, then drove to the O'Hare Holiday Inn and checked in. Mohammed would meet him there when he arrived late that night. Ralph went swimming, had dinner, and returned to his room to wait for Mohammed's call. They agreed to meet at 6:30 for breakfast in the hotel restaurant.

Mohammed was already in the restaurant when Ralph entered. He rose as Ralph approached. "Good morning Ralph. You're looking well. It's good to see you again – good to be off that infernal airplane," he said in a loud voice. There were only two other customers in the restaurant seated in a corner booth a good bit away from Mohammed, but they both looked up at the sound of his voice.

"Good morning," Ralph replied, shaking hands with Mohammed, while frowning and nodding his head in the direction of the other table – signaling Mohammed to take care. Mohammed seemed not to notice Ralph's hint. While they waited for service, he continued to grumble of the complications he encountered with his travel experiences. He had to sit across the isle from some American "Jew Pig," and his loud-mouthed wife.

They griped about everything, and the woman got drunk, stood up and spilled a vodka martini all over Mohammed's new pants. Ralph frowned at him and put a finger to his lips, indicating that he should be quite. This time Mohammed took the hint and sat quietly drinking his coffee until their food was served. Even though the hour was early and the restaurant was almost empty, they were in a public place. A quick glance at the other table proved no one was listening, but Ralph was anxious. *He is usually more cautious,* Ralph thought. *I have never seen him quite so agitated. I do not want to make him angrier, but he is really making me nervous, because the work we have ahead of us is critical to our success.*

Mohammed was in a somewhat better mood, when after a good breakfast they left the restaurant and entered the van. "No one in the world makes pancakes like Americans," he said after a loud burp, and patted his stomach as he settled back for the ride. "I am really excited about our first installation. This is just the beginning of seeing the fruition of all our dreams and plans – and what a beginning. Who would have ever thought that two men alone could have set in motion a plan to topple the mighty American government? Just think Ralph. You will have *pay back* and then some. You will be a hero of Islam. Allah will grant you heavenly riches far greater than an earthly fortune. Americans will burn in hell," he concluded and laughed heartily while shaking his fists with delight. Then suddenly growing quiet he hunched his shoulders and scowled out the window at the dimly lit, empty, early morning streets.

Ralph was becoming increasingly uneasy about Mohammed's mood and his uncharacteristic behavior. *I must direct his attention to the business at hand. We need to both have calm steady hands for this first installation. Nothing must go wrong,* Ralph thought as he enthusiastically announced their upcoming destination. "Our first stop is Walnut Mini Storage to pick up the last ring," he told Mohammed, "If Abdul has not delivered it, we will go to the instrument room in the REM office and start installing the three rings that are already there."

Smiling now Mohammed replied, "I am anxious to see what you have accomplished. Can we visit the diagnostic center?"

"It will be wise to wait until Monday. Then we can visit the center properly dressed. After all, you are a director of the parent company and have every right to inspect the center. I do not wish to be seen dressed like this. By the way, there is another shirt like this one in my duffel bag in the back."

"Good idea, I will put it on in the storage room. I am looking forward to visiting the center on Monday."

Ralph relaxed a bit when he noticed Mohammed carefully noting the entrance code at Walnut Mini Storage and then asking about the key. *He seems to be getting with the program,* Ralph thought and replied, "I have a Chicago set of keys for you. I will do the same for the other cities. The keys are color coded and numbered in sequence to the entrance doors – Reds are for the Mini Storage rooms and greens are for the offices. Abdul will place the final package containing the complete round in this storage room when it arrives. Next weekend he will deliver the first ring to Atlanta."

When Ralph unlocked to the Mini Storage room door, he found the package containing the last ring. Mohammed looked hard at the office furniture, and then realized its purpose. Smiling, he commented, "The furniture is a good idea, a good cover. Well done."

Ralph used the hand truck to load the fourth ring into the van; while Mohammed put on a Lake Instrument shirt – this one, with the name "Mo" embroidered on it. When they had returned to the high rise, Ralph showed Mohammed the color-coded numbered key ring as they rode up in the elevator. No one was in the hall when they exited the elevator. "Ralph" and "Mo" entered the office without incident. Mohammed was all eyes as they moved through the office and instrument room and opened the storage room door. Ralph entered and pointed to the other three packages. Walking up to a shelf where his toolbox was stored, he opened the box and removed a large metric socket wrench set. When he turned to leave he was somewhat unsettled to see that Mohammed was not with him. He quickly stepped back into the instrument room, where he was relieved to find Mohammed looking in fascination at the instrument's computer control panel. "I have not seen it with the real computer installed. Does it operate?" Mohammed asked.

"Yes, it does. Let's turn it on and take a reading before installing the rings. Then we can take a reading with the rings installed and compare the results," Ralph said. Walking to a small table next to the instrument, he picked up a spiral bound book. "This is the operating manual. The key to the computer is hanging on a nail in the storage room." Retrieving the key, Ralph inserted it, turned it and brought the instrument to life. Turning to Mohammed he said, "You can follow the startup procedure in the manual."

Mohammed paid careful attention as he watched Ralph run the diagnostic tests. Next Ralph displayed the gamma radiation readings on the screen, which were slightly above average background. "The room is shielded, and the only source is the uranium-238 liner in the target assembly container," Ralph said.

When they had removed the four ring packages from the storage room, Ralph said, "Let's start with the fourth ring. We can replace the container top after each ring and take a reading. I feel confident that we can install all four rings."

After installing the fourth and final ring and replacing the top, Ralph displayed the radiation reading. "Just as I thought, five milliroentgens above background. There will be no detectable radiation outside of this room. Our first instrument is fully functional. Let's re-install the nuts on the top of the target ring assembly container, cover the instrument and call it a day," Ralph suggested. "I don't know about you, but I am pretty well beat," he told Mohammed, who nodded in agreement.

On the way back to the motel, Ralph was beginning to feel more relaxed and confident that Mohammed would be an asset: rather than the jumpy liability he had feared earlier in the day. He laughed as he joked with Mohammed about the ease with which they had accomplished their task. "Piece of cake, wasn't it? We make a good team. Don't you think? How long do you plan to stay in America?"

"I thought I might stay for a couple of weeks. I want to see all of our locations and storage rooms. We can return to your house in California between visits, hit the winery circuit, eat some more good steaks and discuss plans for the future. I need a rest. You are good for me. I tend to brood a lot, and I need to be with someone who is, as the Americans say, 'up beat.' My frustration with some of our brothers at home is affecting my disposition. I have arranged for the green round to be shipped next week. Abdul can deliver it to the Chicago storage room," Mohammed replied.

"Good! I am glad to see you take some time to relax. I was beginning to worry about you earlier today. You seemed so distracted. The enormity of what we are doing wears on me too. After our visit to the Chicago Center tomorrow, we can fly to Newark. I need your help to install the neutron generators in the other two instruments. By the end of next week one of them can be shipped to Atlanta. The third one can be sent to New York in mid February. When will the last two arrive?" Ralph inquired.

"They should be in Karachi by the end of February. You should plan a trip in early March so that we can complete the conversion. After that, they will be shipped to Newark. Both should be in America by the end of April."

Ralph and Mohammed showered and went out for dinner. Later that evening he called Dr. Ahmad to let him know that they would visit the center the next morning.

As they entered Dr. Ahmad's office, Ralph made the introductions, "Dr. Ahmad, this is our Saudi director Mohammed al-Mihdar. He is visiting our centers. Please show us around and then we will be on our way." After the tour, Mohammed expressed his very favorable impression and commended Dr. Ahmad and his staff. Then they both thanked the doctor for taking time for their tour and said good-bye. A taxi took them to

Midway airport, and they caught a flight to Newark, where Ralph rented a car and drove to the airport Marriott hotel.

The next morning Ralph took Mohammed to the Hudson Instruments building in Newark. Mohammed remained at the building while Ralph drove the company van to Indus Instruments to collect the two Mk 38's. The first red ring had arrived and was also collected. When Ralph returned, he found Mohammed dressed in coveralls disassembling the crate containing one of the instruments. "This is a nice setup. You have done well," Mohammed commented as he helped unload the van. By the end of the day installation of the first Mk 38 was complete.

"We can re-crate it tomorrow, then I will call the freight company and arrange for it to be picked up and delivered to Atlanta. We should be able to complete the second instrument tomorrow," Ralph said.

True to Ralph's prediction, they had completed installing the second Mk 38 and re-crating the second instrument by 6 P.M. the following day. "Tomorrow we will visit the New York building. Abdul will take the first ring to Atlanta this weekend. I want to rent a storage locker here in the Newark area before we leave. I am not comfortable with all of the components and the instruments being stored in this building," Ralph said, "The freight company is scheduled to pickup the instrument Friday morning. They will deliver and install it in Atlanta next Wednesday."

Friday afternoon Ralph and Mohammed flew from Newark to San Francisco on an afternoon flight. During the flight they made plans to visit the Napa Valley on Saturday.

Saturday morning Ralph rose early and went out for his four kilometer run. Five was too much these days. When he returned he found Mohammed in the kitchen making coffee. Ralph joined him and they decided to leave for the wine country as soon as both had shaved and showered. Ralph put the top down and they motored up I-680 to Benicia, where they turned northwest on I-780, then north on I-80 to highway 37 west, which crossed highway 29. Turning north on CA-29 they drove through Napa and continued north to Yountville – where they took a crossroad east to Silverado Trail. Stags Leap winery was about five miles north on Silverado Trail. On the way to their first objective, they stopped to taste at Chimney Rock and Pine Ridge wineries. At Stags Leap, they tasted several of the new vintages. Mohammed purchased a case of his favorite *Cabernet Sauvignon*; and Ralph – at the recommendation of the winemaker – bought several bottles each of *Chardonnay*, *Merlot* and *Syrah*.

Continuing north on Silverado Trail, they stopped to taste the current offering at Robert Sinskey Vineyard, then turned west on Rt. 128 to the town of Rutheford and Beaulieu Vineyard. From Beaulieu Ralph purchase a case of Estate Bottled, Private Reserve, *Pinot Noir*; while Mohammed selected several bottles of different whites. After a late lunch in St. Helena, they headed back to Ralph's house.

"You can really get a buzz on just tasting wine. This has been a fine day," Mohammed said with a laugh. "Are you O.K. to drive?" He asked as he settled back for a nap.

"Yes, the coffee after lunch perked me up. I am fine. I agree with you. This has really been a fine day. It is good to get away from work and our project. I am glad we finally had the opportunity to tour the valley," Ralph replied. "Do you want to stop in Oakland and attend evening prayers?"

"No, I am too tired," Mohammed responded with a yawn – his speech slightly slurred. "Any . . . way, we can't go to a mosque with wine on our breath. Allah will understand. After all, we' re d' . . . oing his work," Mohammed said with slightly slurred speech and a silly smile, a hiccup and a laugh. "We c' . . . nattend prayers to . . . morrow." Mohammed fell asleep.

Mohammed accompanied Ralph to his Livermore office on Monday. Ralph spent the day dealing with management issues pertaining to the Atlanta and New York Centers. It was becoming apparent to Mohammed that Ralph was totally involved with REM's Centers. *I am afraid that my brother is forgetting the real purpose of our venture. He is becoming a capitalist without realizing it. I must steer him back on Allah's path.* After dinner Monday evening, while they were sitting on Ralph's patio, sipping a glass of the Ralph's Stags Leap *Syrah*, Mohammed decided to broach the subject of his concerns – getting locations for the remaining bombs.

"I am amazed at your accomplishments. I had no idea you were so involved in the day-to-day planning and management of REM. Now I understand why you have not had time to find a location in Washington and Boston, but *we* are concerned that you have made so little progress in finding locations in those two cities."

Ralph did not miss the "we" in Mohammed's comment. He knew *we* referred to Usama and he was momentarily caught off guard by the feeling of alarm in the pit of his stomach. *He is telling me I have been spending too much time making money for REM and loosing focus of our original objective. This is Mohammed's not so subtle way of warning me I am not performing up to expectation. I must remind him I am doing more than just meeting the objective. I am making lots of untraceable money for Usama,* Ralph thought in panic.

"Yes, I too have been concerned about both cities," Ralph agreed. "Did I tell you I spent a weekend in Washington looking for a suitable location – to no avail? I asked Patterson to keep his eyes open for a location in both Washington and Boston. Patterson found the New York location. I decided it was more important to open the Atlanta and New York Centers. Having three operational and profitable centers will be an asset in establishing the last two. It will also provide the cover for the first three devices which will be in place and functional."

"I understand your reasoning. However, while I am here in the country, let's spend some time searching for a location in Washington. We consider Washington to be the highest priority," Mohammed replied.

"Washington is also *the most dangerous location.* We have no way of knowing how often and how effective the Government's radiation monitoring is. I have to assume that they do aerial monitoring on a random basis. Why don't we go to Washington from Atlanta?"

"That is a good idea. Let's spend Thursday, Friday and Saturday there. I can fly back to Riyadh from Dulles airport," Mohammed replied.

Wednesday afternoon the freight company delivered and installed the second instrument in the REM office in Atlanta. After running diagnostic tests and checking the radiation level, Ralph and Mohammed covered the instrument, secured the room and left the building. Then Ralph drove to Aunt Lil's storage room; where he provided Mohammed with the entrance code and his set of keys.

Thursday morning they took an early flight to Washington National Airport, and rented a car. Ralph spent the next three days showing Mohammed different locations in downtown Washington and driving around the beltway. By Saturday evening Mohammed was convinced there was no advantageous site available in the DC area for a center and a bomb installation. On the way to Dulles airport Sunday morning he said to Ralph, "I am glad we took the time to do this. Now I understand your problem. Finding a location where the device can be safely stored for a long period of time will indeed be difficult. Your idea of purchasing a warehouse building off New York Avenue has some merit. The building can be fortified into a secure warehouse for high value items. Part of one floor can be completely shielded and sealed so that no one can enter."

"Even so, there are still two major problems that we cannot control. First, the uranium-235 components may be detected while they are being transported to the site; and second, it is very difficult to shield against neutron radiation. Both uranium-235 and uranium-238 undergo spontaneous fission, which release neutrons. If the Government is using aerial neutron detectors our site could be discovered at any time. If we are discovered, it will not take them very long to find the other devices."

"Can't a room be shielded to prevent neutron leakage?"

"Yes, we could use boron or cadmium in the walls and ceiling. These elements absorb slow neutrons. Fast neutrons must be slowed in order to be captured. We do not know the sensitivity of the neutron detectors used by the Government, and the sensitivity will increase in future instruments. The fact that our uranium-235 components will be located in one place for extended periods of time increases the probability of detection."

"I understand. If I have any ideas I will let you know. We will discuss the issue when you come to Karachi for the conversion of the final two instruments," Mohammed said as they approached the car rental return lot. The men parted in the main concourse, each boarding a different shuttle at their respective gates.

The Atlanta Center opened the last week of February. Like Chicago, it was a resounding success. After the opening, Ralph spent the weekend in Boston with Nancy, who had become very interested in the centers. On Monday and Tuesday he met with Professor Bhatti and together they surveyed downtown Boston. Tuesday evening Ralph flew to Karachi.

March, 1992

Events in Karachi were a replay of Ralph's previous trip. The last two devices were converted into Neutron Induced Gamma Spectrometers ready for shipment to America. Both instruments were to be shipped in the next month. Ralph planned to store them in the Hudson Instruments building in Newark. He and Mohammed had decided not to order additional neutron generators from General Neutron, until final locations had been secured. Ralph was concerned about the timing of additional orders. "I do not want to make Bob Johnson or his boss suspicious of us. If we order another Mk 38 this year, Bob will tell Dr. Robertson at Livermore Labs. Someone may become suspicious of our activities and investigate," Ralph told Mohammed as they crated the last instrument. "It will be best if we move the last two instruments to their final location and install the neutron generators during the following year or years. This will allow me to build a cover story with Dr. Robertson and Bob Johnson."

"You do not anticipate any problems in installing the generators at the final sites?" Mohammed asked as he began to gather up tools and put them away.

"No. It is just as easy to install them there. In fact, it is better to do so – eliminates the chance of damage caused by transportation and handling. As soon as the New York Center is opened, I will be able to concentrate on the last two locations. Opening the third center has depleted our main bank account. We are opening the third center before the first center has

produced any significant amount of cash. Braggs expects Chicago to start contributing some cash by the end of March, but additional cash will be required to start the last two centers."

"You should have almost twenty million in the reserve account," Mohammed replied, giving Ralph a funny look. "What is the problem?" he asked in a sarcastic tone and jabbed a screwdriver he was holding in Ralph's direction.

Perplexed at Mohammed's gesture and nasty tone, Ralph, trying to humor him, took a minute before slowly responding in an apologetic tone, "There is no problem, I just wanted you to know that I may have to use some of the reserve capital. I did not want to use funds that might be needed elsewhere until you and Usama had agreed."

"Do not concern yourself with such matters," Mohammed said in a sharp reply and turned to put the screwdriver away in the tool kit.

Still trying to mollify him, Ralph continued, "Well, I just wanted to mention that we could fund REM by going public. Nancy has suggested that we could convert our investment to a loan, and then raise forty million with an IPO. Funds raised by the IPO would be used to repay the loan. She thinks that the stock would triple in a couple of months."

Darkly scowling and slowly turning to face Ralph, Mohammed punctuated each word of his next statement by stabbing the air with the screwdriver, "Just how much does your Nancy *know* about our business?" His icy words hung in the air around them as Ralph frantically sought to ease the situation with some acceptable explanation for his stupid blunder. He could see that he had hit a raw nerve. Mohammed was obviously furious.

Unnerved by Mohammed's continued threatening stance with the screwdriver, Ralph picked up a rag to wipe his soiled hands. Avoiding eye contact with Mohammed, he calmly said, "Nancy is a venture capitalist. Raising money through stock offerings is her business. I have only told her about the success of our Chicago and Atlanta Diagnostic Centers, and she saw the market potential. She has not visited a center, and knows nothing of our activities other than what's public knowledge – REM's a money maker," Ralph replied and laughed in an effort to make light of Mohammed's concerns.

Mohammed would not be laughed off. He continued to hold his stance, and again used the screwdriver to punctuate his words, "It will be best if you break off your relationship *with this Nancy*," Mohammed snarled, his body rigid. "You do not have time to waste with infidel women. If you *must* have a woman," Mohammed continued with a sneer, "find a true believer who knows her place, not some *infidel whore*," he screamed at

Ralph and violently turned around to throw the screwdriver at the wall behind the tool kit.

Taken aback by Mohammed's viciously menacing change of mood and violent reaction to his mention of Nancy, Ralph was perplexed, and responded by innocently asking, "Don't you have a woman?"

"I have no *need* for a woman," Mohammed replied in a sardonic tone as he picked up the screwdriver. "Association with our brothers is *all* that I require. Perhaps you too would benefit from developing *similar* interests," he concluded, throwing the tool in the tool box and slamming the top shut with a resounding bang.

Neither man spoke as they went about completing their work. Glad for the silence and relieved that Mohammed appeared to have calmed down, Ralph decided to let the issue of women drop and to change the subject. *I will be back in America by the end of the week and Mohammed will be in Saudi. I do not wish to have an argument with him. My relationship with Nancy is my business, not his*, Ralph thought, then calmly brought up a non-controversial subject, "Shipments of the components are going quite well. Soon we will have all of the rings for Atlanta. When will you ship the first complete round?"

Mohammed, who had seemingly reverted to his old self, stopped what he was doing and stood as if in a daze, staring into space. When next he spoke it was to matter-of-factly inform Ralph that the first round was in route to Karachi. "It will be shipped next week as a "Shielding Plug, Gamma Spectrometer, Part Number: GS-48321PG. The P is for projectile and G is for green. The next one will be Part Number: GS-48321PR, red for Atlanta. Upon my return from my last visit with you, I met with Usama. He is pleased with our progress, but again instructed me to complete the movement of devices and components to America as quickly as possible," he concluded; while Ralph curiously studied him as he continued staring at nothing in particular on the opposite side of the work room.

Mohammed's uncharacteristically weird behavior had so spooked Ralph that he was afraid to speak. Instead he too stood quietly waiting for Mohammed's return from his apparent reverie. As a result he jumped when Mohammed finally spoke in a raspy half whisper, "Al-Qaeda . . . will soon become active," he said and then slowly turned to walk toward Ralph until the two were almost face to face. With his eyes half closed and trancelike Mohammed moved as close as possible to Ralph's face without touching him. Then tipping his head slightly back and assuming an all-knowing expression, he softly whispered, "Many great things are being . . . planned," and moving even closer – he fixed his eyes on Ralph's parted lips.

Repulsed and fearing the worst, Ralph quickly turned his head to avoid possible contact, stepped aside, and nervously laughed as he awkwardly walked away. "That means you will soon be able to strike a blow for Allah," he said over his shoulder and purposely walked toward the exit door. As he approached the door, he heard a loud snort behind him, and turned just in time to see a red faced, puffing Mohammed clenching and unclenching his fists.

"Noooo!" Mohammed screamed with his head flung back, fists still clinched and arms rigid by his sides. "No," he snarled again, ". . . I am not *permitted* to participate. Usama does not want me involved in any way." Then he continued in a childish sing-song manner, "Allah's Rings are too important. *Neither* of us can do *anything* that will attract attention or worse, get us caught and interrogated."

Afraid to set him off again, but determined for Nancy's sake, Ralph hesitated awhile before asking the one question he desperately wanted answered, "Mohammed, what will you do when everything has been transferred to America?"

"That *is* the question, isn't it?" Mohammed replied in his former sarcastic tone and sneered at Ralph as they exited the room and locked the door.

Ralph, who had – in his mind – spent way too much time with Mohammed, was beginning to see a disturbing trend developing in his nature. A trend that put Ralph on guard for any future reference to Nancy or questions about the future. *He is too mercurial. I can no longer trust him to look after my best interests – if I ever could. He thinks he has me where he wants me and that may be so, but I still hold the key to making this plan come off like clock work. He obviously has his own agenda that goes way beyond the Rings. I must watch my step with him from now on,* Ralph thought.

On the long return flight back to Kennedy airport Ralph continued to brood over Mohammed's comments and irrational behavior, *He as much as ordered me to drop Nancy. I am not sure I am prepared to do that. Then there was his comment about, "that" being the question." Mohammed has nothing to do, once the last component has been shipped to America. It is not in his makeup to do nothing. I wonder what he has in mind.* Ralph would soon find out.

Mohammed flew from Karachi to Peshawar, where he had a brief meeting with Usama. "Praise be to Allah. Three of the instrument devices are in America, and two are in transit. All of the rings for the Chicago device have been installed. Two of the Atlanta rings are stored in a local mini storage facility. The New York device will be installed next week," Mohammed said.

"Allah be praised. What is the status of the other component – the projectiles?" Usama asked.

"The first projectile is being shipped this week. Once it has been received and transported to Chicago, we will have the first atomic bomb in place," Mohammed said with a big smile.

"Have there been any problems?" Usama asked.

"None. The instruments and components have been delivered to the Indus Instrument facilities with no problems."

"How about the cover business, the diagnostic centers. Are they serving their purpose?"

"The diagnostic center in Chicago is a big success and is starting to produce a profit. Atlanta just opened and appears to be following the same path of the Chicago Center. Every indication is that the New York Center will be even more successful. REM Investments will prove to be a very profitable venture for us."

"Allah be praised. Our brother Eid has done well," Usama said with a rare smile.

"Yes . . . perhaps too well."

Usama frowned and studied Mohammed for a few seconds. Finally he asked, "What do you mean by *too well?*"

Mohammed chose his words carefully, "Eid is becoming too absorbed with the success of the centers. He even suggested, or his infidel woman suggested, taking REM public. He seems to be obsessed, both with his infidel woman and building a business empire. I do not believe he recognizes the problem, but a conflict is building within him. The centers are his brain child, and his real mission is to destroy them with the cities in which they reside."

"What do you suggest?"

"At this time he is irreplaceable. He understands the American system and has an unblemished reputation along with excellent contacts. I suggest that I become increasingly more involved in his operations. Once the components have been shipped, my duties here have been completed."

Usama sat quietly for a few minutes, carefully considering what Mohammed had said. Finally he said, "May Allah bless you Mohammed, for you have truly served him and our cause well. I understand that you do not presently see a path to future contributions. You know why I have kept you out of al-Qaeda planning and operations. Allah's Rings is to be our ultimate blow, and it is not to be wasted. Allah's Rings will be our final glorious act against the Great Satan. Allah will tell us when the time has come to use his rings."

"I understand you logic. It is sound. I accept your will," Mohammed replied while bowing his head.

Usama smiled again and said, "Move the remaining components to America as quickly as possible. You will continue to be involved in Eid's operation. Your task will be to keep him focused on his true mission. A mission that may not be completed for many years.

"Now, there are other areas where your intelligence and abilities can be put to use. I wish you to continue to be our contact with The Group. They are greedy men. We have the capital to satisfy that greed – in return for their antiques. I have had some direct contact with the General. However, I wish further contacts to be between you and Colonel Valek."

"Thank you for your faith in me. I will be honored to do as your say."

"I also want you to be my secret ambassador to the senior clerics in Saudi Arabia and Iran. As long as you have no known association with al-Qaeda and me, you will be free to move about as you wish. You will continue to report to me, and only to me in all these matters."

"I understand."

"Now, it is time to establish the code phrase that will activate Eid, and tell him to detonate the bombs. All of the bombs must detonate at the same time. The code word phrase will be: '*Allah has placed rings on his fingers.*' Prior to issuing the code phrase, a time will have been selected and relayed to Eid. How much lead time will be required to arm all of the bombs?"

"I will relay the code phrase to Eid when I next see him. It will take at least a week to arm all of the devices. The complete round has to be transported to the instrument. A panel has to be removed; so that the cannon's breech can be opened and the round inserted. After the panel has been replaced, the instrument has to be turned on, and the circuits tested. Then the timer is programmed with the date and time. Each device will require at least one day. I suggest we start the arming process two weeks before the event. I can arm some of the devices, which will reduce the lead time."

"Allah be praised. You will determine your need to assist in the arming when the time comes. What is the status of the Washington and Boston sites?" Usama asked.

"Washington is a problem. I spent three days there with Eid. His concerns about radiation monitoring – especially aerial monitoring – are valid. The probability of detection in Washington is much greater than in any other city. So far we have not determined a course of action. A site in Boston will be secured after the New York Center has opened."

"Allah will show us the answer," Usama said ending the meeting.

Two weeks later Mohammed flew to Kennedy airport. After clearing customs, he took the helicopter service to Newark airport, then the shuttle bus to the Marriot. All of the red rings and the green and red projectiles had been shipped to the Indus Newark facility – with no problems. Shipment of the blue rings would begin next week, followed by the blue projectile. After that the yellow rings and projectile would be sent. He and Ralph planned to install the New York instrument the next day, then proceed to Atlanta and install the rings the following Sunday. Abdul would deliver the complete round to the Atlanta storage room as soon as the rings had been removed.

The next day Mohammed and Ralph watched as the delivery company moved the instrument into the instrument room of the REM suite. After signing for the delivery, Ralph observed as Mohammed booted the computer and ran diagnostic tests. Satisfied, that all was in order with the instrument, the two secured the room and suite and returned to the Marriot. The following morning they flew to Atlanta. Saturday was a good day to move the rings into the instrument storage room. They planned to install the rings the next day. As soon as the rings were installed, Mohammed returned to Riyadh. Ralph flew to San Francisco, pleased with the knowledge that the New York center was scheduled to open in three weeks.

April, 1992

To celebrate his growing success, Ralph decided it was time to have a party at his house for the Livermore Labs gang. He would invite his former boss, Dr. Jameson and his wife, Dr. Robertson and his wife, Alice and her husband, and a few other friends. He would display photographs of the Chicago and Atlanta Centers. He had a special photo of the Neutron Induced Gamma Spectrometer set aside to privately show Dr. Robertson. The party was important to establish his success and credibility at Livermore. When – after the party – two additional orders were placed for Mk 38 neutron generators, no one would be unduly interested. He would invite Nancy to come and be his hostess.

After calling Nancy, who readily accepted the offer, Ralph called each of his potential guests and invited them to come the following weekend. Next he called Betty, invited her and her husband to come and asked her to find a caterer. Nancy would call her after she arrived and together they could coordinate with the caterer.

Ralph met Nancy at the San Francisco airport on Thursday. Before returning to Rancho Nuevo, Ralph suggested they dine at the Blue Fox, where they could discuss plans for the party. Nancy would purchase liquor for the bar at the local beverage store. She and Betty would plan the food with the caterer, and purchase any needed dishes, glassware and party supplies. Ralph did not want to use plastic dinnerware. He wanted everything to be first rate. He planned to cook the steaks on the patio grill. The caterer would provide everything else. During desert Ralph surprised Nancy by giving her a thank you gift for being his hostess.

"I love surprises and this box is beautifully wrapped," she said as she carefully removed the ribbon and paper. When she saw the sparkling contents she was dazzled. Ralph had purchased one-carat diamond stud earrings, and a four-carat pendant on a platinum chain to match. "Oh, my . . . this is a surprise," Nancy gasped. "I don't know what to say. How can I thank you?"

"You don't have to say anything. Just wear them and think of me every time you do. You deserve to have beautiful things. I am pleased that I can afford to give them to you. Now it is getting late and we really should be leaving. I'll help you put those on later at the house so we can see how lovely you look in them."

"Well they certainly are beautiful, and I thank you very much," she said and gave him a radiant smile and adoring look. "I'll thank you *properly* later," she whispered in his ear as he motioned the waiter to bring their check.

Nancy and Betty had lunch the next day and met with the caterer later in the afternoon. At lunch they agreed that Betty's husband would work the grill, "George is really good with steaks," Betty said, "and I have been told I mix a mean drink. Let us take those two things off you, and both of you can just enjoy yourselves playing host and hostess."

Nancy thanked Betty and happily accepted her offer, "I can use all the help I can get. I was so pleased when he asked me to play hostess, but it is a little awkward. I have never met any of Ralph's Livermore friends, because we live on different coasts. I do not want to do or say anything that will embarrass him. Not having to worry about the food is a great relief."

That evening Nancy filled Ralph in on her day's activities. She had met Betty for lunch, visited the caterer, and purchased the liquor. Betty had already arranged for the caterer to provide everything needed for the party: all the food, tables, chairs, linens, party diner ware and glasses. In addition they would provide two waiters to serve the canapés, drinks, steaks and the side dishes to go with the steaks. They would also take care of set up, take down and clean up. At a local florist Nancy had arranged for the delivery of flowers to be placed throughout the house and on each patio table. Everything would be as Ralph desired – first class.

Guests began to arrive at noon on Saturday. Betty and her husband George arrived first. "We are ready to go to work," Betty said as she hugged Nancy, "You look beautiful and the house with the flowers is elegant. I love your pendant and earrings. Ralph showed them to me at the office. You are one lucky girl. He thinks the world of you." Ralph blushed at Betty's remark and reached around her to shake hands with the gentleman beside her.

"You must be George," Ralph said hoping to keep Betty from embarrassing him further.

"Oh, I'm sorry sweetheart, I didn't mean to ignore you. Ralph this is my husband, George. George this is my boss Ralph Eid and his girlfriend Nancy Hatterson. He is dressed for the occasion," she said and pointed to her husband, who had on a bright white chef's cap and an apron. "Isn't he cute?"

"At your service *mon ami,*" George joked as he shook hands with Ralph.

"We really appreciate you and Betty helping, but I wanted you to relax and be my guests."

"Hey, forget it Ralph. We are both so happy for your success. Betty really enjoys being your secretary. She thinks the work you are doing is very exciting. We are more than happy to help."

"Thank you both very much," Nancy added smiling.

With Betty and George taking care of the food and bar, Ralph and Nancy were free to play host and hostess. Ralph looked the picture of a successful professional dressed in navy blue slacks and an open collared white silk shirt that revealed the gold necklace Nancy bought him in St. Thomas. He charmed the ladies, who privately thought he was a "hunk," and impressed every one by providing several tours of the house as new guests arrived. After viewing the photographs of the Chicago and Atlanta Centers, the men congregated on the patio near the bar. The ladies sat at the tables that were set up around patio. George proved to be an excellent chef, and seemed to really enjoy cooking the steaks.

Nancy, in her black tailored jump suit and wearing her newly acquired diamonds was the hit of the party. Ralph watched her with pride as she circulated between the tables during cocktails and mingled with each guest individually. He was proud to show her off and to tell his friends about her occupation and her gift for raising venture capital.

Many scientists are "wannabe" entrepreneurs. Once they discovered that Nancy worked for a venture capital firm, they made her promise she would speak to each of them after dinner about their special projects. During desert and after-dinner drinks the men congregated around her and bombarded her with questions and ideas for new technology companies. Ralph's former boss Arthur Jameson had numerous questions regarding business plans, raising capital for a start-up company, and types of corporations. By 5 P.M. some of the guests were beginning to leave. Dr. Jameson called Ralph aside to tell him how proud he was of his accomplishments, "You are lucky in business and lucky in love. Nancy is a winner."

When most of their guests had departed, Dr. Roberts approached Ralph and inquired, "How is your research instrument coming along?"

"I am glad you asked. I had planned to show you a photograph of it. Follow me," Ralph said walking into the living room. From a credenza drawer, Ralph took a large manila envelope, which contained an 8 x 10 color photograph. Removing the photo, Ralph handed it to Dr. Roberts. "This photograph of the instrument was taken at the Indus Instrument facility in Newark. We are still experimenting with various samples: liquid, tissue and even blood. As you may know, we have delivered two other instruments to Biotech firms. It will be some time before we know if we have anything other than an expensive toy."

"Are you targeting any specific material?"

"Not yet. So far we are just establishing profiles for various things, like human tissue and blood. Next we will test tumors to see if there are any spikes or markers that could be used in diagnostics."

"I assume the Biotech firms are doing something similar."

"As far as I know they are. We have a confidentiality agreement with them – can't really discuss what they are doing," Ralph said as he put the photo and envelope away, "Let's join the others on the patio to view the sunset."

"Certainly," the doctor said as they walked back onto the patio, "Oh, and Ralph please let me know if you get on to something. If you need any assistance give me a call."

Looking out over the valley Roberts continued, "and Ralph, one more thing. If you ever decide to sell this place – let me know."

"Don't even think about it, Tom," Nancy said, smiling as she walked up to the two men. "We don't have anything like this in Boston."

"True, true. I am pleased to see that Ralph is in such capable hands," the doctor said and thought as he stood looking at the beautiful sunset over the valley below, *God, Nancy is gorgeous. He is one lucky man to have a woman like that and a booming business.*

"Why thank you doctor," Nancy replied.

"Well, it is getting late and I must find my wife. Probably too cool out here for her. She must be inside. It is time for us to leave. Thank you for a fine afternoon."

"We'll go in with you," Ralph said. Ralph joined Nancy and said their good-byes to the departing guests in the warmth of the house.

After Dr. Roberts and his wife left, Ralph and Nancy thanked George and Betty for their help. Betty insisted in helping Nancy clean up the kitchen. There was little to do. All that remained were dirty glasses, which the waiters were collecting and washing. Earlier in the evening the waiters had removed all the dirty dishes, washed and stored them in boxes in the garage. After the party was over, the caterer would collect them, and the tables and chairs on the patio. Nancy declined Betty's help, hugged her good-bye, and sent her home with one of the beautiful bouquets from the living room as a thank you for her help.

Finally alone, Ralph and Nancy sat sipping wine at the dining room table and watching light after light twinkle on in the valley below. "Well, how do you like my group of mad scientists," Ralph said.

"They are a fascinating group – such wide-ranging intellects and interests. So brilliant, yet so naive in matters of business."

Laughing, Ralph said, "Scientists always fail to appreciate the difficulties associated with transferring a successful laboratory experiment into a product. Sometime you must read a book about the Manhattan Project. I have often wondered how General Groves, the Project Manager, kept his wits about him – having to deal with so many scientists. If you are interested I have an fascinating book about the project."

"After meeting these scientists, I *am* curious as to the history of our atomic energy program. Can I borrow the book to read on the plane?"

"Certainly. How do our scientists compare with the doctors you work with in biotechnology?"

"The medical doctors I deal with in biotechnology are more astute businessmen. Most have been in private practice. They are also more difficult to get along with. Many are arrogant and abrasive."

Ralph refilled Nancy's wine glass. "This is an excellent *claret*," Nancy said.

"Thank you, I purchased it for Mohammed al-Mihdar, one of REM's directors. You must meet him the next time he is here," Ralph replied.

"Is he an Arab?"

"Yes, Mohammed lives in Saudi Arabia, but was educated here. He attended Harvard and MIT."

"Both of your are Muslims, and both of you drink wine. How interesting," Nancy said with a sly smile.

243

"Allah makes exceptions for the faithful when circumstances require it," Ralph replied with a pious look, and continued, " You looked beautiful today," he said as he leaned over to kiss her. "Remind me to properly thank *you* later for being the perfect hostess. You made my party a success and were quite the hit with my Livermore buddies. Seriously, I couldn't have done this without you," he said and kissed her again before sitting back to bring up a subject he had been contemplating for weeks.

"Nancy, I'm feeling very pleased with myself tonight, but right now I want to talk to you about your career and the future. A future that I think might include us . . . as business partners. I know you are totally involved with the biotech industry, and Boston is its center. But, how much do you know about the computer industry? I think the potential of the computer industry is much greater than the biotech industry. The area from San Francisco south to San Jose is becoming known as Silicon Valley. A good looking blond venture capitalist could do very well here," Ralph said, intently watching Nancy for her reaction.

Ralph's suggestion caught Nancy by surprise. Actually, she knew very little about computers. Of course she had a personal computer, an IBM 256 or something. It was annoying to use. She hated having to memorize all of the commands. Mostly she used a spreadsheet program, Lotus 123 and Lotus' word processing program. To her, a computer was a tool, not an avocation. "I really know almost nothing about computers. Dr. Jameson mentioned having ideas pertaining to microchips. He said something about 'exponential expansion in computing power,'" she replied.

"Desk top computers will totally change our world in the next decade. Processor speed will double, then double again, and again, and again. With every evolution, software will have to be rewritten and new software developed. Hardware, disk drives, modems, and inventions we have not yet conceived will be purchased; then become obsolete in a year and newer models purchased. Start-up companies will become the new giants. Silicon Valley is going to be the center of the new industrial revolution," Ralph said and pointed in a westerly direction.

Nancy sat staring at the lights for a long time and said nothing. She was thinking, *I thought for a minute there he was going to propose. Thank God he didn't. I adore him, but I am not ready to be tied down to anyone right now. My life in Boston has become rather mundane; and the job, though it pays well and offers security, has lost its challenge. Why not give Ralph's suggestion a chance – do the "due diligence" and see what shakes out?*

"O.K.," she said with emphasis. You have sold me. Give me the book to read and I will examine the industry to see if my company is interested. Maybe they will open an office here," Nancy said smiling.

"Why not open your own office. You have the contacts don't you?"

"You *are* serious . . . aren't you?" Nancy asked in a surprised voice. Now Ralph was smiling.

"Yes, I am *very* serious. California is where the real action is, and is going to be for quite some time. Have you heard of Microsoft, Apple Computer, Intel – to name a few?"

"No, not really. Apple maybe. Oh yes, Microsoft has the operating system, DOS, which runs my computer."

"Microsoft also is developing software: Microsoft Word and Microsoft Excel, a spreadsheet program. A man named Bill Gates heads Microsoft – a real go-getter, like most of the new computer guys. They are going to run over the stodgy east coast companies that are unable to cope with the pace of change. In the new world, obsolescence will occur in two to three years – maybe less. Take hard drives as an example. Today sixty megabytes is a large hard drive. Ten years from now it will be a Model T. I understand that gigabyte drives are possible."

"You really believe the computer revolution will be that large?"

"Ten years from now Wall Street will be driven by companies that do not exist today."

"Read the book on *The Manhattan Project*. A project that redefined America. Computers will do the same in this decade."

All levity gone, Nancy realized that Ralph was very serious. If half of what he predicted occurred, Silicon Valley was definitely the place to be. "I will read your book, investigate the computer industry, and give serious thought to what you have proposed. Starting a new venture capital firm is a major undertaking. I know where to find venture capital investors, but finding the right ventures is the problem. Evaluating technology requires expertise that I do not have."

"You met the answer to that problem today. The scientists at Livermore are in the center of evolving technology. Once you have established a venture capital firm, word will spread through the lab. Business will find you – more than you can possibly handle. Technical evaluations can be obtained by simply asking the right scientist. Throw a little dinner party and mention the technology. Nature will take its course, and you will have more expert opinions than you can imagine."

"You make it sound too attractive. Will you be able to participate?"

"REM's business plan calls for opening two more diagnostic centers in the next year. The only problem is finding the right locations. Once that is done, the rest is simple. New York will open next week, and after that the next two will just be duplication. Cash flow is positive in Chicago. Atlanta will become positive in three or four months. Once New York is operating, REM will generate a great amount of cash. Some of which can be used to back start-up ventures. As soon as my last two centers are operational, I will have free time to participate," Ralph said, answering an unasked question that had been troubling his subconscious mind for some time. Would it be possible for him to join Nancy in a business venture?

"This could mean a gold mine for you financially. It would be great for us too. We make a good team – we proved that today – didn't we? Now, beautiful lady let me take you to bed and thank *you* properly," Ralph said and took her hand as he rose from the table.

The next morning Nancy flew from San Francisco to Boston. Sipping a glass of champagne, she started reading *The Manhattan Project: The Untold Story Of The Making Of The Atomic Bomb*. By the end of the flight she was hooked. *I had no idea that our government could accomplish so much so fast. Unbelievable! If Ralph is correct, and the computer revolution is going to be a modern day version – then computers are definitely the place to be.*

New York Nuclear Diagnostics opened the following Monday. A scientist from Livermore Labs stopped by the center and later reported that it was a first rate state-of-the-art facility. Ralph's reputation at Livermore grew.

The week following the New York opening, Ralph received a phone call at his California office from REM's attorney, Mark Swartz, who reported some disturbing news. REM's registered agent in Delaware, Arthur Lowe, Esq., had received a call from an Aaron Goldstein inquiring about REM and its products. Lowe had provided the basic information that REM was a closely held private company. Goldstein had insisted on obtaining the name and address of the CEO, which is public knowledge. Lowe was not able to ascertain Goldstein's interest in REM.

"As soon as Goldstein hung up, Lowe called me to report the conversation. His opinion of Goldstein was that he is very aggressive. When he contacts you, let me know," Mark said, ending the call.

Ralph did not like the implication that this Goldstein was sniffing around REM. He could cause trouble – big trouble – especially with Mohammed. Trouble is one thing Mohammed will not tolerate. The following day, Betty buzzed Ralph to say that he had a call holding from an Aaron Goldstein. Fearing the worst Ralph took the call.

"Mr. Eid, my name is Aaron Goldstein. My firm, Goldstein and Associates, specializes in marketing high technology products to industry and certain foreign governments."

"What can I do for you Mr. Goldstein?" Ralph asked.

"Actually, Mr. Eid, the question is what can I do for you?" Goldstein answered.

"I am afraid I do not understand what you mean," Ralph replied, feigning indifference and hoping to discourage Goldstein.

"What I can do for you is find buyers for your new instrument, the Neutron Spectrometer that diagnoses tumors," Goldstein replied. "There is a tremendous demand for this instrument. I am sure that I can double your sales."

"I am afraid that you have received incorrect information. REM operates diagnostic centers using state-of-the-art medical instruments. We do not manufacture and sell instruments," Ralph said using a matter-of-fact tone.

"O.K., I understand that you want to market your new instrument yourself. That's understandable, however, I know how to sell technical instruments, that's what I do. You on the other hand are technical people, and technical people just do not know how to market," Goldstein continued.

Ralph realized it was time to end the conversation. "Thank you for your interest Mr. Goldstein, but I must repeat – REM does not develop instruments, nor do we have an instrument that we are marketing. You have received incorrect information."

"Look Mr. Eid, I heard about your neutron instrument and know that you are trying to sell it to biotechnology companies," Goldstein said before Ralph could hang up.

Perturbed, Ralph decided he had better find out what Goldstein knew. "Why don't you tell me what you have heard about our so called neutron instrument?"

"Well, I heard that you developed an instrument that can diagnose a tumor using neutrons. Can it also cure the tumor?"

"Where did you hear this story? Who told you?" Ralph asked, pressing Goldstein.

"Well . . . actually, a friend of a friend has a contact at a Government Lab. I heard about your instrument from my friend," Goldstein replied.

"Again, thank you for your interest. Unfortunately, we do not produce such an instrument, so we have nothing to discuss," Ralph said. "Good-bye Mr. Goldstein."

Ralph sat for a long time frantically thinking after hanging up the phone, *How did this bastard get on to REM? Someone at Livermore – probably Roberts or someone on his staff – has been shooting of his mouth about the spectrometer and tumor detection and treatment. I should have seen this coming. O.K., Ralph calm down . . . think . . . what you need now is some serious damage control. But what should I do? Call Roberts? No, best handle Goldstein myself and try to get him off track. The fewer people involved the better,* he decided as he dialed Mark Swartz private number.

"Swartz here," Mark answered.

"Hey Mark, its Ralph. I heard from Goldstein. Nothing to be concerned about. He is nothing but a blow hard, some kind of hustler. I am sure I convinced him that there is nothing for him at REM. Probably the last we will hear from him."

"I hope your are right buddy, but I don't think so. My guess is that our Mr. Goldstein can become a royal pain in the neck," Mark replied. "Call me if you need legal help with this guy. If he becomes a pest, I'll slap a restraining order on him," Mark concluded, then said good-bye.

Yeah! Call you? Like I'm crazy or something? The last thing I want is front-page legal news. No! I'll deal with this ass. You are a nice guy Mark for a Jew. Why can't they all be like you? Ralph said to himself as he hung up the phone.

Two weeks later Professor Bhatti called to report that he had found a qualified doctor who wanted to start a radiological diagnostic facility in Boston. Hoping to get ideas the doctor had contacted Professor Bhatti to discuss the REM Centers. The doctor liked the upscale format of the REM Centers and had a couple of interested backers. After several discussions, Bhatti had mentioned that REM planned to open a center in Boston and was looking for a center director. Bhatti suggested offering the doctor a deal similar to Atlanta and Ralph approved. Now all that they required was a high rise in the right place.

Mohammed was scheduled to arrive in two days, on a Saturday, at Kennedy Airport. Ralph arrived in Newark Thursday afternoon and rented a car. After checking in at the Marriott, he had dinner and then drove to the Hudson Instruments building. Leaving his car in front of the building, he entered and checked the office to be sure that all of the keys were in place. Then he removed the key ring and folder for Atlanta and Chicago from the desk and placed them in his briefcase. *Abdul has completed his tasks in Chicago and Atlanta and has no need for these.*

Leaving his briefcase on the desk, he entered the building's bay and placed one of the blue ring containers in the van. I can deliver one of the rings this evening and two tomorrow. I can deliver the fourth ring before Mohammed arrives at the office Saturday afternoon. All of the rings will be installed by Sunday afternoon. My last task will be to move the blue projectile to the Walnut Mini Storage locker I rented in Hackensack.

Delivering the rings in New York was an onerous task, because Ralph did not want to use any of the tunnels. He suspected the tunnel entrances had radiation detectors. Avoiding this potential hazard necessitated driving north to the George Washington Bridge; then south on Harlem River Drive, which became River Drive, and finally Roosevelt Drive. After the delivery he could return via the Holland Tunnel.

Ralph and Mohammed completed installing the rings and testing the instrument Sunday afternoon and returned to the Hudson Instruments building via the Holland Tunnel. Ralph had taken a small chance Saturday by taking the round with the blue projectile to the Hackensack storage room on the way to deliver the last ring Saturday afternoon.

"Allah be praised. Three of his instruments of punishment are in place," Mohammed said as they locked the door of the building.

"Yes, only two more to go," Ralph replied. "Speaking of which, I am going to Boston tomorrow to look for a site and meet a potential center manager. Why don't you come?"

Mohammed jumped at the opportunity. "Good idea. While there I can meet Professor Bhatti."

"Change your itinerary and we can catch a shuttle to Boston tomorrow."

Professor Bhatti had agreed to meet them for a late lunch at Quincy Market. They arrived before the professor and walked around the area. "This is an ideal location. I see a building under construction," Mohammed said pointing to the north west." Together they walked in the direction of the building.

"There is the name of the construction company," Ralph said pointing to a large sign. "I will pass it on to Patterson. He seems to know every architect in the northeast."

Returning to the outdoor restaurant selected by the Professor, they sat at umbrella covered table and ordered ice tea while they waited.

"It has been a long time since I was here," Mohammed said, "Things have changed."

Looking up they saw Professor Bhatti walking toward the table. Standing up, Ralph greeted the Professor, "Good afternoon Professor. I am pleased to introduce you to our Saudi director, Mohammed al-Mihdar. Mohammed is the one who encouraged me to start REM. Without his assistance and guidance, I would still be working at Livermore Labs."

Shaking hands with Mohammed, Bhatti said, "It is a pleasure to meet you. I have much to thank you for. Working with Dr. Eid has been a joy. It has added years to my life."

"The pleasure is all mine. Please call me Mohammed. I am used to American customs, and as you know, I was educated in Boston."

"You may call me Umair if you like. I have never been able to get Ralph to do so," Professor Bhatti said.

"I am afraid I am like Ralph. Calling a Harvard Professor by his first name makes me extremely uncomfortable," Mohammed replied and they all laughed.

The rest of the luncheon conversation dealt with the centers. Finally, Ralph asked about the local doctor. "His name is Wesley Murdock, III. He is from an old Boston family and has an excellent reputation and connections. He will make an ideal center director," the Professor said.

"Have you discussed a potential arrangement with him?" Ralph asked.

"Yes, I told him how we structured Atlanta, but did not provide specific details regarding stock. I am sure we can reach an agreement with him."

"Excellent, now all we need is a building," Ralph replied.

"Dr. Murdock's family is very close to several of the partners who are putting up that building," Professor Bhatti said, pointing to the building Ralph and Mohammed had been looking at. "He is sure he can obtain space, but it will be expensive."

Mohammed sat quietly observing Ralph at work. *Things seem to fall into his lap. Surely it is Allah's work.* Deciding it was time to participate, Mohammed entered the conversation, "What do you plan to offer this Murdock?"

Professor Bhatti looked at Ralph, who responded, "We gave each of the two Atlanta doctors fifteen percent of the stock, and fifteen percent of the center's profit each. If Murdock can deliver a suitable location, I will offer him twenty percent of the stock and a twenty percent bonus."

Mohammed thought about the offer. *It is a clever offer. Murdock gets a larger percentage of the stock and a larger bonus than the other doctors, so he will believe he has gotten a better deal. REM ends up with a net gain of ten percent of the stock and ten percent of the profit. Yes, Ralph is a good businessman. REM Investments will make a lot of money. Money that I can use when the time comes. It is well for me to become involved. If . . . or, when . . . something were to happen to Ralph . . . well I would just have to take over.*

Professor Bhatti called Dr. Murdock when they returned to the professor's office. The offer was transmitted and accepted. Murdock hung up and immediately called one of the partners.

A meeting was scheduled with the partner, Arnold Ulrich, Dr. Murdock and the building manager for the next afternoon. Seventeen thousand square feet were available on the thirty-third floor at $36.00 per square foot. Ralph was reluctant to commit. Mohammed pulled him aside.

"Price does not matter – this is an ideal site. We do not care about profit," he said in hushed tones.

"*I* care about profit!" Ralph quickly hissed back. "At any rate I will look foolish if I agree too quickly. Do you know how to play good cop – bad cop?" Ralph whispered.

Mohammed had bristled at Ralph's sharp reply. However, the play-acting made sense and he nodded agreement. Returning to the group, Ralph said, "Thirty-six is too much. We are in business to make a profit."

Ulrich thought for a moment or two then finally said, "If you are willing to sign a five year lease we can drop it to thirty-four."

Ralph frowned, then shook his head, "I think thirty-four is still too high." Mohammed took Ralph by the arm and led him away. The two appeared to argue. Finally, Ralph returned with Mohammed and said, "We can sign a ten year lease at thirty-two."

Ulrich responded, "Done, if an escalation clause is included, based upon increase in the CPI – Consumer Price Index."

Ralph conferred with Mohammed, then agreed, "My attorney will get in touch with you. First he will have to incorporate Boston Nuclear Diagnostics, which will then execute the lease. Dr. Murdock will be the company's president, and I will be the Chairman. How long before we can begin build-out?"

"Your offer is accepted. We should have the floor ready for build-out in six months," Ulrich replied.

Mohammed was obviously disgruntled when they left the building. In an effort to pacify his bad humor Ralph turned to him and cheerfully said, "Let's celebrate our accomplishment and have dinner with Professor Bhatti, Dr. Murdock and my girlfriend, Nancy Hatterson. You have not met Nancy – this will be a good time to do so."

"Are you *still involved* with her? I thought you were going to find a suitable Muslim woman," Mohammed snapped and gave Ralph an angry look.

This time Ralph had enough. "My choice of women is *my* business, not yours," he snapped back and paused to compose himself before continuing, "Do you want to come or not?"

Mohammed did not immediately answer. Finally he said, "Yes. It would not be proper to do otherwise."

At the hotel Ralph called Bhatti, Murdock and Nancy to invite them to an 8 P.M. dinner at *Maison Robert*. Dr. Murdock's wife, Heather, was also included. At dinner, Mohammed assumed the role of host. With a great flourish he showed off his knowledge of fine wines by ordering two bottles of Château Angelus '85, *St. Emilion* – an expensive French white wine – to go with the appetizers.

Dr. Murdock did most of the talking, asking an endless series of questions regarding the other REM Centers. After the main entrées were selected Mohammed ordered another bottle of *St. Emilion*, and a bottle of Dom Leflaive *Batard-Montrachet*, an expensive French red. When Dr. Murdock finally ran out of questions, Heather turned to Nancy and inquired about her profession.

"I am a venture capitalist," Nancy replied. Seeing Heather's confused look, Nancy continued, "My firm raises capital for companies. There are two main levels of venture capital financing. The first is early stage financing, which includes seed capital for product development and research, and start-up capital to begin marketing the product. The second level is expansion financing, which consists of several stages. For example, the first stage is capital for full-scale manufacturing and marketing. The second stage is expansion capital for inventories and working capital. After that comes stage three, 'Mezzanine Financing,' for major expansion. Stage four, 'Bridge Financing,' is preparation for going public – usually by means of an Initial Public Stock Offering or IPO. Capital from the IPO is used to re-structure debt and repay loans. In most cases the stock increases in value; and the initial investors – the venture capitalists – can sell their stock and receive a profit on their investment."

"What types of companies do you specialize in?" Dr. Murdock asked.

"My firm specializes in biotech companies."

"You are certainly in the right place. Boston is the biotech capital," Professor Bhatti added.

"Are you providing capital for REM?" Heather asked.

Mohammed, who had now become visibly irritated, interrupted before Nancy could respond, "REM does not require venture capital. Our stockholders are wealthy and have capitalized the company. REM is a closely held corporation and has no intention of going public," he interjected in a sarcastic voice – all the while sneering at Nancy.

Nancy's face flushed, but she said nothing in reply. Ralph gave Mohammed a hard look. The tension at the table was palpable. Professor Bhatti, observed Mohammed's nasty behavior, and in an effort to defuse the situation asked Ralph, "How is your Filet Mignon? My Chateaubriand is excellent."

Over desert and coffee, Heather attempted to converse with Mohammed by pleasantly saying, "I understand that you attended Harvard and MIT. I am surprised that a good looking man like you doesn't have a former girlfriend or two here in Boston."

"I do not have *time* for women," Mohammed contemptuously retorted.

Searching for something to say, Heather studied Mohammed for a moment, frowned; then turned to Nancy and observed, "It must be difficult for you with Ralph living in California."

Nancy, who had not missed the exchange between Heather and Mohammed, rolled her eyes at Ralph before replying, "Yes, it is. Ralph has suggested I move there and start my own venture capital firm specializing in personal computers."

She immediately knew she had said the wrong thing when she saw Mohammed scowl and Ralph flinch ever so slightly. Before she could say another word, Mohammed leaned back in his chair and sneered, "There is a big difference between computers and biotech. What do you know of personal computers?"

Nancy, who was really annoyed by then, remained polite in her response, "I am researching the market. Ralph and his former colleagues at Livermore Labs think that the personal computer will re-define America in the next ten years," Nancy replied.

"I agree," Professor Bhatti replied.

Not so easily put off, Mohammed continued to patronize Nancy by asking, "Are you willing to *quit* your job, *move* to California, and *start a business* based upon what Ralph has told you his colleagues have said?"

Now Nancy was angry, but held her tongue while she thought, *I know Arabs have no respect for women, but I expected Mohammed, who was educated here, to know better. I will use my 'I've had enough' voice and let it be.* Nancy slowly set her wine glass down in front of her. Looking straight at Mohammed, she smiled sweetly and spoke softly, but pointedly, "Actually, I *am* considering doing so, based upon *my* conversations with Ralph's former colleagues. I met several of them in California last week."

Ralph flinched again and held his breath. *If he was mad before he will be furious now,* he thought and said the first thing that came to mind to ward off another confrontation, "More wine anyone?"

They all declined and Dr. Murdock, sensing that something was terribly wrong, said they really must be going. He and Heather thanked Ralph for a lovely dinner and said their good-byes.

While Nancy and the Professor looked on in dismay, Mohammed, who was slouched over the table, only looked up, nodded and half smiled when they left. He said nothing more while Ralph paid the check, but sat there seething and looking into his wine glass, brooding, *I was on the verge of loosing my temper, and that would not do in front of Professor Bhatti, who is well connected with al-Qaeda. Word would surely get back to Usama. How dare Ralph involve her in our affairs. I will not tolerate her any longer. She has to go, but this was neither the time nor place to challenge*

Ralph on the subject. We are too close to realizing the fruition of our plans. All in good time . . . you infidel whore . . . all in good time.

They said their good-byes to Professor Bhatti, who said he was staying for a cappuccino. Watching the three of them walk toward the door, Bhatti thought, *Something is seriously wrong . . . that lovely, brilliant woman seems to be the source of it. Usama will be most displeased to learn of this dissension.*

When Mohammed, attempting to make amends for his behavior, moved ahead of Ralph to hold the door for Nancy, Ralph followed. Glaring at Mohammed, Ralph turned just as he passed to vehemently say in Mohammed's ear, "Don't *ever* embarrass me like that again . . . I'll see you in the morning."

Just then a taxi pulled to the curb. Hurrying forward, Ralph opened the taxi's door, helped Nancy in and joined her. As they rode away, Mohammed was left standing alone staring after them. They did not hear his parting words to them as their taxi sped away. *"This is not over my brother!"* he yelled after them into the night, and stood shaking his fist as he watched the taxi's tail lights disappear from sight. Then slowly turning, he spat in disgust into the street where their cab had stopped.

In the taxi on the way to Nancy's apartment, Ralph wasted no time broaching the subject that was on both their minds, "I apologize for Mohammed. He is a strict Muslim, a member of the Wahhabi sect. Women are not even allowed to drive an automobile in Saudi Arabia."

"He certainly does not like me."

"He does not like western women."

"I wonder if he likes *women*?" Nancy said with a quizzical look on her face.

Neither Mohammed nor Ralph mentioned Nancy during their morning breakfast meeting, nor during the remainder to their time together. Ralph was disgusted with Mohammed's behavior and knew Mohammed was furious with him about Nancy, but not one for an unnecessary confrontation, Ralph chose to let it go – for now. Mohammed flew back to Saudi the following afternoon.

On the flight back to San Francisco from Boston, Ralph pondered Mohammed's behavior at dinner, and Nancy's comment about his not liking any women. Ralph remembered another comment Mohammed had made, "I have not found the need for a woman," he had said. Then that night at dinner he had said, "I do not have time for women."

When they had discussed Mohammed's open antagonism toward her, Nancy had commented that perhaps it was not antagonism – but jealousy. *If she is right, I have a problem – a serious problem. I never put it together before, but he has always been a little too touchy-feely – and those prolonged hugs . . .* Ralph shivered and shifted in his seat. *I must be even more careful in my dealings with him in the future.* Just then another even more disquieting thought occurred to Ralph when he suddenly realized Mohammed was exhibiting increased interest in the workings of REM and the centers. *Does he think I have out-lived my usefulness? Is he after me – or my job . . . or both? He could be planning to take over completely.*

During his flight home to Riyadh, Mohammed continued to smolder over his loss of control of Ralph. *He has become too damn independent. Success has gone to his head. I will have to take him out if he continues to go against me. I will not tolerate that condescending bitch of his talking to me that way. She is starting to take control of him. That won't do at all. He is going to be mine. . . .*

Yosif, Mohammed al-Mihdar's live in housekeeper, valet and chef, lovingly greeted Mohammed as he entered his apartment. Mohammed towered over Yosif, who was slender, small boned and delicate looking. The two embraced, pressing their bodies together. Finally they parted and Mohammed walked into the main room – where Yosif set about making cold drinks. When they were both settled side by side on the sofa, Mohammed began, as usual, recounting the events of his trip.

Yosif, who was unfamiliar with the world outside of Riyadh, always listened with rapt attention as Mohammed described the wonders of the western world. Normally he would have delighted in hearing about the beautiful house a brother named Eid lived in, but in recent times Mohammed had returned in an angry mood after visiting brother Eid – who had "lost faith" and was "whoring" with some infidel woman. Mohammed made Yosif tremble inside when he was angry. Sometimes when he was mad with others . . . his master could be brutally cruel to him.

"You wouldn't believe how that infidel whore of Eid's behaved at dinner," Mohammed fumed. "She sat there with her blond hair all piled up on her head, and her breasts half hanging out; and prattled on about venture capital, personal computers, and the computer revolution that is coming. As if a woman knows anything about business. Worse still, Professor Bhatti agreed with her."

"I know what Eid wants with her. She obviously gives it to him too – from the way he looks at her like a lovesick dog and hangs on her every word. He even wants her to move to California to start her own venture capital firm to back computer industry startups. I am sure she will move in with him. She has become a bitter thorn in my side. A thorn that may suffer *painfully* from its removal," Mohammed said with sneering contempt.

Yosif, who had no idea what venture capital was, simply nodded in agreement with Mohammed and waited for him to work off his anger. Finally, when Mohammed had vented and life had returned to normal for Yosif, he quietly sighed; then uncrossed his legs, gracefully rose to freshen their drinks and said, "You have a message from Mujahid Shaykh. He said you knew how to contact him." Mujahid Shaykh was an alias for Usama bin Laden.

"Thank you," Mohammed replied, and patted Yosif on the bottom as he joined him at the bar. "The message means that I must take another trip – but not today," he said, taking Yosif's hand and walking toward the bedroom.

June, 1992

Two days later, Mohammed – traveling as Ali al-Libi – met Usama in Peshawar. At the meeting he learned Afghan rebels, with the assistance of General Abdul Rashid Dostam, leader of the government's secret police, had seized control of Kabul and ousted President Najibullah's regime. Sibgatullah Mojadedi, who had been named caretaker president, was not expected to stay in power. Burhanuddin Rabbani, the head of the 10-member Supreme Leadership Council of guerrilla leaders planned to assume control. The Mujaheddin was fragmenting into factions led by warlords – a situation the irritated Usama.

"Praise be to Allah. What is the status of your project?" Usama asked.

The fact that "Allah's Rings" was not mentioned told Mohamed the conversation must be guarded. "Allah be praised. I have completed the first four elements of the project. No solution has been found for the problems holding up the fifth element."

"The most important element. A solution must be found," Usama declared. "We cannot consider your project a success unless all five elements are in place."

"Do we have time to solve the problem?"

"Yes, at least a year, maybe more. We are still active raising funds and training Mujaheddin. We need money to arm them. The political climate is not where I want to be."

"I have given Eid my ideas and requested he attempt to implement them. I am sure he will be able to make one of them work."

"You did well in selecting Eid to be the project manager. He has done exceedingly well. I am confident that with your guidance he will solve the problem. Have you taken any action in the matter of the loose ends?"

"Yes, I asked Colonel Valek to solve the problem at my last meeting with him. He will arrange for the American, Kevin Patterson, to have an accident. His fee was $75,000.00."

"Good, according to your report, Patterson was one of two people who knew enough about the locations to become suspicious of our operation."

"Yes. The other man is Johnson. He knows about the generators, but is no longer associated with them. All the same, I will have Valek deal with him in another year or two."

Bin Laden nodded his head, and said, "I now require your services elsewhere. Soon al-Qaeda will become operational. You are to relay this to the Ayatollah's in Iran and our Saudi supporters. They must know that soon they will see results. I have established a good relationship with the Sudanese President, Hassan Turabi.

"The Yemeni Islamic Jihad have bombed three hotels housing American military personnel in Aden, Yemen. Make sure the right people know al-Qaeda planned and financed the operation.

"Two large operations are planned for next year. The first one will occur in February in the land of the Great Satan. Our brother there expects to cause a great amount of damage by destroying a major building in New York City.

"A second operation will be in Somalia. We have established good relations with the Somali al-Itihaad al-Islamiya group. Our Mombassa cell is in Mogadishu to assist in planning and training."

"What is our status in Iraq since the American's attack?" Mohammed asked.

"Saddam is making the best of a bad situation. He is telling the people that Iraq won; because, the Americans and their coalition stopped and did not advance to Baghdad. We still have a relationship with him, but he is not to be trusted. The man is a *fool*. A fool who would be Caliph. Did you see the photograph of him on his white stallion holding a sword? He was trying to portray himself as the great Caliph Saladin. Worse, he is not a true believer."

"Many in America think Bush will loose the election, because he stopped before taking Baghdad," Mohammed replied.

"Thanks be to Allah. I understand that Clinton is very liberal, does not like the military, and has no stomach for a fight. If this is true, Allah will have opened the door for us."

Aaron Goldstein entered the building on Twenty-fifth Street and looked at the directory. New York Nuclear Diagnostics was located in Suite 5220; and REM Investments, Inc. was located in suite 4926. Goldstein entered an elevator and punched the button for the fifty-second floor. Exiting, Goldstein first looked to his left – where he saw an impressive entrance with large double oak doors. On one of the doors in gold letters was the name, N.Y. Nuclear Diagnostics. Entering the waiting room, he walked to the receptionist and asked to speak with the manager.

"Dr. Weiser is with a patient. Please take a seat and I will let him know you are here. Do you have an appointment Mr. . . ?" The attractive brunette behind the desk asked while she carefully looked over the paunchy, balding man standing in front of her. She noted that he was about five feet, eleven inches tall, moderately well dressed with a flashy Rolex watch on his left wrist, a large gold bracelet on the other wrist, and a diamond ring on the little finger of his right hand. *A salesman,* she thought with disgust.

"Goldstein, Aaron Goldstein. Here is my card."

"Thank you Mr. Goldstein, would you care for a cup of coffee or a soft drink?"

"Coffee would be fine – cream and sugar," Goldstein said and watched as the pretty receptionist left to get his coffee. *Now that's a keeper . . . yes, she most definitely is a keeper.* He thought as he ogled her shapely buns wiggle through the door.

Taking a seat where he could easily observed the other people in the luxuriously appointed waiting area, Goldstein did what he did best – sized up the operation. Everyone was well dressed, he noted with interest. While he waited for his coffee, two older women wearing diamond rings and pins came through the same door the pretty receptionist had used. The women stood talking and holding the door open for a few minutes. In the time the door was open Goldstein deduced that it led to a dressing room area. Before he could get a good look the women let the door swing shut and walked over to the nurse's counter. There they and picked up what looked like prescription slips and left. A couple of minutes later, a tall elegantly dressed man entered, approached the deserted receptionist desk and stood there looking around.

This is a first class operation, Goldstein thought when he saw the 'keeper' returning. In her right hand she was carrying a linen napkin and what appeared to be a porcelain saucer and cup of coffee. *No Styrofoam here – nothing but the best.* Goldstein thought and stood to take his coffee.

"Good morning Mr. Rockefeller, I will be with you in a moment," the receptionist said to the well-dressed man as she approached Goldstein to hand him the cup and saucer. "Mr. Goldstein, Dr. Weiser will be able to meet with you in about ten minutes," she said matter-of-factly, and turned with a gracious smile to assist Mr. Rockefeller.

Goldstein returned to his seat and began reading the Nuclear Imaging brochure he had taken from the receptionist's desk. The brochure listed the types of diagnostic instruments available at the New York Nuclear

Diagnostics Center. A few minutes later the receptionist approached and informed him.

"Dr. Weiser can see you now. This way, please."

Goldstein followed the pretty 'keeper' through the door into a hallway he now saw led to what appeared to be various treatment areas. Turning left they proceeded down the hall to a large office with a spectacular view of Madison Square Park and lower Manhattan. As they entered the office the receptionist turned toward him to make her introduction, "Dr. Weiser, this is Mr. Goldstein," she said and left them alone.

Standing up, Dr. Weiser extended his hand, "Good morning Mr. Goldstein, what can I do for you? Please take a seat."

"Thank you Dr. Weiser, I am interested in learning more about your center and its instruments. I spoke with Mr. Eid and am especially interested in the new neutron tumor diagnostic instrument you are marketing. My firm, Goldstein and Associates, specializes in marketing high tech equipment and instruments to domestic clients and foreign governments."

Weiser was taken aback. Sending an operator like Goldstein to see him without first calling him was totally out of character for Dr. Eid. Goldstein's reference to "Mr." Eid was another indication Eid had not sent him. "I am afraid you misunderstood what *Dr.* Eid told you. We do not market instruments. In fact, we purchase or lease all of the instruments here from companies such as Phillips or GE. I have never heard of a neutron tumor diagnostic instrument. Is there anything else that I can help you with?" The doctor said and stood indicating the meeting was over.

Goldstein realized he had used the wrong approach and that there was no use continuing the conversation. "I must have misunderstood Dr. Eid. Sorry to have bothered you. I can find my way out," Goldstein said as he rose from his chair and exited the office.

Not easily discouraged, Goldstein returned to the elevator, and decided to try the REM office. *REM may be selling the instruments without the center director's knowledge. If it is experimental, that would make sense,* he concluded as he entered the elevator and punched the forty-ninth floor button. Exiting the elevator, he quickly located the REM suite – number 4926. The door to the suite was in keeping with others on the hall, and simply bore the name REM Investments, Inc., in black letters. Opening the door he entered the reception area, walked to the counter and smiled at a woman seated behind a computer.

"Can I help you?" a bleached blond with a twangy Brooklyn accent asked.

Deciding to use a different approach, Goldstein presented his card and said, "I would like to speak to your marketing director or vice president. I had a brief conversation with Dr. Eid regarding your new neutron diagnostic instrument that will be used to detect tumors."

The blond looked confused. "Sir, we do not have a marketing department or director. Please take a seat, and I will see if anyone knows about the instrument. A neutron detector – did you say?" she asked.

"Yes, thank you," Goldstein nodded in reply and smirked as he watched her leave. *No, not a keeper*, he thought. *Too bleached and too nasal. Not bad buns though*, he thought.

Sheila, the blond receptionists, walked down the hall to Tom Braggs' office and informed him that a man, a Mr. Goldstein, was inquiring about some type of neutron instrument. "He mentioned he had spoken with Dr. Eid. Here is his card."

"Thank you Sheila," Braggs said taking the card and looking at it. "I'll walk out and see what he wants."

Entering the reception area, Tom Braggs walked over to the man sitting in a chair and said, "Mr. Goldstein, I am Tom Braggs. Sheila tells me you are inquiring about some type of instrument."

Standing up and shaking hands with Braggs, Goldstein sized him up, thinking, *No jacket . . . tie pulled down . . . and shirt collar unbuttoned – He's either the boss or a flunky.* "Nice to meet you Mr. Braggs," Goldstein replied. "It is my understanding that your company has developed a new diagnostic instrument that uses neutrons to detect tumors."

"I am afraid you are mistaken Mr. Goldstein. REM does not develop instruments. Where did you get your information? Sheila mentioned you had spoken with Dr. Eid. I am sure he did not tell you we are developing instruments," Braggs said as he took Goldstein by the elbow and ushered him toward the door.

What the hell is going on here, Goldstein asked himself. *My friend's wife has a girlfriend . . . who lives in Walnut Creek . . . who has a girlfriend . . . who works at Livermore Labs. She said there was a lot of gossip around the lab about Eid and his new instrument.* "No, Dr. Eid told me the same thing. I just thought that you may be developing a proprietary instrument and wanted to keep it a secret. My interest is in assisting you to market it. That's my business."

At the door now, Braggs opened it and stepped aside to allow Goldstein to exit, "It looks like you are chasing a rumor. I can assure you REM is not in the instrument development business. Thank you for stopping by," he said and let the door swing closed as he returned to his office.

A red-faced Goldstein stood in the hall staring at the closed door. "Somebody's going to pay for this insult," he said out loud. "They *must* be hiding something," he continued to grumble as he walked toward the elevator. "Too, damned determined to get rid of me. I'm not done with them yet."

Waiting on Bragg's office desk was a message from Dr. Weiser regarding a visit from a Mr. Goldstein. After speaking with Weiser, Braggs placed a call to Ralph and filled him in on Goldstein's visits.

"Thank you for the heads-up Tom," Ralph said, choosing his words carefully. "I thought I had gotten rid of Mr. Goldstein, but apparently he thinks we are developing some secret instrument, and he wants to get a piece of the pie. Please fax me a copy of his business card and I will talk to him again."

Just what I need, more trouble from that Jew, Ralph thought. *I'll have to deal with Goldstein before Mohammed hears about him. I don't need to give Mohammed anything else to bitch about. Damn, what a scene he caused at the restaurant. I am very much afraid that Mohammed may be becoming unstable . . . a danger to me . . . and to Nancy.*

Three weeks following his meeting with Mohammed, Usama bin Laden received a disturbing report of the dinner confrontation between Mohammed and Ralph's woman. *It is well that I have Mohammed doing other things,* he thought. *Eid has done very well. Replacing him could jeopardize Allah's Rings. I cannot allow anything to do that. I will continue to receive indirect reports from Professor Bhatti. REM will be generating a great amount of cash – safe cash that provides me a secret source of funds in the belly of the Great Satan. Funds that I can use to bring American infidels to its knees.*

November, 1992

It had been six months since the dinner in Boston. Ralph had exchanged letters with Mohammed, but they had not spoken since they parted at the hotel the following day. In the ensuing months Ralph had grown increasingly worried about Mohammed's true intentions regarding Allah's Rings. In his quiet moments alone he brooded over what was to become of him and Nancy. *Mohammed is a dangerous man,* he thought, *but I have been trained to be dangerous too. While I do not want to do battle with him, I will not be bullied.* In spite of his bravado Ralph always came back to the same disturbing conclusions, *I do not know what Mohammed does when he is in his own country. What he does for Usama. I have never met Usama and have no idea what Mohammed has told him about me and REM. Dare I attempt to contact Usama, or ask Mohammed for an introduction?*

Mohammed's feelings about Nancy are still a big issue between us. One that was never settled – since that scene he made in Boston. With things progressing as they have with Nancy, I am sure to hear more from him when he discovers our plans. I do not want to have a confrontation with him, but she is too important to me to let her go. Her presence in my life has in no way interfered with the fulfillment my duties to Usama. Perhaps there is a way I can explain to him how much she means to my continued stability in light of what lies ahead.

I have been faithful to the cause in all but one regard – I am not practicing my faith with the same dedication. Somehow all that praying and chanting seems to be a waste of time that could be better spent accomplishing the objectives of the brotherhood. Besides the time I spend not going to mosque is devoted to making money for the cause – through REM.

Nancy had made several trips to California and had decided to open her own venture capital firm. She would be moving in with Ralph sometime in the near future. Ralph was looking forward to their future together. However, he was now busier than ever, and more and more consumed with REM's development. Build-out of the Boston Center had begun ahead of schedule. Ralph had made arrangements to lease a small four hundred square foot space adjacent to the center for a REM office. In another two weeks the fourth instrument could be shipped to the Boston office.

Only one instrument remained to be placed, and it was stored in the Hudson Instruments building in Newark. A fourth Mk 38 neutron generator had been purchased and installed in the Boston instrument. General Neutron treated it as a regular order. Bob Johnson had been assigned to another project and was no longer involved. All of the yellow rings were in Boston, two at a Walnut Mini Storage facility and two at Aunt Lil's. The yellow projectile was in a second Aunt Lil's in Medford. The remaining colored rings, the black rings, and projectile were stored in three different storage facilities around Newark. Washington remained the only problem, and Ralph had not yet found the answer.

At least that pest Goldstein had gotten the message, Ralph thought sitting at his desk in his Livermore office. Ralph has just been reminded of Goldstein after finding the salesman's card that Bragg has sent him in his desk drawer. He had called Goldstein following his sales calls to the two New York offices and demanded an explanation for his persistent inquires. Goldstein had been contrite and apologized for being a pest. "Must have gotten bad information," he had said by way of an explanation. Ralph considered the issue closed. *Now, I must bring Mohammed up to date on my activities*, he thought and began drafting a report to his board of directors.

"Chicago, Atlanta and New York are ahead of revenue projections," he wrote, "All three have positive cash flow. REM is earning a nice profit." The last item in the report was the status of the Boston Center. In this section Ralph stated that he planned to have a meeting with Professor Bhatti the second week of December, and that he hoped one of the directors could attend. *This should tell Mohammed that it is time to install the rings.* A week later he received a fax stating that Director al-Mihdar would attend the meeting.

After the rings were installed, Ralph planned to help Nancy close out her apartment. Then they would fly back to San Francisco. Most of her clothes and personal effects were to be shipped to his house via UPS. She had disposed of her furniture, because Ralph had a completely furnished house. Nancy had rented an office down the hall from Ralph's. Once her business was established she would need a suite. For now, PC Capital would be a one-office firm.

Kevin Patterson loved to play poker. He belonged to a poker club that met every other week at a men's club in downtown Atlanta. On poker nights, if he was in town, he had dinner at the club; then joined the game which began at 8 P.M. Most nights, the poker game broke up between 11 P.M. and midnight. Patterson usually parked in the club's lot, behind the building one block east of Peachtree Street – not the safest area in Atlanta. As a rule, he had no difficulty finding a parking place in the club's lot. This night it seemed "Mr. Murphy" was going to be a passenger – everything seemed to be going against him. Upon leaving his office and taking the elevator down to the parking level, Patterson found the right front tire of his BMW 740 was flat. Fortunately, the parking space to the right was empty – making changing the tire easier.

Patterson hadn't noticed the man in the dark green automobile parked several spaces down from him in the office parking garage. After changing the tire, Patterson drove out of the garage and started in the direction of his club. The dark green sedan followed him out of the garage and stayed behind him for several blocks. The man following Patterson stayed behind just long enough to determine he was heading for the club – then used his mobile phone to place a call. A man sitting in a gray van parked on the other side of the street, half a block west of the club's parking lot entrance, answered his mobile phone and heard a German voice say *"Nun"* – meaning *now*. Punching the button to end the call, he got out of a van, opened the rear door and removed several orange colored safety cones used to block traffic, or mark a no parking area. Then he walked into the club parking lot, where he placed a cone in both of the empty parking places. Returning to his van, he waited for Patterson's arrival.

Patterson drove into the club parking lot and quickly discovered there were no empty spaces. Turning around, he stopped at the entrance to the street to look for a parking place. A gray van was pulling out from the curb down the block to his left. *At least something is going right* he thought. After parking in the space vacated by the van, Patterson walked to the club entrance and joined his friends.

The card game lasted past midnight and Patterson had lost most of the hands. After the game he stayed to have a nightcap with one of his friends. Leaving the club, he walked across the dark street and continued down the sidewalk past a few parked cars toward his BMW. He paid no attention to the homeless man sitting slumped in a doorway. Patterson removed his keys from his pocket and attempted to insert the ignition key in the driver's door lock. The key would not enter the slot. *Now what. This just isn't my day,* he thought shaking his head. Walking around the vehicle, he bent over and started to insert the key in the passenger's door lock. Kevin Patterson never heard the man from the doorway approach. He just experienced a blinding flash – then darkness.

The man parked the gray van, which had been stolen early that day, in a fast-food restaurant parking lot; then joined the man from the parking garage in the rented dark green mercury sedan. Together they drove to a motel near the airport. The next day they took different flights to Berlin. Patterson's body was discovered by a police patrol stopping to examine the expensive BMW parked on a deserted street at 3 A.M. The victim's wallet and watch were missing. The crime was classified as a mugging.

1993

Spring of 1993 found PC Capital with two clients and a new opportunity. All of REM's Center's were successful. Mohammed had sent letters of congratulation to Professor Bhatti, Dr. Murdock and Tom Braggs after Boston Nuclear Diagnostics had opened. With Goldstein out of the way, Ralph only had two problems: finding a Washington location; and deciding what to do with REM's large profits. Nancy's reputation in biotech had magically opened several doors for her. She had been told about a hot IPO – America On Line – and was provided an opportunity to get in on the initial offering. Ralph purchased 20,000 shares at $11.50, and the stock began trading on the NASDAQ under the symbol AMER. In addition to being a great investment, AOL provided e-mail, which allowed fast communication among the centers and with Mohammed. PC Capital was provided an additional opportunity to participate in second level financing for a start-up company named Yahoo. REM Investments, Inc. participated in PC Capital's venture fund in the amount of $5 million dollars; and Ralph invested and additional $500,000 of his own personal funds.

Dr. Murdock called Ralph in May. A major medical trade show was scheduled for July in Las Vegas, Nevada. All of the center directors wanted to attend, and they urged Ralph to come also. The newest instrument technology would be on display. Ralph agreed that all of the directors should attend, and decided to go as well.

The Las Vegas Convention Center was full of new products. Professor Bhatti and the center directors were like kids in a candy store. Braggs negotiated upgrades on a number of instruments including a new CAT scan in to replace those currently being leased. On the second day of the conference, Ralph decided to walk through the outside exhibits; where one piece of equipment caught his attention – a mobile CAT scan, mounted in a self-contained forty-six foot trailer. "Small hospital and rural towns cannot support expensive diagnostic equipment, and patients have to travel to large cities," the salesman pitched.

Ralph was fascinated with the concept. *Mobile diagnostic equipment is a natural next step for REM. Even better, it provides an answer to the Washington site problem*, he thought with delight. That afternoon, he met with Professor Bhatti and Tom Braggs in one of the lounges.

"Have you been outside and looked at the mobile laboratory and diagnostic equipment displays?" Ralph asked.

"No," both replied.

"I discovered a mobile CAT scan mounted in a trailer. There were several other mobile units. It occurred to me that mobile diagnostics is a natural area of expansion for us," Ralph said.

"I am not sure I understand," Braggs said.

"That is a wonderful idea," Professor Bhatti agreed.

"I want both of you to tour the mobile exhibits tomorrow. After you see the units, Frank, you will understand what I am talking about," Ralph said, looking at Braggs. "Get all the information and brochures you can. I want you to use any of the center personnel you require to prepare a business plan for a Mobile Nuclear Imaging company. We will also need a market study. I am sure you know a good consulting company that can provide one. In fact, the suppliers of mobile equipment probably have one we can use for a starting point."

Leaving the lounge, with the intention of returning to his room for a nap, Ralph was flabbergasted when he was greeted – accosted might be a better term – by none-other-than Aaron Goldstein. Rushing up to Ralph,

Goldstein offered his hand and gushed in a loud voice, "Good afternoon Dr. Eid, I am Aaron Goldstein. It is a pleasure to finally meet you." Goldstein had seen Eid's name on the attendance list and carefully planned his ambush. One of the hotel employees had pointed Ralph out in return for a fifty-dollar tip. Goldstein stalked Ralph all afternoon, waiting for just the right opportunity to catch him off-guard.

"Good afternoon Goldstein," Ralph replied, appalled by the sight of the bald, overweight, slightly flushed man in front of him. He was outrageously dressed in a loud pink and red Hawaiian print shirt and lime green pants. With his little finger sporting a diamond ring, and his neck and one wrist adorned with heavy gold chains, Goldstein looked every bit the con man.

How in the name of Holy Allah did this fool know who I am . . . and that I was here? Ralph thought and ignoring Goldstein's extended hand and replied, "I'm surprised to find you here. Do you represent any of the vendors?"

"No, I am *trolling* for business. I learn all kinds of interesting things by walking around and talking to exhibitors and attendees. Does REM have a booth?"

"As you have been told, more than once I might add, REM does *not* manufacture equipment – REM purchases or leases equipment for its centers. We're here to looking at the newest instruments," Ralph laughingly replied over his shoulder as he turned and started to walk away.

"Look Dr. Eid, come with me and have a drink in a quite lounge," Goldstein called after him, "Let me tell you what I have to offer. I have *contacts* at Livermore Labs and I *know* that you are working on a neutron instrument."

This unpleasant bit of news brought Ralph up short and he paused to reevaluate the situation. *I had better find out just what this huckster knows.* Laughing again and smiling Ralph turned and agreed, "Perhaps that *is* a good idea Mr. Goldstein. I am sure you know just such a spot," he added – his voice dripping with sarcasm.

Ignoring the barb – for he was used to barbs – Goldstein replied, "Please call me Aaron, Dr. Eid. Follow me . . . if you will," he said with a flourish on his way to the elevator. "There is a quiet lounge on the 14th floor. My favorite place to hold private discussions," he snickered, as they entered the elevator. *At last I have him were I can size him up,* the salesman thought and stood nervously whistling through his teeth and shaking the gold bracelet on his wrist as the elevator ascended. *He's a handsome devil. Women must get hot all over the minute he enters the room. . . .* His thoughts interrupted with the elevator's stop, Goldstein gestured for Ralph to exit first, "After you . . . " he said, snickering again.

"No, you know where we are going," Ralph said in disgust and thought as he followed the waddling Goldstein down the hall, *He is undoubtedly the most aggravating, revolting man I have ever encountered.*

In the small lounge, an attractive redhead greeted Goldstein and led them to a table in the far corner – a table with a spectacular view of the city. Goldstein took a chair that placed his back to the window, ostensibly to provide Ralph the view. In reality it was to make it difficult for Ralph to observe his face. The scantily clad waitress leaned over as she took their drink orders – a Virgin Mary for Goldstein and glass of *Cabernet Sauvignon* for Ralph. Ralph was disgusted as he observed Goldstein brazenly ogled the waitress' bosom, and even more so with his lecherous comments about her buns as she walked away. "Nice," he said, "Very nice," and ran his tongue over his lips before concluding softly to himself, *Yes, I would say she is definitely a keeper.*

His lewd thoughts were interrupted by an exasperated cough from Ralph, who hadn't missed the direction of Goldstein's leering look. Goldstein grinned, and pointing back over his shoulder toward the window said, "Beautiful view isn't it?" Ralph raised one eyebrow, smirked and said nothing. The expression on his face clearly showed his disgust with the salesman. *Allah give me patience to suffer this slimy Jew until I can find out what he knows.*

Undeterred – for he was also used to disgusted looks – Goldstein glibly continued trying to schmooze Ralph by telling him how useful he could be to the development of REM's diagnostic equipment.

"Let me tell you something about *me* and what I have to offer. I've been in the business of putting people with compatible needs and products together for the past twenty years. In the past my main clients were the military and defense contractors. I established a relationship with procurement officers and engineers. By hosting simple after-hours cocktail sessions, similar to this one, I'd learn about problems and opportunities.

"It took a long time to gain the trust of the government personnel, but over time it has allowed me to earn many large fees. No, I didn't *bribe* anyone. I became what is now called a 'facilitator.' For example, in one instance I learned that a company was getting into serious problems with the government engineers, because the company's program manager had a bad attitude. Now, it so happened I knew a vice president of the company," Goldstein bragged with a wave of pinkie fingered hand.

"So I arranged a meeting like this and advised him of the problem. No fee, just a favor. Later, I earned a large fee from the same company as their representative by obtaining a major contract from the same government arsenal. How? Because the government people appreciated me solving a problem for them, and the company owed me a favor."

Just then the waitress returned with their drink orders. Ralph watched with some amusement as Goldstein made a show of not looking at her. Ralph smiled as he thanked the waitress, stifled a yawn and continued feigning interest while Goldstein's big mouth ran on and on.

"After Viet Nam I expanded my area of operations to the Department of Energy and Health and Human Services. Scientists at DOE labs are much more naive than the military ones. That is mostly because DOE labs never seem to be under pressure to achieve results according to a timetable. What I discovered is that the labs are like a diamond field in old Africa – where you could pick up diamonds off the ground. By hosting sessions with scientists and engineers I discover technical diamonds that can be developed into *polished gems*. I think your neutron instrument may be just such a gem. I have contacts with companies that can manufacture it and with government agencies, foreign and domestic, that would buy it."

Ralph sat quietly considering what Goldstein had said. *In spite of my disgust for the man's behavior, some of what he says makes sense. He's smarter than he looks, and he's persistent. He is going to be a problem. He definitely won't be blown off. If I attempt to, he'll keep digging. He may put things together that would be harmful. I think the best course of action is to string him out. Until I find a way to deal with him that will not harm Allah's Rings.* Shaking his head as if in agreement with what Goldstein was saying, Ralph leaned forward and extended his hand to Goldstein, "What an interesting proposition Aaron. Yes, I can see where you could be very helpful to me. Let's shake on that."

"Sure thing, Doc," Goldstein responded and grabbed Ralph's hand enthusiastically. "I knew if you just took time to listen to my approach you'd see I have something positive to offer you."

Ralph continued to placate him, "I *am* impressed Aaron. You are quite good at what you do . . . 'Trolling' . . . Is that what you call it?" Ralph asked.

Aaron nodded in response and snickered.

"Trolling . . . yes that is a good way to put it," Ralph continued. "You have really caught something this time. This time you have a big fish on the line." *One that will turn on you with a vengeance if you don't 'catch and release' Jew boy. Let him think he is really on to something, but it's really hush, hush,* Ralph thought while smiling at Goldstein. "As you have discovered, I am doing research pertaining to developing a new diagnostic instrument. My project is my own, funded by REM – but it *does not* involve any of REM's employees. REM is a closely held corporation. The directors do not wish our research to be known. Not until we have a working instrument, which is still a couple of years away – the competition . . . you know . . . might get wind of it," Ralph said in a conspiratorial voice, while trying hard to keep from laughing at Goldstein, who was sipping his drink through the tiny bar straw and nodding his head in agreement. *He's taking it hook, line and sinker*, Ralph thought with delight as he continued.

"I will relay our conversation, no . . . excuse me, your *proposal*, to our board at the next meeting. I am inclined to recommend we consider your *proposal* in a favorable light. After the meeting, which has yet to be scheduled – I'll get back to you. In the meantime, you *must* stop asking questions," Ralph said. Leaning forward he continuing in a whisper, "You don't want to loose out on this by tipping off our *competition*." Goldstein nodded. "There is no profit in it for either of us if word of my invention gets out," Ralph continued in a hushed tone, "We must keep everything very quiet, until I have talked to the board. If the board approves, and I am *sure* they will, I'll let you know. Once I have successful test results you can start trolling for buyers. Is that agreeable?" Ralph asked with a smarmy smile.

Attempting to keep from smiling too, Goldstein gloated, *Hot damn! I've done it. I just knew they were hiding something. Better sew this up real quick before he changes his mind.* "Yes, that is most acceptable," he said in his best business-like tone, "I am sure we can establish a mutually beneficial relationship."

"Good, we have an agreement," Ralph said continuing to smile and extending his hand to give Aaron's pudgy hand a firmer than usual grasp and hearty shake; before innocently inquiring, "Now tell me about your personal life Aaron. Do you live in New York?"

"No, I live in Palm Springs. I am single, my ex-wife couldn't tolerate my . . . traveling. Do you ever visit Palm Springs? I will write my home address and telephone number on the back of my card – Hope you'll stop by for a visit," Goldstein replied.

While Goldstein continued talking and writing on his card, Ralph signaled the waitress to close out their tab. When she arrived, Goldstein grabbed the check and without even looking at the amount, pulled a hundred dollar bill out of his shirt pocket; which he handed her and said, "Keep the change."

"You really should visit me sometime," Goldstein continued saying to Ralph, who hadn't missed the show with the waitress. *You hundred dollar big shot . . . You'll probably come back later and hit on her to try and get your money's worth. What a pig! How am I ever going to get rid of you?* Ralph thought and took the business card Goldstein was handing him.

"A couple of days off . . . a few rounds of golf . . . some lovely ladies at night – will make a new man of you," Goldstein snickered as Ralph stood to leave the lounge. Standing too he waddled after Ralph to the elevator; all the while keeping up a steady stream of chatter trying to sell Ralph on Palm Springs' grand life style. *There is no way in hell I want to visit you in Palm Springs or anywhere else for that matter. Now how do I dump you, so I can enjoy the rest of my afternoon,* Ralph wondered while suffering through what seemed like an endless elevator ride down to the casino floor.

As they walked back through the casino, an idea occurred to Ralph when a roving photographer offered to take their pictures. He smilingly obliged to pose with Goldstein – and ordered two prints for himself.

A month later the business plan for Mobile Nuclear Imaging, Inc. was delivered to Ralph's office. Ralph carefully read it through, then started rereading it and making notes in the margins. All in all it was a good plan. Market studies provided by the vendors indicated a large nationwide market. Even after discounting the vendor's projections by fifty percent, the opportunity was still attractive. Ralph walked down the hall to Nancy's office. She was on the phone talking to the budding CEO of a computer gaming software company that had just released its first winner. Looking up, she motioned Ralph to come in and used her hand to indicate a talker. Ralph laughed and sat down. A few minutes later Nancy hung up and sighed, "If he can write games anywhere near as well as he can talk he will be a multi-millionaire in six months."

Ralph smiled and laughed, then handed Nancy the Mobile Nuclear Imaging business plan, "See what you think of this."

Looking at the title she said, "This is the idea you told me about after the Las Vegas conference."

"Yes, I have made some notes in the margin. Add your thoughts and then I will send it back to Braggs. I think we can be first in a new market."

"I will read it this evening. Right now I have to finish reviewing 'the talkers' business plan."

"Have fun," Ralph said, walking out the door. "Let's leave early today."

Upon returning to his office, Ralph composed an e-mail to Mohammed.

> I have identified a new area of business for REM. Mobile diagnostic equipment. Instruments mounted in trailers that are parked at hospitals or other convenient locations where fixed facilities do not exist. Washington DC will be a good test market. The trailer can be parked downtown to provide services to Government employees. We are preparing a business plan for a new company – Mobile Nuclear Imaging, Inc.

The following day Ralph logged on to AOL and received the familiar "You've Got Mail." It was an e-mail from Mohammed.

> Sounds like an excellent idea. Please send me a copy of the business plan.

Ralph forwarded Mohammed's e-mail to Braggs and Professor Bhatti. Next he began preparing a memo to be faxed to Omar Mumtaz, "Please order another Mk 38 for delivery to Newark." *That should please Mohammed greatly,* he thought as he sat staring out his office window contemplating the status of their project. *That completes all of the required components for the fifth instrument. I will order one more Mk 38 in six months to be used as a spare in case one of the generators fails.*

Continuing to sit staring out the window, Ralph considered his only pressing problem, *I still have the Goldstein predicament to deal with. I can't let it sit much longer. As much as I dislike the idea, I am going to have to ask Mohammed for assistance. I do not know how to handle this type of problem. Getting rid of him through legal action – a restraining order – is out of the question.*

Turning back to his computer, Ralph logged back on to AOL, and prepared to send Mohammed an e-mail.

> Something important has come up that I need to talk to you about. Can we meet in New York or Boston?

Clicking on the send key, Ralph returned to his mailbox to finish reading his mail. A short time later, he received a "You've Got Mail" chime, and noted that he had a reply from Mohammed. Clicking to open the e-mail, he read:

> I can meet you in New York next Thursday at the Four Seasons.

Ralph confirmed the meeting with another e-mail, then called the travel agent to book his flight and hotel.

The following Thursday afternoon Ralph met Mohammed in his hotel room. After explaining his problems with Goldstein, Ralph said, "I do not know how to get rid of this Jew. He is like a leech. I need your advice."

Scowling, Mohammed snapped, "You should have come to me when this Jew pig first appeared. Never keep a problem from me again. *This Jew* could destroy our project. I will take care of the problem. Do you have his address?"

Ralph was relieved. He had expected a lecture from Mohammed, but instead all he wanted was the Jew's address. So he simply handed Mohammed an envelope containing everything he knew about Goldstein, including the photo from the Las Vegas casino. Mohammed opened the envelope and carefully examined its contents.

"This is everything that I need. I am glad to see that you can do *something* right," Mohammed commented, sarcasm dripping from every word. "Just make sure that the mobile units achieve their real purpose. I would hate to have to report a failure to our leader."

1994

Eight months later, in April 1994, Mobile Nuclear Diagnostics, Inc. (MND) accepted delivery of its first mobile CAT scan, with the optional onboard electrical generator. MND was housed in a large warehouse near Baltimore, Maryland. The first service route included Hagerstown and Cumberland, Maryland; Johnstown, Altoona, Williamsport, and York Pennsylvania. Mobile Nuclear Diagnostics was another winner. Three more units were ordered. After several months of operation, the MND mobile CAT scan was allowed to setup in downtown Washington adjacent to the mall. Over the next several years Mobil Nuclear Diagnostics' trailers became an accepted part of the Washington scene.

Ralph had not heard from Goldstein since Los Vegas, and Mohammed had not mentioned him since the New York meeting. Curiosity finally overcame good judgment and Ralph extracted the card with Goldstein's home phone number written on the back from his desk. First he called the office number and was rewarded with a "not in service" message. He got the same message when he called Goldstein's home number. *Well, if he ever calls me I can honestly tell him that I tried to call him. Best to leave sleeping dogs lie, as the old saying goes,* Ralph thought.

Mohammed had just returned from Tehran where he had met with one of the senior Ayatollahs. The *"shura"* (in this case a council of "radical" clerics) were pleased with al-Qaeda's actions, especially the World Trade Center bombing and Somalia. Mohammed's main mission had been to alert the *shura* to bin Laden's planned letter to King Faisal of Saudi Arabia.

Now seated in his apartment next to Yosif, he boasted, "I am becoming recognized as a man of influence and power by the clerics. While I may not have a visible role within al-Qaeda, I am becoming a powerful man in the Muslim world." Yosif, who had always thought of Mohammed as a great man simply smiled and pressed his head against Mohammed's shoulder. *Yes, I am important. I have the power to issue the command that activates Allah's Rings. Should anything happen to Usama, I will be the most powerful man in the Muslim world, and only I know that. Eid has become a problem. With his infidel woman, he has become a capitalist. He has not yet recognized the conflict. The question is, will he follow Allah's will and arm the devices when the time comes?*

In America the subjects of Mohammed's thoughts, Ralph and Nancy, were happily enjoying the fruits of their collective capitalistic labors. For the past two years, life had been good for them. REM was a success and Ralph was able to spend more time with Nancy, whose venture capital firm, PC Capital, was thriving. When the first attack on the World Trade Center had occurred in 1993, Ralph's first thought had been for the safety of his center. He had not been told that it was an al-Qaeda operation, and did not find out until it became public information. After determining that the center was safe, a disturbing long suppressed thought flashed through his mind, *I will have to destroy all of the centers one day,* but he quickly dismissed the thought.

A year after the first mobile CAT scan trailer had been delivered by Acme Motor Coaches, Ralph found out, quite by accident, that a CAT scan unit, leased to a small company in Michigan, had been damaged in an accident. Ralph purchased the damaged trailer and had it shipped to Hudson Instruments in Newark, New Jersey. Using Saudi and Pakistani workers provided by Mohammed, the damaged instrument was disassembled. Ralph designed a new internal structure for the damaged CAT scan. The remaining Neutron Induced Gamma Spectrometer device was converted into what appeared to be a mobile CAT scan mounted in the repaired trailer. After the conversion was completed, the unit was stored in the Hudson Instruments building. The trailer was jacked up, so that the tires would not go flat. Mohammed assisted Ralph in the installation of the final set of rings during one of his infrequent visits.

"It is too bad Kevin Patterson did not live to see the success of the centers he designed and helped to create," Ralph said to Mohammed while they installed the rings.

"Yes, isn't it," Mohammed said. Ralph did not see the sadistic grin on his face, as Mohammed thought, *Allah's Rings are all in place and ready for the final command – "Allah has placed rings on his fingers."*

"Our terrorism against America is a good terrorism to stop the oppressor from committing unjust acts and to stop America supporting Israel, which is killing our children."

"The call to wage war against America was made because America has spear-headed the crusade against the Islamic nation, sending tens of thousands of its troops to the land of the two Holy Mosques over and above its meddling in its affairs and its politics, and its support of the oppressive, corrupt and tyrannical regime that is in control. These are the reasons behind the singling out of America as a target."
– Usama bin Laden

Part III

Rings On My Fingers

Al Qaeda, 1993 – 2001

President Bush (Bush I) lost the election to William Jefferson Clinton in November 1992. However, Bush I was still the president of the United States and continued to carry the mantel of responsibility held by the leader of the free world. In Somalia, which in 1991 had descended into anarchy after the collapse of the last regime, food convoys were being high jacked, and relief workers intimidated, robbed, and killed by armed Somali clans. Food and supplies were being stolen from the docks as quickly as they were unloaded. Famine had spread across the land. On December 4, 1992, in response to United Nations' request for humanitarian relief in the strife-torn country, Bush I announced operation "Restore Hope": the deployment of up to 28,000 U.S. troops to support "UNISOM I" – the U.N.'s Somalia relief effort. Pakistan, Italy, France, and Turkey also pledged troops.

On the night of December 9, 1992, U.S. Marines hit the beach near Mogadishu, Somalia under the intense spotlights from numerous TV cameras. Those marines were the first of the Restore Hope troops sent to patrol Mogadishu's streets. Within a few months the strife in Somalia was under control and food was reaching the starving population. Although various warlords and their clans continued roaming the streets, they were reluctant to engage U.S. troops in battle.

Seeing a chance to strike at American troops off U.S. soil, al-Qaeda seized the opportunity and began a Middle Eastern campaign against America. American troops on the way to Somalia in 1992 passed through Aden, Yemen, where three hotels were bombed. Initially, the attacks were blamed on the Yemeni Islamic Jihad. Later in an interview with a Pakistani newspaper, Usama bin Laden took credit for planning and financing the attacks and boasted, *". . . the U.S. [had] received the warning and gave up the idea of setting up its military bases in Yemen."* Bin Laden had family ties in Yemen; where his billionaire father, Mohammed, who openly funded Afghan rebels, was born.

William Jefferson Clinton became president of the United States of America in January of 1993, and Usama bin Laden wasted no time in testing him. At approximately 12:18 P.M. on February 26, 1993, an explosion ripped through the parking garage under the World Trade Center complex in New York City. FBI explosive unit personnel determined the crater formed by the detonation measured approximately 150 feet in diameter at its widest point, and was over five stories deep. Evaluation of the damage done to automobiles, concrete and structural steel suggested that the "explosive used" fell into the medium detonation velocity category, and had a detonation rate of between 14,000 to 15,500 feet per second (fps).

Explosives with low detonating velocities (i.e., 40% nitroglycerine commercial dynamite with a detonation velocity of 8,000 fps) produce a pushing effect rather than a shattering effect – making them suitable for pushing and heaving earth. Several commercial explosives are in the medium detonation rate category – water gels, slurries, fertilizer-based explosives, and 60% nitroglycerine dynamite with a detonation velocity of 16,000 fps. High explosives detonate at a faster rate – TNT, 21,000 fps; C-4, 26,000 fps; and Comp-B, 25,500 fps. High explosives shatter rather than push, and their effectiveness is measured in terms of their *"brisance,"* a term that refers to the degree of shattering effect exerted by the explosive.

Initial assessment of the type of damage and size of the crater indicated the explosive main charge had been between 1,200 and 1,500 pounds. Six people in the Trade Center were killed, more than a 1,000 injured, and over 50,000 evacuated from the complex in the hours immediately following the blast.

In the wake of this attack there was shockingly little American outrage, and no military response directed against terrorists by William Jefferson Clinton, America's new president. Ramzi Youssef's trial and conviction for the bombing in 1998 established that Youssef had direct contact with Usama bin Laden and was funded by al-Qaeda.

Emboldened by his Trade Center success, bin Laden pushed on. The Mogadishu, Somalia incident – described in the movie *Blackhawk Down,* and a book with a similar title – began on October 3, 1993, and can only be classified as a resounding success for al-Qaeda; as well as the first true indication of the Clinton administration's policy for dealing with terrorism.

A historical look at Somalia indicates that America's involvement with the country had its roots in Soviet's cold war efforts to seize control of Somalia's government. Somalian President, Said Barre, backed by Russia, seized power on October 21, 1969 and established a Supreme Revolutionary Council. War with Ethiopia's socialist government followed, and the Soviets withdrew support of Barre and backed the Ethiopians. America, then under the Nixon administration, backed the Somali regime in return for the use of the navy base at Barbera.

Somalia was made up of six major clans, each of which was made up of sub-clans, whose territories were defined by their nomadic migrations. War and drought brought famine and starvation to people already on the brink of extinction. Relief food began arriving at the port in Mogadishu in the early 1980s. Barre's government used that food to build its power base and control people in the hinterlands.

Opposition to President Barre grew, forcing him to flee on January 27, 1991. Somalian warlord, Mohammed Farah Aideed, who had gained prominence in the United Somali Congress (USC), had his eye on the presidency. However, USC Somalian ex-patriots in Italy proclaimed Ali Mahdi President of the Republic of Somalia. Inside the country the claim was disregarded. Civil war erupted after the collapse of Barre's regime when various clan-based military factions competed for control. Aideed's Somalia National Alliance Forces (SNAF) militia gained the upper hand. Confining Mahdi's supporters to a portion of Mogadishu, Aideed concentrated his efforts on factions in southern Somalia. The famine of 1991 resulted from a power struggle among the clans.

Ali Mahdi was elected chairman of the USC by a two-thirds vote in June 1991. By October he had formed a government of eight ministers and held the promise of massive financial backing and support from the Italian government.

President Bush I's 1992 decision to protect distribution of food and prevent a devastating famine had the desired effect. Operation Restore Hope's 28,000 American troops with proper in-country support were able to enforce the goals of UNISOM I – to feed the starving people of Somalia. By May 1993, all the parties involved in the civil war agreed to a disarmament conference proposed by Aideed – now Somali's leading warlord. "UNISOM II," the second phase, began when the U.S. handed over the mission to the U.N. on May 4, 1993.

When the Clinton administration took office in January 1993 they immediately began making changes. By June 1993 Clinton had decreased Bush I's 28,000 U.S. troops to 1,200 combat troops and 3,000 support personnel.

Encouraged by al-Qaeda operatives and the diminishing presence of U.S. forces in Somalia, warlord Aideed – promoted to "General" by the press – sent his SNAF to ambush and kill 24 Pakistani soldiers assigned to UNOSOM II on June 5, 1993. The next day, the United Nations Security Council issued Resolution 837, calling for the arrest and trial of those responsible for the ambush.

The Clinton administration authorized a paltry $25,000 reward for the capture of General Aideed – pocket change for the warlord. Admiral Jonathan Howe, Special Representative to the U.N. Secretary General responsible for mediating the peace process, asked the U.S. to send Special Forces to capture Aideed. General Joseph P. Hoar, Commander, U.S. Central Command, requested four AC-130H gun ships to carry out air strikes against the Somalis. In response four Special Operations Aviation Regiment (AFSOC) AC-130H gun ships (fixed wing aircraft) were deployed on June 7, 1993.

The gun ships remained in country until July 14th and flew a total of 32 interdiction, reconnaissance, and PSYOP missions in support of UNOSOM II. Between June 11th and the 17th, eight combat sortie missions were flown over the streets of Mogadishu. Using 105 mm, 40 mm cannons, and 7.62 mm Gatling guns, the AC-130Hs demolished: two weapons storage facilities; an armored tank compound; Aideed's "Radio Mogadishu" propaganda station; and weapons storage areas and vehicle compounds belonging to Aideed and his key supporters. The AC-130H gunship missions and related ground operations together drove Aideed into hiding.

In late July 1993, six months after Clinton took office, America's Commander and Chief ordered the AC-130Hs out of Somalia. Shortly thereafter, four American soldiers were killed by a remotely detonated mine. Forced to take additional action, Clinton's Administration formed "Task Force Ranger," which consisted of: a group of Delta Force commandos; one company of Army Rangers; and pilots from the 160th Special Operations Aviation Regiment (SOAR) – the "Night Stalkers."

Under the command of Major General William F. Garrison, Task Force Ranger, numbering four hundred and forty brave men, arrived in Somalia on August 26, 1993. Their mission – *to capture Aideed and his lieutenants.* General Garrison's request for Bradley Fighting Vehicles, and the powerful, combat proven AC-130H gun ships was summarily denied by Clinton's Secretary of Defense, Les Aspen – effectively denying Garrison's troops the best possible support available for house to house urban warfare.

On October 3, 1993 members of Task Force Ranger received information that Aideed and some of his lieutenants were planning to meet in a Mogadishu house next to the Olympic Hotel. A detachment of Army Rangers and Delta commandos boarded the lightly armed MH-60 "Blackhawk," and MH-6 "Little Bird" helicopters and moved out to capture their target.

In the ensuing battle, two of the Blackhawk helicopters were shot down. Two crewmembers were captured, and the rescue attempt was delayed by U.N. chain of command problems. Two Special Forces sergeants – snipers who volunteered to rope down to the downed Blackhawk – were killed after they ran out of ammunition. Images of one of the bodies being dragged through the streets of Mogadishu were played and replayed on TV, while American viewers recoiled in horror.

279

If the Clinton Administration had provided Task Force Ranger the requested Bradley Fighting Vehicles and AC-130h gun ships, the "Blackhawk Down" incident may never have occurred. As it was, the lack of readily available armor and air support resulted in a demoralizing disaster for America's armed forces.

Secretary of Defense, Less Aspin, *who had no military experience,* had withheld crucial air and ground support until it was too late. Usama bin Laden had taken the measure of the new American president and found Clinton wanting.

Bin Laden's Saudi Arabian citizenship was revoked in 1994, because of his irresponsible behavior and fanatical opposition to the Royal Family. In August 1995 bin Laden wrote a letter to King Faisal of Saudi Arabia calling for a guerrilla war to expel American troops from the kingdom. According to a story published in The London-Based *AL-HAYAT* daily, a 1995 plot to assassinate Egypt's President Hosni Mubarak – in Addis Ababa, Ethiopia – was planned at al-Qaeda camps in Somalia and Afghanistan. The plot, with a budget of $200,000, was foiled. The three would-be assassins were sentenced to death in Ethiopia in March 1998.

As a result of this foiled plot, bin Laden was expelled from Sudan in 1996. He returned to Afghanistan and joined the Taliban militia in its initial conquest of Afghanistan. Once established in Afghanistan, bin Laden issued a *fatwa* – a formal legal opinion or religious decree issued by an Islamic leader – calling for a jihad to end the presence of *"American crusader forces"* in Saudi Arabia. Bin Laden is reported to have said:

> *"The call to wage war against America was made because America has spear-headed the crusade against the Islamic nation, sending tens of thousands of its troops to the land of the two Holy Mosques over and above its meddling in its affairs and its politics, and its support of the oppressive, corrupt and tyrannical regime that is in control. These are the reasons behind the singling out of America as a target."*

Softly spoken words followed by violent action became bin Laden's trade mark. His fatwa was followed by the June 25, 1996, 10:30 P.M. bombing of the Khobar Towers military housing complex at Saudi Arabia's King Abdul Aziz Air Base near Dhahran, Saudi Arabia. Five thousand pounds of explosives contained in a truck detonated: ripping the front off an apartment building and creating a crater thirty-five feet deep. Nineteen U.S. service members were killed and scores of others injured. President

Clinton promised that those responsible would be hunted down and punished.

A second small bomb was detonated in the market area of Saudi city on the morning of October 7, 1996. Two people were killed, including an American, and four others were injured. Bin Laden is reported to have said:

> *"The two explosions that took place in Riyadh and in Khobar recently were but a clear and powerful signal to the governments of the countries that willingly participated in the aggression against our countries and our lives and our sacrosanct symbols."*

Bin Laden and al-Qaeda established training camps in Afghanistan where 15,000 to 20,000 terrorists were trained since 1996. One such training camp was located south of Kabul in Rishkhor, Afghanistan. Upon graduation, the extremists pledged their loyalty to bin Laden and al-Qaeda; returned to their home countries; and initiated local jihads.

In February 1998, bin Laden created a new terrorist alliance, the International Islamic Front for Jihad Against the Jews and Crusaders, which included the Egyptian Islamic Jihad and the Harakat ul-Ansar. The following excerpts are from bin Laden's then released *fatwa*:

> *". . . in compliance with Allah's order, we issue the following fatwa to all Muslims:*
> *"The ruling to kill the Americans and their allies – civilians and military – is an individual duty for every Muslim who can do it in any country in which it is possible to do it, in order to liberate the al-Aqsa Mosque and the holy mosque [Mecca] from their grip, and in order for their armies to move out of all the lands of Islam, defeated and unable to threaten any Muslim. This is in accordance with the words of Almighty Allah, [who says] '. . . and fight the pagans all together as they fight you all together. . . .' and '. . . fight them until there is no more tumult or oppression, and there prevail justice and faith in Allah.'"*

The February 1998 *fatwa* was followed by the August 7,1998 bombing of American embassies in Dar es Salaam, Tanzania, and Nairobi, Kenya that killed two hundred fifty-eight and injured more than five thousand people.

In response to these brazen attacks President Clinton *finally took military action* and ordered cruise missile attacks on al-Qaeda training camps in Afghanistan and on a pharmaceutical factory in Khartoum, Sudan. Again the president promised that those responsible would be hunted down and punished.

An August 2003 *American Legion* magazine article, "The Terrorist Next Door," by John Stone, reported that: during the New York trial of four terrorists, convicted for the 1998 East Africa, American Embassy bombings; a former al Qaeda member named several American based Muslim charities that funded the terrorist group. *Mercy International Relief Organization* was one such charity. Trial documents also indicated that Mercy had smuggled weapons from Somalia into Kenya where one of the embassies was attacked.

In 1999 bin Laden continued his attempts to attack the United States – this time on American soil. When Ahmed Ressam, an Algerian al-Qaeda member, was apprehended while attempting to enter the United States by ferry from Canada, sixty kilograms of explosives were discovered in his car. During interrogation he disclosed his plan to blow up the Los Angeles airport on New Years Eve.

The year 2000 was an election year in America, and al-Qaeda planned to celebrate the end of the Clinton administration with a bang. An attempted January 2000 attack on the American destroyer, U.S.S. Sullivans in the Aden, Yemen harbor failed. The Sullivans got lucky when the Yemen attack had to be aborted because the attackers' boat almost sank under the weight of explosives it carried. Later that year, a second attack in the same harbor was successful.

Commissioned in 1996 with its homeport in Norfolk, Virginia, the U.S.S. Cole was not so lucky. 17th of 51 planned Arleigh Burke Class guided-missile vessels to join the U.S. fleet, the Cole departed Norfolk on June 21, 2000 for its deployment and was scheduled to return home December 21. As part of the U.S.S. George Washington Battle Group, the Cole was in transit from the Red Sea to a port visit in Bahrain. When the ship stopped in Aden for routine refueling on October 12th, a small boat loaded with four hundred to seven hundred pounds of C-4 high explosives managed to pull along side. The terrorists on board detonated a charge that blew a hole sixty-feet wide by forty-feet deep (extending below the water line) in the side of the ship: disabling it, injuring thirty-nine crewmembers and killing seventeen. Repair cost exceeded $250 million dollars.

President Clinton promised again, in one final grand stand for his Administration, that those responsible would be hunted down and punished. Sadly no substantive moves against al Qaeda were undertaken. Sadder still, for Clinton's legacy, was his failure to publicly recognize bin Laden's obvious war against America by properly informing the American public. There can be no doubt that Clinton was aware of bin Laden's and al-Qaeda's successes and failures. History records numerous al-Qaeda plots that thankfully were not successful. Plots to assassinate Pope John Paul II during his visit to Manila in late 1994; simultaneously bomb U.S. and Israeli Embassies in Manila, and other Asian capitals in late 1994; and attempts at midair bombings of a dozen U.S. trans-Pacific flights in 1995. Clinton himself was a potential victim in a planned assassination plot in the Philippines in early 1995, and again in April 2000 in Bangladesh. None-the-less Clinton failed to adequately recognize and openly identify the true threat bin Laden's war held for America and for her unsuspecting citizens.

In consequence Bush II's Administration began its term woefully uninformed and therefore unprepared to protect the American public from the inherent dangers lurking in America's open society. The significance of the Cole bombing faded into the background of the 2000 presidential election's fiasco, when the state of Florida became center stage for recounting, recounting, and recounting thousands of elections ballots. "Chad," the small circle of paper usually punched out by the stylus to indicate a vote; along with several new terms – hanging chads, dimpled chads, and pregnant chads – entered America's vocabulary. If not for the seriousness of the issue – electing the next President of the United States of America – images of election officials holding up ballots, attempting to divine the voter's intent by the condition of the ballot's chad, would have been great theater.

While Al Gore turned the election process into farce, the world watched and tried to understand the American system. Some did. Others severely misread the situation and assumed that the winner, George W. Bush – Bush II – would not be able to govern.

Further hampering Bush II and fueling contempt for the effectiveness of his leadership were the prolonged confirmation proceedings orchestrated by the Democrats in congress, who stood in opposition to the president's appointments – thereby impeding his ability to set up his administration.

It is likely that, given what the world viewed as Bush II's ineptitude, Usama bin Laden assumed that America's president would be a toothless tiger – even easier to run over than President Clinton. Despite his reputation for gifted planning and plotting, underestimating Bush II may have been bin Laden's biggest mistake.

On September 11, 2001 al-Qaeda committed their ultimate mistake when they hijacked four American commercial airliners, and flew them into a Pennsylvania field, the Pentagon and New York City's Twin Trade Center Towers, incinerating and maiming thousands of people from many lands. In the wake of the horrific events that followed, America awakened to its vulnerability to terrorism. For a second time Muslims and Islamic fanatics had totally misjudged the resolve of the Bush family and the American people. Perhaps the American reaction to Pearl Harbor and the history of the war in the Pacific was omitted from the curriculum of the madrasaes. President Bush II rallied the nation and led an angry nation to war. Once again America was blessed by having the right man as president in a time of great crisis.

* * * *

1997

Ralph visited each center once every four months. He scheduled his trips so that he could make a clandestine visit to the unmarked office and run diagnostic tests on the spectrometer. All of the centers and Mobile Nuclear Imaging were profitable and growing.

Ralph and Nancy had out-grown their small Livermore office and moved their offices to San Jose. Each had leased an office suite on different floors of the same building. REM's office consisted of an office manager and Ralph, while PC Capital now had several employees. Betty's husband, George, had been transferred to Sacramento. Betty's leaving prompted the relocation decision. Ralph and Nancy had purchased a large condo near their office building, and returned to Rancho Nuevo on weekends.

REM's and Ralph's personal investments in PC Capital venture funds had quadrupled in value. Nancy had arranged for several Livermore scientists to get in on two IPO's that had netted them a better than one hundred percent return. All in all, life was good.

Avoiding publicity associated with REM's success was Ralph's major problem. Nancy Hatterson had been featured in a venture capital magazine. Somehow a reporter from INC Magazine heard about the diagnostics centers, and that Ralph Eid was responsible for their success. The INC reporter, an attractive female, had made several attempts to interview the elusive Dr. Eid. Finally the reporter, Sally Baker, caught up to him. Ralph was forced to talk to her off the record. Ralph finally convinced her that REM's majority stockholders were foreign and prohibited him from giving an interview. Doing so would cost him is position. Ms. Baker reluctantly agreed to pen a short article about Radiological Diagnostic Centers without mentioning REM or Dr. Eid. Ralph had been sorely tempted to grant an interview. After all he was a very successful businessman and would enjoy being recognized as such. Two things had dissuaded him from the interview – Mohammed's certain anger; and the fact that Nancy was convinced Sally Baker had her eye on him. Ralph found that Nancy's jealousy pleased him.

To his great relief Ralph had little contact with Mohammed. Quarterly REM financial reports sent to the Saudi director were acknowledged by e-mail. The relationship between Al-Qaeda and the purpose of REM's special diagnostic instruments were becoming surreal to Ralph, but that had to change.

November 1997

Mohammed al-Mihdar had become a recognized figure in the radical cleric's world. He regularly traveled to Syria, Egypt, Iraq, Iran, Pakistan, Afghanistan, and Uzbekistan. He was the "back door" channel of communication to Usama bin Laden; however, all was not well between Mohammed and the clerics. They were becoming concerned. Why did the Americans ignore al-Qaeda's attacks? What would it take to get the evil American's attention? What would it take to put the fear of Allah in them? Mohammed's answer was that Americans were so self-centered they disregarded the attacks. "It's like swatting a fly. You swat it as a reflex, but are not really conscious of the fly," he told them. Not satisfied with his own answer, Mohammed decided it was time to visit Eid. Logging on to AOL he sent Eid an e-mail.

> I will be visiting you in the next two weeks in San Francisco. I will advise you of my arrival time and hotel. Plan to meet me at the hotel."

Mohammed had heard about the Tenderloin District of San Francisco and planned to investigate the local attractions and bathhouses.

Later the same day in a different time zone, Ralph logged on to AOL and received the usual "You've Got Mail" announcement. Scanning the list of messages, Ralph opened Mohammed's and read it. *I have been wondering when he would show up. I hope he does not start on Nancy again*, he brooded.

Two weeks later Ralph left his new Mercedes SL 500 convertible with the hotel valet. In the main lobby, he picked up a house phone and asked to be connected to Mr. Mohammed al-Mihdar. Mohammed answered and invited Ralph to come up to his suite. Upon entering, Ralph shook hands with Mohammed, who then hugged him and greeted him in an unusually friendly manner, "It is good to see you my brother. You are looking fit and prosperous."

"It is good to see you too my brother," Ralph said while Mohammed continued to hold his hand. "Allah be praised for your safe arrival," Ralph replied as he gently pulled his hand away and adjusted his tie. *Something is different about him*, Ralph fretted, *I've never seen him act so congenial, and he has a new look about him. I have a gut feeling there's been a radical change in his agenda – one I may not agree with.*

"Praise be to Allah. The Director sends you his greeting and congratulations for your success with REM." *The Director* was a code phrase for Usama bin Laden.

After the usual small talk about relatives and Saudi, Ralph filled Mohammed in on REM's progress. One additional center had been opened in Dallas, Texas. Two additional mobile CAT scan trailers, and one mobile MRI trailer had been placed into service in the southwest.

Several minutes passed while Ralph continued to expound on the profits REM was earning. The conversation took an abrupt turn when Mohammed interrupted Ralph in mid-sentence by gruffly asking a question that revealed the real purpose for his visit. "Some of my associates are wondering at America's lack of concern about Somalia, our attacks on the World Trade Center and Khobar Towers in Saudi. Can you explain this?" Mohammed asked with a hard edge in his voice and a scowl.

The unexpected question, coupled with Mohammed's abrupt change of demeanor, took Ralph by surprise. Careful not to show it, and caught off guard by the change of subject, Ralph looked out of the window while he considered Mohammed's question. *I didn't anticipate this question and I haven't really given much thought to the issue. I only followed the stories because of my association and obligations to al-Qaeda. Perhaps that is the answer, but how to express it.*

Using carefully measured words, Ralph replied, "I am not sure how to phrase this. The simple answer is that the two events you referred to didn't seem to be important – or important enough to override everyday things. America's economy is roaring. The president and the media have not made them an issue. People are content, and don't wish to be bothered with problems not directly effecting their daily lives – so they ignore them. In other words, 'It's not my problem.' Does this make sense to you?" Ralph asked.

"That is the answer that I have formulated too . . . but no, it does not make sense to me – nor to our sponsors," Mohammed said, staring at Ralph with a malevolent expression. "They want to see Americans *suffer*," he sneered, "but our attacks are being ignored and we are being pushed to do something that will get a reaction."

"Are you telling me it is time for the rings?" Ralph asked with an unexpected tightening in his chest.

"No . . . not yet," Mohammed snapped.

Somewhat relieved by Mohammed's quick reply, Ralph sat quietly composing himself and tried to formulate an response to dispel Mohammed's dark mood. Finally Ralph calmly said, "The problem is so fundamental it may be beyond the ability of your – no our – sponsors to grasp. The reverse may also be true. Muslims, educated in Muslim countries cannot understand, cannot *relate* to the western concept of Democracy and separation of church and state – especially the separation of church and state. Who teaches and influences Muslim thinking? The clerics. Who looses the most if Democracy is accepted in Muslim countries? The clerics. Who really runs Muslim countries, yours for example? Again the clerics. I assume it is the clerics who are pushing for action."

Mohammed sat in silence, staring out of the window, his face almost expressionless. This was not what he wanted to hear. Suddenly turning, he glared at Ralph with a maniacal expression on his face and said, "What you say has merit. Yes! In reality the *clerics* are the final authority – therefore the *church is the state.* As far as our people are concerned, it has always been that way, and it *always will be that way.* Iran is an excellent example. The elected government answers to the Guardian Council of Ayatollahs. In Saudi, the King actually serves at the pleasure of the clerics. Western Democracy is an alien concept that will *never* be accepted in our world."

"Correct," Ralph quickly replied, realizing that Mohammed's demeanor was unnerving him. "The American government believes its prime mission is converting the world to its vision of Democracy. Americans in particular cannot grasp that some people do not *want* Democracy. The conflict is so fundamental, so basic as to defy solution. Don't your see. . . ." *He is not hearing me.* Ralph thought. *I can tell be the look in his eyes. Without the freedoms afforded by democracy we would not have been able to pull off our plan. He was never quite so vehement . . . .*

Suddenly slapping his hands on the arms of his chair and rising, Mohammed interrupted Ralph's thoughts in a continuation of his earlier tirade, *"Allah has commanded the faithful to convert or kill the infidel.* We are making plans to carry out his will in America," he raved as he began pacing around the room. "America *will* become an Islamic state," he snarled through clenched teeth while he shook his head back and forth and waved his fist in the air.

The intensity of Mohammed's new fanaticism further unsettled Ralph, who attempted to show no disquiet, and sat very still watching as Mohammed continued to breath through clenched teeth and pace back and forth. "Are you saying that our ultimate goal is to convert America to Islam by force?" Ralph quietly asked, and jumped in response to Mohammed's booming response.

"*Absolutely*," Mohammed stormed, "Nothing else is acceptable. You have no idea how many cells al-Qaeda has in this immoral land," he hissed. Then as if completely unaware of the scene he had just made, he calmly took his seat next to Ralph, cocked his head to the side and matter-of-factly sneered, "When the final day comes, the clerics will arouse the faithful and send them out of the mosques to convert or kill all infidels. The streets will run red with infidel blood," he concluded with a smirk.

Desperate now to change the subject, Ralph felt sick at his stomach as he remembered his enthusiasm and pride when he accepted the project. Now he was assailed by doubts – terrible doubts he acknowledged for the first time. He knew that he was no longer the wide-eyed youth bent on changing the world at all cost. He had grown and matured. What to do? What to say? Certainly not confront Mohammed. Mohammed had obviously become a wild-eyed raving fanatic. No, he had always been a fanatic, Ralph suddenly realized. *When we set our course of action years ago, Mohammed showed a more rational approach to changing the world, but over time he has become unbalanced. Do I still believe that America must be punished for its actions? Yes, punishment is due, but forced conversion to Islam through genocide and slaughter? I just do not know anymore,* Ralph thought. Careful not to antagonize Mohammed further and to learn more of his plans, Ralph returned to Mohammed's earlier question, "What are your plans to introduce fear among Americans?"

"An escalating series of strikes – each larger and more spectacular than the last. I am sure Allah's Rings will be the final act that destroys America's will," Mohammed calmly said. Then reverting to his earlier maniacal self, he pounded on the arm of his chair for emphasis as he shouted out his final vengeful prediction, "*The shock of Allah's Rings will stun America. Our brothers will easily rise up and assume control. Americans are cowards – cowards who hide behind their high-tech weapons. They have no stomach for real combat. After a short period, they will be glad to embrace Islam.*"

Mohammed's last outburst confirmed Ralph's fears and he sat very still before quietly asking, "When will the attacks begin?"

"Next year . . . in Africa."

Spring, 2001

Three years had passed since the emotionally charged meeting with Mohammed in San Francisco. Ralph had recognized he had an all consuming fear of Mohammed, who he now realized was an unbalanced maniac. After their meeting, he went through a period of obsessive paranoia. He couldn't tell Nancy what was troubling him. She knew something was wrong when he had security systems installed in their offices, the condo, and their house. When she asked why he was so nervous, he told her that they needed more security because he feared the competition. He also bought a gun which he kept with him on most occasions. Even though she had grow up around hunting guns, the hand gun really disturbed Nancy. Ralph told her he had a close call with a mugger while in San Francisco, and that prompted him to buy the gun for self-protection. "You can never be too careful," he told her when she protested, "The world is full of drug addicts, who would slit your throat for a fix." *How do I tell her that Mohammed may have us killed at any time – even before the signal is given to set off the bombs? After all he knows how to set the timers on the devices. I really am of no further use to him,* Ralph thought.

It was that realization that prompted Ralph to begin making serious plans for his and Nancy's future. He contacted Mark Swartz and authorized him to prepare a will making Nancy the sole beneficiary of his estate including his life insurance policy. He also added her name to his offshore accounts, the condo and house.

On the advice from a friend he had learned of an vacation property in Ensenda, Argentina that could be acquired and time share leased through a management company in San Francisco. The hacienda had a pool and lovely guesthouse that he and Nancy used on several occasions for their vacations. Nancy loved it there. The climate was wonderful and the people were warm and friendly. They both loved to ride, and the hacienda horses were beautiful and spirited. Ralph surprised her by buying the estate for her birthday and announcing the purchase by showing her the deed in her name during a romantic dinner celebration.

"What have you *done*? She beamed when she saw the address on the deed. "I can't believe you bought the entire estate."

"You know I always think big," Ralph jokingly said with a laugh. "Besides it pays for itself by renting time shares in the main house. We don't need all that room and the guesthouse is charming. You know you love it there," he concluded, with a kiss on her cheek, while thinking, *You must never suffer for my misdeeds. I am in too far to get out, but I must do everything I can to keep you from being caught up in what I have done. This will serve as a retreat – I hope one day for both of us.*

Over time Ralph's communication with Mohammed all but ceased. *The madman,* as Ralph privately thought of him, slowly faded from

Ralph's conscious thoughts. To compensate, Ralph devoted himself to his growing love for Nancy and to REM's growth. He had no way of knowing that Mohammed was busy doing Usama's bidding, interfacing with the senior radical Islamic clerics and principal contributors to al-Qaeda.

By the end of 1998 Ralph had all but suppressed his reservations about completing al-Qaeda's final mission, the destruction of five American cities, and of course his baby – REM. Operating in a state of denial, Ralph continued expanding REM, increasing his personal fortune, and enjoying his relationship with Nancy. There were nights though, when Ralph woke covered in sweat from a reoccurring nightmare in which he was trying to scream, but making no sound with his fear stricken throat. In his terrifying dream he saw Nancy smiling and emerging from the water in that beautiful blue bikini. Then to his horror she was consumed in lake of fire. The dream always ended with him jerking awake: after seeing his own distorted, terrified face and wide gaping mouth.

Nancy was always there to comfort him when he lay trembling. He kept the truth of his dream from her by saying he was dreaming of his parent's death. In reality he knew deep in side that his obsessive fear was of Mohammed, and of facing the future moment of truth when he would hear Mohammed say, *"Allah has placed rings on his fingers."*

Now in the spring of 2001, on this exceptionally beautiful spring day, the object of Ralph's dread had unexpectedly returned for yet another meeting. Mohammed had e-mailed Ralph the time of his arrival and stated that this time he would drive himself out to Ralph's house for their meeting. Ralph felt that now familiar knot in his stomach when he saw the e-mail. His first reaction was to praise Allah that Nancy was in New York for the week, setting up funding for another IPO. Then he frantically prayed, *Allah, help me! I don't know what to expect from that maniac. Protect us from his insanity. . . . Why is he coming?* Ralph continued talking to Allah. *His e-mail said nothing about the signal code. Is he coming to kill us and arm the bombs himself? Maybe he is just coming to check on things for himself and to talk about the elections. I know from Mohammed's previous questions at past meetings that Usama follows the American political climate very carefully. The elections have had worldwide coverage. A new Bush in the White House could be causing the brothers serious concerns. That may be why he is coming – or maybe it's just a friendly visit. . . . Allah, give me wisdom in this time of mortal danger,* Ralph prayed. After several hours of stewing over their safety, Ralph finally concluded he must be really close to loosing it. If Mohammed planned to kill them he finally reasoned, why would he let me know he was coming? I cannot afford to let him see how anxious I am over this meeting. I just have to ride out the storm and hope he is only here for information and insight into the elections.

Sitting on the patio, Mohammed gazed out onto the valley. "Just as I remembered it – such a beautiful view. I understand why you still choose to live here.

"Yes, but I am spending more and more time at my San Jose condo. I can walk to the REM office from it." *Praise Allah, He's acting like his old self – not wild eyed and agitated,* Ralph thought, relieved by Mohammed's calm demeanor.

"I must visit your new office before I leave," Mohammed said, raising his wine glass in a toast to Ralph who was placing steaks on the grill. "This brings back memories of our early meetings here." Mohammed. said, while thinking, *But you are not the naive young pup you were then. Are you my beautiful Brother? Look at you, wearing a gold necklace and bracelet. When did you acquire those I wonder?*

"Yes, those were heady times. Two young men planning to climb Mount Everest, do great deeds and change the world," Ralph replied.

Mohammed smiled and answered, "In our way we did climb the mountain, and one day we will certainly change the world." *At least I will,* he thought and pleasantly asked, "What is the condition of the instruments?"

"I check each of them every six months." *Every four months was just too much trouble,* Ralph thought. "There is one complete backup neutron generator at the Newark facility. I can order parts from the supplier if needed. Did I tell you that my original contact, Bob Johnson, was killed in an automobile accident?" Ralph asked.

"No . . . but now that you mention his name, I seem to remember you telling me about him in Karachi," Mohammed said as he got up and walked over to the patio table to refill his wine glass. Turning his back to Ralph, he sneered then pleasantly asked, "What is your opinion of the new president?" He asked.

Ah, that is why you are here – the elections, Ralph realized and relaxing a bit laughed at Mohammed's question before responding, "I was wondering when you were going to ask about him. A lot of us are wondering about him. Actually, I don't have a handle on him. The press and the Democrats have dismissed him as a pretender: a man with no mandate to govern, a weak man."

Mohammed nodded in agreement. "We believe that the second Bush will be unable to be more than a puppet president. He will just sit in his office for the next four years. This second Bush is Allah's gift to us. Soon he will be tested, and proven to be. . . . what is the American expression? Oh yes, a *wimp*," he said and laughed heartily at his own joke.

Ralph removed the steaks from the grill. *He is in an unusually lighthearted mood, but I still need to be wary,* he thought and carried their steaks into the dining room. Behind him Mohammed smirked and picked up the almost empty wine bottle. Following Ralph into the house he said, "It really is a lovely night and this wine is wonderful. Do you have another bottle? I . . . I think will stay in your guest room tonight."

"Yes, I will get a bottle." *I wonder what prompted that? I'd best be very careful how much wine I drink,* Ralph concluded as he retrieved the second bottle.

Ralph removed the cork, and still feeling cautious set the bottle on the table before saying, "It's good to see you again my brother. Good to have you in my home after so long an absence. You really look well. Life must be agreeing with you," Ralph said to relieve his tension.

"Yes it is. It truly is," Mohammed responded. "You too look well, my brother, and very prosperous – a beautiful new car in the garage. I looked in when I went to use the bathroom. An expensive silk shirt and jewelry too . . . When did you come by those? Mohammed asked gesturing toward Ralph's necklace and bracelet.

"Oh, thank you. They were a gift," Ralph responded hesitating to say from whom. Then abruptly changing his mind he looked at Mohammed and exclaimed, "From Nancy . . . I know you don't approve of our relationship, but I need her. She is the only thing that has kept me sane through all these years of waiting. Can't you understand?" Ralph all but pleaded.

I knew who they were from you fool, Mohammed thought, but looking away from Ralph took a sip of wine before looking back and glibly changing the subject to Afghanistan and the Taliban. Mohammed told Ralph that Usama was now living near Kabul. "Usama lives with his brothers. He has never been *pretentious*. He is one of them; that is why they love and follow him."

Ralph caught the sarcasm in the "pretentious" remark, as it related to his jewelry. He said nothing in response, but simply stared at his guest before quietly saying, "Let's eat. Our food is getting cold."

After dinner Ralph became somewhat more at ease as the conversation turned back to President Bush II and planned al-Qaeda strikes. Mohammed said, "Soon there will be a major strike into the heart of this evil country. This time America will be staggered by its weakness and vulnerability. Bush is too weak to do anything. America will feel the wrath of Allah and tremble," Mohammed boasted.

"I would not underestimate Bush II, just because the press does. We do not have the measure of the man. I do not know what he is capable of, and to make assumptions based upon the prattlings of the press is foolish. It would have been better if Gore had won."

Mohammed suddenly became very serious. "Why do you say that?"

"In my opinion Gore is weaker than Clinton. Al-Qaeda's attack on American embassies and the Cole were acts of war, and what did Clinton and Gore do? They shot up a bunch of empty training camps and a pharmaceutical plant with cruise missiles. There was no follow up – just a big fireworks demonstration. The sitting vice president, who was running for president, had a perfect opportunity to assert himself, and he did nothing."

Mohammed considered Ralph's comment; then asked, "What do you think Bush II would have done?"

"I don't know, and that is the problem. If the planned attack is of greater magnitude than the embassy bombings, then al-Qaeda may be providing the new president a platform from which he can claim the power of his office."

Albuquerque, New Mexico, Summer 2001

The Defense Special Weapons Agency (DSWA) was a tri-command – Army, Navy and Air Force – with headquarters is in Alexandra, Virginia. The technical work of DSWA, however, was done by its Field Command, located as a tenant on Kirkland Air Force Base, Albuquerque, New Mexico. DSWA Field Command originated as the Armed Forces Special Weapons Project in 1947 in support of the Manhattan Project. In 1959 it became the Defense Atomic support Agency (DASA), which became the Defense Nuclear Agency in 1971, and finally evolved into the DSWA in 1996. Its mission was to provide support to the Secretary of Defense; Joint Chiefs of Staff; and military departments in matters concerning nuclear weapons, nuclear effects, and nuclear weapons testing. In the 1960s, DASA was responsible for developing nuclear and thermonuclear warheads; weapons testing; managing the nuclear weapons stockpile and stockpile sites; and providing nuclear weapons training. Training courses ranged from the Weapons Orientation Advanced (WOA) course, limited to GS-15s and O6s and above; to the Nuclear Emergency Team Operations course for enlisted personnel. Field Command DASA also housed the world's most extensive nuclear weapons museum in Building 600. The museum, which included cut-a-way displays of the most advanced nuclear and thermonuclear warheads, was constructed in such a manner that certain displays could be hidden. Thus, the museum could be quickly reconfigured to match the security classification and "need to know" of different groups admitted for a tour. Nuclear and thermonuclear weapons were once referred to as "Special Weapons." The definition of Special weapons has been expanded and now includes both nuclear and advanced conventional weapons.

When Kirkland AFB absorbed the Army's Sandia Base in 1971, it inherited Field Command, DASA and the Department of Energy's Sandia National Laboratory as tenants. Sandia National Laboratory began operations in 1945, when Division Z of the Manhattan project was transferred to the Army's Sandia Base (the only Army installation with the name "Base") as an ordnance design, testing, and assembly facility. President Harry S. Truman wrote a letter to American Telephone and Telegraph Company President, Leroy Wilson in 1949, ". . . offering the company an opportunity to render an exceptional service in the national interest by managing Sandia Laboratory for the Atomic Energy Commission (AEC)." The AEC later became the Department of Energy (DOE). AT&T accepted, and began managing the Laboratory on November 1, 1949 on a non-profit, no-fee basis, and continued in that role for forty-four years. On October 1, 1993, Lockheed-Martin was awarded a contract to manage the laboratory. Sandia National Laboratory has over 6,600 employees in Albuquerque, and approximately 850 more in Livermore, California.

In 1998 as part of the Department of Defense Reform Initiative, the Secretary of Defense directed the merger of the On-Site Inspection Agency, the Defense Special Weapons Agency, the Defense Technology Security Administration, and some program functions of the Assistant for the Secretary of Defense for Nuclear, Chemical and Biological Defense Programs into the newly created Defense Threat Reduction Agency (DTRA). The civilian director of DTRA reports directly to the under secretary of Defense for Acquisition and Technology.

Newly promoted Major General George Robert Alexander, USAF, Deputy Director of the DTRA, and the former Commanding General of the Field Command, DSWA, looked out his office window in the DTRA building on Kirkland AFB toward Sandia Crest. His mind was occupied with thoughts of terrorism and how it threatened his country, *We are still trapped in the cold war mentality,* he thought. *The bureaucracy cannot change its mindset. Fifty years experience in dealing with the Soviet Union – successful dealings because there has not been a nuclear war– has created a mindset that cannot be changed short of a catastrophic event. MAD has been the foundation of U.S. policy. The concept of an enemy that does not care about consequences is beyond comprehension, therefore beyond reality. The CIA is barred by law from conducting activities in*

America, and the FBI is not structured to deal with Islamic terrorists on U.S. soil. Customs, CIA, FBI and the State Department do not share information. God bless the State Department – they have become nothing more than a super chamber of commerce, catering to the desires other countries, our enemies included. Our embassy in Riyadh is still issuing visas through travel agencies. Perhaps there is a special tour package for terrorists. I hope the new administration puts a stop to it before it's too late.

A highly intelligent man, Alexander had risen rapidly through the ranks after graduation from North Carolina State University with a bachelor's degree in Nuclear Engineering and a ROTC commission as a 2nd Lieutenant in the Air Force. The fact that his family was friends with the family of the current Chairman of the Joint Chiefs, who was also an N.C. State alumnus, had not hindered his career; however, the Chairman would soon retire. Alexander was frustrated. American embassies and a war ship had been attacked, acts of war, but the military had not been ordered to respond. Bin Laden had chosen the ideal time for the attack on the Cole. President Clinton, at the end of his second and therefore his last term, had taken no substantive action. The new president, severely crippled by the highly contested election, was effectively hamstrung. *Another round to al-Qaeda, and this is most certainly not the last. Next time it will be worse.*

The dilemma was that no one in authority appeared to realize what the true nature of the world's problem was – or they were unwilling or unable to face it. A culture clash that began with the Prophet Mohammed was still raging. 1st Lieutenant Alexander had been in Tehran, Iran when over three million Iranians had taken to the streets to welcome Ayatollah Khomeini. Khomeini stepped from his plane and the Iranian revolution began.

In his nightmares, Alexander could still hear the crowds surging through the streets chanting *Allah Akbar*. Watching the mob surge down the street reminded him of a wall of brown water rolling down a dry arroyo in New Mexico after a violent rainstorm in the Sandia Mountains. Anyone foolish enough to camp in what appeared to be a dry creek bed would be swept away without warning – just like the mobs were sweeping away the Iranians' freedoms. Whipped up by the *mullahs*, the mob was unlike anything he had ever experienced or seen in the movies or on TV. The fury they disgorged demonstrated hatred and rage on an unimaginable scale.

Alexander's training detachment had been pulled out of Iran a few days later, but not before he had seen the true face of Islam. A face that he recognized was totally alien to western philosophy. Soon after his return to Wright Patterson AFB, Alexander's tour was completed and he was assigned to the Air Force Weapons Laboratory at Kirkland AFB.

After completing his tour at Kirkland, Captain Alexander attended Harvard and obtained his master's in political science. His next assignment was assistant military attaché in Amman, Jordan. Major Alexander's experiences in Jordan and other nearby Arabian countries re-enforced the views he had formed in Iran. Views he wisely kept to himself.

After Jordan, he was assigned to Special Operations at Macdill AFB, where he was "loaned" to the CIA on several occasions. Next came the Pentagon, where Lt. Colonel Alexander was assigned to the Air Force Chief of Staff. Alexander caught the attention of the White House, and was reassigned to the National Security Advisor (NSA). The White House tour opened his eyes to how things were really done in Washington and in global politics. His work pleased the NSA and the Secretary of State.

After completing his White House assignment, Colonel Alexander became the Air Force Military Attaché in Riyadh, Saudi Arabia. By the time he left Saudi Arabia, his understanding of the Arab and Islamic world was nearly complete. Next came Command and General Staff College, his first star, and command of Field Command, DSWA.

Still looking at Sandia Crest, Major General Alexander was contemplating his future. His third star was in doubt. General Donneley, the Commander of DASA, had retired and then taken a senior position with the Department of Energy. This door was probably closed to Alexander, because he had been highly critical of the lack of security at Livermore and Los Alamos Labs.

The new president had serious problems, because of the contested election and the resentment of the Democratic Party. *No matter the man's intentions,* Alexander thought, *he was hamstrung and rendered impotent by the constant hammering of the press and his political rivals – perhaps a position at State. I have a fairly good rapport with the Secretary, a former Army General. On the other hand, I am not very popular with the bureaucracy at State; because I have hammered them for opening the door to potential Arab terrorists.*

Alexander and his wife, Jane, missed New Mexico. Neither liked the Washington DC area, where they were now quartered. DTRA headquarters was in Alexandria, Virginia, and they lived nearby. Jane wanted him to retire so that they could move back to New Mexico.

Several radical Islamic groups posed a threat to the U.S. Al-Qaeda was at the top of the list. Iraq, Iran and North Korea were developing nuclear weapons. A fact that had been studiously ignored in the past. Attacks against the U.S. were escalating, and the threat was not being recognized. The former Secretary of DOE had scoffed at the idea of terrorists being able to bring a complicated nuclear weapon into the U.S.

No, Alexander didn't think he could take any more of the Washington bullshit – *perhaps a position with Lockheed-Martin. I am one of the most knowledgeable people in the world in the field of special weapons, and I do not see a meaningful use for this knowledge. We are going to be hit with a weapon or weapons of mass destruction, and no one will admit to this until it happens. I have tried to warn the Joint Chiefs, State, and the White House to no avail. Except for the World Trade Center bombing, no serious attack has occurred on U.S. soil. No one will pay attention until we are hit over the head with the proverbial two by four. I just hope it is a two-by-four and not an ax. Well, Jane likes New Mexico, so I will sit tight and complete my tour. Am I ready to retire and build a house on our property north of Santa Fe in the Sangre de Cristo Mountains? I do not have to make a decision until I receive my next assignment,* Alexander concluded to himself.

On the morning of September 11, 2001 al-Qaeda struck and the world changed. Once again America demonstrated that it was a Janus, switching from its face of peace to its face of war in the blink of an eye. President Bush II cast off the restraining chains forged by the contested election and led an angry nation to war. Once again American resolve had been evaluated solely on the basis of its peaceful intentions, and once again the price for the enemy's miscalculation would be great. Al-Qaeda's follow-up plans for additional chemical, biological and nuclear attacks were thrown into disarray by the ferocity of the American military attacks in Afghanistan. American hypocrisy toward Israel was also demonstrated. American liberals and the press were constantly criticizing Israel for doing less to the Palestinians than the Americans were doing to the Taliban and al-Qaeda in Afghanistan.

Ralph and Nancy were watching CNN in their San Jose condo. When the scenes of the first airplane striking one of the twin towers in New York were aired, Nancy screamed "OH NO!" While Ralph sat breathlessly hoping this was not what he thought it was: the beginning of the end of all he had worked for. Like most Americans, they sat glued to the TV watching the second plane impact the other tower. After a while, Nancy was able to compose herself and left for her office. Ralph stayed in the condo and watched events unfold. Would the dreaded command to activate Allah's Rings come? Ralph was still unable to face the question of what he would do when it finally came.

Fortunately, bin Laden's timetable for using the rings was totally upset. Instead of gloating over America's collapse, senior al-Qaeda members in Afghanistan were running for their lives. Two months had passed and Mohammed was dumfounded. What had happened? "Holy

Tuesday," the name given to September 11th by the fundamentalist, was supposed to have scared and cowed the Americans, forcing them to call for the abandonment of support of Israel. Just the opposite was occurring. He had totally lost contact with Usama and with every passing day he became more furious.

The Mujahedeen, who had faced the great Soviet army and sent them packing, was being picked apart by bombs – bombs that fell out of thin air, directly onto their positions. Stinger missiles that had decimated the Soviet helicopters and airplanes were useless against the highflying bombers.

Mohammed raged to Yosif as he berated the new American president. "We underestimated the man. He is the devil in disguise," he raved. Yosif sighed and nodded in agreement as his master shook his fists in the air and screamed. "Our brothers are bleeding and dying at the hands of that demon. Our leaders are lost and we are in disarray. Who is to take control and return our people to the great nation Allah intends us to be?" he ranted. Openly bitter and murderous toward Bush II, Mohammed privately recognized the greatness of his enemy. Though he hated to admit it he now knew Ralph had been correct in his assessment of Bush II. In his response to the destruction of the World Trade Center, Bush II had seized the moment, taken strong immediate action, and emerged as America's undisputed leader.

Once the initial shock of America's retaliation had passed, Mohammed was able in his quiet moments alone to calmly reflect on the worldwide status of the brothers, *All is not lost. Fortunately, compartmentalization appears to be saving the other al-Qaeda cells that were to make the next attacks. As long as our cells remain quiet, blending into the background, they remain safe. In the mean time I must move toward solidifying my position with the clerics. With Usama in hiding or dead I alone hold the key to America's destruction.*

2002

Four months after Holy Tuesday Mohammed was summoned to a *shura* meeting in Qom, Iran. Explanations were demanded, but Mohammed had none to present. Contact with Usama was difficult. "What are the plans for future actions against the Great Satan? When will the plans be implemented? Why haven't there been calls in America to abandon Israel? To make concessions to the Palestinians?" The questions continued. Mohammed realized that Ralph had been correct. The clerics just could not, or would not, understand the West – especially America. Fortunately for Mohammed, the messenger was not killed, and he safely returned to Riyadh. *Things had to get better*, he thought. But this was not to be.

Mohammed had received no messages from Usama for several months. No videotapes had been released showing Usama bin Laden in locations that established the place or date. By the end of the year, Mohammed began to wonder if Usama was alive. He had no direct contact with the visible leadership of al-Qaeda. In fact, none of the visible leaders knew who Mohammed was. The man controlling al-Qaeda's most powerful weapon was completely isolated from al-Qaeda's remaining leadership. Apparently Usama had been true to his word, no one but Ralph and Mohammed knew of Allah's Rings. *What shall I do if Usama is dead?* he thought. As fate would have it, Mohammed happened to be looking at an old framed photograph of Saddam astride his white horse brandishing a sword; when Usama's words came back to him – "He thinks of himself as the next great Caliph, the next Saladin." *We shall see about that Saddam. We shall see,* Mohammed thought.

Meanwhile the wannabe Caliph, Saddam Hussein, watched as events unfolded in Afghanistan. Taliban and al-Qaeda fighters were being slaughtered. His trusted advisors told him he was next. With typical Arabian arrogance – even after having his army destroyed by Coalition forces in 1991 – he still told himself Iraq could not be conquered and occupied. Bush II had several reasons to target Saddam, not the least of which was the stupid assassination attempt on his father, Bush I. Iraq was at one end of Bush II's "axis of evil," and its weapons of mass destruction program had been exposed in the 1991 Gulf War.

An arrogant Saddam could not believe that America would return. Had he not cleverly hidden his WMD program? U.N. inspectors had been run around the country like traveling circus performers. Finally they just gave up and left. Manufacturing chemical weapons had been abandoned. They were too difficult and dangerous to store and maintain. The massive storage facilities were easily identified. Nuclear weapons could be hidden, but not uranium and plutonium separation facilities and breeder reactors. Biological weapons were another story. They did not require large facilities, and commercial facilities could be quickly converted to manufacture biological agents. Mobile manufacturing "labs" that were almost impossible to find and destroy were in use. As the year 2002 ended, Saddam still felt safe; however, a little contingency planning never hurt.

2003

Still no word from Usama, and Mohammed was frustrated and worried. Several tapes had appeared, but no Usama. Usama's number three, Khalid Shaikh Mohammed, had been arrested in Pakistan in March. The clerics were pressuring Mohammed for answers. Answers he did not have. When would al-Qaeda strike and bring the arrogant American infidels to their knees? Where was bin Laden? And so it went. *I am loosing credibility with the clerics,* he worried. *I must do something soon or all will be lost. Praise be to Allah that the clerics are occupied with Palestine and Iraq. I now have no doubt that America will invade and conquer Iraq. I hope our Baghdad brother has secured the biological agents and taken them to a safe location. Anthrax is very easy to conceal and use; however, smallpox scares me. It is too easy to make a mistake and cause a release. Colonel Valek warned me of this at our first meeting; and again when he provided the smallpox sample that we shared with Saddam. As far as I know, both bio agents are hidden in America, but I do not know who the cell leaders are. Should I identify myself to the existing al-Qaeda leadership; and if I do, will they believe me?*

Saddam Hussein was becoming concerned. Contrary to assurances, the French, Germans and Russians were not deterring the U.S. from its course. Bush II and his lackeys were beating the war drum, and more and more nations were beginning to listen. Bush had just blown through the U.N., and the striped-pants crowd was in a tizzy. *Bush will never find my secret weapons. When the inspectors fail, Bush will look like an ass,* Saddam thought. *On the other hand, he just might invade. If he does . . . I will charter three ships, each under a different flag. The important stuff will be loaded onto them. For the present, they will just sail around, making port calls at friendly nations. If necessary, the cargo can be off loaded in several different locations; where the equipment, fissile materials, and bio agents can be well hidden.*

On May 20, 2003 a coalition led by the U.S. military swept across Iraq and took Baghdad in three weeks. Like the al-Qaeda terrorists in Afghanistan, Saddam, his two sons and the Baathist party members were running for their lives. America's military had once again stunned the world with is power. Bush II's Axis of Evil had been reduced to two countries. Saddam's two sons, Oday and Qusay were killed in a gun battle on July 22, 2003. Then came the hard part – finding the WMD's and governing the country. After a chaotic summer and fall when terrorists' attacks against collation forces increased, and the new Iraqi army was plagued with desertions of the new recruits, good news was received. On December 13, 2003, the larger than life – at least in his own mind – dictator of Iraq, Saddam Hussain, was captured without a shot being fired. Hiding in an eight foot deep, six foot by eight-foot spider hole, looking like a homeless person, the bedraggled ex-dictator, who would be caliph, was video taped having his scraggly hair and beard examined for lice.

General Alexander had finished reading the newest intelligence report. Comparing it with the news on CNN and FOX, he was depressed. After displaying its prowess in the field, America was demonstrating its ineptness in managing Iraq. The clerics had finally understood that they could not beat a western army on the battlefield, but they could in the streets. Without identifiable targets, America's military was stymied. Collateral damage, especially killing civilians was repulsive and against American beliefs. Terrorist snipers had been hiding behind women and children for years.

Now a few Iraqi clerics were haranguing the faithful in the mosques, inciting them to rebellion against the very people, who had just liberated them from a brutal dictator. The *shura* had finally understood America's weakness. America had won the battle, but could loose the war for the minds of the Iraqi people. In August a Black Hawk helicopter had blown a Shiite religious banner from a communication tower in Sadar (Saddam) City. *Imam* Abdul al-Hadi al-Daraji, speaking at Fridays prayers in the Ahil al-Bati mosque in Sadar City to an estimated 25,000 people, equated the American occupation to Saddam's brutal government. The Imam stopped just short of calling for an uprising. No one would consider doing what needed to be done – hanging the radical clerics in front of their mosques.

The situation continued to deteriorate. By winter suicide bombings had spread throughout Iraq, Afghanistan, and Turkey. Several helicopters had been shot down, and a mob in Mosul, Iraqi had dragged the bodies of two American soldiers from a wrecked vehicle and mutilated their bodies.

WMD's were another problem. Alexander had warned the Joint Chiefs that they might not find any WMD's in Iraq by the end of the war. If Saddam had concentrated on bio weapons, as Alexander suspected, then the actual bio agents and unique equipment used to produce them could easily be removed from the country. After all, Saddam had sent his fighter planes to Iran during the Gulf War. One should never forget the Arabic adage: *The enemy of my enemy is my friend.* If Iraq still had any fissile material or enriched uranium, it would accompany the bio weapons. Sensitive to politics, Alexander watched the president's political enemies begin to use the absence of WMDs in Iraq to attack him. September 11th's terrorist high jacking of four civilian aircraft had made him, and the missing WMD's could ruin him.

We are our own worst enemy, Alexander thought. *Nobility is fine if taken in small doses. Self-preservation must come first. We understood this, and were able to win our independence from England. Now we have forgotten the formula of our success. Safe behind our oceans, no enemy has been able to attack us on our mainland since the battle of New Orleans with the British in 1815. Japan was able to attack the island of Oahu in Hawaii in 1941, but not the continental United States. That perception changed on September 11th, and the lesson still has not been learned. We will be hit again, next time with bio weapons, or worse, with nuclear weapons.*

Ralph Eid was frantic as he sat in his condo watching FOX news report yet another al-Qaeda capture. Al-Qaeda was constantly in the news. One key member after another was being captured. He had not heard from Mohammed is several months. He kept trying to convince himself that he was safe; that only bin Laden and Mohammed knew of the devices. *No, that is not entirely true,* he thought, *Omar Mumtaz and Abu al-Aziz know enough to point the FBI in my direction. Mohammed has assured me that both of them would not talk about what they had seen. That leaves Bob Johnson of General Neutron, Kevin Patterson of LRM, Tom Roberts and Arthur Jameson, my old boss at Livermore Labs. But both Johnson and Patterson are dead. . . .*

"Oh, no!" Ralph gasped aloud to himself, "Could Mohammed have had them killed?" he wondered aloud; and instinctively jerked his head around to see if Nancy, who had already left for the office, had heard him. Relieved that he was alone, he continued to mutter softly to himself, "I am trapped. No way out. If the devices are found I have no place to go. If they are used, and I help set them off, then what . . . ?"

His mind hysterically racing, Ralph continued to stare at the TV screen, but was aware of nothing but his own silent desperate thoughts, *I certainly cannot remain in America. Where can I go that they will not find me? On the other hand, who would ever be able to connect me to them? All evidence would be destroyed. Dr. Roberts is the only person who might make the connection. I never got around to mentioning him to Mohammed. Why didn't I see this coming? Mohammed is a madman. How do I approach him on the subject of Johnson and Peterson deaths? Are Nancy and I next in line? Once I have served my usefulness . . . .*

Later that same evening, Ralph and Nancy were sitting on the patio of their house in Rancho Nuevo, enjoying a glass of Merlot. Fall was in the air, even in central California. "I think it is time to get completely out of the market," she said. "I have been slowly selling off our stock. Foreign capital is fleeing to the Euro and Swiss pound. Our interest rates are so low that it is not worth investing in bonds. Election politics usually drive the market in this part of the presidential election cycle. A few months ago I thought Bush was a sure thing, now I am not so sure. The Democrats do not have a good horse in the race. Their candidates are destroying each other. The market is nervous. Anything can happen. One more big mistake and Bush will be severely wounded."

Still unnerved by his own awakening to Mohammed's instability and the morning news, Ralph responded, "Yes, you are correct"; while frantically thinking, *I am certain I'm marked for death. But how can I protect Nancy? I love her. She is an innocent bystander in all of this.*

Nancy's gesture to have her wine glass refilled brought Ralph back to reality, *I cannot let her see that I am so troubled . . . must keep the subject on business . . .* "How is PC Capital doing in this market?"

"Not very well. I am considering closing the firm. We both have made more money than we will ever need. Shock waves from the "dot com" collapse are still rumbling through Silicon Valley. Why keep trying to ride a dying horse?"

All the money in the world won't fix the burden I am carrying, Ralph brooded and asked, "What would you do?"

"I have been giving that a lot of thought for the last few months. Teaching sounds interesting," Nancy answered.

"Professor Hatterson, that has a nice ring to it," Ralph light heartedly joked, but continued to struggle with the dread that was consuming him. He had considered marrying Nancy for years. His other life prevented it.

Religion had never been an issue with them. Nancy was protestant, but not a practicing churchgoer. His own Mosque attendance had all but ceased in the wake of his rush to business success. *Teaching? That's a switch for someone who is so ambitious. But she is, above all things, very patriotic,* Ralph thought as he remembered the time she had asked him a question about Allah after a news commentary on the Saudi government and Muslim terrorists.

"How can those people claim to be doing Allah's work, when they kill and maim innocent women and children? And how can the Saudi's, who look like a grade B movie production of 'Fat Cats,' wearing their silly archaic robes and headdresses, sit inside ostentatious golden palaces on gold gilt chairs while their fellow Islamists encourage men, women, and children to blow up themselves and others – Arabs, Jews and Christians alike – in the name of *their* God? What kind of God would ask that of humans he supposedly loves. What kind of friends are the Saudis?"

How do I answer her when I am one of those few who are preparing to commit mass murder? Ralph thought and hating himself for the hypocrite he had become answered, "Allah teaches true believers through the Koran that we are to be tolerant of one another. We are by faith a gentle, loving people. These terrorists have distorted Allah's teachings for their own purpose," he said in reply to her question.

No! Nancy would never understand or be able to forgive me once Allah's Rings were used, Ralph groaned to himself and dredged the depths of his conscience trying to decide if he could ever forgive himself. Somehow he sensed that he would soon have to face his quandary head on.

Mohammed was also facing his own crises. Usama was either dead or incapacitated. It didn't matter. It was apparent that no one knew about Allah's Rings. The clerics had quit calling for him to brief them. *My star is falling. If I do not act soon, no one will remember my name,* he thought. For the last several months, Mohammed had spent hours sitting in a chair staring at a framed photograph of Saddam Hussein astride a white horse holding a sword. Yosif had become concerned about his master and lover. He could not understand Mohammed's fascination with the photograph. After all, it was of poor quality.

Mohammed had just returned from a meeting with Eid. Ralph, who was unusually jumpy during their time together, had once again brought up the subject of the dead co-workers. *He knows I was involved in that, but doesn't have the guts to ask. He covered himself pretty well though when I asked what he was so nervous about. Claimed he was worried about the economy. I still have not decided what to do about him and that loathsome woman he finds so appealing.* Mohammed thought.

For once she had proven to be useful, Mohammed thought, even though it galled him to have to agree with her concern about the American economy. REM's money would be transferred to a Liechtenstein anstalt, a holding company under the extremely secret and protective laws of Liechtenstein, and Swiss banks. Low interest rates had precipitated a wave of home refinancing and borrowing. Capital was beginning to flee America to markets paying higher interest. Deflation was in the wind. Treasury notes could no longer compete with foreign bonds paying several more interest points. Banks and lending agencies were realizing that a large portion of their money was committed for long terms at low interest rates. The price of gold had increased by more than $100.00 per ounce.

Reflecting on their time together, Mohammed realized that he had two growing concerns regarding Eid. *First,* he wondered, *will he arm the devices when he receives the order; and second, what to do with him after he did?* Mohammed decided that he would have to assist Ralph to make sure he accomplished his task. *Then,* he thought with a sneer on his face, *Well . . . one will just have to wait and see. I am quite fond of Ralph . . . but, that meddling infidel woman Nancy will definitely have to go.*

The radical *shura* was accomplishing its three main goals: defeating democracy in Iraq. After all democracy would mark the beginning of the end for the cleric's dictatorial power; disrupting the "road to peace" connecting Israel to Palestine; and deflecting attention away from Iran's nuclear weapons program. By successfully fomenting minor revolts throughout Iraq and Afghanistan, they were defeating America's goal for democracy in these countries, and painting the liberating forces as hated occupiers. Saudi Wahhabists were attempting to start a religious war between the Sunni and Shiites, and between Shiite sects in Iraq, by assassinating leading clerics. Grand Ayatollah Mohammed Baqir al-Hakim, one of Iraq's most esteemed clerics and the leader of the Supreme Council for the Islamic Revolution, was assassinated with a car bomb in Najaf in August as he left the gold-domed, Imam Ali mosque after preaching a sermon calling for Iraqi unity. The bomb, the third such in August, left a three and a half foot crater and killed eighty-five people. The Imam Ali mosque is Iraq's most sacred Shiite shrine, the burial place of Ali, considered by the Shiites to be the Prophet's heir. 64 year old Grand Ayatollah al-Hakim, was considered to be the voice of moderation. His brother was a member of the U.S. appointed Iraqi Governing Council. Both were supporters of the U.S. effort to form a new government.

A noble cause was being been turned inside out; and America was desperately trying to determine what had gone wrong. The potential for another Vietnam was in the making. It was easy to keep Palestine in a state of chaos – give the faithful a few hundred dollars and they would send their children off with bombs strapped to their bodies. All of these disruptions ensured success of the cleric's third goal – deflecting American attention away from Iran's nuclear weapons program.

2004

The Council of Radical Clerics continued to stir the Iraq pot. Using the young, militant, firebrand Shiite cleric Muqtada al-Sadar and his militia as their *agent provocateur*, they engineered the infamous Fallujah atrocities. A civilian convoy of was lured into an ambush. A mob of cheering Iraqi's inflicted horrendous atrocities on the bodies of four American civilians that were burned, mutilated, dragged through the streets, and then hung from the top of a bridge so that the corpses dangled over the road. While

Americans watched in horror, liberals and Islamic scholars explained that such acts of barbarism were not condoned by the Islam. A few Iraqi clerics condemned the desecration of the human bodies, but not the perpetrators of the gruesome acts. In the following month two cities neared revolt.

Al-Qaeda stepped up attacks in Saudi Arabia. Large car bombs were detonated. The truce was over and the Royal family and government personnel and buildings were targets. Attacks also increased in Jordan. Al-Qaeda and the council of radical clerics viewed both countries as weak and pandering to the west. Strong Islamic leaders were required. Expanding its horizons, al-Qaeda scored a major success with simultaneous bomb attacks on trains in Madrid. The cowed Spaniards elected a trembling appeaser who pulled Spain's troops out of Iraq. The first step toward Spain's forced conversion to Islam had been taken.

Alexander watched the TV coverage and read accounts of the atrocities in news papers and magazines. The *New York Times* story of the young Iraqi boy in Fallujah, who used his heel to stomp the burned head of one of the four American corpses summed up the whole Islamic situation for him. "Where is Bush? Let him come here and see this." the article quoted the boy as yelling. *Animals, all of them are animals,* Alexander thought. *Instead of the careful, controlled response made by the U.S. Marines, we should have used the B52s to carpet bomb the center of the city, and used the militant mosques for bombing practice.*

Predictably, the Republican convention nominated the incumbent president and vice president as its presidential ticket. After all, there was no one else, with the possible exception of the Secretary of State. Things in the other party were different. The primaries had been hateful, each wannabe trying to out do the others. Instead of attacking the Republican president, the Democratic candidates had turned on each other, and the surprising leader was so liberal that his ability to beat the incumbent president was in doubt. The apparent winner, a self proclaimed Vietnam war hero who served two tours in Vietnam – one on a navy ship off the coast and a second short tour on "Swift" Boats in Vietnam rivers – had an anti-military voting record in the Senate and rumored ties to Jane Fonda. Stories circulated on the internet that the senator had only served four months of combat duty on the river patrol boats in Vietnam, and in that short period of time had earned three Purple Harts, a Bronze Star, and a Silver Star – which must be a record for winning medals in any army or navy. It was alleged that the senator, then a navy lieutenant, did not require hospitalization for any of his wounds, and that three Purple Hearts was a "get out of Vietnam" card; the recipient could request immediate transfer back to the U.S. These allegations were not addressed by the main stream media.

As the time for the Democratic convention drew near, the party leadership was severely depressed. So far any Bush II blunders had been overshadowed by an ever increasing improvement in the economy; and the handover of power in Iraq had occurred without a major uprising or civil war. The apparent Democratic nominee had made several major blunders and his voting record had come back to haunt him in the form of Republican political ads. Something had to be done. The week before the Democratic convention a former president floated an idea, actually an old idea – draft a candidate at the convention. So it came to pass that the 2004 Democratic presidential candidate was the Senator from New Hampshire, Hilda Rodman. The incumbent president found himself in an unexpected horse race.

Iraq moved back to center stage. Iraq's WMD's, or to be more precise Iraq's missing or nonexistent WMD's became the Democrats WRD, "Weapon of Republican Destruction." Rodman hammered on the Iraq war fiasco, and the economy – because the effect of increasing oil prices had finally had a major negative effect. "It's the economy, stupid," had a familiar ring. The president was a statesman, but not a good, down and dirty, in the gutter politician. An accident at the president's ranch one month before the election had removed him from the campaign trail, thereby tipping a close election, and Hilda Rodman became the first woman president of the United States.

Mohammed was overjoyed. The news that Rodman had won had just been announced, and Mohammed was so elated that he jumped up and hugged Yosif – then began dancing around the room. "Yes! Yes! Yes! Allah has blessed us, blessed me. Now it is time to act," Mohammed cried out in joy. After the euphoria had passed, Mohammed sat down and began to plot. Looking at the photograph of Saddam on his white stallion, Mohammed thought, *my time has come.*

A month later Mohammed entered the conference room in a private house in Qom, Iran. It had been very difficult to obtain an audience with the radical *shura*. Mohammed had chosen the words of his request with extreme care. One did not lie to this group, at least not twice. He had to make them think that he was delivering a message from Usama, and do so in such a manner that he would not be called a liar when he appeared at the meeting. *This is my chance to grab the brass ring. Funny I should think of an American idiom, but it does fit,* he thought. Nine clerics from Saudi Arabia, Syria, Morocco, Iraq, Pakistan, Egypt, Afghanistan, and Yemen were seated behind a long table facing the door. At the center of the table was Iranian Grand Ayatollah Hamid Khomeini. Standing before the table, Mohammed received the signal to begin.

"Praise Allah, for he has shown me the path to accomplish our most holy goal. For some years you have know me as Usama bin Laden's messenger. Today I will reveal to you my other role, my most secret role that only three people in the world know about. These three people are Usama, my cell leader in America, and myself," Mohammed paused and looked carefully at each of the stern clerics sitting at the table. He had their attention.

"Usama bin Laden was a great leader, a man able to see into the future and make plans that would take years to come to fruition. You have seen the evidence of his planning. Usama was also a man, and men make mistakes. The timing of his attack on the infidel's twin towers was such a mistake. His mistake provoked the devil Bush to attack and occupy Muslim lands, and to support the abomination called Israel. For four years we have had to endure this insult. Perhaps Allah allowed this to happen in order to test us and give us the strength of will to do what now can be done.

"Allah is great. Many years ago he provided us the means to destroy the Great Satan. Allah, be praised, for he chose Usama bin Laden to be the keeper of his wrath, and Usama chose me to prepare the way for the Great Satan's annihilation." Looking around, Mohammed saw that he had them. All were looking at him, waiting for his next words. *Yes, I can do it,* he told himself.

"Allah has blessed us beyond our dreams. He has given us, with me as his instrument, the power to totally destroy five American Cities." Mohammed paused and carefully looked at each of the stern old men seated in front of him. No one spoke. All waited in rapt attention for him to continue. Satisfied, Mohammed went on, "Allah has given into my hands five atomic bombs." Again Mohammed paused for effect, then continued, "Yes, five atomic bombs that are in place in five of the Great Satan's cities. Five atomic bombs that I can cause to be detonated at my command."

Enough had been said. It was time for a response from the council. Mohammed waited, making it obvious that he had said all he planned to say. After what seemed to Mohammed to an eternity, the senior Ayatollah asked, "Where did you get these atomic bombs? Did al-Qaeda make them? Did you get them from Saddam Hussein?"

The point of the questions was obvious to Mohammed. In either case, the bombs could not be assumed to be reliable. There could be no guarantee that they would function properly. After all, Iran and Iraq had attempted to make such items, but unless they were tested one could never be sure they would function. "The five bombs were obtained from a nuclear super power. They will function," Mohammed replied. "I myself received the weapons from the source; and I tested them to be sure that they were genuine."

"Allah be praised. What is the source of the weapons?" another Ayatollah asked.

"By Allah's blessings I have been given this gift. The source of the weapons must remain Allah's secret. I can tell you that the source government does not know that we have the bombs. There can be no talk of them after we leave this room. Even the hint of their existence would start a search that could result in their discovery. This must remain our most guarded secret until the day comes for their use," Mohammed replied. The critical moment was at hand. Either they believed him, thus elevating him to the stature he deserved, or he would have to try to assemble the scattered al-Qaeda leadership.

Mohammed stood quietly while the assembled members talked among themselves. After several minutes, the senior Ayatollah spoke, "We are thankful to Allah for his blessing, and to you for making us aware of them. What is it you propose?"

Mohammed strove to maintain his humble appearance while thinking, *I have done it.* Addressing the Ayatollah, he said, "We must wait for the right moment. We must allow the new woman president to take office. Allah will show us the appointed time."

"We should strike now, while the Devil Bush is still president," one of the lesser clerics said.

"No," another said with contempt, "Mohammed is right. Wait until the infidel *woman* is their president."

After several more exchanges, the senior Ayatollah addressed Mohammed, "I assume you have additional thoughts on this matter."

"Allah bless you. Yes, I have. After the attack, the faithful in America should be ready to rise up and start conversion of the infidels to Islam. There can be no delay. This will also be the time to drive the infidels from our sacred lands. Islam's holiest sites must be secured. After that, it will be possible to reclaim our heritage – to reestablish the great Islamic empire, the Caliphate."

2005

President Rodman was comfortably installed in the White House. Many familiar faces had reappeared in the Cabinet and bureaucracy. Policy and culture of the previous administration had been swept away with frightening speed. Drastic cuts in the military had been made within days of her inauguration. New rules of engagement (ROE) had been issued for Iraq and Afghanistan. Rules that immediately resulted in an increased number of casualties. Along with new ROE's, troop strength was being reduced. The smoldering embers of civil war in Iraq began to catch fire. It was quickly becoming apparent that America would exit Afghanistan and Iraq as they had in Viet Nam. Grumblings that had started in the field were spreading throughout the military and from some in congress. President Rodman was warned that the situation was becoming dangerous. Something had to be done to relieve the pressure.

Major General Alexander had retired on the last day of December 2004. The following month George and Jane Alexander moved into their mountain chalet, a four thousand square foot house that had a spectacular view of the upper Rio Grand River. In spite of his promise to himself and Jane, he continued to worry about his country.

President Rodman was a true believer in liberal ideals. Her philosophy of appeasement of Islamic fundamentalists was leading the country down a previously trodden path – a path that led to more violence, not peace. It seemed that this simple lesson could not be learned. Perhaps it was because the alternative was so repugnant to civilized people. Every concession to the Islamic fundamentalists and the Palestinian Authority was met with demands for more concessions and additional violence to emphasize each new demand. A consummate politician, Rodman was unable to understand that her opponents had an entirely different value system. In just a few months, her administration was in trouble. Alexander had received a series of phone calls from active duty and retired officers. All gravely concerned about the direction Rodman's administration was taking. Her National Security Advisor was Sarah Blumberg, a left wing liberal, full professor from Columbia University: whose lack of real world experience was balanced by her huge ego. Professor Blumberg was the center of a gathering storm.

Alexander had just placed another log on the fire. Jane was reading the Sunday edition of the *Santa Fe New Mexican*. The telephone rang, and Jane said, " I hope it is not another of your friends calling to jaw about the sorry condition of the military." Alexander walked over to couch and picked up the phone on the side table, "Hello."

"Is this General George Alexander?" a voice asked.

"Yes, this is General Alexander."

"Please hold for the President of the United States."

The expression on George's face told Jane that something was up. As she started to get up, he motioned for her to sit and be quite. A minute later he heard a voice from the past, "Hello George, I hope I am not disturbing your Sunday morning."

"Not at all, Madam President," George replied, watching the shocked expression on Jane face.

"Please give my best wishes to Jane, and tell her I hope she will understand the need for my call. George, the country needs you. I need you. Will you answer another call to duty?"

Completely taken aback, and unsure how to reply, Alexander thought, *What is she up to? I am dealing with a very shrewd, calculating and savvy lady. I have not seen or spoken to her for at least eight years. Why now? She is in trouble with the military and congress. Her National Security Advisor is a disaster, and the Department of Homeland Security under Charlene Tatz is in total disarray. Better make her expose her reason.* "Madam President, I am always ready to serve my country if I have something to contribute."

"I am glad to hear that George. As I am sure you know, I am having problems in the Middle East, and some dissatisfaction at home pertaining to the military. My main problems are at Homeland Security. Some are saying that I am getting bad advice. I think you can help me in that area."

"I am not sure I understand what area you are referring to."

"Military affairs, the Middle East, and terrorists, specifically their capabilities to attack us here – the types of weapons and how they can be used."

"I will be honored to advise you in these areas; however, your National Security Advisor, Professor Blumberg and I do not see eye to eye. I do not think I can work with her."

"That will not be a problem. I am offering you the position of Secretary of Homeland Security. Secretary Tatz will tender her resignation as soon as I have a replacement. Will you accept the offer?"

"When do you require my answer?"

"Now."

"Please give me a minute to talk to Jane."

"Keep the line open, I will be back on in five minutes," the president said.

Jane had been following the conversation with growing uneasiness. "What does she want you to do?" she asked.

"The short version is that she is in trouble and needs someone who is respected to bail her out. She wants me to take the position of Secretary of Homeland Security."

"That will mean going back to Washington."

"Yes, I am needed. The country needs someone like me now. I can limit my acceptance to, let's say, the remainder of her first term."

"If you really think it is that important, then take the job. You can get an apartment in DC. I will spend part of the time here. I want to be near our kids." James Alexander, their son, was a senior at the University of New Mexico, and Jenna, was a freshman at the same school.

"That's a good idea. My job will require a great amount of traveling. You can fly to DC when I am in town."

A voice in the telephone receiver said, "Are you there General?"

"Yes"

"Hold for the President." *Like I was not holding for her*, Alexander thought.

"Well George, have you made a decision?"

"Yes Madam President, I will accept the position for the remainder of your term. No longer."

"Fine. Thank you. Secretary Tatz will announce her resignation in the morning, and I will submit you name for conformation the following day. How soon can you come to Washington? I need you ASAP."

"We can come next week on a TDY basis. Jane can look for an apartment, while I get up to speed. I hope that is acceptable to you."

"I am looking forward to your arrival. Check with Kirkland flight operations. A plane will be placed at your disposal." The president broke the connection.

"Well, we have moved up the pecking order. The president has placed a plane at my disposal. Maybe you will like Washington this time."

"I doubt it. Do what you have to do, so that we can get back here on a permanent basis."

Alexander laughed. "If you thought I was getting calls from my old military buddies before, wait until the announcement of my new position hits the news."

Jane smiled, "Just turn on the answering machine."

Mohammed was back in America. Ralph was meeting him in New York at the Waldorf Astoria hotel that evening. Mohammed could sense that the time to strike was near. Just as he had hoped, the new woman president had played into the hands of the clerics. Iraq was in turmoil, close to civil war. Reductions in U.S. troops had been met with even more attacks and assassinations. The pot was boiling in Israel. Palestine was near revolt. The road to peace had turned out to be a circle instead of a straight line. As soon as a target date was selected, the clerics would start preparing Syria, Jordan and Egypt to join in another attack on the Jews, and this time there would be no America to come to their aid. *Soon . . .very soon,* Mohammed thought.

Ralph took a limo from Kennedy airport to the Waldorf, checked in, and called Mohammed's room.

"Let's have dinner at the *Le Bernardin*," Mohammed said as soon as Ralph said hello.

"Sounds good to me," Ralph replied. He is in a good mood. I wonder why?

"I have reservations for 9 P.M. Meet me in the lobby at 8:30," Mohammed said, hanging up.

Le Bernardin is a four star French restaurant that specializes in seafood. Entering, Mohammed palmed a fifty dollar bill and gave his name to the Maître d.' Smiling, the Maître d' led them to their secluded table. Mohammed requested the wine sommelier attend them. After discussing the choice of seafood and their order, the sommelier selected a vintage for them to taste. Mohammed approved and he and Ralph sipped the crisp cool white *claret* with pleasure. Looking at Ralph, Mohammed said, "Allah has smiled upon us. His punishment for not following his will is complete, and he has blessed us with another opportunity in the *woman* president. Our time to act is near – only selecting the time remains."

For Ralph, the dreaded day had arrived. After years of indecision and being assailed with misgivings and doubts, his decision was really quite a simple. *I have no choice,* he realized, *I must do as he says or he will have Nancy and me killed . . . and he will arm the devices anyway.* "Has Usama picked a date?" he asked forcing himself to eat his meal.

Smiling, Mohammed answered, "No, he has left the selection up to me. That is why I am here. Your advice and predictions have always proven to be very accurate. I am seeking your council in this matter."

Ralph was both sick at heart and relieved, *at least this way I have some control,* "Thank you, I am pleased that you consider my thoughts important. A major celebration has been announced for Memorial Day, the end of May. The administration is attempting to rally the country. A joint session of congress will be held on Friday afternoon; so that the president can present a report on the accomplishments in the Middle East, and honor some soldier who was killed in Iraq and awarded the Medal of Honor. The word is that *Madam* President will use the occasion to give a rousing speech – an effort to increase her ratings. She will attempt to put a good face on her accomplishments. A big celebration will be held on the mall following the speech. The festivities will last late into the night and continue on Saturday. Large celebrations are being planned for Saturday in many of the major cities. The NAACP is calling for rallies, and there may be a million man march. The last Friday in May will be an excellent time."

Mohammed was elated – *So easy. I had anticipated spending days going over potential dates. Yes, Ralph is right again. Praise Allah. I will bring the infidel nation to its knees – and I will be the next Caliph. After all, who is better qualified?* he gloated to himself. "Then that is the date. What about the time?"

Ralph slowly sipped his wine while he considered the question. Looking up he said, "4 P.M."

"As Allah wills it, so it shall be," replied Mohammed. We will discuss details later. Now eat up – let us enjoy our excellent meal."

Later back in Mohammed's suite, they agreed that arming and setting the timers of the devices would begin two weeks before the zero hour. Mohammed would return to assist. Arming would be completed at least two days prior to the zero hour, so that both Mohammed and Ralph would have sufficient time to be well clear of the areas. Ralph was debating leaving the country. Mohammed planned to be in Qom, ready to address the *shura* and claim his position as Caliph, but first, he had to set the stage.

Returning to his suite, Ralph finally had to face the reality of his situation. The time had come to arm and detonate the devices. He had to perform his duty – otherwise Mohammed would arm the devices himself. *Would Mohammed kill him when the job was done? I just don't know*, Ralph thought. *I must be careful not to give him the opportunity. But then what? What is Mohammed's real plan? There have been a few taped interviews with Usama, but I wonder if he is really in charge. I wonder if he gave the command to detonate the devices? This could be Mohammed's operation. Best that I stroke his ego and make plans for Nancy and me to disappear. Mohammed knows nothing of our Argentine retreat. It is best if we are there when the devices detonate.*

The day following his dinner with Eid at Le Bernardin, Mohammed flew to Paris. On the plane he mused about his pending triumph, *Soon I will be known as one of Allah's greatest warriors – no as his greatest warrior – a great hero of the Islamic world. No one can oppose my becoming caliph. Shall I establish my capital in the traditional capital city of Baghdad or in Riyadh – or perhaps Cairo? This will require more thought. I must have one last dinner at Le Bernardin. A pity such a fine restaurant must be destroyed.* Mohammed spent the night in Paris, partaking of the local pleasures, and then flew to Tehran. He would meet with the radical *shura* in three days and announce the date for the destruction of the Great Satan. The clerics would set their timetable accordingly. *By the grace of Allah I will succeed and become the greatest Caliph,* he thought.

After Mohammed's meeting with the radical *shura*, word went out to the faithful to be prepared to rise up and drive all of the infidels out of Muslim lands. Allah would provide the signal, and the signal should occur in the next two months. In some Islamic countries, the rulers were made aware of the pending event, and they began to prepare their armies to invade and destroy Israel. In countries with weak leaders, who were pawns of the west, plans were made to overthrow the current government and convert the country to Islamic rule. In all such places, there were strong military officers, who were prepared to assume command and follow their brothers in the annihilation of the hated Jews. No infidel would be left alive. Islam would rise. The holy land would again belong to Allah.

General, now Secretary, Alexander was settling into his new position. The department welcomed a strong, knowledgeable leader – and that was good. Unfortunately, the other agencies had reverted to the old hostilities. Turf wars were raging – and that was bad. Alexander was totally dissatisfied with the intelligence he was receiving. Professor Bloomberg, still NSA, was a major impediment to obtaining accurate human intelligence from the Mideast. She believed in the good intentions of the Arab leaders, and did not want to hear anything that contradicted her opinions.

Something had to be done. Alexander had quietly established contact with military attachés in Saudi Arabia, Egypt, Jordan, Morocco, and Israel. The picture he was getting from the attachés was not compatible with the accepted intelligence. Again, Alexander found himself at odds with the establishment. *I was a fool to accept this position. I have served her purpose. She has a well-respected military man in Homeland Security. That satisfied the public. Now I have been pushed to the sidelines. I am tempted to resign, but I won't and she knows it. God, I hate having to attend the Memorial Day pageant she is planning. Another super PR scheme for the public, and they will eat it up. The NAACP is in on the act with a huge rally planned for Saturday. There will be fireworks Friday night and parades throughout the country,* he thought.

Numb from the stress he was under Ralph was in a dream-like state as he planned to begin his arming duties in Chicago. If there were a problem he would have to fly to Newark to get spare parts. After Chicago, he planned to go to Newark and pick up the company van and spare neutron generator. While he was there he would install the complete round in the gun assembly disguised as a mobile CAT scan; then he would have the trailer made ready for use. Tires would be checked and replaced if required, and then the blocks removed.

315

He had a surreal feeling when he arrived in Chicago at 6 P.M., rented a minivan, and drove to the Walnut Mini Storage facility. After entering the security code in the numeric keypad, the gate opened and he drove into the facility. Parking the van near the door to the storage building, he entered the building and opened the storage room. *I must put all thought of everything but surviving this out of my mind, if Nancy and I are to have a future*, he told himself as he removed an old chair and several boxes to expose the container holding the complete round. *Nothing else matters. We have money enough for a lifetime. Just do your job safely and get out of the country,* he continued prompting himself; then stood the container on end and used the hand truck in the storage room to move the complete round to the van. Placing the container and hand truck in the van, he locked the van and returned to the storage room to replace the junk items and lock the door. Returning to the van, he drove into Chicago and entered the underground parking lot of the Chicago Nuclear Diagnostic's building. There he parked near the freight elevator, locked the van, and took the elevator to the forty-second floor to make sure there was no one in the area who might interfere with his mission. Satisfied, he returned to the van where he placed the container on the hand truck and returned to the REM office. After locking the outer door and the double locks on the instrument room behind him, Ralph removed the cover from the instrument. Opening the toolbox located in the storage room, he selected the special fastener tool and used it to remove the instrument's end panel, where he exposed the breech of the gun.

Ralph wiped the grease from the breechblock and inner chamber using rags from a box in the storage room. Next he used a large mop with a long handle to swab out the barrel to remove the grease. Making sure the shunt was still in place; he closed the breech, booted the computer, and ran the diagnostic program. All circuits checked out. Ralph used his watch to set the computer's clock. He had decided to use his watch to set all of the clocks so that all would be on Eastern Standard Time. Next, Ralph opened the container, removed the round with its uranium-235 projectile, and inserted it into the cannon. Then he removed the electrical shunt connecting the two contact pins on the breechblock and carefully closed the breech. He then re-ran the diagnostic program. This time the diagnostic program checked the bridge wires in the squibs and found at least one of them to be intact. The weapon was ready to be fired. Ralph replaced the instrument's end panel. Now it was time to set the Event Timer. Accessing the Event Timer program, Ralph set the date to be May 27, 2005 and the time to 1600 hours. Next the CRT display was turned off; so that it would not be apparent that the computer was running. Without the CRT drawing power, the backup power supply would be able to provide power for one month. All that remained was to cover the instrument. Leaving the hand truck in the room, he locked the doors for the final time.

Secretary Alexander hung up the phone. The Israelis were nervous. Colonel Sam Combs, U.S. Army, military attaché in the American Embassy in Israel, had just reported that you could feel the tension in the air like static electricity. Something was up, but no one knew what. It was on the faces of the Palestinians, it was in the air. Alexander had received similar reports from Jordan and Saudi. Inquires to CIA had been dismissed by the new Director. Professor Blumberg just laughed at his concern. Homeland Security was on alert; however, the president had vetoed raising the threat level from green, the lowest level. After all, the Memorial Day festivities were designed to sooth the public. Raising the threat level was out of the question.

Ralph caught a late morning flight from Chicago to Newark and took a taxi to the REM building. Using the REM van, he drove to Hackensack where he removed the container with the complete round from the Aunt Lil's storage room. Returning to the building, he spent the next three hours repeating the arming procedure in the trailer. By late afternoon, the job was completed. The next morning Ralph instructed a local tire company to replace all of the tires on the trailer, check the air shocks, and then remove the blocks so that the trailer was ready for pickup. Finally he called the dispatcher at Mobile Nuclear Imaging, Inc. in Baltimore and instructed him to move the backup instrument trailer from Newark to the storage building in southeast Washington, DC. Using his notebook computer and a inkjet printer in the office, Ralph prepared a memo to the Mobile Nuclear Imaging, Inc. driver The memo stated that the Mobile CAT scan trailer No. 5 was to be moved to the parent company's facility in Washington, DC to serve as a backup instrument. Should the driver be stopped for any reason, formal paperwork usually solved any problems.

Two years ago Ralph had become lost in Washington while attempting to find his way from the Library of Congress to South Capital Street. Somehow he had gotten on New Jersey Avenue and ended up on K Street SE, where he discovered an area containing old warehouse buildings, one of which was for sale. The neighborhood was not good, but the location was. Ralph had arranged for REM to purchase the building and fix it up so that vehicles and trailers could be pulled into it if required. Now the investment was paying off.

Before leaving REM's Newark building, Ralph carefully went through the office and placed any documents, or items such as maps and keys that might connect REM to the devices, into a box. After loading the spare neutron generator, the box containing the records, and the empty container that had held the round into the van, Ralph departed for Boston. He spent that night at a motel near an exit on I-95, and arrived in the Boston area the next afternoon. It was too early to move the round, so he checked into a Holiday Inn Express near Medford. He decided to relax at the motel until 6 PM, and then have dinner. After dinner he drove to Aunt Lil's to get the container with the Boston round. It was after 8 P.M. when he entered the parking garage in Boston. Ralph took the empty round container, and the box of records with him on his first trip to the REM office. The floor was deserted, and he encountered no difficulty in entering the office. Leaving the empty container and box next to the instrument room door, he returned to the garage with the hand truck to get the container with the round.

When Ralph ran the first diagnostic test, the number one neutron generator tube showed a fault. Ralph returned to the van and removed one of the sealed neutron generator tubes from the extra generator. *I am glad this did not happen in Chicago,* he thought. Returning to the instrument, it was necessary to remove the back access panel in order to install the new tube. After removing the damaged tube, Ralph was confronted with the problem of how to pull the connector cable through the conduit. *We never thought about this,* he thought. *I can disconnect the cable from the junction box, tie a string to it and pull it through from the back – if I had a string.* Ralph stood up and started walking around the instrument. *Of course – cut the cable at the base of the bad tube and tape the connector end of the cable from the new tube to it. Then I can use the old cable to pull the new cable through from the other side.* Ralph completed arming the Boston device. The final diagnostic tests showed no faults and the Event Timer was set for 1600 hours, May 27, 2005. After placing both empty containers and the box in the storage room, Ralph covered the instrument, locked the doors and left the building. It was 2 A.M.

Returning to the motel, Ralph slept until 10 A.M. Following a late morning run, he shaved showered and had a late breakfast. Returning to his room, he called Nancy at her office, "Good morning hon, I miss you."

"I miss you too," Nancy replied. "When are you coming back?"

"Tuesday or Wednesday. Why don't we leave for Argentina on Thursday? Your IPO is ready and you can monitor the market from there. Let's get out of town before the big weekend; we can stay for two weeks."

"That sounds like a plan. A good plan. I am ready to get away. I will be ready when you get back. Love you," Nancy said.

After the call, Ralph sat thinking, *I love you too. Why didn't I tell you.* Then checking out, he started back to Newark.

Mohammed arrived in New York, rented a minivan and drove to the REM building in Newark to meet Ralph. When Mohammed arrived at the building Ralph was surprised to see him with a full, well-trimmed beard, but Ralph did not comment on it. The trailer was off its blocks and ready to go. As they were preparing to leave, the tractor arrived and they watched the driver hook up to the trailer. Ralph showed the driver the envelope containing the memo and explained that the trailer was being sent to DC as a backup unit. Ralph cautioned the driver to drive slowly and be especially careful because the instrument was very sensitive. That night they removed the container with the complete round from the Walnut Mini Storage room in Hackensack, and armed the New York City device. The Event Timer set to the same date and time as the previously armed devices.

The next day they returned to the REM facility so that Ralph could leave the company van in the building. Ralph and Mohammed walked through the building looking for anything that might connect them to the coming detonations. Finding nothing, they placed the spare neutron generator in Mohammed's minivan, locked the building and started south toward Atlanta. Ralph detoured to drive by the old Indus Instruments building. It was now a storage warehouse for NEC Electronics. Indus Instruments had been phased out three years ago. All records had been "lost" when the American branch was closed and the personnel recalled to Pakistan.

Arriving in Atlanta the following night, they repeated the arming procedures. No faults were found in the equipment. The pair departed Atlanta in the minivan for Washington, DC the following afternoon. "Four down, one to go," Ralph said to Mohammed as they entered North Carolina. After spending the night in Durham, NC, the two continued their drive northward to Washington. Ralph was driving and decided it was time to broach the subject of what happens next with Mohammed.

Choosing his words carefully, Ralph brought up the subject, "By Saturday I expect that you will be a hero of Islam. Usama *will* give you credit for your accomplishments won't he?"

Ralph's comment jarred Mohammed out of his daydreams . . . daydreams of being caliph. "Yes . . . I will receive credit for humbling The Great Satan," Mohammed answered with a grin. "Unfortunately, I will not be able to share my glory with you, for if I do you will be in serious trouble."

"I am glad that you will receive credit. After all, this was your plan, and you made it all happen. All I did was follow your instructions. Mohammed, you are truly a great man, a real hero of Islam. Your deeds will establish you as one of Islam's greatest heroes," Ralph gushed, pumping up Mohammed's ego. "I am not worthy of sharing your glory. In fact, the less known about me the better for me. Only you and Usama know who I am. I would prefer to leave it that way."

"Yes, that is best for you isn't it," Mohammed replied while thinking, *Maybe I should leave Ralph and his infidel whore alone. I may need him in the future when I take over this godless land and bend them to the true faith.* "What are your plans?"

Deciding it was time to play his cards close to the vest, Ralph replied, "We are going to the Riviera on Friday morning. We will be out of the country when the event occurs."

Entering Washington the next afternoon, Ralph and Mohammed encountered a traffic jam as they approached the Fourteenth Street Bridge. Ralph was driving and Mohammed was looking out the side window at the Potomac River. A black limousine slowly passed on their right side. The windows were dark and Mohammed wondered if it was a government vehicle. Secretary Alexander happened to be looking out the left side window of his limo as the two vehicles passed each other. Lost in thought, Alexandra's attention was momentarily drawn to the middle eastern looking man staring out of the maroon van's window. It struck Alexander as odd that the man seemed to be so extremely animated – his expression intense, almost threatening. The minivan moved forward and eventually pulled in front of Alexander's vehicle. George Alexander had briefly seen the face of evil. A face he would see again.

After passing the disabled taxi on the bridge, traffic began to move and Ralph continued on I-395 to the South Capital Street exit. A few minutes later, they entered the REM warehouse and closed the door behind them. The Number 5 trailer was inside the building. Ralph used his keys to unlock the door and enter the trailer. Everything appeared to be in order. From a storage locker in the trailer, he removed a power cord, which he used to connect the trailer to building power. Returning to the trailer, both men entered, went to the instrument console, and booted the computer. A blue screen appeared. Two more re-boots resulted in the same blue screen. Mohammed became more agitated after each boot. Turning to Mohammed, Ralph said, "The computer is damaged. I will replace it with the spare in the van."

Extremely upset, Mohammed left the trailer and started pacing back and forth. Ralph opened the rear door of the minivan and opened the General Neutron box containing the computer. Deciding that Mohammed was not going to be any help, he removed the computer and returned to the trailer. The configuration of the fake CAT scan was similar to the Neutron Induced Gamma Spectrometers. Unscrewing the front access panel, Ralph removed the computer, and carefully disconnecting the cables. The spare computer was installed and the access panel replaced. Returning to the console, Ralph booted the computer. This time the expected menu appeared. Selecting the diagnostic program, Ralph ran the program. Mohammed entered the trailer as the diagnostic program began its analysis and said, "Allah be praised, the spare appears to be working."

Both watched until the diagnostics were completed. "All systems go," Ralph said. Returning to the main menu, set the clock, then selected the Event Timer and proceeded to enter the date and time. After turning off the CRT, they covered the instrument with a large cloth cover. "It is now in Allah's hands," Ralph said.

"Yes," Mohammed replied, "Allah has blessed us and our jihad. Four days from now the Great Satan will be mortally wounded, and Allah's word will be spread across this godless land. It is time for us to go. I can take the evening flight to Cairo."

"If I cannot get a direct flight to San Francisco, I will go to Dallas or Houston," Ralph replied. "Open the door, and I will pull the van out."

Once the van was outside, Ralph closed the roll-up door and secured it with two padlocks. Exiting through the small steel door, Ralph locked the two dead bolt locks. Looking up at the video camera that covered both doors, he smiled. Yes the camera is on, but it is only connected to the monitor that was visible through the small, barred window. Anyone contemplating robbery would see the monitor through the window and assume a security company was monitoring the building. Turning back toward the van, he could see a small portion of the capitol dome over the roof of the building across the street.

Ralph was able to purchase a first class seat on the last flight to San Francisco International Airport from Dulles. Mohammed took a later flight to Paris. An hour into the flight, Ralph sat sipping a glass of Merlot, lost in thought, *In four more days it will be over. It is time to take care of Nancy and me.* A year ago Ralph had incorporated an Argentine company, Argentine Radiological Imaging. The company was owned by Ralph through a law firm in Buenos Aires. It would be very difficult to trace the ownership to Ralph Eid. There was over $64 million U.S. dollars in accounts in Switzerland alone. A large portion of the funds had been earned by Ralph through PC Capital. *I will transfer thirty million from the Swiss accounts to Argentine Radiological Imaging tomorrow. I will route the transfer through New York, Atlanta, the Isle of Man, the Bahamas, and Panama. After Friday it will be impossible to trace the money. After all we earned it, and we are entitled to a share,* Ralph decided, turning back from the window to his dinner.

Alexander was becoming more concerned. He had just spoken with military attachés in Morocco and Egypt. The reports were the same as those from Saudi, Jordan and Israeli. Trouble was in the air. Getting up from his desk, he walked down the hall to the FBI liaison office. Entering without knocking, as was his practice, Alexander asked, "Hi Fred, have you picked up any unusual activities or chatter from the al-Qaeda bunch?"

"Yes, starting on Saturday there has been an increase in e-mails and phone calls. From what we can tell, most are asking each other what is going on. If something is being planned, no one seems to know what or when. There is a lot of unusual activity at some of the mosques, but we do not know what is going on."

"Yes, I understand," Alexander replied.

Rodman's new FBI Director had ordered all clandestine monitoring of American mosques to stop; in spite of the allegations that Saudi Arabia had spent \$35 billion dollars to spread Wahhabi Islam around the world. Approximately half of the mosques and Islamic schools in the U.S. received funds from the Saudis. Those same schools, which contained an estimated thirty thousand students, were being pressured to use Wahhabi-influenced textbooks. Included in the textbooks was the teaching that Muslims should not befriend *"kuffrs,"* an Arabic word that means unbeliever (*i.e.,* Christians and Jews).

John Stones *American Legion*, article, "The Terrorist Next Door," reported that many of the Islamic school's textbooks contained the message, "The day of judgment will not arrive until the Jew hides behind a tree or a stone. Then the tree and the stone will say, 'Oh Muslim, oh, servant of God, this is a Jew behind me. Come and kill him'" The article also states that the Saudi Embassy was distributing copies of the Quran to prison inmates, and paying the expenses of two hundred prison chaplains, who had been schooled in Saudi Arabia; and that Wahhabi Inman Warith Deen Umar, who helped run New York's Islamic prison program, was reported to have said, "The 9/11 hijackers should be honored as martyrs." The purpose appeared to be the conversion of black Americans to the Wahhabi brand of Islam.

Fear of interfering with religious freedom and fostering intolerance against Muslims was making mosques a sanctuary for terrorists. The CIA had been handcuffed again. "Unsavory characters" were not to be used in intelligence gathering. As a result, meaningful intelligence had for all practical purposes ceased.

"Given the constraints we are all working under, I just have a gut feeling we are missing something, and we are ripe for a hit . . . a big hit," Alexander said.

Fred nodded his head in agreement and solemnly asked, "Are you staying for the weekend festivities?"

"Yes, I have to attend the joint secession and the parties afterward. Jane is planning to fly in Friday morning."

"The wife and I haven't decided yet, but I will probably stay. Washington will be a madhouse Friday evening. Trying to go home will be futile" Fred responded.

Alexander grunted, waived goodbye and returned to his office thinking, *Something is up and I haven't a clue what.*

Mohammed mailed a letter in the Cairo airport to *Al-Majalla*, a Saudi owned magazine in London. The letter claimed responsibility for attacks that would occur in five American cities on May 27th. Retrieving a videotape from a locker in the airport, he boarded a flight to Doha International Airport, Qatar. Two weeks earlier Mohammed had made the videotape. Now it was time to arrange for its broadcast. Later in the day, he entered the Al-Jazeera all-news satellite television station, asked to speak with the communications director, and was escorted to Khalid Ali's office. Mohammed introduced himself as he approached the desk, "Allah be praised. I am Muraaqibu al-Khawaatim and I have a video message from al-Qaeda. If is extremely important that this tape be broadcast at exactly 9 PM, on May 27, 2005. Broadcast time is critical, because it will precede the event by a short interval. You must keep the tape a secret until it is broadcast."

Ali studied the well-dressed man standing in front of him. He had never heard of Muraaqibu al-Khawaatim, but that did not mean anything. "How can I be sure it is from al-Qaeda?"

"When you screen the tape, as I am sure you will, your questions will be answered."

"Is this a message from Usama bin Laden?"

"No, from me. By May 28th I will be the leader of al-Qaeda . . . and much more. Failing to follow my request to the letter would be – as the evil Americans say – a career ending decision."

Ali looked at the man, who was staring at him with a fanatical intensity that was frightening. *Another fanatic, but this one appears to be very dangerous*, he thought. "Allah bless you, it will be as you have requested. Will you contact me after the event?"

"Yes, within a few hours if possible. You will want to spend the night at the station in order to cover the most important story of your life. When I contact you, I will use the phrase 'Allah has used the power of his rings.' May Allah bless you," Mohammed said, turning and leaving Ali's office and the building.

By the time Muraaqibu al-Khawaatim, which means keeper of the rings, had reached the main door, Ali had lifted his telephone and speed dialed the Chairman of the Board of Directors of Al-Jazeera, a member of Qatar's royal family. Relaying his encounter with Muraaqibu, Ali waited for a reply.

"Do you think this Muraaqibu al-Khawaatim is a real member of al-Qaeda?" the Sheik asked. "I have never heard of him. I wonder why he is calling himself the keeper of the rings."

"Yes. I think he is genuine. He is a fanatic with the coldest eyes I have ever seen. He reminded me of pictures I have seen of Hitler . . . a frightening man."

"I will come over this afternoon and we will screen the tape."

Mohammed returned to Riyadh. He planned to travel to Teheran early Friday morning. He had notified the clerics that he would provide the date and time of the event that morning. They could send out the alert code words that afternoon. Activation orders would follow the event, except in America, where the events would be the activation order. *Soon I will be Caliph*, he gloated to himself.

Secretary Alexander was not the only one picking up the vibrations of pending disaster. Retired Lt. General Valrie Yatchenko, now Chairman of the Board of The Group was also tuned in. The buzz was getting louder. *The whole Mideast is wound tight, and no one knows why,* he thought as he sat in his dacha. Yatchenko picked up his phone and dialed a Berlin number. Alexei Valek answered on the second ring, *"Guten Tag."* Hearing the General's voice, Alexei switched to Russian and said, "It is a pleasure to hear your voice, Boris. What can I do for you?"

"Sergey thinks that his old antique collector may be getting ready to place the antiques he purchased on the market."

"That can be troublesome. How soon do you think they will hit the marketplace?"

"I do not know, but it appears imminent."

"Then we must make preparations."

"Yes, we must," the General said, ending the call.

Alexei sat quietly, looking out the window. *How vulnerable am I?* he wondered. *Ivan passed away in 1999 – his wife the year before. No loose ends there. Major Yury Kyrillov was killed in Chechnya. So was Sergeant Umov. I do not know what happened to Lieutenant Anatoly Borisov and Sergeant Vanin, but I am sure the General does. As for the men, well, who would believe one of them? Even so, it may be time for me to take an extended vacation in South America. Venezuela is nice this time of the year. As soon as I arrive, I will order a Mercedes E55. Yes, it is time to go, but I do not have to hurry.*

Alexei enjoyed Berlin, but never planned to settle there. He was prepared to depart at a moment's notice from where ever he was when the time came. Identities had been established in several countries, complete with bank accounts and property deeds. In Venezuela he was Herr Ludwick von Graften, a retired German industrialist. Proper "contributions" had been made, and Ludwick could assume residence in his *casa grande* with no questions asked. Alexei Valek would cease to exist. The General had no knowledge of Alexei's secret identities. Just as he had no knowledge of the General's. It had to be so for mutual protection. A method of reestablishing contact was available, but doing so was strictly voluntary.

By the time Mohammed had boarded a plane for Riyadh, the Chairman of al-Jazeera was departing for the station. Two hours later Khalid Ali and the Chairman placed the tape in a VCR and Ali pressed the play button. Fifteen minutes later the two sat staring at the blank TV screen. Neither man spoke for some time. Finally, Ali asked the Sheik, "Are you going to tell the Americans?"

"I do not know. I must discuss this with others – a most difficult decision. Can we take this Muraaqibu seriously? Can we afford to ignore him? If he can do what he says he can . . . and, we do not tell the Americans? I . . . cannot make such a decision. It is for the Emir to make."

"What will happen if he does make good on his threats?" Ali asked.

"May Allah have mercy on us."

Thursday morning Jim Alexander and a friend decided to attempt to climb the face of Sandia Peak. Having just started in the sport the previous year, Jim was not an experienced climber. His friend was more experienced, but certainly not an expert. They began their climb early Thursday morning. Jane Alexander was on a field trip in the mountains near Taos. She was unaware of her son's climb, and her cell phone did not work in the remote mountain area. Therefore she was not informed about the accident until late that afternoon when her cell phone made contact with a tower, and she was able to get her voice mail. Jim had been taken to the University of New Mexico Hospital in Albuquerque. Calling the hospital she determined that her son was seriously injured. It was going to take her at least two hours to reach the hospital. She decided not to call her husband until she had seen Jim and determined the extent of his injuries.

One hour and fifty minutes later, Jane Alexander entered the hospital. The highway patrol trooper, who had stopped her for speeding, recognized her, and provided an escort to the hospital when she told him the reason for her haste. Jim was asleep when she reached his room. Locating the doctor,

Jane determined that he had broken one leg – a compound fracture – and a back injury. The extent of the back injury could not be determined at this time, but spinal surgery might be required. Jane walked back to the lobby and used her cell phone to call her husband.

It was 9:28 P.M. in Washington when General Alexander's cell phone buzzed. Alexander was in his apartment, preparing to go to bed. When he picked up the phone, he saw that the call was from Jane, "Hi hon, did you have a good field trip?"

Not one to waste time, Jane said, "Jim has been hurt in a fall. He was trying to climb Sandia Crest with his friend Burt and he fell. He is in University Hospital."

"How seriously is he hurt?"

"Compound fracture of his left leg and a spinal injury. The spinal injury is the problem."

"How bad is it?"

"The doctors do not know yet. Surgery may be required. The doctor has ordered an MRI."

"I will get there as quickly as I can. Get a room near the hospital. I will call you when I get to Albuquerque. I love you."

"I love you too," Jane said, ending the call.

Alexander's next call was to Andrews AFB to alert the duty officer at flight operations that he required immediate transportation to Kirkland AFB. What kind didn't matter. Time did. "I will be at flight operations in one hour," he told the duty officer.

"Sir," Major Rogers replied, We have an F-15E scheduled to Kirkland in the morning. The pilot is in the BOQ. I can wake him up and you can depart as soon as both of you are ready."

"Thank you major, the F-15E will be fine. My son has been injured in an accident. I do not know how badly."

"We'll get you there ASAP Sir. There is a major weather front forming that looks like it will move eastward tomorrow afternoon. This way you will arrive ahead of any bad weather."

Grabbing a previously packed emergency overnight bag, Alexander hurried to his car. On the way to Andrews, he called the duty officer at the White House and left the president a message explaining why he had to go to Albuquerque. "Please tell Madam President that I regret missing her speech tomorrow. I will alert my deputy in the morning to cover for me." Alexander next called the Homeland Security duty officer, relayed the same information, and requested that his deputy be alerted to take his place at the ceremonies.

Secretary of Homeland Security, George Alexander arrived at Kirkland AFB at 3 AM, on Friday, May 27, 2005. The Wing Commander and two Air Force cars were waiting for him. Getting out of the F-15E, Alexander greeted his old friend, Colonel Charles Young, "Charlie, you didn't have to get up and meet me at this ungodly hour, but thank you for doing so."

"Hell George, you would have done the same for me. How is Jim?"

"I don't know. Jane told me he had a broken leg and a spinal injury. When she called the doctors did not know how serious the spinal injury was."

"Let's get you out of the flight suite and we will go the hospital and find out. I will assign a car and driver to you if you need it."

"Thanks. I will not need it. Jane is here with her car."

Turning to the F-15E pilot, Alexander shook his hand and thanked him for the ride. Colonel Young turned to his aid and instructed him to make sure the pilot, Captain Bass, was taken care of.

A few minutes later, the Alexander and Young got into Young's staff car and headed for the hospital. Partially to get Alexander's mind off of his son, and partially to obtain information, Colonel Young said, "Guess you are going to miss the big hoopla in Washington tomorrow. I mean today. What's going on? Things are going to hell in a hand basket and our Commander-in-Chief is throwing a party to celebrate."

"What can I say? It is pretty much self-evident. She is putting a good face on it."

"How come the threat level is so low? Green is the lowest level. The Washington blowout is an open invitation to our enemies. Why not paint a bull's eye around the Capital or White House?"

"Off the record, Charlie, I recommended raising the threat level, but that contradicted the purpose of the party. I have been getting very unsettling reports from the Mideast for the past week. Something is up, but no one knows what."

"Do you think something is going to happen?"

"I wish I knew. My gut is telling me to watch out. Anyway, thanks to my son's inability to recognize his limitations, I am here and will miss the party. At least some good has come from his accident."

The driver stopped at the entrance to the hospital. "Thanks for the ride Charlie. I will let you know how Jim is doing as soon as I find out."

"Any time George. I think I will put the base on alert for the next three days. By the way, did you notify the FBI you were coming?"

"No."

"I will alert the field office you are here. Give my best to Jane," Colonel Young said before the staff car left.

Alexander went to his son's room. Jim was asleep, and he was not surprised to find Jane and their daughter, Jenna, asleep in chairs. After meeting with the staff doctor, Alexander and Jane returned to their motel to get a few hours of sleep. Jenna returned to her dorm room.

While General Alexander had been flying across the United States in the F-15, Mohammed was entering the city of Qom. Soon he would meet with the clerics. Filled with a feeling of elation, Mohammed waited to be crowned caliph.

The problem of the videotape finally reached the Emir late Friday morning. After being briefed on its contents, the Emir dismissed the problem as one more boastful would-be terrorist trying to impress the world with his bravado. The Sheik disagreed. "You have not seen the tape. This Muraaqibu is frightening. He does not rant and rave; rather he is very calm, like bin Laden. I think we must take him seriously."

"He claims to have atomic bombs in place in America, and they will be detonated in the near future?" The Emir asked.

"Yes, and he was very specific as to the time the tape is to be aired. He also told Ali that he should stay at the station all night so that he could cover the greatest story of his life."

"What do you recommend we do?"

"I think we must inform the Americans. Perhaps even let them see the tape."

"Unofficially inform the Americans, but do not show them the tape. Air the tape as requested," the Emir concluded.

Two hours later, Lt. Colonel Ryder, USAF, military attaché at the American Embassy in Qatar received a call from the al-Jazeera station manager informing him of the tape and the time that it would be aired. Colonel Ryder reported the information to the Ambassador and to the CIA station chief. Both of who made reports to their respective agencies. The messages arrived in Washington at 8 AM, Friday and started making their way up the chain of command. CIA Director Stella Humphrey dismissed the report on her way to the Capitol building. The Secretary of State did not receive the massage, and National Security Advisor Blumberg dismissed the report as utter nonsense. President Rodman was not immediately informed.

Frustrated, Colonel Ryder called his friend, Colonel Combs, "Good afternoon Sam, how are things in Israel?"

"Funny you should ask. Nervous. Very nervous."

"Why?"

"That is the problem. No one knows why. There is tension in the air unlike anything I have ever experienced. You can almost touch it. Our hosts are on edge. How is it in Qatar?"

"Quiet here, nothing like your are describing. Perhaps I may have a reason for the tension. I received a call from the station manager at al-Jazeera this morning. They have a tape from a new player, who claims to be al-Qaeda. Apparently the government is taking it seriously enough to authorize him to tell us about it on an unofficial basis."

"Have you seen the tape"?

"No. I was told that it is a typical al-Qaeda tape – one man reading a prepared message. What seems to have worried the Emir and his staff was the demeanor of the man, and his message. The man brought the tape to the station and issued instructions. The station manager said his eyes reminded him of Hitler. He claims to have positioned five atomic bombs in the U.S., and that they will soon be detonated. He requested the tape be broadcast at exactly 9 P.M. today."

"That's 2 P.M. in Washington. Have you sent an alert message?"

"Yes, but no one in DC is paying any attention. There is a Joint Session of Congress scheduled for the afternoon, followed by a big party on the mall."

"Hell of a time to set off a bomb. Do you know General Alexander?"

"No, who is he . . . oh, do you mean the Secretary of Homeland Security?"

"Yes. He has called me a couple of times. Seems he doesn't trust the intelligence reports. He has requested unofficial reports from several of the military attachés in our part of the world. I'll pass on your report to him if it O.K. with you."

"You bet its O.K. Thanks Sam. Let me know what he says."

"Roger that," Combs said ending the call.

George and Jane Alexander returned to Jim's room at 7:30 A.M. Their son was awake and the neurologist was examining him. The parents waited until the exam was completed, then entered the room. After introducing themselves, they asked the obvious question, "How serious is it Doctor?"

"My preliminary examination indicates a badly bruised spine, however, I am waiting for results from the MRI."

"How soon will you get the results?"

"Should be this morning. I can provide a firm diagnosis as soon as I evaluate the film."

"Thank you Doctor," Jane said, handing the doctor her card with her cell phone number printed on it, "Please call us when you know something."

Turning toward the bed, both parents looked at their son, who was looking very sheepish with a large cast on his left leg. "Hi Mom, Hi Dad, guess I goofed."

"That's one way to put it," his father answered. "At least you did a proper job of it."

The comment earned Alexander a hard look from his wife, and a laugh from his son.

"I am sorry Dad. I guess I made you miss the big event in DC."

Alexander laughed and smiled, "Well I guess there is always some good in every bad event. I would much rather be here than in Washington. That is one party I am glad to miss."

Jane and George settled into chairs and spent the next two hours sharing experiences with their son.

Colonel Combs placed a call to General Alexander's phone. The call was answered by the duty officer who informed him that the Secretary was not available, and transferred the call to the Secretary's voice mail. Frustrated, Combs hung up. Replacing the call, he attempted to explain to the duty officer that it was extremely important that he immediately reach the Secretary. He had urgent information. The response was that he should forward a report through proper channels. Combs called a friend in the Pentagon, one of the eager beavers who get to work at 6:30 AM, who said he would try to find out how to reach Alexander. An hour later Combs received a call from his friend informing him that the General had left town to deal with a family emergency. He had hitched a ride in an F-15 to Kirkland. After thanking his buddy, Combs called Kirkland and spoke to flight operations. "Yes Sir, General Alexander did arrive this morning. Colonel Young met him and they left the base. The only person who can reach him is Colonel Young. Would you like to be transferred to the Colonel's office?"

"Yes, thank you Major."

"Colonel Young's office, Captain Thomas speaking."

"Good morning Captain, it is morning where you are isn't it? This is Colonel Combs calling from Israel. I need to speak to the Colonel. I am trying to locate General Alexander, it is extremely important that I do so."

"Yes Sir, it is 10:14 A.M. here. Colonel Young is expected back in a few minutes. I know that he met General Alexander early this morning. I think his son had a climbing accident. Can I have him call you when he returns?"

"Thank you Captain. Yes, please tell him it is very important. Very time sensitive," Combs said, leaving his direct phone number.

Five hours earlier, Mohammed, dressed in the traditional flowing Islamic robes with headgear entered the same conference room in Qom. Tehran and Kabul time is 30 minutes ahead of other times. To convert 4

P.M. or 1600 hours in Washington, DC to Tehran time you add 7 hours and 30 minutes. After being shown into the room he stood before the radical *shura*, who were sitting at the same table, and waited for their undivided attention. He began by expressing a formal Islamic greeting; then looked directly at the Grand Ayatollah Hamid Khomeini and said, "Praise Allah, for He has shown us the path. The path to destroy the Great Satan. . . . The path that will lead us to reclaiming our holy lands. . . . The path to recreate our *great new Islamic Empire.*

"Allah has chosen me to be his instrument of destruction – *the keeper of his rings.* The *rings* that are the key that will open the door to his holy path. Henceforth, I shall be known by the name Muraaqibu al-Khawaatim.

"By Allah's will, the time has come. By Allah's direction his humble servant, Muraaqibu al-Khawaatim, has set the place and hour of the destruction that will bring the Great Satan to its knees.

"By Allah's will, I, his chosen warrior, have set the time of that destruction to be 11:30 P.M. today, which is 4 P.M. in the capital of the Great Satan.

"By Allah's will, I will cause the destruction of five of the Great Satan's major cities.

"Praise be to Allah. At 11:30 P.M. today, the cities of Chicago, Boston, New York, Atlanta, and the Washington, DC will be destroyed by atomic bombs.

"Allah has chosen this humble person to be his ultimate warrior, to accomplish what no other has been able to accomplish, to provide the means to reclaim our holy lands, to provide the means to drive the infidels from our lands, to provide the means to reclaim our heritage, our birthright . . . *Our Empire!*

"Now it is up to you. Rally the faithful in Allah's name and send them out to do His work. Send them out as soon as the mushroom clouds have formed over the Great Satan's cities.

"Praise be to Allah."

Muraaqibu al-Khawaatim stood with his head slightly bowed. The clerics sat in stunned silence for almost two minutes – an eternity for Muraaqibu. Then they stood as one. The senior Ayatollah spoke for them all, "If the destruction of the Great Satan's cities occurs as you have predicted, we will honor you as Allah's greatest warrior. Word will be sent forth to alert the faithful that they must be prepared to act when an event occurs that could only be caused by Allah. That the event is expected in the next twenty-four hours. Please return here at 10:45 P.M. tonight; and we will all await the event you have promised."

Muraaqibu, trembling and using every bit of self-control he possessed, calmly announced, "I have prepared a video tape that will be shown on al-

331

Jazeera at 9:30 P.M. today," then he bowed to the clerics, turned and left the room. *Yes, I have done it. I will be the caliph of the greatest Islamic Empire the world has ever seen,* an elated Muraaqibu thought.

Walking into his office at 10:23 AM, Colonel Young was greeted by Captain Thomas. "Sir, a few minutes ago a Colonel Combs from the American embassy in Israel called. He said he had to reach General Alexander pertaining to an extremely important matter that was, as he put it, time sensitive."

"Do you have a contact number?"

"Yes Sir."

"Get him on the phone ASAP."

A very worried Colonel Combs was sitting at his desk, thinking, *We were blamed for not knowing about 9/11. Yet, when something even worse may be about to happen, no one will listen. I wonder if the same thing happened then.* The buzzing of his phone interrupted his thoughts. Picking up the phone and pushing the blinking light button he said, "Colonel Combs."

"Colonel Combs, this is Colonel Young at Kirkland. I understand you are looking for General, or should I say Secretary Alexander. I understand it is important."

"Yes Sir, I have information of extreme importance. I must reach the Secretary."

"Does this have anything to do with the situation in the Mideast? George told me about his concerns this morning on the way to the hospital. You may not know it, but his son had a climbing accident, a fall. He just called me to tell me the injury is not too serious, just a broken leg and a badly bruised spine." Young used Alexander's first name and included information about the accident to establish his relationship with Alexander: which should encourage Colonel Combs to tell him what was going on.

"Sir," Combs, said, "I have information pertaining to a possible terrorist strike using WMDs that may occur at or around 2 P.M. EST. Al-Jazeera will broadcast a videotape at 2 P.M. EST today – from an unknown man claiming to be al-Qaeda. In the tape he says he will detonate *five atomic bombs in five American cities.*"

"Have you sent out an alert message?"

"Yes Sir, but no one is listening."

"All right, I will find Secretary Alexander and have him call you. Keep me posted. If I am not here, my aide, Captain Julian Taylor, will take messages and relay information," Colonel Young said and hung up.

Then Young turned to Taylor, who had been listening to the Colonel's side of the conversation, and said, "Julian, have communications set up a

TV tuned to the Arab station al-Jazeera in my conference room. Also tell them to tape the broadcast. Al-Jazeera will broadcast a tape at noon our time. This may be very serious. Notify my staff to be here to watch the tape. Also call Major Dobson at DTRA as well as the FBI office, and tell them about the broadcast." Young pointed toward the door to direct his aid to get moving; while he used the other hand to pick his telephone. Quickly dialing Alexander's cell phone, he waited for an answer.

George and Jane were checking out of the Marriot when his cell phone rang. Caller ID said Kirkland AFB. Answering, he said, "Hello."

"George, Charlie here. Where are you?"

"Just about to leave the Marriot. What's up? You sound worried."

"I am. Do you know a Colonel Combs?"

"Yes, Sam Combs in Israel. Why?"

"I just finished talking to him. The short version is that al-Jazeera will broadcast a video at noon our time that claims an attack with WMDs today. How fast can you get here?"

"I should be at your gate in ten minutes, fifteen max."

"An escort will be waiting."

Turning to Jane, Alexander said, "Let's go, now!"

Jane saw the expression on her husband's face and asked no questions. Walking quickly to Jane's white Audi A6, George entered the driver's door. As they were exiting the parking lot, Jane asked ,"Where are we going in such a hurry?"

"Kirkland, something's up – something big."

Approaching the gate, the AP signaled the vehicle to stop. Approaching the driver, the AP said, "Please provide your name, and state the purpose of your visit."

Alexander noticed that the base was on high alert. Producing his military ID, which would mean more to the AP than his Secretary ID, he handed it to the AP saying, "I am General Alexander, this is my wife. Colonel Young is expecting me."

Coming to attention, the AP saluted and pointed to a Hummer parked just inside the gate. "Please follow that vehicle Sir." Returning the General's ID, the AP signaled to the driver of the Hummer.

Alexander followed the AP vehicle to the headquarters building, and parked in a visitor's space in front of the building. An AP escorted them to the Wing Commander's office. Colonel Young was waiting for them in the outer office. "I am sorry to interrupt you during a family crises, but this cannot wait. Jane, forgive me, but you will have to wait here. Captain Taylor will see to your needs," Young said, motioning Alexander to enter his office. Young followed Alexander into his office, closed the door and walked to his desk; where he picked up his phone and dialed a number, then pushed the speaker button.

"Colonel Combs speaking."

"This is Colonel Young," Young responded. "Secretary Alexander is here. Please tell him what you told me."

"Hello Sam," Alexander said.

"Good morning Sir," Colonel Combs replied. With your permission I would like to include Lt. Colonel Ryder in Qatar in this call. He is the one, who was contacted about the tape."

"Good idea," Alexander said.

Placing the Generals on hold, Combs speed dialed Ryder, who was expecting the call. "Jim, I am going to patch you into a conference call with Secretary Alexander and Colonel Young. Tell them what you told me, and answer their questions."

Combs completed the connections and informed them, "Colonel Jim Ryder is on the line. Jim, please tell them what you told me."

"Good morning Sirs, thank you for taking my report seriously," Ryder said. Then making it clear that he had not seen the video, he quickly related the facts as they had been told to him.

"If I understand correctly, the tape says that there are five atomic bombs in place in five different cities, and that they will be detonated very soon," Alexander said.

"Yes Sir. That is correct," Ryder replied.

"And the specified time of the broadcast is 9 PM, which is 2 P.M. in Washington."

"Yes Sir."

"And your alert messages have not been taken seriously."

"Yes Sir."

"Do you think this is a real threat?" Alexander asked.

"Yes Sir, and so does the Emir. The station manager said that the man on the tape was a terrifying fanatic, cold, calm, totally dedicated. He compared the look in his eyes to that of Adolph Hitler."

"Thank you Colonel. The broadcast is ten minutes away. We will monitor it. In the mean time, I will try to raise the alarm," Alexander said, ending the call. Opening his wallet, he extracted a card with emergency numbers on it. Selecting the number of the president's security detail, he dialed the number and punched the speakerphone button.

"Hello, who is this?" a voice asked.

"This is Secretary Alexander, I must speak to the President – *Clarion* priority."

"Sir, the President is preparing to enter the House chamber to address a joint secession of Congress. She left specific instructions that she was not to be disturbed for any reason. All emergencies are to be referred to Dr. Blumberg. I will get her for you."

A couple of minutes later, Alexander heard Bloomberg's voice, "What can possibly be so important that you would bother the President at this time? Especially since you could not find time to be here."

Colonel Young's face flushed, and he muttered, "Who the hell does that bitch think she is?"

"Did you say something George," Bloomberg said.

"I do not have time for your sarcasm, Sarah. Have you received the report from Qatar regarding the al-Jazeera video?"

"Is that what you are all hot and bothered about. Of course I am aware of it. Just another bullshit and bravado tape. We will tape the broadcast, and our analysts will go over it when they have time."

"Have you taken any actions based upon the threatened use of weapons of mass destruction?"

"The President and I told you the threat level will not be raised. It will stay at green. Use your head, George, President Rodman is soothing the fears of the people, this is not the time for hysterics. I will tell her of your concerns when she has completed her address."

"When do you expect that to be?"

"Some time after 3:30 P.M. I am sure she will call you. Now, I have to get to my seat. She will be entering the chamber soon," Bloomberg said, and then the line went dead.

"God, George, how do you put up with her," Young asked.

"I ask myself that every day."

"What are you going to do?

"Not much I can do. I have been ordered not to raise the threat level. I will instruct my Department to monitor and tape the transmission."

"I have arranged for us to monitor it from here. Have you told Jane what's going on?"

"Not yet. I will in a little while. Please ask her to join us for the broadcast. First I have a few calls to make."

ABC, CBS, NBC, CNN and FOX had received calls from their sources informing them about the al-Jazeera video broadcast. All had determined to make a copy of the tape and decide about its use later. At 8:55 PM, the announcer at al-Jazeera informed his audience that the station had received a videotape from a representative of al-Qaeda. At precisely 9 P.M. the videotape began.

On TV screens in Homeland Security, FBI and CIA headquarters, the Pentagon, the headquarters of the major networks, Colonel Young's conference room, and in millions of Islamic and Arabian houses, businesses, mosques, and government buildings the image appeared of a thin Middle Eastern man.

Sporting a neatly trimmed beard and dressed in a flowing black *bisht* embellished with gold trim worn over a white silk *thob* and wearing green *ghoutra* held in place with a black *agal*, he sat behind an intricately carved inlayed wooden table. In the background behind him, gold leafing could be seen covering the molding on the paneled walls. Above the molding and hanging on the wall directly behind him was an Islamic flag – different from those currently in use. On the table in front of him lay a scimitar, a large Arabian sword, with a bejeweled handle.

For ten seconds the man sat staring into the lens of the camera without speaking. His dark eyes riveting. His demeanor radiating intensity. Finally he spoke. When he did, English subtitles appeared at the bottom of the picture.

"Oh Muslim brothers and sisters, our great leader, Usama bin Laden, has asked us to devote our lives to martyrdom in the way of Allah. He has said to you, *'Do not be afraid of their tanks and armored personnel carriers. These are artificial things. If you started suicide attacks you will see the fear of Americans all over the world.'*"

Pausing, the man raised his right hand and turning it slightly punctuated certain of his next words by cleaving the air for emphasis as he spoke, "I am *proud* of those martyrs who answered our leader's call, *including members of my own family*, who sacrificed their lives for the sake of Islam."

Then lowering his hand the man leaned slightly forward and continued speaking in a deliberate tone, "Usama bin Laden's call to wage war against America was made not only because America has spearheaded the crusade against the Islamic nation, by sending tens of thousands of its troops to the land of the two Holy Mosques, Mecca and Medina; but, moreover, because of America's meddling in Islamic affairs and politics; and its support of the oppressive, corrupt and tyrannical regime that is currently in control. These are the reasons for selecting America, The Great Satan, as our target.

"The Great Satan has attacked Afghanistan, Iraq, Somalia, and Sudan. The Great Satan has supported the hated Jews against our brothers and sisters in Palestine.

"On Holy Day we attacked the Great Satan in their capital of greed, New York City; and in the capital city of their infidel empire, Washington . . . *But this was not enough.* No, the evil ones were only stung, not wounded, not destroyed. Instead, they attacked our brothers and sisters in Afghanistan, destroying a true Islamic government, the Taliban." Again he raised his hand up and down in a chopping gesture to emphasize his message.

"The time has come to take the Great Jihad to the Great Satan – America.

"The time has come to make the infidels, especially the Jews, bleed and die.

"The time has come to place fear in the heart of every infidel in America and Israel.

"How can this be done? Only with the help of Allah."

Lowering his hand and once again pausing for effect, he stared menacingly into the camera's lens. Then matter-of-factly he continued.

"Over a decade ago, Allah provided al-Qaeda with the power to destroy the Great Satan. A power that had to be horded, protected, secreted. A power to be placed in the land of the Great Satan. Placed in such a manner that the infidels were completely unaware when Allah's gift was put in their belly.

"Allah's power is represented by rings," the man said, raising his arms and holding up both of his hands: this time with his palms facing him, and displaying a brilliant array of ruby, emerald, sapphire and diamond rings.

"Allah has chosen me, *Muraaqibu al-Khawaatim*, to be the keeper of his rings, *Allah's Rings*." Then slowly lowering his hands to place them on the arms of his chair, Muraaqibu rose and stood erect looking straight at the camera.

"With Allah's guidance, I have, over many years, carefully placed Allah's Rings in the land of the Great Satan, in the heart of five of America's large cities.

"Now, Allah has granted me the authority to release the awesome power of his rings. . . . The power of *the Atomic Bomb!*" Muraaqibu said, lifting the scimitar from the table with his right hand and holding it beside his head. Again he paused, his eyes burning with religious fervor, and glared into the camera's lens.

"Today I have given the command to release the power of the rings," he announced, holding the scimitar over his head, and continuing to stare into the lens. Finally he lowered the scimitar, returned it to the table, and boldly said,

"It is time for the faithful to reclaim our lands for Allah.

"Time to return our lands to Islam.

"Time to cut down rulers who proclaim themselves to be true Muslims, but sell out the interests of their own people. Rulers who betray their nations, and commit offenses that furnish grounds for expulsion from Islam. Rulers who drink alcohol. Rulers who listen to evil western music. *Rulers who forsake the teaching of the Prophet and embrace western idea*s

– like the equality of women. One such is the ruler in Riyadh. He and men like him, who are false rulers, and the influential people, who stand by them – *all must be cut down.* People, who have sided with the Jews and the Christians, and given them free reign over the land of our two Holy Mosques. *Such people must be wiped out – wiped out now!*

"In the name of Allah the Most Compassionate, the Most Merciful, I call for the Great Jihad to begin when the power of Allah's rings is unleashed, which will be very soon. Then it will be time to expel . . . *NO . . . to kill the infidels in our holy lands.*

"Time for Palestine . . . *a Palestine without Jews.*

"Time for our righteous brothers living in the land of the Great Satan *to rise up* . . . to convert the infidel to Islam . . . *to impose sharia on that godless land.*

"Those who do not convert must perish.

"To my al-Qaeda brothers in America I say, when the power of the rings is released. Rise up. Implement your plans. Kill the infidels in Allah's name."

Now standing very erect, with both arms by his sides, Muraaqibu again stood quietly staring straight into the camera for a full twenty seconds before continuing.

"Once Islam was a great empire. The Prophet brought the word of Allah to us and united us. The first Caliph, Abu Bark began the spread of Islam. Other great Caliphs followed, Umar, Uthman, Ali, and Muawiya spread the word by jihad and increased our empire. So it shall be again. Under the great Caliph Saladin, our empire stretched from North Africa, to Egypt, to Sicily, to Spain. When our great jihad has achieved its goal, Islam will again be a great power. Even greater than before."

Picking up the scimitar again, and turning slightly to his right, he used the scimitar to point to the Islamic flag behind him.

"When our Great Jihad has been completed, the flag of our powerful Islamic Empire will again fly over our holy lands. . . . The flag created by the great Caliph Saladin."

Turning slowly to again face the camera, Muraaqibu returned the scimitar to the table, stared into the lens for about ten seconds, then somberly concluded, *"Praise Allah . . . My words are spoken with the divine guidance of Allah and are the blessed fruit of our Great Jihad."*

The tape faded to white, then ended.

In the Kirkland conference room, there was dead silence. *I have seen that man somewhere,* Alexander thought, *I remember the eyes. Where have I seen him?*

Finally a staff member spoke, "Is he for real? Maybe he has been reading too much Tolkien, or he saw *Lord of the Rings*. The nut is hung up on rings."

This comment encouraged others to add their thoughts. Finally Alexander asked, "Have any of you been over to the Nuclear Weapons Museum? If not I suggest a quick trip. Pay special attention to the Little Boy. Who can tell me how the Little Boy worked?"

None of the staff wanted to take the bait. So Colonel Young said, "As I recall, Little Boy was a gun-type atomic bomb. One component was shot into the other component."

"That is correct," Alexander replied. "Do you recall the names of the components?"

"Yes," Major Dobson responded, "The component that was fired down the gun tube was the projectile. I think they called the other component the target."

"Correct again," Alexander replied. "What else do you recall about the target?"

"Nothing else, why?"

"The target was actually several pieces, large washers actually – *called rings.*"

"Oh my God!" Dobson responded, half rising from his chair.

"Yes," Alexander said, "He was telling us that he has five gun-type weapons. Weapons that he could disassemble, and bring into the U.S. as components. If he has been at this as long as he claims – and, his claim makes sense – then the detonations will occur very soon."

While everyone else sat watching him, Alexander rose from his seat at the table and began pacing up and down the room. Thinking and slowly nodding his head up and down, he began to mumble to himself as he puzzled over the Arab's message, "He *wants* us to know he has them. Why else would he have included English subtitles? I must assume he is smart enough to know we will find them – if we have time. But I do not think he plans to give us time to find them."

Suddenly turning toward the table, he quickly said, *"No! He doesn't plan to give us time to find the bombs – the subtitles!* He *wants* us to understand his message *when* it is broadcast. The event will happen *before we have time to get a translation."*

As he spoke Alexander rushed to the conference table; where he picked up the phone, pressed the speaker button and dialed the number of the president's security detail. Identifying himself he again requested to speak to the President. The agent answering the phone replied, "I am sorry Mr. Secretary. I have specific instructions not to interrupt the President or Professor Bloomberg if you call."

Leaning over the table and desperate to make the agent understand, he tried again, *"The President's life is in danger. Everyone's* life is in danger!"

"I am sorry Sir, but I have my instructions," the agent calmly replied. Is there anything else sir?"

Alexander stood for a moment in stunned silence still holding the phone to his ear. He had the speaker on. Everyone in the room had heard the conversation.

" No, thank you," he sighed and hung up.

"I must do something to try to avert this disaster," Alexander told them and with the speaker phone still on quickly made another call. Others in the room listened as a voice answered. "Homeland Security, Jefferson speaking."

"This is Secretary Alexander, I am ordering you to immediately raise the threat level to Threat Condition 5, Severe, color red."

Alexander and those present were shocked to hear the reply, "Mr. Secretary, I have received specific instructions from the National Security Advisor, acting for the president, not to change the threat level without presidential authorization."

Alexander looked at the stunned faces of the officers sitting at the conference table. *"Fucking unbelievable,"* someone said, then "excuse me Mrs. Alexander." The others just nodded their heads.

"Jefferson, order the radiation detection choppers to start a sweep of area, using the Capitol building as the center. Concentrate on neutron emissions," Alexander ordered.

"Yes Sir. It will take a half hour to get them in the air. We have orders not to fly any aircraft within one mile of the Capitol."

"Get the choppers up!" he snapped, "And immediately order similar sweeps of New York. I will add additional cities later – if there is time. And alert the NEST teams to be prepared to disarm gun-type nuclear weapons. That is all for now," he concluded and slowly hung up.

Looking around the table, he saw Jane's anxious expression, shook his head and sighed again, "God help them."

Then moving quickly he walked to the large U.S. map hanging on the wall, gestured toward the East Coast, and said, "The Arab said five cities."

"Two are obvious. Any suggestions for the remaining three cities?" he asked.

Chicago was a unanimous choice, followed by Denver, Dallas, San Francisco, Seattle, Atlanta, Philadelphia, Houston, Miami, New Orleans, San Diego, and New Port News.

Alexander turned from the map to go to the phone, "I had better add Chicago to those sweeps ASAP."

Colonel Cobb held up his hand, "There is a major weather front approaching the Midwest. Let me call operations and check the weather in Chicago."

A quick call determined that major storms were approaching Chicago. Heavy winds and rain was expected within the hour, making an aerial radiation survey impossible.

Colonel Young, like everyone else present, desperate to try to do something, reached for the phone. "I can at least alert the Chairman of the Joint Chief's office and tell the adjutant that a terrorist nuclear attack on five cities is eminent."

He dialed the office, quickly identified himself as calling for Homeland Security Secretary Alexander, and reported the grave news. "Alert the Chairman immediately. A terrorist nuclear attack is eminent. The most probable locations were Washington, Chicago and New York."

It was 12:45 P.M. mountain standard time – 2:45 P.M. in Washington.

There was nothing else left to do. The television set in the conference was changed to FOX to watch the president's speech. The announcer said that he expected the speech to end around 3:30 PM; however, the president was running a few minutes behind schedule.

The computer in the Chicago device had compared the current month with the month stored in the Event Timer's memory and found a match, which told the computer to go to the next set of instructions. Next, the current day had been compared with the day stored in the Event Timer's memory and found to be the same. The computer advanced to its next set of instructions – comparing hours. Hours were compared to the hour set in the Event Timer's memory minus one hour until they matched; prompting the computer to go the next set of instructions, which required second by second comparison of the minutes. When the time was determined to be five minutes from the time set in the Event Timer, the heating elements in the neutron generator tubes would be activated; and the seconds would be compared every tenth of a second. The computer was unaware of the storm raging outside.

President Rodman completed her speech, and after prolonged applause, left the rostrum and started toward the door. As is usual in such events, she paused to shake hands and kibitz with supporters. Finally she exited the chamber and started toward the building exit and her limousine. It was 3:50 P.M.

As she exited the building, Professor Blumberg caught up with her. Both stopped and Bloomberg whined, "Alexander is causing a problem. He called just as you were getting ready to enter the chamber. He was all hot and bothered about the terrorist tape that was going to be broadcast. He wanted to speak to you and raise the threat level. I intercepted the call and told him get a grip," she gloated.

President Rodman laughed and smirked, "Well, he has served his purpose – time for him to go. He is the only Cabinet member not here. Look around, all of the Supreme Court Justices, the Joint Chiefs, every senator, and almost all of the house members. His absence will be noted."

A member of her security detail approached and said, "Madam President, Secretary Alexander has been trying to reach you. He said that it is a *Clarion* priority."

"Thank you, Bob," the President said.

The computer in the Washington device determined that the time was five minutes before the time stored in the Event Timer, and activated the heating elements in the sealed neutron generator tubes.

Three Senators approached the President and the National Security Advisor. "A brilliant speech," one said.

"Yes, your plans for increasing funding for AIDS was right on the target," another said.

"President Rodman, I would like to sponsor your initiative for schools for women in Iraqi. I will be pleased to introduce a bill in the Senate."

"That is very gracious of you, Tim. I will have my staff contact you to work out the details."

General Donald O'Neill, Chairman of the Joint Chiefs, approached, "Madam President, I have received a very troubling report concerning the al-Qaeda video that was broadcast at 2 P.M. My staff considers it to be a valid threat. Secretary Alexander is at Kirkland Air Force Base with Colonel Young. Both think the nuclear threat is real and imminent."

"We have been all through that before," Bloomberg snapped. "Energy Secretary O'Riley has determined that it is impossible to smuggle a working nuclear warhead into the U.S." Bloomberg and President Rodman turned, facing east.

The entire eastern seaboard was experiencing good weather. Winds were light and the sky was clear: those conditions were forecast to change around midnight as the severe weather front approached. In the REM warehouse, approximately a quarter of a mile away from the capital building, the computer in the Washington device was comparing the time – every tenth of a second, to the time stored in the Event Timer.

When the programmed time matched to the second, the computer sent a signal to close the relay: thereby introducing a twelve volt current into the firing circuit that heated the bridge wires in both squibs; causing ignition of the sensitive compound surrounding the bridge wires; and causing a hot flame to be injected into the main propellant charge of the cannon round.

Almost instantly the smokeless propellant grains began to burn, producing hot gases that increased pressure. As the propellant grains were consumed, pressure built up in the case, causing it to expand and to push against the breech, the walls of the cannon barrel, and the base of the projectile. Only the projectile could move, and it began to accelerate down the cannon barrel toward the target assembly container.

Approximately six milliseconds later, the projectile exited the barrel, and began its entrance through the hole in the target assembly container into the target rings. The projectile was now traveling at 617 meters per second (2,028 feet per second). As the nose of the projectile, which had a smaller diameter than the base of the projectile, passed through the hole in the target assembly container, part of the plastic sabot also entered. The hole in the steel target assembly case acted as an extruder die, allowing part of the plastic sabot to be "extruded" into the target rings.

Neutrons from natural fission began to bounce around in the fissile material comprising the projectile and the target rings. Because of the shape of the projectile and rings, the nuclear reaction was still sub critical. Less than one millisecond later, the projectile had almost completely entered the target rings. The three sealed neutron generator tubes fired, introducing 2.5 Mev neutrons into the target rings and the projectile at three locations. Some of the neutrons that leaked from the forming supercritical mass were reflected by the depleted uranium reflector liner called a "tamper." The plastic from the sabot that had entered the target rings acted as a moderator, slowing the neutrons to thermal energy. A supercritical mass was created, seeded with millions of neutrons, many of which would quickly slow to thermal energy levels. The resulting nuclear reaction released energy equivalent to fifty thousand tons of TNT.

Walking toward the presidential limousine, Professor Blumberg said to President Rodman, "That fool Alexander has the military taking that terrorist seriously."

President Rodman was starting to reply when a brilliant white light, thousands of times brighter than the sun, appeared directly in front of her. The fireball vaporized everything within sixteen hundred feet from the center of the detonation. Energy was released as gamma, X-ray and particle radiation that produced heat, which caused flammable materials to spontaneously ignite, flesh to char and metal to melt or soften. The resulting super heated air created overpressure – thereby producing a powerful blast wave.

Radiating outward from the fireball, the blast wave created overpressure on surfaces causing walls to collapse and glass to shatter and become lethal fragments. Houses and buildings in the area were flattened. Some of the more solidly built government buildings survived, but were gutted and contaminated. As the fireball cooled it created a vacuum at the point of detonation, which created a second blast wave: this time inward – as air rushed back to fill the vacuum.

By the time the first blast wave reached the Capital building, approximately a quarter of a mile distant, every exposed person was already dead. All that remained of President Rodman, Professor Blumberg and the others outside of the Capitol building were black shadows on the concrete where they had been standing. Because the point of detonation occurred at ground level, destruction of buildings and direct effects from radiation would be less than destruction caused by an air burst. A ground burst, however, would produce more radioactive fallout. Within one minute of the detonation, the main government buildings of downtown Washington, DC were destroyed or contaminated.

Prompted by Alexander's and Young's warnings, the key personnel at the Pentagon, Andrews AFB and Ft. Meade had gone to protected areas and some survived. At the CIA, flying glass killed and injured many. Aircraft at Andrews AFB, Bolling AFB, and Regan National Airport, and planes in the air were destroyed, or the pilots blinded by the flash. Those airplanes that could still fly landed at Dulles airport. The remainder crashed.

Similar devastation occurred in New York City, Boston, and Atlanta. Chicago faired a little better, because the storm had driven people indoors. The airports were closed and the rain washed the radioactive contamination from the air. The major front sweeping in from the west would soon push the radioactive fallout clouds from Boston, New York, and Washington out to sea; where the rain would drop it into the ocean. In the southeast, the radioactive cloud would drift eastward until the rain finally knocked it down onto the land.

Television sets tuned to ABC, CBS, CNN, NBC, FOX C-Span, and BBC lost their pictures. After a few minutes, local stations switched to local broadcasting or displayed notices of "Network Problems." No one could determine why the satellite links had been interrupted. Those who tried to call New York or Atlanta received a pulsing busy signal.

In the Kirtland conference room the TV screen went blank – just static. In unison they all turned to look at the clock mounted on the wall. The time was 2 P.M. – 4 P.M. in Washington – exactly two hours from the start of the al-Jazeera tape.

"Oh my God," one of the Colonels said.

"Switch to one of the other channels," Young ordered. Colonel Cobb turned to CBS, then CNN, then each of the major networks. Only stations broadcasting local programs were on the air. "Get NORAD on the phone," Colonel Young ordered.

NORAD is the North American Aerospace Defense Command.

Lt. Colonel Osborne answered the phone. "This is Colonel Young at Kirkland, do you have any indication of a nuclear detonation in the U.S.?"

"Hold for Lieutenant General Fox," Osborne said.

General Bruce Fox came on the line, "Hello Charlie, we're kind of busy right now. What makes you ask about a nuclear detonation in the U.S.?"

"Did you see the al-Jazeera tape that was aired just over two hours ago?"

"No, and I do not have time for that right now . . . did the tape have something to do with nuclear detonations?" Fox asked.

"Yes, General Alexander, I mean Secretary Alexander is with me. I am putting you on speaker so he can hear," Young said, punching the speakerphone button. "The Arab on the tape said he had planted five atomic bombs in five of our cities, and that they would soon be detonated."

"Bruce, this is George Alexander. I considered the video to be a valid threat, and tried to warn the president. Couldn't get past Bloomberg, who thought it was a hoax. We were watching live feed on C-Span when the picture went. Nothing since on any of the other major networks."

"Shit, we are getting preliminary satellite info that nuclear detonations occurred in Chicago, Boston, New York, Washington, and Atlanta. That's five, just like the Arab said," General Fox replied.

"Chicago is blanked in bad weather. We are trying to zoom in on Washington. It is my understanding that the whole Government was there, Cabinet, Joint Chief's, and both houses of Congress. Is that correct Mr. Secretary?" Fox asked.

"Yes, Bruce, that is correct. I would have been there too, if my son had not been injured in a climbing fall yesterday," Alexander replied.

"Mr. Secretary," Bruce continued, "According to the Presidential Succession Act of 1947, as amended in 2003, you are eighth in line to assume the Presidency. At this time I must assume that the President, Vice President, Speaker of the House, President Pro Tem of the Senate, Secretary of State, Secretary of the Treasury, Secretary of Defense, and the Attorney General were all killed in the explosion. Do you have any information that any of these persons were not in Washington?" General Fox asked.

A stunned Alexander answered, "No. As far as I know they were all there. Probably outside of the capital waiting for the president to leave."

"In that case, I must recognize you as National Command Authority. We will have teams entering the Capital areas within hours. We expect severe weather on the entire east coast by midnight. Sir, what are your orders?" General Fox asked.

Oh my God, Alexander thought. *The last thing in the world I wanted or expected was to become president. Assuming General Fox is correct, I am going to have to start thinking like the Commander-in-Chief.*

Without another moment's hesitation Alexander took command. "General Fox," he ordered, "Send a message to all military commands advising them of what has happened. Request that they inform all U.S. personnel worldwide. Inform the Air Force and Navy to immediately prepare to evacuate our personnel from Middle Eastern countries. We must consider the possible actions of our enemies: especially North Korea, Iran, and maybe some of the other Middle Eastern countries.

"Also, issue orders to ground all commercial and civilian aircraft and seal our borders. No one is to leave or enter the country until we sort this out. Inbound aircraft will only be allowed to land if they do not have fuel to return to their point of origin. Instruct the FBI to detain and question all passengers arriving from a foreign destination.

"Issue bulletins to all concerned that I will take temporary leadership and establish my command post here at Kirkland; and that a state of war exists. The U.S. is at war with unidentified enemies. Our first priority is to establish communications and a chain of command. Next in order will be to obtain precise information on conditions surrounding the blast sights: the levels of radioactivity and extent of destruction. Only then will we be able to determine who survived in Washington.

"I will have to make some type of statement to the nation in the next few hours, otherwise we will have full scale panic." Alexander paused and reached for a nearby glass of water.

"Sir," Fox said, "I suggest we raise the alert status to DEFCON-TWO."

"Approved," Alexander replied. *I have full force of America's military at my command, he thought, and by God I'm going to use every thing we've got to protect this country from further attack,* he thought and with the full war time power of the presidency began issuing critical orders.

"Also, I am ordering release of tactical nuclear weapons to area commanders. Let's get some ready for use." "I want the Navy armed with

Tomahawk TLAM-Ns ASAP. Also order the Navy to arm the carriers with B61s.

"In my name order CINC STRATCOM to arm additional B-1s with AGM-129s, and B-2s with B61s and B83s and to get the TACAMO birds in the air, and then establish communications with me here at Kirkland. We want to make sure that none of the hot heads think this is a good time to hit us."

The enduring stockpile of tactical nuclear weapons had been reduced to a few types of bombs and missiles. The Navy's Tomahawk sea launched Land Attack Missile Nuclear or TLAM-N, and the Air Force's Advanced Cruise Missile or ACM-129 – both cruise missiles are armed with the W80 200 KT warheads. Gravity nuclear bombs consisted of the B61 nuclear bomb with yields between 10 to 340 KT, and the B83 thermonuclear bomb with variable blast heights and yields up to 2 MT; both bombs have FUFO, which stands for "full fusing and firing option," sometimes called a dial-a-yield bomb because the yield and burst height can be set in flight;

The Strategic Air Command (SAC) was disestablished in 1992. The command, control, and communications mission of all elements of the nuclear triad was placed under the newly-formed U.S. Strategic Command (USSTRATCOM), commanded by a four star Admiral or Air Force General, located at Offutt AFB, Nebraska. USSTRATCOM's mission is to: "Establish and provide full-spectrum global strike, coordinated space and information operations capabilities to meet both deterrent and decisive national security objectives. Provide operational space support, integrated missile defense, global C4ISR and specialized planning expertise to the joint warfighter." The Secretary of Defense directed the Air Force and Navy secretaries to consolidate the "Looking Glass" mission aboard the Navy's E-6B "Take Charge and Move Out" (TACAMO) aircraft located at Tinker AFB, Oklahoma. The E-6B is a Boeing 707 airframe loaded with high-tech communication equipment: which has the ability to communicate directly with the nation's ballistic submarine fleet. Its battle staff, when airborne, is under the command of a flag officer – an Air Force general officer or a Navy admiral. General and flag officers are from: USSTRATCOM; the Air Force's Air Mobility Command (AMC); Air Combat Command (ACC); Air Force Space Command (AFSPC); the Navy's Commander, Submarine Group NINE, Pacific (COMSUBGRU NINE); the Commander, Submarine Group TEN, Atlantic (COMSUBGRU TEN); and the Air Force and Navy Reserve.

"Have your staff contact the Air Force, Army and Navy. Tell them to sort out who is their senior officer and have him or her establish contact with me ASAP.

"Charlie, I need your PR people. Tell them what we know, and have them start drafting a short announcement for me. Also, have them contact the local TV stations. Alert them that I will be making a statement to the nation shortly. I will also need a method to communicate with our embassies and foreign governments. Designate one of your officers to set up a conference call with the governors of Illinois, Indiana, New York, New Jersey, Connecticut, Maryland, Virginia, and Georgia. Have another officer get in touch with the FBI's local Agent In Charge. Have him set up communications with other field offices, then report to me. Also tell him to alert all other FBI agencies and the CIA that we are now at Threat Condition 5, Severe, color red, and to take appropriate actions regarding suspected terrorists – and to watch the mosques, there may be trouble there. We must assume that there will be more attacks.

"We also need to contact the Director of Los Alamos Laboratory and have him get the Department of Energy in the loop. Have the DOE director establish a chain of command and then report to me. We need response teams at each of the detonation sites. Let's get moving people.

"Captain Thomas, call Colonels Combs and Ryder right now and fill them in. Have them contact their counterparts in our embassies in the Middle East. All hell may break loose in their area. We need to get our people out of there."

After the shock of the terrorist's videotape and the realization that America had been attacked, Jane Alexander watched in fascination as her husband assumed the awesome responsibility of the Presidency; then quietly rose to leave the command center to be with her children.

Muraaqibu al-Khawaatim and the clerics were watching the live broadcast from Washington. Six TV's were set up, five tuned to a different American station and one to the BBC. As the clock reached programmed detonation time, they sat nervously watching the feed. Three of the monitors showed the President and National Security Advisor as they turned and started toward their limousine. Then the all but one TV screen went blank – the one tuned to BBC.

All the clerics sat and watched the static on the screens for several minutes. Only the set tuned to BBC had a picture, and the announcer said that they had lost the signal from Washington. Then Muraaqibu proclaimed, *"Thanks be to Allah. The Great Satan has been brought to its knees."*

"How can you be sure?" one of the clerics asked.

"Loss of signal," Muraaqibu replied with confidence. "CNN broadcasts from Atlanta. If Atlanta was not destroyed, we would see feed from their headquarters. The same is true for the major networks broadcasting from New York. Only the English station – BBC – is on the air."

"We will wait for confirmation before acting," the Grand Ayatollah Hamid Khomeini replied. "As soon as one of the major news networks confirms the detonations we will issue the final message to the faithful."

Tom Braggs, REM's President and COO, and his family were driving west on I-80. They had just entered Pennsylvania when they noticed a bright flash of light behind them. "That was awfully bright for lightening," his wife commented.

Ralph and Nancy were sitting in main room of their guesthouse watching CNN's coverage of the president when the screen went blank. Quickly switching to other satellite news channels, he found that only regular broadcasts were available. BBC had a message posted saying that the signal from Washington had been lost.

"Must be a satellite glitch," Ralph said, and leaned over to kiss Nancy. "How about a swim before dinner? Go change to your suit and I'll join you shortly. I want to chill a bottle of white wine to go with dinner," he told her and watched as she left to change.

It is done, he lamented as he put the wine in to chill. Then crossing the patio to enter the bathhouse, Ralph stopped for a moment to gaze out over expanse of the Rio De La Plata River and consumed by fear and remorse wondered, *What shall I do? Can the bombs be connected to REM . . . to me? Can we go home? Should we go home? Should I tell Nancy? If I do, what can I say to her? Allah, please help me.*

At 6 P.M. mountain standard time Alexander faced print, radio, and local TV reporters in a hanger at Kirkland AFB.

"Good evening. I am George Robert Alexander, the Secretary of Homeland Security. According to the Presidential Succession Act of 1947, as amended in 2003, I am eighth in line to succeed the president.

"At 4 P.M. Eastern Standard Time today, our country was attacked by terrorists using weapons of mass destruction. Simultaneous nuclear detonations occurred in Washington, New York, Chicago, Boston, and Atlanta. The center of each of the cities has been destroyed. The military has assumed the attacks were made by terrorists, because there was no indication of missile or aircraft delivery of the nuclear weapons. Preliminary information indicates that the detonations were in the ten to fifty kiloton range.

"As most of you know, at the time of the detonation, a joint session of Congress had just ended. Most of our senior Government officials and members of Congress were outside of the Capitol when the detonation occurred. The only reason I escaped being killed was my return to Albuquerque to be with my son, who had been injured in a climbing accident.

"I am the acting President of the United States of America. I will remain in an acting capacity until it has been verified that no one above me in the succession chain has survived.

"Who is responsible for these attacks?

"We do not know at this time.

"Two hours prior to the attack a videotape was broadcast by al-Jazeera in which a man, identifying himself as Muraaqibu al-Khawaatim, and claiming to be al-Qaeda, said he would soon detonate five atomic bombs in five of our cities. Local network providers did not pick up the al-Jazeera broadcast. Homeland Security was alerted just prior to the broadcast. Not knowing which cities were targeted, I immediately ordered radiation detection helicopters to begin searches in the obvious cities of New York and Washington. But there was not enough time to obtain results. Bad weather prevented aerial searches in Chicago. We were unable to identify the remaining two cities; but we had compiled a list of eleven cities as possible targets. Radiation detection searches are currently underway in those cities to determine if others have been targeted.

"The American system of government, so wisely structured by our forefathers and the forward thinking leaders who drafted the constitution, has prepared us to endure such an attack. Our government and our military are still functioning and in control. I therefore issue this caution, in the strongest possible terms, to the leaders of other nations.

"Do *not* to contemplate taking advantage of the situation.

"The United States is at war with yet to be identified enemies.

"While I am temporarily acting as president, I do have the authority to use military force. I have ordered our defense status raised to DEFCON-TWO, the United States Air Force to arm B-1 and B-2 bombers with nuclear weapons, and the Navy to arm ships and submarines with nuclear cruise missiles. Any attack on American interests will be met with a nuclear response.

"I have directed that the internal threat condition be set to Condition Severe, color red. All airports are closed and all flights, except military, are grounded. Only inbound flights that do not have sufficient fuel to return will be allowed to land.

"I have ordered our borders sealed. No one will be allowed to enter or leave the United States until we have had time to evaluate the situation.

"Citizens take heart. Your government has been disrupted, but it is functioning. Our military and disaster response capabilities have not been damaged. Relief activities for the survivors of the attack are underway.

"I have spoken with the Governors of the affected states and they are coordinating activities with the Department of Energy and Department of Defense. As I am speaking to you, help is on the way to the stricken cities. Top priority is being given to the injured. Civil defense measures are in effect. Citizens in the areas of the detonations must follow instructions being broadcast on radio and local TV. Martial Law has been declared in the areas surrounding the five cities. Governors have activated their National Guards.

"Looting will not be tolerated.

"It will take some time to complete reorganization of our Government. Citizens in the unaffected areas of the country should attempt to continue their lives in a normal fashion. Stock markets will remain closed until they can be reorganized. Banks will be closed for one week. We are assembling a task force to deal with the banking and credit card issues. I will provide additional information as soon as it is available.

"Do not attempt to place telephone calls to cities that have been attacked. Except for emergencies we ask that you limit all telephone calls, so that government and relief agencies will have use of the telephone network.

"Command posts are being established near each of the attacked cities. As quickly as accurate data is available, information bulletins will be issued by each command post. Emergency shelters and medical facilities are being established. It will take time to identify survivors. Identification of all of the dead may never be possible.

"Do not to accept unsubstantiated reports. Now is the time for responsible reporting by the press. This is not the time for wild speculation, rumors and armchair quarterbacking. The press must only report verified facts.

"Once we have reorganized and bandaged our wounds, we will determine who was responsible for these attacks – *then and only then will we seek retribution.*

"I have established temporary headquarters here at Kirkland Air Force Base in Albuquerque, New Mexico. I request that citizens make no attempt to contact me. Information bulletins will be issued keeping you up to date on events and our progress. Remember, it will take time for your government to reorganize and establish a nationwide communication system.

"The greatness of America is its people. Now is the time we must help each other. America has been sucker punched, but we are not down – and we are definitely not out. In the past great tragedy has united us. So it *will* today.

"Good evening, and God bless America."

Saturday morning the sun rose over a nation filled with resolve and a thirst for retribution. The course of western civilization, and indeed the world, was about to change.

Main Fictitious Characters

Abdul, Al-Qaeda leader in charge of cave in Afghanistan.

Qaiser Ahmad, M.D., Center director, Chicago Nuclear Diagnostics.

Georgi Akademii, Engineer at test site on First Lighting, and Ivan's friend.

Abu al-Aziz, Manager, Indus Instruments New Jersey facility.

Major General George Robert Alexander, USAF, Secretary, Department of Homeland Security.

Khalid Ali, Communications director, Al-Jazeera all-news satellite television station, Doha, Qatar.

Mohammed al-Mihdar, Second in command to Usama bin Laden for Allah's Rings. MS International Finance Harvard, and a Ph.D. in Physics from MIT. Director of REM Investments, Inc.
    Alias: Uncle Saleh and Cousin Ali
                The antique collector Ahmed al-Hijazi
                Ali al-Libi (Afghanistan)
                Muraaqibu al-Khawaatim (Keeper of the Rings).

Steven R. Arlington, M.D., Director, Erie Diagnostics.

Betty, REM secretary in Livermore, California.

Umair Bhatti, Ph.D., Pakistani, Medical Director, REM Investments, Inc. Professor of Radiology, Harvard.

Sarah Blumberg, National Security Advisor (NSA).

Lieutenant Anatoly Borisov, Second in commander of special KGB unit at Semipalatinsk test range.

Tom Braggs, Arthur Anderson accountant. President and COO of REM Investments, Inc.

James Clark, M.D., Co-director, Atlanta Nuclear Diagnostics center.

Colonel Sam Combs, USA, Israeli military attaché.

William Cox, Manhattan building manager.

Major Dobson, USA, Defense Threat Reduction Agency

Ralph Eid, Ph.D., American born, Egyptian. Father and mother killed in an automobile accident. Ph.D. Nuclear Physics from the University of California, MBA in Business Administration from Harvard. Cell leader for Allah's Rings in the U.S., and founder and CEO of REM Investments, Inc.
    Alias: Saif Abdullah (Afghanistan).

Leonid Fedotov, Ph.D., Nuclear weapons physicists at the All-Russian Scientific Research Institute of Experimental Physics (VNIIEF).

Lieutenant General Bruce Fox, USAF, CINC-NORAD.

Boris Glukhih, The Group's KGB agent at Saravo.

Simon Goldberg, M.D., Little Neck Radiology Associates, co-director New York Nuclear Diagnostics center.

Aaron Goldstein, Goldstein and Associates, marketing representative.

Nancy Hatterson, Venture capitalist, Ralph Eid's girlfriend. Founder of PC Capital.

Thomas Hornell, M.D., Co-director, Atlanta Nuclear Diagnostics center.

Kamal Hussain, Colonel, Pakistani Inter-Service Intelligence (ISI).

Ivana, The General's secretary. Her loyalty to the General was unquestionable.

Arthur Jameson, Ph.D., Ralph Eid's boss at Livermore Labs.

Bob Johnson, General Neutron sales engineer.

Abdul Khalifa, REM's al-Qaeda New Jersey driver.

Grand Ayatollah Hamid Khomeini, Head of the radical *shura*, the council of radical clerics.

Captain 3rd Rank Yury Kyrillov, Commander of special KGB unit at Semipalatinsk test range.

Usama bin Laden, Founder and leader of al-Qaeda.
  Alias: Usama bin Muhammad bin Ladin,
         Shaykh Usama Bin Ladin,
         Osama bin Laden
         the Prince,
         the Emir,
         Abu Abdallah,
         Mujahid Shaykh,
         the Director.

Omar Mumtaz, General manager, Indus Instruments, Karachi Pakistan.

Wesley Murdock, III, M.D., Center director, Boston Nuclear Diagnostics center.

Joanne Murphy, Ralph Eid's house sitter.

Kevin A. Patterson, Senior Vice President, LRM Associates, Atlanta, Georgia

Thomas P. Roberts, Ph.D., Livermore Lab Scientist, neutron activation technology.

Hilda Rodman, 44th President of the United States of America.

John Rogers, Rogers Construction, Inc., Chicago.

Samuel Rossman, Chicago business broker.

Lt. Colonel Jim Ryder, USA, Qatar military attaché.

The Sheik, Chairman of the Board of Directors of Al-Jazeera, and a member of Qatar's royal family.

Mark Swartz, Esq., REM's attorney and son of Swartz, Kaplan and Goldberg's Managing partner.

Senior Sergeant Umov, Special KGB unit at Semipalatinsk test range.

Colonel Alexei Valek, Member of The Group, formally Lieutenant Colonel KGB, Border Guards.
> Alias: Sergey of Volga Antiques,
> Herr Ludwick von Graften, a retired German industrialist in Venezuela.

Sergeant Vanin, Special KGB unit at Semipalatinsk test range.

Saul Weiser M.D., Little Neck Radiology Associates, co-director New York Nuclear Diagnostics center.

Lieutenant General Valrie Yatchenko, KGB, Leader of The Group.

Yosif, Mohammed's live in housekeeper, valet, chef, and lover.

Colonel Charles Young, USAF, Commanding Officer, Air Wing, Kirkland AFB.

Anna (Anya) Zeldovich, Ivan's wife.
> Alias: Maria Karpov – Cuba

Ivan Zeldovich, Senior test engineer, Soviet gun-type atomic bomb team.
> Alias: Nicholas Karpov – Cuba

Appendix A

Uranium and Highly Enriched Uranium

Uranium was discovered in 1798 by Martin Klaproth, a German chemist, who isolated an oxide of uranium while analyzing pitchblende samples from the Joachimsal silver mines in the former Kingdom of Bohemia located in the present day Czech Republic. Uranium was isolated in 1841 by French chemist Eugène Péligot. Uranium was named after the planet Uranus, discovered only eight years earlier in 1791. Uranium ranks 48th among the most abundant elements found in natural crystal rock.

Uranium is present in the Earth's crust at an average concentration of 2 parts per million. Acidic rocks with high silicate, such as granite, have higher than average concentrations of uranium, while sedimentary and basic rocks have lower than average concentrations. Uranite or pitchblende (U_3O_8), is the most common uranium-containing ore. The richest ores are found in the western United States, Canada, Australia, South Africa, the former Soviet Union, and The Congo (the former Belgian Congo, and Zaire). The concentration of U_3O_8 in ores can vary from 0.5% in Australian ores to 20% in Canadian ores. Solvent extraction, a continuous process, is the preferred method, employing tertiary amines in an organic kerosene solvent. The solvents are removed by evaporation in a vacuum. Ammonium diuranate, $(NH_4)_2U_2O_7)$ is precipitated by adding ammonia to neutralize the solution. The diuranate is then heated to yield a purified, solid (U_3O_8) known as yellow cake.

Uranium Enrichment Technology – The Manhattan Project

America chose gaseous diffusion as its primary HEU separation technology. Code-named K-25, the massive Oak Ridge gaseous diffusion plant was a U shaped two level building, one mile in total length and 400 feet in width. Building a gaseous diffusion plant was a mammoth under taking. Separation technology was being developed at the same time the facility was being constructed. By 1944 completion of the K-25 facility was behind schedule; and the Americans needed a quick source of enough HEU for at least one uranium bomb. In order to quickly produce the oralloy needed for the first uranium bomb, the Manhattan Project Director, General Leslie Groves turned to electromagnetic isotope separation (EMIS) calutron separation technology. Construction of the Y-12 calutron separation facility at Oak Ridge began in July 1942.

EMIS technology was based upon the cyclotron, both invented by the renowned American physicist and Noble Laureate, Dr. Ernest Orlando (E.

O.) Lawrence, from the University of California in Berkeley. Dr. Laurence named the technology the "calutron" (calu for California University and tron for cyclotron), and was chosen to be chief scientist in developing America's calutron separation technology at Oak Ridge.

The heart of the calutron processing facility was a huge oval shaped magnet. Production calutrons, designated XAX calutrons, and later "alpha calutrons," had a steel core magnet that was 122 feet long by, 77 feet wide by, 15 feet tall. Magnets this size required a large amount of copper wire, and copper was in short supply. General Groves obtained 14,700 tons of pure silver from the American government depository at West Point to make the wires for the huge Y-12 calutron magnets,

Ninety-six vertical C shaped tanks were placed around the outside of the huge magnet. The entire assembly was called the "racetrack." Five racetracks that produced slightly enriched uranium-235 were built in the Y-12 Oak Ridge facility.

The calutron process started with Tuballoy, uranium oxide, which was converted to uranium tetrachloride that was used to create uranium tetrachloride ions. The ions were accelerated into the C shaped chambers maintained under a vacuum. Uranium tetrachloride ions traveled in a straight path; until subjected to the strong magnetic field generated by the oval magnet that bent them into elliptical paths. The radius of the path was a function of the ion's inertia. Heavier uranium-238 ions had a slightly larger radius than uranium-235 ions; thus each stream of ions was deposited into separate collectors. One can conceptualize the workings of a calutron by visualizing a large powerful magnet. Next, picture an air rifle or BB gun that shoots a BB past the magnet. The path of the BB curves toward the magnet. Heavier BBs will travel farther than lighter ones.

Five alpha calutrons produced 12 percent enriched uranium by early spring 1944; however, output from the five alpha racetrack calutrons was not enriched to the degree required for an atomic bomb. A second smaller calutron, the beta calutron had been designed; and six beta calutrons with thirty-six C shaped tanks were added to the Y-12 facility. The beta calutrons processed the 12 percent uranium-235 from the alpha calutrons and produced HEU; however, the output from the alpha calutrons was still insufficient to provide enough HEU for an atomic bomb. Additional feedstocks had to be found. Some EU feedstock was provided by the partially completed gaseous diffusion facility, but still more was needed.

General Groves re-evaluated thermal diffusion technology being developed by the Navy, and determined that the Navy's technology could produce feedstock for the beta calutrons. Thermal diffusion technology consisted of a pipe within a pipe, within a pipe: a small nickel pipe within a larger copper pipe that was in a still larger galvanized pipe, creating an assembly called a "column." The center nickel pipe was heated with 280 degrees centigrade steam. Uranium hexafluoride gas was passed through the center copper pipe and around the outside of the heated nickel pipe. The outer pipe contained water used to cool the outside of the center copper pipe. Uranium-235 hexafluoride molecules concentrated along the outer wall of the hot center nickel pipe (now the inside wall of the copper pipe) and moved upward where they were skimmed off at the top. Heaver uranium-238 hexafluoride molecules were cooled by the outer wall of the copper pipe and moved downward where they were siphoned off. Wall thickness of the forty-eight foot extruded nickel and copper pipes had to be controlled to tolerance of .002 inch. A new manufacturing process for uranium separation column had to be developed.

A contract to build a thermal diffusion facility at Oak Ridge, code named the S-50 facility was awarded in late June 1944. S-50 was built next to the K-25 power plant (the largest electrical power generating plant in America at the time) in order to take advantage of the excess steam capacity (the gaseous diffusion plant was only partially completed). Clearing for the S-50 facility began on July 9, 1944. S-50 was a large structure (525 feet long, 82 feet wide and 75 feet high) that contained three groups of processing columns. Each group contained seven racks of 102 columns for a total of 2,142 columns. Processing began in the partially completed building on September 16, 1944 when rack number 21 began operation.

HEU, required for subsequent uranium atomic bombs, came from the enormous Oak Ridge gaseous diffusion plant after its completion. As the name implies, gaseous diffusion technology converted natural uranium to uranium hexafluoride gas. Hot uranium hexafluoride gas was then pumped under pressure into a series of separation chambers; where the lighter uranium-235 isotopes passed through porous barriers in the first chambers and on into the next chambers; where the process was repeated thousands of times until HEU was obtained. The barrier had to be resistant to the highly corrosive hot uranium hexafluoride gas; strong enough to contain the pressure differential between chambers; and able to contain billions of uniform holes so small that only the smaller uranium-235 hexafluoride molecules could pass through. Three of the major components (the pump design, pump seal and the barrier) had to be invented while the plant was being constructed. During this period, Bendix Corporation constructed a plant to build the yet to be designed pump.

Nuclear terminology

Atom

An atom consists of three main parts: a proton which has a positive electrical charge; an neutron that has no electrical charge; and an electron that has a negative electrical charge. The proton and neutron are located in the nucleus or center of the atom, and the electron orbits around the nucleus much like the planets orbit around the sun.

Element

An atom is the smallest unit of an element that possesses all the characteristics of the element. An element is a substance that can not be separated into simpler substance by chemical means.

A substance which consists wholly of atoms having the same atomic number is called an **element**, and is given a chemical symbol. The number of protons in the nucleus of an atom is referred to as the element's **atomic number**, and the total number of protons and neutrons is called the element's **atomic mass number**.

Atomic number.

Hydrogen, the lightest element consists of one proton in the nucleus and one orbiting electron, has an atomic number of 1 and is written $_1$H. Helium, the second lightest element, with 2 protons and 2 neutrons in its nucleus and 2 orbiting electrons, is written $_2$He. Uranium (depletealloy), a very heavy element, has 92 protons and 146 neutrons in the nucleus, and it is written $_{92}$U.

Atomic mass number.

Hydrogen has one proton and no neutron, and its atomic mass number is written ^{1}H. Helium that has 2 protons and 2 neutrons in its nucleus and its atomic mass number is written ^{4}He. Uranium has 92 protons and 146 neutrons and is written ^{238}U.

Electrons are not counted when determining the atomic mass number because the electron's mass is so small it is insignificant – approximately 1/1837 of the weight of a proton or neutron. One proton weighs approximately .00000000000000000000000017 grams.

Combined atomic notation

The chemical symbol, atomic number and atomic mass number can be combined as follows: $_1^1$H, $_2^4$He, and $_{92}^{238}$U.

<u>Isotopes.</u>

Elements can have variations caused by a different number of neutrons in their nucleus and are called **isotopes**. An isotope of an element always has the same number of protons but has different numbers of neutrons. The two important uranium isotopes are $^{238}_{92}U$ (depletealloy) and $^{235}_{92}U$ (HEU or Oralloy).

Coming in 2005

The Story Continues,

The Rings of Allah: The Caliph

President Alexander tackles the problems of forming a new interim government, stopping additional terrorist attacks in America, dealing with a worldwide Muslim uprising, and finding those responsible for the 5/27 attack. The radical *shura* takes control of Muraaqibu al-Khawaatim and bends him to their purpose.

Excerpts from *The Caliph*.

A civilian representing the Department of Energy spoke up, "Err, . . . Mr. President," *I guess I have to call him that, even though I don't accept him as President,* he thought, "won't that send the wrong message to the world community? I mean, shouldn't we allow the United Nations to handle aggression?"

Tired and very annoyed, Alexander turned his attention to the speaker, saying, *"And you are?"*

Shocked by Alexander's sharp tone and hard look, the man replied, "I am Dr. George Landry, from DOE, representing the Director of Los Alamos Labs Mr. President."

Fixing Landry with a cold stare, Alexander said, "Well Dr. Landry, make no mistake, *the United States is at war and our survival is at stake.* The United States has never, and will never place its survival in the hands of others. We will identify, and then destroy, our attackers. Nothing less is acceptable. Quit worrying about what the world thinks of us. It is time for the world to worry about what *we* think of them."

A shocked Dr. Landry blanched – his face drained of color – looked at Alexander in trepidation. Nodding to the imposing man sitting at the head of the table, the man who was being recognized as President, Landry meekly mumbled, "Yes sir."

Damn. Admiral Vazquez thought, *We have a leader.*

* * * *

362

By 5:45 A.M. the ambush was set. Twenty minutes later the OP reported that the truck was pulling out, followed by the van. Two terrorists were in the truck, the remaining four in the van. Previously the OP had reported that several cases of explosives had been loaded onto the truck, then the forklift had removed a crate that appeared to be very heavy from a room partially concealed by a false wall. After the crate was loaded onto the truck, the remainder of the explosives were loaded and then one of the men had placed detonators connected to a box in the explosives. After locking the truck's rear door, they got out rugs and knelt to pray. The EOD team had arrived and been briefed. All that remained was for the truck and van to encounter the cows.

A jubilant Faysal was driving the truck – today he would go to paradise. *Will Allah himself welcome me,* he wondered. *Will I meet the brave warriors who had given their lives to destroy the Great Satan's cities. Surely they would be the most honored of all.* Engrossed with thoughts of heroes, 72 virgins, and food, he crested the hill, and suddenly came face to face with reality in the form of two startled cows – their woeful eyes shining in the headlights. Faysal had a fleeting impression of more cows behind them. Without thinking, he slammed on brakes and tried to stop, but couldn't. After striking the first cow, Faysal instinctively turned the wheel to the right and ran into the ditch. The van driver, caught off guard, rammed into the back of the truck and was knocked unconscious. The other three men in the van were stunned and therefore slow to react. Faysal, and his companion Yahya holding an AK-47, jumped out of the truck to assess the damage. When they were clear of the truck both were illuminated with spot lights and told to freeze. Yahya fired a quick burst at the light and was cut down by M-16 fire. Faysal attempted to draw a pistol and was severely wounded. The three terrorists in the van saw the light and reacted by attempting to exit with their AK-47s. All were cut down by M-16 and light machine gun fire.

* * * *

Trucks carrying 130 mm and 155 mm projectiles moved forward to deliver their cargo to artillery batteries. Other trucks delivered special 122 mm rockets to pre-positioned launchers. At 1700 hours, the Syrian commander issued the order to fire. 122 mm rockets streaked skyward, then slowly pitched over, following a parabolic path towards the Jordanian armor dug in on a ridge line. Seeing the smoke trails, the tanks and armored personnel carriers buttoned up, expecting high explosive warheads or bomblets. Instead, the rocket warheads burst upon impact, creating clouds of vapor, which was pulled into the armored vehicles by the ventilation systems. Before anyone had time to react, vision dimmed because the eye's pupil pinpointed. Shortly thereafter the limbs of the body began to jerk and the body went into spasms. By this time, breathing had been affected and the person had lapsed into unconsciousness. Finally the body arched backwards and death followed. A few frantic calls of "gas" and "gas attack" were heard on radio nets. As is always the case, some survived. Those who had gas masks donned them, which protected them from the GB/GF nerve gas carried by the 122 mm rockets. Next came a barrage of 130 mm and 155 mm projectiles fired by the Syrian artillery. These round bust over the target, releasing a yellowish cloud of mustard gas. The survivors wearing gas masks experienced severe skin burns that would scar them for the remainder of their lives. Some of Saddam's missing WMD's had surfaced.

About the Author

After graduation from college with a degree in nuclear engineering Lee Boyland served as an Officer in the U. S. Army Ordnance Corps. Upon completion of the U.S. Navy's Explosive and Nuclear Ordnance Disposal Schools, he was assigned to the Defense Atomic Support Agency's Nuclear Emergency Team responsible for nuclear weapons accidents including the rendering safe of armed nuclear warheads. He had access to the design details of every nuclear and thermonuclear warhead developed by the United States through the Mark 63 warhead. His duties took him to the Nevada Test Site on many occasions. After leaving the Army, he designed conventional and special ordnance and later demilitarized chemical weapons at Rocky Mountain Arsenal and Tooele Army Depot.

After Viet Nam, his interest shifted to hazardous waste, and he made the transition by applying aerospace combustion technology to incineration of Agent Orange. He went on to found a successful full service medical waste service company. He has started and purchased businesses, and is currently involved in the management of medical and special wastes.

LaVergne, TN USA
27 December 2010
210172LV00007B/26/A